Celtic Cosmology and the Otherworld

Mythic Origins, Sovereignty and Liminality

SHARON PAICE MACLEOD

McFarland & Company, Inc., Publishers

Jefferson, North Carolina

LIBRARY OF CONGRESS CATALOGUING-IN-PUBLICATION DATA

Names: MacLeod, Sharon Paice, 1960– author.
Title: Celtic cosmology and the otherworld : mythic origins, sovereignty
    and liminality / Sharon Paice MacLeod.
Description: Jefferson, North Carolina : McFarland & Company, Inc.,
    Publishers, 2018. | Includes bibliographical references and index.
Identifiers: LCCN 2018017779 | ISBN 9781476669076 (softcover :
    acid free paper) ∞
Subjects: LCSH: Ireland—Religion. | Great Britain—Religion. |
    Celts—Religion. | Mythology, Celtic.
Classification: LCC BL980.I7 M33 2018 | DDC 299/.162—dc23
LC record available at https://lccn.loc.gov/2018017779

BRITISH LIBRARY CATALOGUING DATA ARE AVAILABLE

ISBN (print) 978-1-4766-6907-6
ISBN (ebook) 978-1-4766-3029-8

Front cover: painting Standing Stones (Sharon Gadonniex)
The artist may be contacted at sgadonniex@gmail.com.

Printed in the United States of America

McFarland & Company, Inc., Publishers
    Box 611, Jefferson, North Carolina 28640
    www.mcfarlandpub.com

This book is dedicated to those
who have helped along the way:
family and friends, teachers and mentors,
professors and students,
storytellers and tradition bearers,
well-guardians and poets, scholars and seekers,
and, to quote the *Dindshenchas* poem on *Carn Máil*,
all those who seek to "weave the web of knowledge."

Table of Contents

Introduction

In order to see the shape of a myth, one has to shine light on it from as many different sides as possible in order to illuminate its many various surfaces…
—Wendy Doniger O' Flaherty, *Women, Androgynes and Other Mythical Beasts* (University of Chicago Press, 1982, p. 5)

This book has been many years in the making and reflects a wide variety of research projects I have undertaken over a period of almost twenty years. It includes the first academic paper I ever wrote, prior to formal Celtic Studies training, which was based on ten years of independent academic reading. Oddly enough, that paper has been the most cited of all my published works. Other chapters have arisen from conference themes, questions that my students have asked (for which there was insufficient data available), and areas of inquiry in which I myself sought the answers. At conferences, while teaching and during the publishing process, I have been the grateful recipient of much encouragement and assistance from professors, librarians and graduate students, many of whom find these topics as fascinating as I do.

I believe some of this interest is due to the types of questions I am asking and the themes I am pursuing. Some of these have fallen outside those areas of inquiry that were, at the time, considered sufficiently mainstream (or advisable) for those pursuing a tenure track position. As a Harvard-trained Celticist and teacher, grant-funded researcher and author, and Celtic musician and Gaelic singer, I wear many hats, and the brass-ring of tenure has not been my primary focus. As a result, I have been fortunate enough to work within academia and make use of its remarkable resources, as well as the deep learning and camaraderie that comes with it. In addition, I have had the freedom to research and explore many unmarked trails. While I am sometimes led by the Muse, I am also hard-wired to seek truth. This has resulted in many remarkable experiences and opportunities, and I am grateful for all the incredible teachers, mentors and colleagues who have shared ideas over a pint at The Burren or a cup of tea in the Kates Room at Harvard, who have listened to my thoughts and supported my research every step of the way.

Celtic cultural and language-based beliefs and traditions, mythology and folklore, and religious practices in general are of interest to many inside academia (and outside the academy as well). There is often a divide between academics and non-academics, set up on one side by the rigor and requirements of academic work, and on the other by the widespread circulation of historically inaccurate information that abounds in non-academic sources (not to mention the tenacity with which some outside of academia cling to that misinformation). Part of the blame must be directed at popular publishers who often do not know enough about these topics to properly edit or reject certain ideas, and who choose to publish whatever might sell, regardless of content. Sadly, these are the types of books to which most people have access. A quick on-line search of books on Celtic spirituality and the like seems to push these titles to the forefront.

This situation is something I am working to change through my writing and teaching. My book *Celtic Myth and Religion: A Study of Traditional Belief* (McFarland, 2012) appeared in first place under "Celtic Studies" and in third place under "Celtic Mythology" on Amazon.com for a quite a number of years. I believe this is indicative of the deep level of interest that exists in the general populace and suggests new avenues of information-sharing that have yet to be fully explored. Academics can find ways to share their training and wisdom with those outside of academia, many of whom are hungry for the knowledge they possess. Those outside of academia must shake off the cloud of naiveté and access reliable materials, rather than believing everything that books, groups, teachers and websites claim to provide.

In his book *Comparative Mythology* (Baltimore: Johns Hopkins University Press, 1999), Jaan Puhvel writes about the importance of this field of study (p. 128):

> Myth in the technical sense is a serious object of study, because true myth is by definition deadly serious to its originating environment. In myth are expressed the thought patterns by which a group formulates self-cognition and self-realization, attains self-knowledge and self-confidence, explains its own sources and being and that of its surroundings, and sometimes tries to chart its own destinies.... Myth operates by bringing a sacred (and hence essentially and paradoxically "timeless") past to bear preemptively on the present and inferentially on the future....

Over the last few years, there has been quite a bit of new academic research into these topics, resulting in conferences, proceedings, and collections of essays. This is an exciting development, one that I hope will pave the way for more books, articles, classes and on-line resources that can open up this field of study. New translations and studies of materials first edited in the late 19th or early 20th centuries are sorely needed. There are also many topics that would benefit from a collation of source materials and analysis that allows room for the materials to speak for themselves—a "bottom-up" rather than "top-down" approach, one that I heartily espouse. In addition, with the job market so radically changed over the last decade, younger academics are looking for new and creative ways to teach, publish and interact with those inside and outside of academia. I believe this has the potential to vastly improve the current situation and can provide islands of refuge amidst the stream of inauthentic "Celtic" information that continues to flood the market. It is important to remember that there are many wonderful, intelligent and hard-working people interested in Celtic languages and literatures who just don't happen to be Celticists. They are doctors, lawyers, nurses, teachers, business executives and military personnel, as well as writers, poets and artists, and parents who wish to raise their children to be well-versed in the actualities of their Celtic heritage (even teaching them a Celtic language before they learn a cultural-majority language).

In order to provide sources of useful and authentic material, we must examine aspects of the archaeological record, as well as historical sources, linguistics, and comparative religion. We have to be cognizant of the dates of manuscripts, as well as likely dates of composition based on language forms and even veiled references to current events. Other important aspects like cultural context, the intentions of a particular patron or scribe, and actions and objects that were important in the daily lives of ancient or medieval people, all play a part in the interpretation. We must also work to discern which elements may be native in origin and which reflect Biblical, Classical or other Medieval sources. At this point, the wearying and decades old categorization of researchers or methodologies as "nativist" or "non-nativist" has thankfully pretty much run its course. That debate did bring up many interesting and important considerations, but in the final analysis, choosing the middle road has proven to be of most service in considering areas that ultimately fall under the category of the humanities, rather than the hard sciences. This is not to say that science doesn't have a role to play, for it does, and I myself am encouraged by recent efforts in cross-disciplinary research. The archaeologist digging at a ritual site, the historian who knows the history of the area, and the Celticist who understands the ins-and-outs of the literature have much to share with each other. Edel Bhreathnach has written eloquently about these topics in *Ireland in the Medieval World AD 400–1000* (Dublin: Four Courts, 2014). In Part Three, entitled "Religion, ritual and ritualists," she writes the following [pp. 130–131]:

> Too often, the complexities of the religious human experience and the complexity of a society's conversion from one religion to another have been lost in the frequently naïve and confrontational discourse on pagan and Christian in Ireland. Religion comes under the scrutiny of many disciplines, some of which have been rarely intro-

duced to early medieval Irish religious studies. These include anthropology, comparative religious studies and cognitive science. The extension of the narrative of religious beliefs in early Ireland into these fields has the potential to offer new and rational insights into the practice of religion, custom and ritual in this society, which, in turn, elucidates aspects of its distinction between "the sacred and the profane," if that distinction existed at all....

These models prove invaluable in comprehending the process of conversion and the survival of traces of the older religion into the Middle Ages. This subject is fraught with difficulties, and scholars in recent decades have stressed the many pitfalls when attempting to define or disentangle earlier belief systems from an omnipresent medieval Christian culture....

While it is clear that Christian literate culture inspired many early Latin and vernacular Irish texts, the range of texts in Ireland, especially in the vernacular, is so varied and so close in date to the continued existence of strong elements of the old religion that, combined with archaeological and other evidence and with the use of models from other disciplines, it is possible to identify genuine non–Christian religious practices and practitioners.

In addition to cross-disciplinary work and the results that will undoubtedly flow from those processes, it is also exciting to witness the work of new members of the academy, as well as new ventures from more established scholars. I am heartened by the open-mindedness of up-and-coming scholars who were not reared on the nativist v. non-nativist debate, but have been trained to consider all aspects of the strands of tradition and history that comprise medieval literature and look at it with fresh eyes. Researchers are now exploring topics that were once deemed too inconsequential, "fringe" or even taboo (from the standpoint of Classically-inspired models of ethnocentrism and colonialism that have formed the basis for the educational model for too long), as well as monotheistic-derived judgments and assumptions that are far from objective. It is imperative that we approach these cultures, and their beliefs and traditions, with as much objectivity and respect as possible, and when possible, to let them speak for themselves.

In an illuminating article, "Symbol and Mystery in Irish Religious Thought" (*Temenos Journal* 13, 1992), John Carey writes about the importance of this mythic symbolism (p. 102):

The literature is as rich in metaphor and image as it is poor in theory and abstraction, and it is surely here that the key is to be found. The indigenous Irish mentality tends to find expression in symbolic rather than in analytic terms: concepts are not extracted from phenomena in order to be manipulated on the plane of "pure reason," but are instilled and contemplated in concrete entities ... a symbol, unlike an abstract concept, is alive, and therefore inexhaustible: it can embrace contraries, point the way into deeper or subtler realms of thought, or be itself transformed and reinterpreted by the unfolding of history.

In this book, I have endeavored to provide a scholarly exploration of certain aspects of Celtic cultures and their religious beliefs, including how those aspects of the human experience which are concerned with non-mundane topics and themes may have been expressed in written form. I have sought to delve deeply into patterns, reflections and elements that may pertain to indigenous beliefs, practices and perceptions among Celtic-speaking cultures. These include tales concerning the origins of things, the presence of the pre–Christian Otherworld and its inhabitants, and the all-important concept of Sovereignty, especially as personified in female form. I am also interested in the ways in which people may have attempted to interact with the Otherworld, whether ritually utilizing (or avoiding) certain parts of the landscape, making use of music or poetic recitation to invoke or praise supernatural beings, and what role religious offerings or rites may have played in all of this. It is fascinating to track the theme of the Otherworld as the source of wisdom, healing, prosperity, victory, guidance and truth (a theme that has persisted over many centuries), as well as the importance of boundaries—and liminal times and places—in regards to that theme. One must be able to recognize the Otherworld, and act according to traditional precedents when in its presence, in order to gain access to its gifts.

This book is arranged in three parts based upon three major themes: Cosmology, Sovereignty and Liminality. In Chapter 1, we will look at a wide range of materials that come under the general heading of cosmology, including beliefs about how the cosmos is arranged, and aspects of tales that may pertain to sacred origins. Chapter 2 contains a unique exploration of the pseudo-historical aspects of medieval literature to see what patterns regarding native origins may be found. While the first two chapters explore both temporal and spatial concepts, Chapter 3 explores the temporal aspect in more depth, and looks at layers of data pertaining to cyclical time, as well as seasonal celebrations and related deities.

The next three chapters have to do with Sovereignty, specifically with goddess figures whose tales have much to say about how people viewed the stewardship of the land and the divine beings who inhabited it. In Chapter 4 (an updated version of that first paper mentioned at the start of the Introduction), I explore a wide range of materials pertaining to the figures of Danu, Anu and the Mórrígan, and discuss how they may be interconnected, and subsequently re-examined and re-understood. In Chapter 5, I present a new look at the figure of Guinevere (Gwenhwyfar), and through comparisons with the Irish figure of Findabair and an exploration of the Welsh Triads, seek to reveal the presence of Sovereignty in places where it has been disguised or lost under layers of medieval accretion. In Chapter 6, I have brought together a wide range of references to the little-studied figure of Flidais, exploring her "wilder side" and her independent nature, which tie into concepts related to Sovereignty in unexpected ways.

The final three chapters each relate in different ways to the theme of

Liminality, particularly exploring how people may have attempted to cross boundaries, access arcane knowledge, or "walk between the worlds." Chapter 7 looks at the theme of the Nine Otherworldly maidens, and explores early Classical accounts of priestesses and Otherworld islands, as well as a Gaulish inscription and other materials relating to holy people who lived and worked in relation to (as well as devotion to) the sacred Otherworld realms. In Chapter 8, I have gathered together a wide range of resources pertaining to the arch-druid figure Mug Roith and his equally fascinating daughter Tlachtga, who was associated with the site where the pagan Irish were said to have held their Samain rituals. Through genealogies, poems, glossary references and sagas, we can follow literary depictions of their training and perceived power, as well as images of druids and their magic (including their association with a bewildering array of magical objects). Finally, in Chapter 9, I explore the relationship between Water and Wisdom, both as it was believed to relate to (and flow through) the physical landscape, but also the role it played in relation to the quest for Otherworldly knowledge and poetic inspiration (a theme that will play a major role in my next book).

At this point, I would like to take a moment to thank a great many people who have been of immeasurable assistance and support throughout this process. First and foremost, I must thank my family who, although slogging through hundreds of pages of arcane information pertaining to our Celtic ancestors isn't necessarily their cup of tea, have in their own special ways been absolutely unflagging in their support and encouragement, never slow to express their happiness for my successes, and quick to express pride in what I have accomplished. Next, I must thank many dear friends who have watched and supported me as I have explored these pathways in great depth, have sometimes fallen and gotten back up again, and ultimately arrived at a place where I can joyfully weave together all the threads of knowledge I have been blessed to possess. They have remembered the struggles of the journey and have understood what it all meant and why it was so important to do. These include academic colleagues, many of whom have become close friends, who have never judged my areas of research or the ways in which I explored them (and have unwittingly often served as "dealers" for precisely the type of research materials they know I like). I offer my gratitude and warmest wishes to Dr. Benjamin Bruch, Dr. Charlene Eska, Dr. Michael Newton, Dr. Kate Olson, Dr. Joe Eska, Dr. Michael Linkletter, Dr. Dorothy Africa, and many more. I am humbled and grateful for the direction and tutelage that has been so generously provided by the faculty and staff at Harvard University, including Professor Patrick Ford, Professor Tomás Ó Cathasaigh, Professor William Gillies, Dr. Kathryn Chadbourne, Dr. Barbara Hillers, and many others in the Department of Celtic Languages and Literatures.

I am also so very grateful for long-time friends—many of whom are more like family, at this point—who have encouraged me along every path I have sought to explore intellectually, creatively and personally: James Möbius and Donna Martinez, Bart Mallio and Sharon Gadonniex (whose painting graces the cover of this book), Daphne Bishop and Iain Stewart, Jean Teneriello and Diane Gatchell, Charlie Maguire and Stephanie LoGrande, Mark Bilokur and John Powell, Sarah McKee and Gina Martin, Michael Verrilli and Deborah Uller, Carin Roberge and Kevin Gregg, Thomas Leigh and Maggie Carchrie, Laurie Gale and Bruce Imber, Caris Visentin and Dave Liebman, Diane Champigny and Gypsy Ravish, Laura Wilson and Kris Thompson, Tracy Wilkinson and Tim Saunders, Rich Taylor and Brett Bevell, and Walter Lavash (who stands alone in his prodigious power).

I would also like to thank the members of The Moors and Trouz Bras; the staff and students at The Omega Institute, Kripalu Center, Arlington Center and Rowe Center; Joseph Keane and Danny O'Flaherty, Ji Hyang of Wellesley College and Dr. Julia Jean, Sisters of Sophia and Tintagels Gate, Tim Swallow and brothers and sisters of the Inipi Lodge, and Scott Dakota and the inhabitants of Nine Cambridge Terrace, where all this Celtic madness first began. In Ireland, warmth and blessings to Dr. Jenny Butler, Mary McKenna, Dr. Gearóid Denvir, Prof. John Carey, Declan Forde, and a great warrior-poet of the old style, Alan Ó Domhnaill. In Scotland, a sprig of heather and a Gaelic song to Liam and Valerie Gillies, Dr. John Purser and Barbara, Dr. Emily Lyle and Professor Rob Dunbar, friends and colleagues at the University of Edinburgh and Sabhal Mòr Ostaig, as well as all the wonderful beings who live in and around the hills of my beloved *Siorrachd Pheairt* (Pitlochry, Fortingall, Gleann Lìomhann, Loch Tatha) and the Isle of Mist (Eilean a' Cheò), *An t-Eilean Sgitheanach.*

Tapadh leibh–Go raibh maith agat–Diolch yn fawr–Meur ras–Wopila

A Note About
Indo-European Root Words

Linguists have worked backwards in time to bring to light a parent language—referred to as Proto-Indo-European (PIE) and assumed to have been in existence between 4500 and 2500 BCE—from which many descendant languages have their origin. Even if not attested in an inscription or document, by following known linguistic rules of sound and spelling change, we do in fact arrive at the extant languages. Throughout the text, Indo-European words or word segments that are theorized and linguistically feasible but not directly attested are preceded by an asterisk.

1

Cosmology and the Celtic Dreamtime

A sacred spot never presents itself to the mind in isolation. It is always part of a complexus of things which include plant or animal species which flourish there at various seasons, as well as the mythical heroes who lived, roamed or created something there and who are embodied in the very soil, the ceremonies which take place there from time to time, and all the emotions aroused by the whole.
—Lucien Lévy-Bruhl[1]

Our knowledge of traditional Celtic cosmology might be likened to a shining, multi-hued cloak whose strands have not yet been woven together into a unified whole, a garment with potentially threadbare places due to information that has been lost over time. Archaeology and Classical reports pertaining to the Celts and their cultural and religious traditions can provide us with some useful insights. In addition, a number of mythological and cosmological elements may be discerned in some early Irish literary sources, the subjects of which are found in association with cosmology in other cultures. In Tomás Ó Cathasaigh's article, "Pagan survivals: the evidence of early Irish narrative," he makes the following observations:

> ...what is remarkable about the Irish situation is the extent and richness of the vernacular literature which has come down to us from the early medieval period. Much of this literature is firmly rooted in ancient myth and remains robustly pagan in character; it has been used, along with other evidence, to build up at least a partial picture, not only of the pagan religion of the Irish, but also that of the Celts, and it has even been laid under contribution in the comparative study of Indo-European mythology.[2]

Attempting to reconstruct a native system of ideology from a patchwork of sources that differ in both temporal and spatial realities requires a keen eye and an awareness of the potential alterations that may have taken place over time; we need to examine each thread carefully.[3]

Scholars have long lamented the fact that Irish myth is not an intact mythology in the usual sense of the word, for archaic elements have been interwoven with a variety of Biblical and medieval materials. In terms of the debate between "nativist" and "non-nativist" viewpoints, Mark Williams notes the complexity of the backdrop to vernacular literary culture. He quotes Elva Johnston's proposition that we think in terms of "interlocking intellectual elites, imagining neither a nativist gulf between indigenous and ecclesiastical men of learning, nor an anti-nativist fusion between the two".[4] Williams notes that we can picture the *filid,* members of a highly trained learned class of medieval Irish poet-seers, as bridging the ecclesiastical and secular worlds, sharing their intellectual and religious thoughts with their clerical colleagues.[5] In terms of the timeline of the various cultural processes at work, especially in relation to cosmology, Marina Smyth writes:

> It is most unlikely … that within a mere two centuries Christianity had completely wiped out all indigenous cosmological doctrines, all the more so as Ireland was no more universally Christian at that time than any other area of western Europe. It is more believable that the tendency to recognize the inherent value of pre–Christian wisdom inasmuch as it did not conflict with the new religion, was applied in the realm of natural science as well as to traditional law—in other words, if indigenous cosmological perceptions were not threatening, why reject them?[6]

In this book we will be making use of native literary sources, augmented by evidence from archaeology, comparative religion, linguistics, Indo-European studies, and Classical accounts pertaining to the Celts and their culture.[7] It is important to have an awareness of the potential for diversity between various Celtic regions and eras. Something that was reported about the Gauls in the 1st century BCE may not reflect the beliefs or practices of the Irish or the Picts in the fourth century CE. However, by casting a fairly wide net and keeping a number of important caveats in mind, in some cases we may be able to discern patterns of symbolism and belief which can help us begin to weave together a tapestry that reflects some aspects of cosmology and religion amongst some of the Celtic-speaking nations.[8] Roseanne Schot writes:

> It appears that historians and literary scholars by and large agree that despite censorship, revision and deliberate omission on the part of Christian redactors, some residual motifs or themes of pre–Christian origin remain … this is an area where each case needs to be assessed on its own merits and one in which multi-disciplinary studies clearly have a major role to play.[9]

The Vertical Cosmos

In numerous traditional cultures there is a perception that the earth on which we live is just one of many worlds. This belief frequently manifests in the perception of one or more additional and separate Otherworld realms, which may exist above or below our world, or which may function as parallel realms contiguous with our own. Sufficient evidence exists to support the assumption that in earliest times the Celtic Otherworld or Cosmos was conceived of as being triune in nature.[10] This reflects a widespread cosmological conception of the threefold nature of the divine realms, often categorized as "Earth, Sky, and Sea/Underworld." R. Mark Scowcroft states that the division of the land into three is likely to have been an early native concept, a triune system which corresponds to what Mircea Eliade identified as "the three cosmic zones" (actual, celestial and chthonic) which are frequented by shamans around the world.[11]

From the evidence that we have, it appears that the Celtic Otherworld (or worlds) were conceived of as existing nearby (and parallel to) our own plane of existence. These were most often said to be located in or underneath hills, beneath lakes or under the sea, on islands situated in lakes or off the coast, or in halls or buildings encountered by chance in the night which disappear with the dawn.[12] Certain aspects of the Otherworld mirror those of the mortal realm, yet in many ways it was considered superior to our world.[13] Let us examine in detail some of the historical accounts and texts which contain information pertinent to the layout of the cosmos.

Early reports of encounters between the ancient Celts and members of other cultures provide us with some hints as to how the Celts perceived the cosmos. One of the earliest accounts pertains to Alexander the Great, who lived from 356–323 BCE. When the Celts living on the Adriatic met Alexander on the Danube, he asked them what they feared most. They replied that it was the sky falling on them (rather than Alexander himself, as he had hoped).[14]

Aristotle, writing around 330 BCE, described the Celts as "fearing nothing, neither earthquakes nor waves," even to the point of taking up arms against the ocean waves.[15] The integrity of the cosmos depended on the stability of these elements, and an early Irish poem remarks on the lack of divine retribution against a group of criminals by bemoaning that: "...the sky did not fall on them ... the great ocean did not drown them ... the heavy earth did not swallow them."[16]

Liam Mac Mathúna has written extensively about native Celtic perceptions of a three-fold cosmos consisting of sky, earth and sea.[17] He states that this three-fold division of the cosmos in Irish sources was traceable back to their Continental Celtic forebears, and that it was central to the thinking of the Irish in the early historical period.[18] Exemplars from early Irish sources demonstrate what Mac Mathúna describes as an inherited triangular division of the observable cosmos: Old Irish *nem, talam, ocus muir* ("sky, earth and sea").[19] In the first recension of the Irish saga *Táin Bó Cuailgne, Sualdam,* the father of the great hero *Cú Chulainn*, hears a report that his son is fighting outnumbered in a very dangerous situation and cries out:

> *In nem maides fa muir thar chricha fa thalam conscara fa gáir no maice se,' ol se, "re n-éccomlonn?*[20]

> "Is it the sky that cracks, or the sea that overflows its boundaries, or the earth that splits, or is it the loud cry of my son fighting against odds?"[21]

He travels to warn King Conchobar, and again cries out about the warfare and destruction that is taking place. Conchobar responds to his alarm by saying:

> *Muir ara cendaib, in nem húasa mbennaib, talum foa cosaib, dobér-sa cech mboin ina hindis díb ocus cach mben ocus cech mac dia tig iar mbúaid chatha.*[22]

> "[I swear by] the sea before them, the sky above them, the earth beneath them, that I shall restore every cow to its byre and every woman and boy to their own homes after victory in battle."[23]

In the version of the *Táin* from the Book of Leinster, Conchobar's response is even more cosmologically explicit. As in the First Recension, the king is not initially impressed with the urgency of the situation:

> *Romór bic in núall sa,' bar Conchobor, 'dáig nem úasaind ocus talam ísaind ocus muir immaind immácúaird, acht munu tháeth in firmimint cona frossaib rétland bar dunadgnúis in talman nó mono máe in talam assa thalamchumscugud ná mono thí inn fairge ethrech ochorgorm for tulmoing in bethad, dobér-sa cach bó ocus cach ben díb cá lias ocus cá machad, co'aitte ocus co'adbai fadessin ar mbuaid chatha ocus chomlaind ocus chomraic.*

> "A little too loud is that cry," said Conchobor, "for the sky is above us, the earth beneath us, and the sea all around us, but unless the sky with its showers of stars falls upon the surface of the earth, or unless the ground bursts open in an earthquake, or unless the fish-abounding, blue-bordered sea comes over the surface of existence, I shall bring back every cow to its byre, every woman to her abode and dwelling, after victory in battle and combat and contest."[24]

Elsewhere in the tale, Cú Chulain himself invokes the aid of this cosmic triad:

> *Adeochosa inna husci do chongnam frim. Ateoch nem ocus talmuin ocus Cruinn in tsainrethaig.*[25]

> "I beseech the rivers to come to my help. I call upon heaven and earth and especially the river Cronn to aid me."[26]

William Sayers writes that while much of the evidence we have is allusive, "durable sets of motifs and widespread homological correspondences among these sets suggest an archaic Celtic conception of a tripartite cosmos composed of three domains:

(1) The sky or heavens
(2) The earth's surface, our familiar world, and
(3) The underearth and undersea, subterranean and submarine."[27]

This triune perception of the cosmos was at variance with the dualistic "heaven/earth" opposition of Christian belief, but in a few instances the inherited triad of *nem, talam, muir* survived, as in this example from the poems of *Blathmac* (257–260):

> *Ba deithbir do dúilib Dé,*
> *muir mas, nem nglas, talam cé,*
> *co imro-imchloítis a ngné*
> *oc coíniud a ngalgaite.*

> "It would have been fitting for God's elements,
> the beautiful sea, the blue heaven, the present earth,
> that they should change their aspect
> when keening their hero."[28]

While most Christian descriptions of the act of creation state that God created "the heaven and the earth," an enumeration of the native triune cosmos was preserved in *Leabhar Breac*:

> *Dia ... is e do-roine nem ocus talam ocus muir...*

> "God, it is he who made heaven and earth and the sea..."[29]

Scowcroft notes that the native threefold division of the cosmos appears to have suffered alteration over time, being presented later as a binary system composed of polar opposites more in keeping with the Christian concept of good and evil, Heaven and Hell.[30] These changes in the interpretation, representation and perception of the sacred realms resulted in a great deal of confusion regarding the nature of the Celtic Otherworld (and well as the nature and origin of its inhabitants).[31]

Some of the earliest clues we have pertaining to Celtic conceptions about the cosmos come from linguistic evidence. Victor Kalygin has explored this evidence in detail and his work provides us with extremely helpful insights into these concepts. He points out that in Old Irish there are two different words meaning "world": *domun* and *bith*. *Domun* refers to "earth, land, soil" while *bith* refers to what lives in or on the world. *Bith* is cognate with Welsh *byd*, which is etymologically connected with Gaulish *Bitu-*. Both *bitu-* and *bith* derive from Common Celtic **bitu-* which comes from an Indo-European root word meaning "living." Thus, the words *bith* and *domun* reflect two different semiotic classifications, "living/moving" vs. "inanimate/staying."[32] Here we will be concerning ourselves with the sense of "world" as reflected in the word *domun*, as we explore the concept of "other worlds."

The Old Irish word *domun*, the obsolete Welsh word *dwfn* ("depth/world") and Gaulish *dubno-* ("world") come from Common Celtic **dubno-* meaning "dark" (< I.E. root **dheubh-* "black, dark"). This word could be used as an adjective ("deep, dark") and occurs in a number of compound words referring to water or the depths of waters. Kalygin states that the semantic development in the Celtic languages from "deep/ bottom" > "world" may be interpreted as remnants of a cosmological conception.[33]

Another word to be taken into account is the Welsh word *elfydd*, which derives from Common Celtic *albijo* (< Proto Indo-European [P.I.E.] *albho-* "white"; Cf. Gaulish *albio-*). This word has no direct equivalent in Irish, except perhaps in the Gaelic name of Scotland, *Alba*, which may be a borrowing from Brittonic. *Elfydd* seems to refer to "land, surface,(this) world." This word occurs in an excerpt from a poem in the Black Book of Carmarthen which reads: *oetun blodev guit/at vinep eluit* ("I was forest blossoms on the face of *elfydd*").[34] In the Book of Taliesin, a poem which refers to the ordering of poetic inspiration states that it exists: *Yn Annwfn is eluyd/yn awyr uch eluyd* ("in *Annwfn* below the earth/in the air above the earth").[35]

Annwfn was an early Welsh term used to refer to the Otherworld, which Kalygin suggests derives from *ande-dubno-* (denoting either "under/below/ beneath/lower" + "deep/dark," or "very" + "deep/dark"), referring to a Lower World or Underworld realm.[36] He points out that *Annwfn* would have been a secondary semantic development stemming from a primitive Proto-Celtic word for "Otherworld" which was probably *dubnos-*, later prefixed by *ande-* (Cf. Gaulish gen.pl. *anderon*). The prefix reinforced the original meaning of "dark/deep" and may have been used to name the Otherworld in particular by describing it as "very dark/deep" or "lower dark/deep." He feels this change occurred because *dubnos* had lost its special significance and had become a general word for "world," alongside *albios* and *bitus*.[37]

John Koch has also written about the words *elfydd* and *alba* in relation to Celtic cosmogonic concepts:

> It would of course be extremely valuable to know how the pagan Celts conceived of the world or earth…. Plainly *elfydd* does not mean the whole of the universe nor even what we would call the earth. It excludes *awyr* … the lower atmospheric air or sky, *gwynt* "wind," *gweilgi* "sea," and it sits above…. *Annwfwn* … which is, clearly enough in the Welsh tradition, the subterranean realm of the old pagan gods. *Elfydd* is where the trees and flowers grow. It is that part to which *dynyon*, "human beings" belong.[38]

Koch refers to an additional line of poetry from *Canu Taliesin—y dynyon eluyd—*"to the human beings of *elfydd*." He has suggested that *Elfydd* is not considered "white" (*albho-*) in contrast with the sky above, but in contradistinction to the underworld below:

> When the ancient Britons called themselves *Albiones,* this signified, essentially, dwellers on the earth's surface, and the primary distinction was … against supernatural beings thought to inhabit the infernal regions and watery depths—in other words, an essential opposition between mortals vs. immortals. This cosmology had changed drastically from that which prevailed in Indo-European times. The Common Celtic word for a human being was *(g)donjos* (> Welsh *dyn*, OIr. *duine*), the

etymological sense of which is "belonging to the earth." Its exact cognate is Greek *khthoniós,* "underworld supernatural being." The concept which had originally opposed this was that behind **deiwos,* which had meant in Indo-European a divine being of the shining sky.[39]

So where does all this lead us? First we might visualize a linguistically well-supported theory of Indo-European cosmology in which deities inhabited the bright sky realm, and human beings—those that "belonged to the earth"—lived below them.[40] In Celtic cultures, at least, there appears to have been a shift; human beings lived in the realm above, and the gods lived below in the Underworld.[41] This may be the result of changes in religious belief and practice which started in the late Bronze Age in Europe, in which the religious focus on the heavens (as evident from pre–Iron Age monuments and alignments) changed to a focus on the lower world. All across Europe, offerings began to be made into bodies of water (and ostensibly, into the earth as well). It has been theorized that this took place due to deterioration in climate in the later Bronze Age.[42] Whatever the cause, by the time of the Iron Age Celts the primary focus is on the Lower World and the supernatural beings who dwell there.[43] It should be noted that in Celtic tradition the Lower World was not a dark or gloomy place; descriptions of it depict a lush, almost dreamlike region. The Celtic Otherworld was "deep" in the sense of being below us, existing in the depths under the surface of the earth and beneath the waters. However, it was not "dark" in terms of aspect or condition, but in terms of "that which is not commonly seen."[44]

Belief in a world which existed beneath our own can be surmised from descriptions in medieval Irish texts. Apparently some of the Irish may have still clung to these beliefs even after conversion. In the year 748, Pope Zachary wrote a letter to Saint Boniface and mentions a complaint he received concerning an Irish cleric named Virgil, who at that time was working in Bavaria. Virgil was teaching his Bavarian flock that there was another world and other men beneath the earth, as well as a sun and moon. As a result of these heretical teachings, the Pope directed that Virgil be expelled from the church. It appears that this did not happen, for in 767 Virgil was elevated to the bishopric of Salzburg, and was later canonized in 1233.[45]

The Horizontal Cosmos

In addition to a three-fold vertical structure, the universe also possesses a horizontal structure. Many religious traditions refer to the four quarters of the world (or the four cardinal directions).[46] In the tale *Aided Dhiarmada meic Cherbaill,* Diarmait is trying to return to Tara for the *Feis Temro* ("Feast of Tara") at Samain after his royal circuit. The text states that his circuit traditionally took him first to Leinster, then to Munster, from there to Connacht and finally to Ulster, outlining a sun-wise circle starting in the east. This type of movement was considered auspicious in Indo-European cultures.[47] In Celtic sources, there is often a focus on the central point as well, making a total of five sacred points.[48] In many cultures, the four quarters are associated with particular elements, colors or attributes. Alwyn and Brinley Rees have discussed the Irish manifestation of this concept in some detail,[49] as has Grigory Bondarenko in his work on Irish mythology.[50] The topic has also been explored by Proinsias Mac Cana in his book on the sacred center.[51]

One of the most fascinating of the early Irish narratives is *Suidigud Tellaig Temra*, "The Settling of the Manor of Tara." It is contained in the Yellow Book of Lecan (late 14th or early 15th century) and the Book of Lismore (late 15th century). In this story, during the reign of *Diarmait mac Cerball* (545 CE–565 CE), the nobles of Ireland refused to attend the feast of Tara until some arrangement was made concerning the limitation of the royal domain. *Fintan mac Bóchra*, a figure who was said to have lived before the Flood, was summoned to make a judgment on the matter, due to his learnedness regarding the history of Ireland.

Fintan's authority on this matter is a mysterious figure named *Trefuilngid Tre-eochair*, who had appeared at a gathering in the past. Fintan states that Trefuilngid had asked that seven people from each quarter of Ireland be assembled, especially the wisest, most prudent and most cunning among them, together with their principal *seanchaidh* ("historian, custodian of traditional lore"). Once this had happened, he would communicate to the people (and especially to Fintan) the manner in which the land should be partitioned. After hearing his story, the nobles of Ireland accompanied Fintan to the hill of Uisnech, the cosmological center of Ireland. There he set up a pillar-stone marking the five provinces and recited a poem describing the boundaries of each.[52]

The scene in which the manner of the partitioning of the land is revealed is quite remarkable. Trefuilngid asks Fintan how Ireland had been partitioned and what things had been in each partition.

> *Ni ansa, ar Fintain, Íaruss fis. Tuadus cath. Airthis bláth. Teissus séis. Fortius fláith.*

"Easy to say," said Fintan: "knowledge in the west, battle in the north, prosperity in the east, music in the south, kingship in the center."[53]

To this answer, Trefuilngid replies:

> *Is fír ém, a Findtain, ar Tréfuilngid, at senchaid saineamail. Is amlaid robái ocus bias co bráth béos.*

"True indeed, O Fintan," said Trefuilngid. "You are an excellent seanchaidh. It is thus that it has been, and will be forever."

Trefuilngid then relates the properties or attributes which reside in each quarter of the land:

West: Learning, foundation, teaching, alliance, judgment, chronicles, counsels, stories, histories, science, comeliness, eloquence, beauty, modesty, bounty, abundance, wealth

North: Battles, contentions, hardihood, rough places, strife, haughtiness, unprofitableness, pride, captures, assaults, hardness, wars, conflicts

East: Prosperity, supplies, bee-hives, contests, feats of arms, householders, nobles, wonders, good custom, good manners, splendor, abundance, dignity, strength, wealth, householding, many arts, accoutrements, many treasures, satin, serge, silk, cloths, green spotted cloth, hospitality.

South: Waterfalls, fairs, nobles, reavers, knowledge, subtlety, musicianship, melody, minstrelsy, wisdom, honour, music, learning, teaching, warriorship, *fidchell* playing, vehemence, fierceness, poetical art, advocacy, modesty, code, retinue, fertility.

Center: Kings, stewards, dignity, primacy, stability, establishments, supports, destructions, warriorship, charioteership, soldiery, principality, high-kingship, ollaveship, mead, bounty, ale, reknown, great fame, prosperity.[54]

Taking into consideration the lateness of the manuscripts in which this story has been preserved, if the attributes presented here do represent aspects of native belief (at whatever stage of development or transmission), this is a remarkably detailed, nuanced and illuminating representation of how the early Irish may have perceived the horizontal cosmos.

In other Irish texts, the four cardinal directions and the directions between them seem to have been associated with certain winds, which were credited with particular attributes. A poem edited by Meyer, which he ascribes to the 10th century, mentions eight winds which might blow on the 1st of January and their attributes. This appears to have been a form of weather divination that took place at the New Year. The first stanza begins: "Guide us, O Christ, that rulest the sea around the mighty vast world; that I may tell what signifies the voice of the wind (*gair gaithi*) on the calends of January." The attributes of the winds in this text are:

East: It is fruitful though productive of plague; it rejects chiefs only; many are its diseases.

South-east: Not bad; it signifies especially good fruit, fish and corn, while it lasts; it is unique in its excellences.

South: It signifies a rich harvest; a great quantity of full fruit; marvelous huge fish.

South-west: Goods will be destroyed; a track not narrow; it signifies every crop laid low; battles and scant harvests.
West: It denotes the death of a king; great bloodshed; slaying of men; and plague on sinners.
North-West: Death and slaughters.
North: There will be noise of red-sworded battle; death of the sinful; plague and heat; drought and heavy distress.
North-east: A fair multitude of fish, but a petty commemoration, as there are sicknesses in it; battle with venom; "many fruits it brings to us."[55]

Taking into account the association of east with prosperity and north with battle in the story of Fintan, we can perceive a general sort of agreement between the two texts. A proverb from Irish folk tradition may also be relevant: "In every land, hardness is in the north of it, softness in the south, industry in the east, and fire and inspiration in the west."[56]

Another example of attributes associated with the winds and the directions comes from a tract pertaining to the creation of the world. It is found in its entirety in Egerton 92 (15th century) and appended to the prologue of the *Senchas Már,* a collection of law texts which came into being in the Old Irish period (Harleian 432, early 16th century).[57] *Saltair na Rann* describes the creation of heaven and earth; the sun, moon and stars; "the birds of the air, the serpents of the sea" and "the beasts of the earth." In the third section of the text there is a passage enumerating the creation of twelve winds, each of which was associated with a specific color. There were four chief winds, each of which had two secondary winds located spatially after the chief wind.[58] The four chief winds and their associated colors were:

East: Purple
South: White
West: Dun
North: Black

Starting in the east and proceeding in a sunwise direction (the direction of auspicious movement in Indo-European traditions), the colors of the twelve winds were described as follows (with the chief winds capitalized)[59]:

Purple, red, yellow; White, green, blue; Dun, gray, jet-black; Black, dark, piebald
Corcor, dearg, buide, Geal, uaine, glas, Odhar, liath, ciar, Dub, temen, alad[60]

We can perceive a logical progression from Purple, red and yellow; towards White, green and blue; Dun, grey and jet-black; and finally to Black, dark and variegated hues.

A set of colors similar to those of the *prímgaetha* ("primary winds") is found in Isidore of Seville's *De natura rerum*. Isidore's writings are known to have been widely read by the learned classes in early medieval Ireland. In this work, the colors are associated with the rainbow:

> For it has four colours, and takes to itself appearances from all the elements. For from heaven it takes the colour of fire, from the waters purple, white from the air, and black from the earth.[61]

In comparing the two texts, we can see that *Saltair na Rann* has "dun" instead of "fire-coloured" (*igneus*), but otherwise the four colors are the same. It is important to note that the concept of four "elements" (earth, air, fire and water) associated with the four directions originates in Greco-Roman contexts, but does not form part of Celtic cosmology.

The color "dun" is familiar to people in modern times primarily in relation to the color of horses or cattle. In horse breeds, it denotes a variety of colors, including light yellow, sandy yellow, reddish brown and steel grey, although a range of light, creamy tan to deep, rich gold is most commonly associated with the term. In cattle breeds, dun denotes a range including yellow, brown and a dull shade of brownish grey. The English word "dun" literally means "dark or dusky," which fits well with the position of dun in the western quarter. John Carey writes that on an intuitive level it does not seem inappropriate that purple—especially the Irish *corcur,* which tended towards crimson—should be associated with the region of dawn, and dun with that of evening, or that north and south should be black and white respectively.[62]

Carey notes that the system seen in *Saltair na Rann* is quite isolated in medieval Europe, even when taking into consideration the passage from Isidore, the association of colors with the four principal winds in the book of Zechariah, and the assigning of colors to the heavenly quadrants by Arabic and Jewish writers between the ninth and twelfth centuries. None of these examples agrees with the Irish system in its arrangement of the colors, and in the absence of other evidence, he notes that there appears to be nothing against the hypothesis that the *Saltair*'s color scheme originated in Ireland.[63]

> It seems most reasonable to suppose that the system as we have it was devised in Ireland; at any rate, no foreign exemplar has yet presented itself. This being so, it is likeliest that in an earlier version the colors were four in number, related specifically to the cardinal points (*arda*) which, unlike the winds, played a major part in native Irish conceptions of cosmic order.[64]

The color scheme associated with the four primary winds in *Saltair na Rann* also reflects the results of Berlin and Kay's well-known research on color terminology. They concluded that that in numerous cultures, the first stage of color differentiation and naming relates to white and black (or more accurately, light and dark). The third color stage or category differentiated and named is red, and the fourth is green or yellow. This is followed by a fifth stage (blue), sixth stage (brown), and seventh through eleventh stages (in varying order: purple, pink, orange and grey).[65] An analysis of color terms in Celtic contexts by Heidi Lazar-Meyn showed that Old and Middle Irish had a "stage four" color system. That is to say, according to Berlin and Kay's system, it had only five basic colors: *dub* "black," *bán* "white," *derg* "red," *buide* "yellow" and *glas* ("green and blue").[66] By slightly emending the set, from red to purple/crimson, and from yellow to dun, we arrive at the colors of the four primary winds in the Irish text.

If, as an exploratory exercise, we note the range of meanings of the colors of the winds, and arrange them in relation to the primary attributes of the four quarters as outlined in *Suidigud Tellaig Temra* (with their attendant range of meaning), some symbolic patterns may emerge.

> *East:* Prosperity/*Bláth* ("flower, blossom; bloom, (bright) color; flourishing appearance, condition; prosperous, prosperity")
>
>   *Corcur* (Cf. Latin *purpura*): "purple/crimson," often used of cloth, plants or flowers.
>
>   *Derg* "red, ruddy," used of the color of blood, flame; also orange or tawny hue as of ale, gold, etc.; used to describe eyes, cheeks, complexion, hair; animals, plants; as well as earth or clay turned up; In a figurative sense "full-blooded, flushed with pride"; as an intensive: raging, bitter, fierce, intense; note the verb *dergaid* "reddens, makes red; makes red-hot, heats, kindles, burns; reddens" (soil), hence "turns up" (soil), digs, ploughs.
>
>   *Buide* "yellow," used of hair, flowers, honey, pollen; used in phrases or compounds with the word *bith* "the world; land, territory, soil; existence, life; age, period of time."
>
> *South:* Music/*Séis* ("sense, meaning; design, plan; order, arrangement; commentary, explanatory treatise; air, strain, melody, noise, sound")
>
>   *Gel* "fair, white, bright, shining"; used of complexion, limbs; metals, weapons; the sun, scenery, foliage, animals; inanimate objects. The word *gelach* means "moon" (*Cf.* the verbs *gelaid* "makes white, bleaches"; intransitive use "grows white, shines" and *gelaigid* "brightens, gives light to; grows white (with blossom), blossoms")
>
>   *Uaine* "green, verdant"; of fields, hills; estuaries, rivers (blue or green); animals (a duck's head); eyes, eyelashes; clothes, armour; drinking horns; walls, ramparts; ice or stars
>
>   *Glas* "various shades of light green and blue, from grass-green to grey"; differentiated from *uaine* "green" and *gorm* "blue." "Green or greenish hue," especially of growing things such as grass and trees. Blue, greenish blue or greyish blue: of eyes, the sea; the blue dye

extracted from woad (hence called "*glasen*"), seen in the phrase *crecad glas ar na roscaib* "blue tattooing on the eyelids" (Laws v 108.30 Comm.). Grey or blue-grey: of metal; frost or ice; shades of grey (birds, stones, mist, thread; the silvery skin of the birch); wan (complexion); faded (of garments). Green hues may figuratively denote "fresh, young," Grey hues may denote "fresh, raw, sharp" (of weather, probably originally "grey, overcast") or neutral tints, hence "plain, unassuming, inconspicuous."

West: Learning/*Fis* ("Act of finding out or ascertaining; knowledge, information")

Odur "dun or greyish-brown colour," of faded plants; cows and horses; dark or sallow complexion.

Liath "grey"; of persons: grey-haired, aged; used of eyes, dew, horses, deer, birds; used as a substantive referring to old men, veterans.

Ciar "dark, murky, black"; of animals, birds; woods ("shady, gloomy"); of hair or general appearance.

North: Battle/*Cath* ("Battle, fight; troop, battalion")

Dub "black, dark"; used of eyelashes, hair, complexion; berries; seasons; Used figuratively to denote "dark" (in a moral sense); dire, gloomy, melancholy; pigment, ink.

Teimen "dark, obscure"; enigmatic; or, plain, inconspicuous.

Alad "piebald, variegated"; used of animals, or the appearance of ground or landscape.

The patterns suggested by these images appear to follow the cyclical movement of the sun, the progression of the seasons of the year, and the stages of the lifetime of a living being:

(1) In the east, the primary attribute is Prosperity ("blossoming, flourishing, prospering"): the colors *corcor* "purple"; *derg* "red" (of blood; flame; ale; gold; heating, kindling, burning); and *buide* "yellow" (of flowers, honey, pollen; used with the word *bith* "world; land; existence, life"): dawn/spring/birth and infancy.

(2) In the south, the primary attribute is Music: *gel* "white, bright, shining"; *uaine* "green, verdant," of land, waters; and *glas* "light green, blue, grey-blue," of growing things, grass, trees; the ocean; "fresh, young": noon/summer/youth to adulthood.

(3) In the west, the primary attribute is Knowledge: *odur* "dun, greyish-brown," used of animals; faded plants or complexion; *liath* "gray," used of the natural world, grey-haired, aged; and *ciar* "dark, murky, black": sunset/autumn/maturity.

(4) In the north, the primary attribute is Battle: *Dub* "black, dark";
     Teimen "dark, obscure, enigmatic"; and "piebald, variegated," of
     various shades and hues, as the pattern changes and prepares to
     emerge into the next cycle: midnight/winter/old age.

Here we might also note the widespread Indo-European association
of colors with social tripartition. In Indo-Iranian, Hittite, Latin and Celtic
contexts, the color white was assigned to priests (Dumézil's first function:
The Sacred), red to warriors (Dumézil's second function: Protection), and
the third function (Fertility: farmers/herders) was connected with either
black/blue or blue/green or green/yellow. A fourth function or position was
sometimes associated with a goddess figure who represented all three functions (and could be associated with one of the other colors from those associated with the third function).[67] If we map out the directions and their
attributes, with these colors and their attendant social functions, we arrive
at the following:

East: Prosperity—Purple/Red—Warrior Caste
South: Music—White—Priestly Caste
West: Knowledge—Dun/Yellow—Farmers/Herders
North: Battle—Black—Tri-functional Goddess

It is not a perfect mapping, as one might wish to see the Priestly caste
associated with Knowledge, the Warrior Caste associated with Battle, and
the function of Fertility associated with Prosperity. However, it is a topic
worth considering, and as a separate line of inquiry it may prove fruitful in
a further study.[68]

Another medieval Irish text which may include materials relevant to
perceptions or beliefs concerning the horizontal or lateral aspects of the cosmos is *Cath Maige Tuired*. In the beginning of the narrative it states:

*Bátar Túatha Dé Danonn i n-indsib túascertachaib an domuin, aig foglaim fesa ocus
fithnasachta ocus druídechta ocus amaidechta ocus amainsechta, combtar fortilde for
súthib cerd ngenntlichtae. Ceitri catrachai i rrabatar og foclaim fhesai ocus éolais ocus
diabuldánacht .i. Falias ocus Goirias, Murias ocus Findias.*

The Túatha Dé Danann were in the northern islands of the world, studying occult
lore and sorcery, druidic arts and witchcraft and magical skill, until they surpassed
the sages of the pagan arts. They studied occult lore and secret knowledge and dia-
bolical arts in four cities: Falias, Gorias, Murias and Findias.[69]

The text then goes on to enumerate four magical talismans that were
brought from these "northern islands" to Ireland, followed by a listing of four
wizards (actually *druid*, "druids") who were in the four cities.[70] The outline
suggested by the passage is as follows:

City	Druid	Talisman
Falias	Morfesa	Stone of Fál
Gorias	Esras	Spear of Lug
Findias	Uiscias	Sword of Núadu
Murias	Semias	Cauldron of the Dagda

An account of the Túatha Dé Danann's training in the occult arts and the list of their four talismans also appear in *Lebor Gabála Érenn,* a pseudo-historical account of the history of Ireland compiled in the medieval era, which we will discuss in depth in Chapter 2. The account appears again as a separate anecdote in the Yellow Book of Lecan, the Book of Ballymote, and Egerton 105. However, in *The First Battle of Mag Tuired,* the account of their arrival emphasizes their mastery of all the arts and their journey from the northern islands of the world, but does not include the wizards, cities or talismans. While the language of these initial paragraphs in *Cath Maige Tuired* is later than most of the rest of the narrative, suggesting that this anecdote may have been added to the beginning of the tale, Elizabeth Gray notes that the traditions themselves may predate the earliest surviving version of *Lebor Gabála.*[71]

Whatever the original form may have been, in *Cath Maige Tuired* it is conceivable that the four "cities" represented the four directions. The word *cathair* denotes "a stone enclosure, fortress, castle or dwelling." In light of the fact that cities were a relatively late development in Ireland, the word "fortress" or "dwelling" may be preferable in this context.[72] By examining the names of the fortresses and the druids who were in them, as well as the mythic associations of the talismans, we may be able to discern patterns relating to the four directions.

> *Falias:* The Old Irish word 1 *fál* denotes a "fence, hedge or enclosure," hence a wall or barrier; 5 *fál* refers to the name of the stone at Temair (Tara) generally known as the *Lia Fáil,* which was associated with kingship. The text states that the stone would cry out beneath every king who would take Ireland. The name *Morfesa* is comprised of *mór* "great" and a form of *fis* "knowledge."
>
> *Gorias* may derive from *gor* "fire," or "heat."[73] The name *Esras* seems to derive from *esrais/esrus* "outlet, passage; means, way, opportunity." As for the spear of Lug, no battle was ever sustained against it, or against the person who held it in their hand.
>
> *Findias* contains the word *find/finn,* "white, bright, lustrous; fair, light-hued; fair, handsome; bright, blessed (frequently used in religious poetry); fair, just, true (in a moral sense)." *Uiscias* appears to derive from *uisce* "water." Of the sword of Nuadu, the text states that no one ever escaped from it once it was drawn from its deadly sheath, and no one could resist it.

Murias appears to include the word *muir* "sea." *Semias* may derive from *séim*, "slender, thin; rarified (of air)" (*Cf. séimide* "transparent, bright, limpid"). Regarding the talisman, it was said that no company ever went away from the Dagda's cauldron unsatisfied.[74]

It is unfortunate that the text does not directly connect the four fortresses, druids and talismans with specific cardinal directions. If, as an exercise, we assign them to the four directions, starting in the east, we have the following arrangement:

East: Findias–Uiscias–Sword of Nuadu
South: Gorias–Esras–Spear of Lug
West: Murias–Semias–Cauldron of the Dagda
North: Falias–Morfesa–Stone of Fál

It is, of course, possible that errors in copying may have occurred at some stage. If we switch Uiscias and Semias, a fairly coherent pattern may be discerned:

East: Findias (<"bright, white, blessed")
    Semias (< "transparent, rarified—of air")
    Sword of Nuadu
South: Gorias (< "fire, heat")
    Esras ("outlet, way, opportunity")
    Spear of Lug
West: Murias (*muir*, "sea")
    Uiscias (*uisce*, "water")
    Cauldron of the Dagda
North: Falias (< *fál* "enclosure, wall")
    Morfesa ("Great Knowledge")
    Stone of Fál (associated with Kingship)

As regards the first set of associations, Nuadu's sword may be the predecessor of the "Sword of Light," a talisman found in a number of Gaelic folktales. In *Cath Maige Tuired*, Nuadu acknowledges the newcomer Lug's many skills and steps aside, allowing Lug to sit in the seat of kingship.[75] By advancing in a sunwise direction, we proceed from Nuadu to Lug. If this arrangement is correct, the east is connected with a "bright, white" location, perhaps associated with air (or wind?) and the Sword of Light. In the south, we have fire or warmth (a common association in a number of cultures in the northern hemisphere), "passages or opportunities," and the spear of a newcomer to the gods, who is many-skilled. The west is associated with the sea, water and a cauldron of abundance, and the north is connected with enclosures, kingship and knowledge. This is not to suggest that native Celtic cosmology included the four elements of Classical tradition (although these could have crept into the system as a result of early Irish clerics and poets' familiarity with Classical writings).

In relation to this, it is interesting to consider Section 23 of Plutarch's *De Defectu Oraculorum* in which he discusses the assignation by Plato of the principal parts of the universe:

> In the like manner, Plato, assigning unto the principal parts of the universe, the first forms and most excellent figures of the bodies, calls them five worlds—those of the earth, water, air and fire, and finally, of that which comprehended all the others, which he calls Dodecahedron (which is to say, with twelve bases), which, amply extending, is of easy motion and capacity, its form and figure being very fit and proper for the revolutions and motions of the souls...[76]

Perhaps a text like this served as an inspiration for Irish scribes to work the Classical system of four elements into a native system associated with the four directions.[77] Plato's twelve-fold model may have inspired (or brought to mind) the twelve winds.[78] However, there does appear to be native symbolism associated with the number 12, such as the cosmological model in *Togail Bruidne Da Derga* discussed by Bondarenko. In the tale, four roads radiate from Tara in the four cardinal directions, and there were three kings on each road, making a total of 12.[79] It is a fascinating conundrum, one which reflects the complexities of the various modes of intermingling of native Celtic and other cultural concepts in early medieval Ireland.

The Bile: Tribal Centers and Sacred Trees

In many cultures, the three worlds are connected by the *axis mundi,* a central tree, pillar or mountain, often referred to as the World Tree or Tree of Life. A widespread focus on the central point of Celtic ritual sites, and the abundant evidence pertaining to the veneration of trees (including single sacred trees or *bile*), may point to native belief in a concept similar to that of the World Tree. Tree imagery plays a very prominent role in iconographic and literary sources from a variety of Celtic regions and eras.[80]

As we saw above, in "The Settling of the Manor of Tara," Fintan describes his previous encounter with Trefuilngid. He says this gigantic, heroic figure approached the assembly from the west at sunset, with a shining crystal veil upon him and golden hair falling in curls to the level of his thighs. In his left hand he carried stone tablets and in his right hand was a branch with three fruits on it: nuts, apples and acorns. As he strode around the assembly with his golden many-colored branch, one of the people at the assembly asked him where he had come from, where he was going, and what his name was. He replied that he had come from the setting of the sun and that he was going to the rising of it. He said he was responsible for the rising and setting of the sun and that his name was Trefuilngid Tre-eochair (Is é m'ainm Tréfuilngidh Tre-eochair). At that point, he said he would like to see all the people of Ireland gathered together in one place. The king said it would be a hardship on the people to support him during that period. Trefuilngid replied there would be no hardship, for the fragrance of the branch served him for food and drink as long as he lived.

The people of Ireland gathered together and he says he will establish for them the progression of the stories and chronicles of the hearth of Tara itself, with the four quarters of Ireland all about, for he is a truly learned witness "who explains to all everything unknown." After Fintan responded to his query about the primary attribute of each of the directions, Trefuilngid related all the lore concerning the full range of attributes associated with each direction. He left this ordinance with the men of Ireland forever, and gives Fintan some of the berries from the branch that was in his hand so he could plant them in whatever places he thought it likely that they would grow. Fintan planted the berries, and five trees or bile grew from them: the ancient trees of Tortu, Ross, Mugna, Dathe, and Uisnech.

Fintan remained, relating stories to the people of Ireland, until he survived the ancient trees and they had withered during his time. When he perceived his own old age and that of the trees, he recited a poem in which he declares himself a seanchaidh over a period of a thousand years. Afterwards, the nobles of Ireland accompanied him to Uisnech where he set up in their presence a pillarstone of five ridges on the summit. He assigned a ridge to each province in Ireland, "for thus are Tara and Uisnech in Ireland, as its two kidneys are in a beast." He marked out a forrach there, the portion of each province in Ireland:

"the five divisions of Ireland, both sea and land … the points of the great provinces run towards Uisnech, they have divided yonder stone through it into five."[81]

It is difficult not to see aspects of this narrative as reflective of native Irish cosmology, which included the four directions and the sacred central point.[82]

In the tale, the medieval narrator expresses uncertainty about the identity of Trefuilngid, musing that he may have been an angel of God, or even God himself. While he carries stone tablets in his left hand, a recognizable Judeo-Christian motif, he carries in his right hand the branch of a magical Otherworld tree, a potent and often-used native Celtic symbol. Once again, we encounter the co-mingling or co-existence of native and foreign iconography and symbolism.

Here we should note that the first part of his first name, Trefuilngid, appears to reflect a meaning along the lines of "through / by means of" +

"one who supports, sustains, maintains, endures; a supporter, defender."[83] His second name, *Tre-eochair* is given in DIL as meaning "three-edged," as well as being the name of a poetic metre.[84] There are seven possible meanings for *eochair,* one of which is "a key" (in a literal sense) as well as "a clue, solution, explanation, guide, means of access" (in a metaphorical sense). It is this sense that pertains to our story. In the Triads of Ireland we encounter the following: *tri heochracha aroslicet imráitiu: mescca, tairisiu, serc* ("Three keys that unlock thoughts: drunkenness, trustfulness, love").[85] There are also several references to keys of knowledge or divination. The first occurs in "The Wooing of Étain," as the king Eochaid Airem asks his druid to find Étain:

> *Ba tromm immorro laisin druid dicheilt Étainiu fair fri se bliadna, co ndernai .iiii. flesca ibuir, ocus scrípuidh oghumm inntib, ocus foillsigthir dó triana eochraib écsi ocus triana oghumm Étain do bith i Sith Breg Leith iarna breth do Midir inn.*
>
> "Now it seemed grievous to the druid that Étain should be hidden from him for six years, so then he made four rods of yew and he writes an ogham thereon, and by his keys of knowledge and by his ogham, it is revealed to him that Étain is in the Fairy Mound of Breg Leith, having been carried there by Midir."[86]

Another example appears in *Baile in Scáil. Conn Cétchathach* ("Conn of the Hundred Battles") asks one of his poets about the origin and meaning of a stone that had cried out under his feet. The poet said he would provide the answer to Conn's question in fifty-three days. During that time he meditated, "until his keys of poesy" (*eochra éccsi*) revealed the information to him.[87] Here we might recall that the word *éicse,* here translated as "poesy," has a wide range of meanings: "divination, the faculty of divination; wisdom, the profession of a seer; revelation, lore, learning; especially used of poetry; poetic composition; the poetic art, poetic skill or faculty, the calling of a poet; the poetic profession, the bardic order; poets."

Trefuilngid ("through? + one who supports, sustains, maintains") *Tre-eochair* ("the three keys [of knowledge]"), provides important cosmological and socio-religious information to the sages and elders of Ireland. He comes from the west, the direction associated with learning. The "three keys" could refer to the keys of divination, poetry, and wisdom as seen above. Perhaps they are represented by the three objects on his magical branch—nuts, apples and acorns—which are associated with the Otherworld and its wisdom in numerous narrative and poetic contexts.

Another possibility is that his branch—symbolic of the *bile*—provided access to the three worlds (a common function of the *axis mundi* in many cultures). The five sacred trees that grew from the berries given to Fintan are mentioned in several poems from the *Dindshenchas.* The trees are directly called *bile,* a word which refers to an ancient or sacred tree, as well as a pillar or mast. This word may be have been used in Irish contexts to refer to the

World Tree (or its local representative) which was believed to connect the three cosmogonic realms.

In Ireland and Scotland, at least, the *bile* could serve as a symbol of the center of tribal territory. A variety of Dindshenchas poems mention the sacred trees planted by Fintan: *Éo Rossa* (a yew), *Éo/Dair Mugna* (an oak), *Cróeb Dathi* (an ash), *Bile Tortan* (an ash), and *Unnius Uisnig* (also an ash).[88] The poem on *Bile Tortan* bemoans the fact that this ancient, venerated tree had fallen down after many years, after being blown over by a mighty windstorm. The people of the region mourn the huge tree, for they used to meet together under it. The poem states that the plain of Tortu is "a plain without a ruler since it lost its noble tree."[89]

Trees were also associated with one form of the *ogam* alphabet, a system of writing devised in Ireland around the fourth century CE. It consisted of horizontal or diagonal strokes made across a spine or vertical line, representing the letters of the Irish alphabet. It was used to mark graves and territory markers, send messages, and may have been used in divination.[90] There are many versions of the ogam alphabet that formed part of the training of the medieval Irish *filid* or poet-seers.[91] In one version of the alphabet, the letters were associated with certain trees or plants. Each of these was associated with "kennings" or cryptic phrases, probably intended to test students regarding the symbolic and practical attributes of the trees, or used to covertly allude to letters (and thus "spell out" messages) amongst themselves without having others understand their communication. The plants, trees and shrubs in the "tree" version of the ogam alphabet were arranged into four categories:

> Chieftain trees: *oak, hazel, holly, apple, ash, yew, fir*
> Peasant trees: *alder, willow, birch, elm, whitethorn/hawthorn, aspen, mountain-ash (rowan)*
> Shrub trees: *blackthorn, elder, spindle-tree, test-tree, honeysuckle, bird-cherry, white-hazel*
> Herb trees: *furze (gorse), heather, broom, bog-myrtle, rushes, vine/ivy, pine*[92]

Tree symbolism in Celtic contexts is quite extensive, and it would require far more than one section of a chapter to fully explore this aspect of Celtic belief. We have iconographic evidence of deities whose names appear to connect them with certain trees, and literary evidence suggests that in some cases the pagan Celts held ceremonies in sacred groves. In Ireland there are clear references to sacred assemblies being held under or near the *bile* of the tribe or its territory. Trees were widely associated with tribal and sacred ceremonies, and were also potent symbols of the Otherworld and its wisdom. In addition, in a cosmos containing three cosmogonic realms and four primary directions, it is the *bile* or World Tree, located at the sacred central point, which connects the three and the four (perhaps accounting for the symbolism of the number seven).[93]

There is quite a bit of evidence supporting the sacral importance of this central point. The central region of Ireland was known as *Mide* (modern Co. Meath), which means "middle." This region contained four sacred assembly sites: *Temair* (Tara), *Tlachtga* (The Hill of Ward), *Tailtiu* (modern Telltown) and *Uisnech*. The hill of Uisnech was considered to be the cosmological center of Ireland. In one of Fintan's poems he says it has been a long time since he drank a drink of the deluge over the *navel* of Uisnech. The sacred center was sometimes referred to as the *omphalos* or "navel" of the land (or the cosmos). Classical accounts note that the druids of Gaul used to gather periodically in the region of the *Carnutes,* a tribe whose territory was considered the center of Gaul.[94] Similar rituals may have taken place at *Medionemeton* ("Middle Sanctuary/Grove"), an ancient place-name in Scotland. Possibly analogous was *Mediolanum* ("Central place/plain," modern day Milan).[95] Those interested in pursuing this facet of cosmology in more depth, in Irish, Gaulish and comparative Indo-European contexts, are referred to Proinsias Mac Cana's work, *The Cult of the Sacred Centre.*[96]

One of the most common representations of the primordial sacred site consisted of a round area of land surrounded by ocean, with the World Tree at its center. Sometimes a well of wisdom was located underneath the tree. Descriptions of locations in the Celtic Otherworld mention sacred trees which were associated with wells of wisdom. In "Cormac's Adventures in the Land of Promise," and in several Dindshenchas poems, we are given descriptions of an Otherworld well surrounded by hazel trees. We will explore this archetypal scenario in more detail in an upcoming chapter. The Norse world tree was said to have branches that stretched over heaven and earth and roots that passed into the Underworld realms. Two sacred springs or wells, one connected with wisdom and one with fate or destiny, were located beneath the tree.[97] The Norse tree was threatened by living creatures which continually fed upon it. An eagle and a hawk lived in its uppermost branches, a great serpent gnawed at its roots, and horned creatures such as harts and goats fed upon the branches and tender shoots.[98]

An interesting description of a tree associated with a variety of animals comes from the Irish tale "Finn and the Man in the Tree." The man in question is *Dercc Corra mac hUi Daighre,* (perhaps "The Red Peaked One, Descendant of the Flashing One"), a figure whose name may suggest some primeval or divine significance. The pertinent scene is as follows:

> One day as Finn was in the wood seeking him, he saw a man in the top of a tree, a blackbird on his right shoulder and in his left hand a white vessel of bronze, in which was a skittish trout and a stag at the foot of the tree. And this was the practice of the man: cracking nuts; and he would give half the kernel of a nut to the black-

bird that was on his right shoulder while he himself would eat the other half; and he would take an apple out of the bronze vessel that was in his left hand, divide it in two, throw one half to the stag that was at the foot of the tree and then eat the other half himself. And on it he would drink a sip of the bronze vessel that was in his hand so that he and the trout and the stag and the blackbird drank together.[99]

In Celtic contexts, the hazel tree and its nuts were associated with divine wisdom or the gift of prophecy, and hazel trees are described as growing around a well of wisdom. The apple tree, and its fruit and branches, seem to symbolize journeys to and from the Otherworld. Drinking sacred water (or ritual beverages) was sometimes connected with the gift of divine knowledge. That all of these sacred elements appear together may suggest that the scene is representative of an Otherworldly or cosmogonic landscape.

The Norse world tree was associated with animals which fed upon certain parts of it. In the Irish example, the man and his animal companions (who are located in or near the tree) feed upon the produce of sacred trees. In the Norse scenario, a serpent, a deer and several birds are associated with the world tree; in the Irish tale a trout, a deer and a blackbird appear in connection with the tree. In Irish and Scottish folk tradition, the salmon and the trout may serve interchangeable roles in connection with holy wells whose waters possess healing or other magical powers.[100] While there are no snakes in Ireland, they do exist in Scotland, and in Scottish contexts the snake or serpent is sometimes substituted for the salmon in stories associated with the acquisition of gifts or skills (including prophecy or healing).[101]

This being the case, the similarity between the animals in the Norse description (serpent, deer/goat, birds) and the Celtic example (trout, deer, bird) is all the more striking. In addition, the animals mentioned in the Irish tale (fish, deer and blackbird) are the same creatures mentioned in association with kennings associated with the word *ébad* ("yew tree") in the system of ogam described above.[102] The yew may have been considered a symbol of the *axis mundi*; *Eo Rossa* was a yew, and the evocative word *eó* may mean either "salmon" or "yew." In light of this, the scene depicted in "Finn and the Man in the Tree" may reflect native traditions pertaining to the world tree and its sacred manifestations in the Irish cosmogonic landscape.[103]

The Concept of Síd: Finding the Celtic Otherworld

Early Irish literature provides us with numerous intriguing tales that describe interactions between human beings and the inhabitants of the Otherworld realms. For simplicity's sake, the term "The Otherworld" is often used in translating aspects of these encounters, but there may well have been a number of Otherworlds, or at least a number of Otherworld locales.[104] Kathryn Chadbourne writes:

> Our convenient term, the Otherworld, implies a single realm, a unified kingdom. The truth is more complicated. To map the relationship of the human world to the Otherworld, a mapmaker would need to demonstrate not just place, but dimension ... the Otherworld is all around us, omnipresent. Human beings can access pieces of it which are whole in themselves (like a fortress or a plain), but these "other worlds" are not necessarily connected to or adjoining one another. That is because the Otherworld is at once local and universal...[105]

These Otherworld locales are often described as somewhat analogous to their earthly counterparts, but are more beautiful, numinous, and desirable. Colors are heightened, music is more wondrous, and the senses are delighted at every turn (at least in instances when Otherworld encounters are positive). Early Irish tales provide descriptions of human beings having encounters with Otherworld beings in this world, or travelling to Otherworld locations. In most cases, the Otherworld exists in (or is accessed through) dwellings or regions beneath hills (natural or made by humans, as in the case with Neolithic burial mounds), as well as beneath lakes, springs or the sea; on islands in lakes or off the coast; or in houses encountered in darkness, storm or mist.[106]

An Otherworld location beneath the earth is wonderfully described in *Serglige Con Chulainn* ("The Wasting Sickness of Cú Chulainn") (my translation):

> There are, in the doorway to the west,
> In the place in which the sun sets
> A herd of horses with speckled manes
> And another chestnut herd
>
> In the doorway to the east
> Are three sacred trees of bright purple
> From which a gentle, everlasting flock of birds
> Calls to the offspring of the royal fortress.
>
> There is a tree in the doorway of the court,
> Not unseemly [are] the nuts from it,
> A tree of silver that shines as the sun
> With a brightness like that of gold...
>
> There is a vat of intoxicating mead
> That pours out for the folk there
> It exists yet, enduring is the custom,
> So that it continues, ever-full.[107]

An evocative description of a supernatural location associated with the ocean and an Otherworld island occurs in *Immram Brain* ("The Voyage of Bran"). In the story, Bran is being enticed to the Otherworld by a woman bearing a magical branch (also my translation):

A branch of Emain of the Apple Trees
I bring, like those that are familiar
Twigs of white-silver on it
Brightly fringed with blossoms.

There is an island in the distance
Radiant around the path of sea-horses
A shining course towards bright-sided waves
Four feet sustain them

Feet of white bronze underneath
Gleaming throughout the exquisite worlds
A fair land throughout the ages of the seas
On which many blossoms fall

Glistening is the appearance of every colour
Throughout the gentle winds of the plain…
From its view, a shining tranquility
Of no comparison is existence out of the mist.[108]

In the literature, there are a variety of names for the Otherworld realms. As we saw above, in Welsh contexts the Otherworld is generally referred to as *Annw(f)n*. It is often located underground, but can also be under or over the sea.[109] The Otherworld in Irish literature is frequently located in a *síd* mound (often translated "fairy mound"), which appears to serve as a portal to the chthonic realms.[110] Names for the Irish Otherworld include *Tír na mBeó* ("Land of the Living"), *Mag Mell* ("The Plain of Honey"), *Mag Dá Cheó* ("Plain of Two Mists"), *Mag Argatnél* ("Plain of Silver Clouds"), *Tír na mBan* ("Land of Women"), *Tír Tairngire* ("The Land of Promise," a term influenced by Christian literature) and later, *Tír na nÓg*, ("Land of Youth").

In many cases, the Irish Otherworld is simply referred to as the land of the *Síd*. This word derives from the Indo-European root **sed-* "sit," originally denoting "seat, abode" (as in "the seat of power"), later specialized as "abode of divinities" (i.e. "the seat of the Gods.") In Irish contexts, the word was further specialized to refer to the "hollow hills" of the landscape in particular.[111] In some tales, an unusual or extraordinary figure (who is eventually recognized as an Otherworld being or a deity) might simply be referred to as being "from the *síd*." The term *Áes Síde*, "People of the *Síd*" was used to refer to the supernatural inhabitants of the *síd* realms.[112] As Tomás Ó Cathasaigh has shown, in addition to referring to the location of the Otherworld realms and the divine inhabitants of those realms, the word *síd* also refers to a state of peace that ensues from being in a right relationship with the Otherworld, a condition which can be brought about by the good and truthful reign of an ideal ruler.[113]

The state of peace secured by kings of the mythical past—whose kingship was sanctioned by the Otherworld—protected a worldly order that was founded on truth. The Otherworldly support of human sovereignties was also dependent on (in Ó Cathasaigh's words): "…the respect for the superior sovereignty of the gods and the sense of limitations inherent in every human delegation of the divine sovereignty."[114] If a false judgment is given, this destroys respect for the Otherworld beings who have bestowed sovereignty upon the ruler. As Otherworld interventions in the affairs of human beings are not always benign, the Otherworld dimension of kingship also has its dark side: "What the gods bestow, they can also take away."[115]

Despite the dates of the various texts concerned with these themes, and because of parallels with other Indo-European cultures, Ó Cathasaigh feels they do reflect ancient tradition. He writes: "The Otherworld of Irish tradition must also have its roots in ancient ideas … and the Otherworld dimension of kingship … is likewise of great antiquity."[116] Marion Deane has written about literary forms which express the principle of symbiosis that governs mythic thought, stating that these forms "characteristically express the coexistence of parallel worlds in which human conduct finds its counterpart in the world of the gods."[117]

In an article concerning the nature and location of the Celtic Otherworld(s), Kate Chadbourne poses some important questions we must ask ourselves:

> Why must these worlds come in contact at all? Why can't they remain isolated, existing alongside each other without ever touching? What compels them time and again to spill over their borders and affect each other so profoundly? The short answer is they need each other; one supplies to the other what is lacking. Patrick Ford writes: "Just as man cannot do without gods, so gods are imperfect without man." Each world embodies qualities that potentially can transform the other, that are required to release the world from stagnation and bring about renewal. Conversely, each world contains treasures that the other would greedily take. Thus there is the potential for devastation and death alongside the hope of rebirth.[118]

Native Flood Myths and the Lands Beneath the Waves

In addition to horizontal and vertical spatial components, traditional cosmology also includes temporal components, including the concepts of sacred and cyclical time. Annual cycles of seasonal rites and celebrations are included in the temporal aspect of cosmology, and Celtic concepts pertaining to the yearly round will be explored in detail in Chapter 3. In the annual cycle, the quarter days were not only connected with herding and agricultural concerns, but were also considered "time outside of time," that which is betwixt and between (*idir eatarthu*). Kate Chadbourne has written:

...these temporal interstices were charged with power and danger; the barrier between the worlds grew thin and less substantial, allowing two-way traffic of the good and the bad ... the space of time in which any ritual—large or small—is performed can also hold open the door.[119]

Another aspect of temporal cosmology is what Australian aboriginal peoples call "The Dreamtime." This refers to an ancient period in which the gods are active in or on the earth, the landscape is formed, and sacred precedents are set forth. Floods, deluges or the eruption of sacred waters appear in connection with the creation legends of numerous cultures. A number of native flood myths may also have existed in Irish tradition. John Carey has examined the legend of Cesair (the first of the pseudo-historical "invasion myths"), a tale whose origin may exist in flood myths which were native to Ireland prior to the creation of *Lebor Gabála*.[120] The original matrix of these tales involves the theft or abduction of a woman, which is followed by the destructive eruption of water (ocean, lake, well or spring). These flood myths reflect local legends and traditions, without any necessary connection to Biblical traditions concerning floods or primeval migration.[121] Quite a number of traditional cultures have flood myths that are not connected to (or reflections of) the Biblical Deluge. John Carey and other scholars have explored and discussed scattered references to flood narratives in early Irish literary sources.[122]

One such reference comes from *Lebor Gabála*, in which *Cesair*, the daughter of *Bith* (a word meaning "the World; land, territory, soil; existence, life") was alleged to have come to Ireland forty days before the Flood with fifty maidens, and three men: her father Bith, the steersman Ladru, and Fintan mac Bóchra (properly *bóchna*, "sea, ocean"). The fifty women were divided among the three men, with Cesair marrying Fintan. This apportioning took place at *Commar na Trí nUisce*, ("confluence/assembly/meeting place of the three waters"). In the tale, Ladru, Bith and Cesair die, but Fintan flees to Tul Tuinne where he hid in his cave dwelling. He slept there until God raised him up to be a witness to the ancient past.[123]

In a passage ascribed to *Cín Dromma Snechta* (a lost text dating to the eighth century), the name of the woman in the tale is not Cesair but Banba, one of three goddesses of the land of Ireland who was encountered by the Gaels in the pseudo-historical tradition (as well as a poetic name for the land of Ireland).[124] A similar account is given in *Chronicon Scotorum*, a set of annals compiled by the poet *Dubhaltach mac Firbhisigh* from a number of sources. In this account, the name of the women is given as: "Eriu or Berba or Cesair." Berba is the name of a goddess associated with the River Barrow. In another passage attributed to *Cín Dromma Snechta*, Banba stands on Tul Tuinne ("Crest of a Wave") and claims to antedate the Flood.[125]

There are other independent tales in which female figures are associated with floods, some of which are clearly local in nature. In the Dindshenchas poem on *Tuag Inbir,* a princess named *Tuag* was tended by a company of maidens at Tara. When men began to woo her, the god Manannán mac Lir sent messengers to seek her. The messenger was named Fer Fí, and he was a fosterling of Mannanán's, as well as a druid of the Túatha Dé Danann. Fer Fí turned himself into the shape of a woman and stayed with Tuag's women for three nights. On the fourth night, he chanted a spell and bore Tuag off in her sleep, playing a sleep-compelling strain of music. He bore her from Tara to the "point of green-topped Banba." Fer Fí laid her down upon the shore sleeping, and went to seek a boat. While he was away, the flood-tide came in and drowned her. Manannán killed Fer Fí, and the place where she drowned was named Tuag Inbir.[126]

The Dindshenchas account then provides a triad: "The Three Waves of all Ireland," which are listed as "the Wave of Clidna, the Wave of Rudraige, and the Wave that drowned Mac Lir's mate, that visits the shore by Tuag Inbir."[127] Next it recounts a story that begins by saying that the River *Banna* had once been narrow enough to jump over. This is followed by a story of two fleeing lovers who are given a magical horse by the god Oengus mac Óc. The horse had to be returned before it could pass water. The journey was long and the horse was weary, and its urine created a deep well. King Eochu (who was in strife with Clann Rudraige) built a house around the well with a lid placed over it. A woman was set to watch the well. One day she lifted the lid and the waters swelled up and drowned many people, except Eochu's son Conaing. This created the "sea of Liathmuine" or the outbursting of Lough Neagh, which gave force to the river Bann.[128]

Another flood story occurs in the Dindshenchas, where two separate poems give an account of *Tond Chlidna,* "The Wave of Clidna." A gathering was held by the people of the Otherworld, and Clidna Cendfind ("Clidna Fair-Head") was queen of that gathering. However, she was carried off by Ciaban mac Eochu by boat over the sea. He left her alone while he went hunting, and a wave came and drowned her. The poem then mentions another location, north of Tond Clidna, known as Tond Téite, where a woman named Teite (a daughter of Flidais, in some accounts) was killed. In the second poem, Clidna, daughter of Genann mac Tren, was carried off by Ciaban. Her father declares that a day will come when a wave "whose crest shall sparkle" will overwhelm her home on an island. As they sail to the south-west, the wind and storm of the sea carry them onto the sand and Clidna met her death.[129]

Carey suggests that taken collectively, these legends represent a matrix from which the Cesair tale may have arisen. In these stories, the theft or disrespect of a woman is followed by a destructive eruption of the waters and a drowning (which most often occurs on the shore). A group of Otherworld women features in these tales, and Carey states that: "it seems reasonable enough to discern in this material the elements of an essentially pagan narrative."[130] The floods in these stories are local in origin and take place in a number of regions. The concept of lake-bursts which cause an inundation are also widespread in Irish literature, and a list of the names of plains which were said to exist beneath the lakes of Ireland occurs in a small codex written in the late 16th century. Well-known tales of lakes engulfing kingdoms exist, such as those pertaining to the origins of Lough Neagh and Lough Ree, but this list includes other submerged plains, some of whose tales occur elsewhere and others whose tales have not survived.[131]

Two of the most fascinating origin tales associated with bodies of water are *Immacaldam Choluim Chille ocus Ind Óclaig oc Carraic Eolairg* ("The Conversation of Colm Cille and the youth at Carn Eolairg") and *Immacaldam in Druad Brain ocus inna Banfatho Febuil ós Loch Febuil* ("The Conversation between Bran's druid and Febul's prophetess above Loch Febuil"). Both stories are associated with the legendary origins of Lough Foyle and probably date to no earlier than the eighth century.[132] We will discuss the second of these colloquy tales first.

In this conversation, Bran's druid states that he is a man of knowledge and that when he was in Bran's stronghold drinking during the cold winter, his knowledge "went to the high clouds" and bound strong men in the presence of witnesses. He also says that his knowledge reached a pure well in which was the snare of a troop of hundreds of women. The treasures of this troop of women would be a great find for the man who could locate it."[133] This description of the druid's knowledge traveling upwards to the clouds and downwards into a well seem to support the concept of an Irish perception of three worlds which included an Upper World and a Lower World. In addition, he notes a group of women associated with a water source and treasures that exist beneath the well (a theme which occurs in the above-mentioned tales).

The prophetess responds by saying that she was worthy in the eyes of the king of *Mag Fuindsidi* (< *fonn* "base, bottom, foundation; soil, ground; piece of land, territory (land or sea)" + *síd*), "The Plain of the Land/Territory of the *Síd*." She says that the plains they used to ride over, the lands where they used to go and encamp, and the music that they used to hear, were very beautiful. However, *Mag Febuil* "of the white flowers" is now a "stony grey sea." She also notes the beautiful companies of women in Bran's assembly. Her final lines state that the king used to say sweetly, "Though he goes, let him come back again" (*Cia téit, taet a frithissi*), perhaps referring to the welcoming hospitality shown to guests in this remarkable Otherworld location.[134]

The other colloquy is between Colm Cille (Saint Columba) and an unnamed young man (who the text conjectures could be Mongán mac Fiachna). Columba asks the young man where he comes from and the youth answers:

"From lands of strange things, from lands of familiar things, so that I may learn from you the spot on which died, and the spot on which were born, knowledge and ignorance."[135]

Columba does not respond to this statement, but asks the young man to whom the lake they are standing near formerly belonged. The youth does not say who "owns" the lake, but recounts how it used to be yellow and flowery, green and hilly, rich in liquor and strewn rushes, and abundant in silver and chariots. He then makes a series of remarkable statements:

"I have grazed it when I was a stag; I have swum it when I was a salmon, [and] when I was a seal; I have run upon it when I was a wolf; I have gone around it when I was a human."[136]

The young man seems to allude to a series of lifetimes in which he existed in or near the lake, and his apparent ability to shape-shift (a theme we will encounter again below). Columba asks him what is under the sea to the east of them, and the youth says there are long-haired men with broad territories beneath it, great, fearsome pregnant cows (whose lowing is musical), oxen and horses, and two- and three-headed beings.

At this point Columba says, "That is enough," and while looking at his followers, he rises and steps aside with the young man to speak with him alone and ask about "the heavenly and earthly mysteries." They converse for half the day (or from one day to the next), while Columba's followers watch from a distance. When the conversation ends, they realize they can no longer see the young man and have no idea where he has gone. They ask Columba to reveal something of the conversation, but he says he cannot tell them even a single word of anything that had been said and "that it was better for mortals not to be informed of it."[137] This narrative is a remarkable counter-play to the numerous medieval stories in which the pagan Irish learn about the mysteries of life, the cosmos and so forth from Christian clerics. Columba shows great interest and patience in listening to what the young man knows, but in the end must stay true to his own path.

There is one additional passage from this story which is of great interest in terms of temporal cosmology. After the young man tells Columba that he had gone around the lake when he was in human form, he also says that he had landed there "under three sails":

Ro gabus fo thríb seólaib: seól mbuide beres, seól nglas bádas, seól nderg foa combretha feóili.

"I have landed there under three sails: the yellow sail which bears, the blue sail which drowns, the red sail under which bodies were conceived."[138]

He then makes the cryptic statements that women have cried out because of him, although father and mother do not know what they bear, with labor for living folk, with a covering for the dead. Carey interprets this imagery as descriptive of the processes of birth, dying and conception, "points of transition within a continuum."[139] I suggest that if we take into consideration the position of these three colors as represented in the scheme of the twelve winds in *Saltair na Rann,* as well as the cosmological associations with the colors and the four directions, the meaning of the "three sails" will clearly emerge as representing conception/birth; life; and waning/death.

In the sunwise pattern of the twelve winds, red (*derg*) appears just after the eastern point (*corcur:* prosperity/sunrise/spring), en route towards the south (*gel:* music/noon/summer). However, it is closest to the east (and may directly represent the east), the point at which Indo-European cyclical and ritual movement begins. It is in connection with this sail that "bodies" (literally "flesh, both of living and dead bodies") are brought into living form.

Next is yellow (*buide*) which is also found between east and south, but closer to the south (music/noon/summer). We have seen that the color yellow, *buide,* was often used to describe hair and flowers, honey and pollen, and used in phrases or compounds along with the word *bith* "the world; land, territory, soil; existence, life; age, period of time." The yellow sail is associated with the verb *beirid:* "carries, bears, brings forth, yields; spends (time), lasts, endures." This is the sail of living and existence.

The blue sail (*glas*) occurs between the south (music/summer/noon) and the west (learning/autumn/sunset), but is closer to the west, the waning portion of the cycle. When *glas* denotes "green" it describes living things; if "blue-green or blue-grey" it is used of the sea, metal, frost or ice; if "grey" it denotes a waning life force, that which is faded or overcast. This sail is connected with the verb *báidid,* "submerges, drowns; sinks; extinguishes, quenches; destroys, overwhelms" and clearly represents the waning cycle of life, as one moves towards the north which is the point of death and also, ultimately, of rebirth.

Sages, Shapeshifters and Elders

Also associated with native legends pertaining to floods, the eruption of waters, and the beginnings of things are characters who exist throughout the ages in a variety of human and animal forms. One of the most famous of these figures is someone we met above: *Fintan mac Bóchra mac Bith* ("Fintan, son of Sea/Ocean, son of the World/Life or Existence/Age"). He exists in Ireland prior to the flood and survives in various animal forms throughout the ages as a witness to all that has taken place.[140] Fintan is briefly mentioned in a number of Irish texts, including The First Battle of Moytura, *Cethri arda in domain, Echtra Cormaic, Bruiden Beg na hAlmaine,* and the *Metrical Dindshenchas.*[141]

A poem attributed to him appears in *Lebor Gabála,* in which he outlines the events associated with the invasion of Cesair.[142]

The earliest surviving reference to Fintan is in the tale *Airne Fingein,* which is believed to date to the ninth or tenth century. In this text Fintan is not associated with the "invasion" of Cesair and her women, but is still said to have lived in Ireland before the Flood. In this text, it says that Fintan was mute or without speech from the time he heard the flood-waters until the time he was called from his seclusion to attest to all he had seen (in "The Settling of the Manor of Tara"). Prior to that event, all the inherited knowledge, prophecy, tradition and just laws of Ireland were hidden (presumably guarded by Fintan in his cave).[143] Fintan is likely to have originally been independently associated with the period before the Deluge, later becoming part of the artificial history of Ireland's invasions as recounted in *Lebor Gabála Érenn.* He was closely associated with the province of Munster, and connected with *Tul Tuinne* as well as the fortress or dwelling *Dún Tulcha* which was located in Kerry.[144]

In "The Settling of the Manor of Tara," the five elders of Ireland are summoned to confer with the king about the division of the land: *Finchad* from *Falmag* in Leinster, *Cú-alad* from *Cruachu Conalad, Bran Bairne* from *Bairenn, Dubán mac Deg* of the *Fir Olnegmacht,* and *Tuan mac Cairell* from Ulster (a figure we will discuss below). The five elders come to Tara, but say it is not proper for them to provide information about the division of the land as long as their senior (and fosterer) was not at the assembly: Fintan son of Bóchra son of Bith, who was at that time at Dún Tulcha in Kerry. The king sends for Fintan who arrives with a retinue of eighteen companies, nine who went before him and nine who went behind him. All of these people were said to be his descendants (attesting to his great age).

Fintan is hailed as the senior figure of the wise elders of Ireland and is invited to sit in the judge's seat. He states that his foster mother is the island of Ireland, and the familiar "knee" of the island (at which one would sit to be fostered or receive knowledge) is the hill of Tara. He also says that it is the nut-crop and produce, and the flowers and food of the island that sustained him from the time of the Deluge until the present time. He is welcomed at Tara, and, as we saw above, he begins to relate to the king and the wise men of Ireland his remarkable encounter with Trefuilngid Tre-eochair.[145]

Fintan is credited with reciting several poems which are inserted into the tale. In the first poem he says he knows every group of people who have lived in Ireland (presumably from the list of "invasions" from *Lebor Gabála*) since the beginning of the world, and that he was a year under the Deluge at *Tul Tuinde.* He says "there has not been, nor will there be, any better sleep" than that which he experienced during that era. He mentions the Túatha Dé Danann, who "arrived in clouds of dark mist." Fintan says: "I lived along with them, though it was a long life." He ends the poem by declaring: "I am bright Fintan, son of Bóchra, I will not hide it; since the Deluge here I am, a high, noble sage."[146]

After this poem, the people ask Fintan how reliable his memory was. He tells them how one day he passed through a wood in west Munster and took away from the wood a red yew berry. He planted the berry in his garden and it grew until it was a big as a man. He moved it from his garden and planted it on the lawn of his dwelling-place, and it grew in the center of that place so that he could fit a hundred warriors under its foliage. The tree protected him from wind and rain, cold and heat. He and the yew tree remained, flourishing together, until it finally shed its foliage from decay. He cut it from its stock and made from the wood seven vats, seven churns, seven pitchers and numerous other objects. He remained with these yew vessels until they too decayed from age.[147]

Fintan is then told by the elders that they have summoned him to pronounce a true judgment for them, "for it was a transgression of an elder's judgment to transgress his [Fintan's] judgment." Fintan assures them that he is skilled in every just judgment that has been given since the beginning of the world until that very day. He then recites a poem in which he lists a number of Biblical judgments, followed by those associated with native Irish lore (including judgments attributed to *Fénius Farsaid, Cai Cáin-brethach,* and *Amairgen*). After this poem, Fintan tells them of the arrival of Trefuilngid Tre-eochair and the information concerning the attributes of the four directions and the sacred center.[148] Fintan had planted seeds given to him by Trefuilngid, from which grew the five sacred trees of Tortu, Ross, Mugna, Dathe and Uisnech. It was said that Fintan remained, relating stories and lore to the people of Ireland until he himself was the survivor of the ancient trees, for they had withered during his long existence. When he perceived his own old age and that of the trees, he recited another poem which ended as follows:

> So long as *Ess Ruaid* resounds,
> so long as salmon are disporting therein,
> *Dun Tulcha,* to which the sea comes,
> it will not depart from a good *seanchaidh*.
> I am a *seanchaidh* myself before every host,
> a thousand years, and no mistake,
> Before the Sons of Míl, an abundance of strength,
> I was bearing clear testimony.[149]

After this poem, the nobles went with Fintan to the summit of the hill of Uisnech where he set up the pillar-stone with five ridges, one for every province. There he recited another poem which concluded with the following stanzas:

> Wise the division which the roads have attained,
> perfect the arrangement dividing it into five

> The points of the great provinces run towards Uisnech,
> they have divided yonder stone into five.[150]

He then took his leave and went to *Dún Tulcha*, where he declared that he was feeling weakened and that decay had arrested his motion. He states: "I change not shape any longer, I am Fintan son of Bóchra." The following poem tells of the people he encountered during his many years, and the women he had wed (including Éblenn, sister of the god Lug.) He then felt death approaching, and recited a final poetic utterance. In Fintan's final poem, he says he had drunk a "drink of age" in the secret places of *Mag Mais*; his final stanza is as follows:

> I am Fintan, I have lived long,
> I am an ancient *seanchaidh* of the noble hosts

> Neither wisdom nor brilliant deeds repressed me
> Until age came upon me and decay.[151]

As is the case with some of the other medieval Irish tales, the story is appended with a scene in which a native Irish figure receives communion or converts prior to their death. In this case, the story relates that the spirits of Patrick and Brigid were present at Fintan's death. However, the tale ends by saying that the place in which Fintan was buried was uncertain, and that some think he was taken away in his mortal body to some divine secret place ("as Elijah and Enoch were borne into paradise"), where the people awaited the resurrection of "that venerable long-lived elder, Fintan son of Bóchra."[152]

In one of the poems from "The Settling of the Manor of Tara," Fintan alludes to having lived in various shapes throughout the ages. Another figure associated with shapeshifting is *Túan mac Cairell mac Muiredach Muinderg* (also known as *Túan mac Starn mac Sera*). He was said to be the son of the brother of Partholón, another of the pseudo-historical invaders from *Lebor Gabála*. He alone of Partholón's people survived a great plague, and God transformed him into many shapes. He lived from the time of Partholón until the time of Saints Finnian and Columba; it was he who related to them the story of the various invasions of the land.[153]

Scél Tuain meic Chairill tells how Tuan lived through many generations in a variety of shapes, existing as a stag, a boar and an eagle. He then changed into the shape of a salmon, which was caught and eaten by the wife of Cairill who gave birth to him again in human form.[154] A poem pertaining to Tuan– *Tuan mac Cairill ro clos*—describes how he existed for a hundred years in human form, three hundred years in the shape of a wild deer, a hundred years in the shape of a wild boar, three hundred years in the shape of an ancient bird, and one hundred years in the shape of a salmon, before he was caught and eaten by the queen.[155]

In one version of Tuan's tale, he relates that each time he passed from one form to another, he would return to his own dwelling in Ulster, as he felt old age coming upon him. Each time, he would fast for three days, after which he would remember his previous incarnations. Here Tuan describes one of his shape-shifting experiences:

> I remembered every shape in which I had been before. Old age and wretchedness fell upon me. I had no strength left. Then I changed into the shape of a hawk. I was eager and lusty; I would fly all over Ireland and everything that happened I would find out.... For a long time I was in the shape of that hawk, so that I outlived all those races who had invaded Ireland.[156]

The theme of aged ancients, who have experienced extraordinarily long lives and have lived in the form of other creatures, seems to have been important in native Irish tradition. In a poem known as "The Hawk of Achill," Fintan has a conversation with a bird in which they discuss their lives and experiences. Fintan addresses the hawk, for he is able to converse in bird-language. The bird lives in Achill where he says he enjoys warm thickets, noble streams, and fruitful chases in which he gets his fill of fish, wild game and venison. The two end up realizing that they are the same age. The hawk addresses Fintan as a poet and seer, and asks him about the evils and wonders that befell him during his lifetime(s). After the loss of the people associated with the invasion of Cesair, Fintan says he was in the shape of a salmon and swam in many rivers. He came to a waterfall known as *Ess Ruaid* and tried to leap upwards, but the icy water was like clear blue glass. A crow flying above the river-mouth came and took away one of his eyes, and from that night onwards Fintan was known as "The Blind One of Assaroe."[157]

The hawk confesses that it was he who swallowed Fintan's eye, and Fintan asks him for compensation for the act. The bird threatens to take his other eye, but Fintan says it would be better for the bird to wait and hear more about his lifetimes. In Fintan's transformations, he lived for five hundred years as a salmon, fifty years as an eagle, and one hundred years as a blue-eyed falcon, before returning to human form. He tells the hawk of the changes he has seen in Ireland, from the time of Slainge, "the first king of Ireland who invented festivals" (tribal assemblies or gatherings) to the coming of Patrick during the reign of King Loegaire. The bird then recounts the battles he has seen and the prey he carried away from battlefields. He claims to have found the hand of the god Nuadu, which he kept for seven years in his abode. The bird speaks of the Second Battle of Mag Tuired and the battlefields he frequented during that event. Fintan responds by relating more of the "invasions" from *Lebor Gabála*.[158] Then he tells the bird about the coming of

Trefuilngid with his magical branch. In Fintan's narrative, he tells how the branch that Trefuilngid held in his hand had the ability to satisfy all needs for human beings, including cold, hunger and thirst. He says that Trefuilngid recited the following stanzas about the branch:

> If you eat it facing northward, the fruit of the tree of virtues,
> The old man who partakes of it straightaway becomes a youth again.

> If you eat it facing southward, the fruit of this fruiting tree,
> You need have no fear of painful disease so long as the blackthorn lasts.[159]

These lines support the interpretation of the direction of north as the point of both death and rebirth, as well as the connection of south with auspicious attributes, as we have seen above. Fintan then tells the bird how Trefuilngid spent three days conversing with the people at Tara and left with them the branch, which contained a nut, a sloe-berry and an apple. Fintan picked up the fruits and kept them in his garment, and until he had finished planting them, no one was able to harm him. The planting resulted in three trees, rather than five as in "The Settling of the Manor of Tara": the trees of Ross, Mugna and Tortu.

Fintan asks the bird for a tale. The bird gives his blessing to Fintan, and relates his adventures during the wars of the time of Cú Chulainn, including the bodies he fed upon on the battlefield. He says he came upon Cú Chulainn severely injured, his face drenched with blood, and his back against a pillarstone. The hawk landed upon him with the intent of eating his eyes, but Cú thrust a small javelin into the bird. Although he was able to remove it, the head of the weapon remained in his body. The hawk goes on to say that it was he who killed the solitary crane of Mag Léna, the eagle of Druim Bricc, the solitary crane of Inis Géidh, and other famous birds of Irish legend. He says that in his early days he could carry away the bodies of fighting heroes, a year-old boar, a yearling fawn, a pig or piglet, or a wild fawn. As he became older, however, he would become weary carrying a blackbird. He asks for Fintan's blessing before he dies, and Fintan says he too will go to meet death on the same day.[160]

The idea of relationships between the lifetimes of animals and those of human beings is found in many cultures. There are a number of Irish and Welsh narratives in which heroes are born on the same day as a particular animal. The motif of longevity associated with specific beings occurs in a number of texts. In the Book of Ballymote we find the following comparisons:

Three fields to a tree
Three trees to a hound
Three hounds to a horse
Three horses to a human

Three humans to a deer
Three deer to a chain
Three chains to a salmon
Three salmon to a yew
Three yew trees to an age...[161]

A later form occurs in a manuscript from the British Museum (Egerton 133, Art. 20):

Three winters, a stake
Three stakes, a dog
Three dogs, a human
Three humans, a deer
Three deer, an eagle
Three eagles, a male salmon
Three salmon to the end of the world.[162]

The Book of Lismore gives a variant as well:

A year for the stake
Three years for the field
Three lifetimes of the field for the hound
Three lifetimes of the hound for the horse
Three lifetimes of the horse for the human
Three lifetimes of the human for the stag
Three lifetimes of the stag for the blackbird
Three lifetimes of the blackbird for the eagle
Three lifetimes of the eagle for the salmon
Thee lifetimes of the salmon for the yew
Three lifetimes of the yew for the world
from its beginning to its end.[163]

In the Welsh Triads, we encounter the following aged creatures grouped together:

Three Elders of the World: The Owl of Cwm Cowlwyd, the Eagle of Gwernabwy, and the Blackbird of Celli Gadarn.[164]

A more elaborate set of "oldest animals" is found in the tale *Culhwch and Olwen,* and consists of (from younger to oldest): the Blackbird of Cilgwri, the Stag of Rhedynfre (who outlived an oak), the Owl of Cwm Cawlwyd (who outlived three forests), the Eagle of Gwernabwy, and the Salmon of Llyn Llyw.[165]

Variants of these lists have been found in both Ireland and Scottish folk traditions (the first is from Ireland and the second from Scotland):

Three stakes equals a hound's life
Three hounds a steed
Three steeds a man

Three men an eagle
Three eagles a salmon
Three salmon a yew tree
Three yew trees a ridge
Three ridges from the beginning to the end of the world.[166]

Thrice a dog's age, the age of a horse
Thrice a horse's age, the age of a man
Thrice a man's age, the age of the deer
Thrice a deer's age, the age of an eagle
Thrice an eagle's age, the age of the oak.[167]

If we compare the elements of these proverbs, we may be able to postulate the original form in which this bit of Celtic lore may have once existed (noting that the chain, the owl, and the ridge only appear once, and the blackbird and the oak appear twice but in different positions):

Three winters to a stake, three stakes to a field, three fields to a tree, three trees to a hound, three hounds to a human, three humans to a stag, three stags to a chain, three chains to a blackbird, three blackbirds to an owl, three owls to an eagle, three eagles to an oak, three oaks to a salmon, three salmon to a yew, three yews to a ridge.

The most common progression appears to include the following nine elements: field, tree, hound, human, stag, eagle, oak, salmon, and yew. Tuan existed in the form of a falcon, an eagle and a salmon in one source, and as a stag, a boar, an eagle and a salmon in another. Fintan lived as a salmon, an eagle and a hawk. As his name may derive from the proto–Celtic *vindosenos ("white/bright/blessed ancient [one]"), it is likely that some form of a tale reminiscent of the stories of Fintan or Tuan—without references to the pseudo-historical invasions of Ireland—could have formed part of native traditions about earliest times.

Cosmogonic Time: Otherworld Temporal Realities and Sacred Cycles

We have seen that Irish literary sources contain materials that may reflect aspects of what could be termed the Celtic "dreamtime," an ancient mythic past when the gods were active, waters covered parts of the land, important socio-religious precedents were set, and ancient beings in both human and animal form lived through the ages and gathered wisdom to guide future generations. As we saw above, the native three-fold cosmos underwent a change to conform with the dualistic opposition of Heaven and Hell in Christian thought.[168] A change in perception concerning the structure of temporal cosmology also appears to have taken place. The Christian concept of the Trinity required of all creatures (whether organic, inorganic or intelligential) a beginning, a middle and an end. Christian historians therefore assumed all temporalities to be linear, with movement from a beginning, through a middle stage, and on to an ending point.[169]

This was implicit in the belief in one life in this world, which progressed linearly towards one of several options (but which did not cycle or repeat). This is quite different from the native concept of time, a topic which has been discussed by Patrick K. Ford and Alwyn and Brinley Rees, among others.[170] In many native cultures, time is perceived as being cyclical in nature, rather than linear.[171] The cyclical nature of time was often associated with perceptions about creation. Hence in many societies it is customary to commemorate or re-enact events associated with creation at the New Year, the start of a new temporal cycle. We will explore the annual cycle of sacred time in Chapter 3.

There is another important temporal aspect that may be called "Otherworld Time." In numerous tales, people visit the Otherworld and experience events that would normally take place over many days or weeks in our world. However, when they return they find that almost no time has passed here at all. Conversely, they may spend some time in the Otherworld and return to find that hundreds of years have transpired and the people they formerly knew have passed on. A good example of Otherworld time comes from the tale *Tucait Baile Mongáin,* one of the Mongán anecdotes believed to have formed part of the lost manuscript *Cín Dromma Snechta.* In the story, Mongán's wife *Findtigern* asks him to relate to her all of his adventures. He asks her to grant him a seven-year respite before he does so, to which she agrees. They attend a great assembly at Uisnech, and Mongán and his retinue come upon a wondrous habitation where they are treated to the luxurious hospitality of the Otherworld. Mongán becomes intoxicated and gives a trance-inspired recitation of his adventures to Findtigern. In the morning they awake to find that an entire year has passed, rather than a single night. In addition, they are no longer at Uisnech, but at Mongán's own stronghold in Dál nAraide.[172]

Carey describes Otherworld Time as not only being out of alignment with mortal time, but of a fundamentally different kind as well:

> The moment in which one may be ensnared for centuries, [and] the years which can be hidden within an instant, partake of the character of eternity—a mode of being transcending yet comprehending time and duration. The tales reflect this in two ways. First: the Otherworld continues, in the midst of the present, the conditions of a vanished Golden Age; the journey to the Otherworld may in fact also be a return to the distant past. Second: In the Otherworld all of time exists simultaneously in an eternal present.[173]

The ambiguities associated with the Otherworld in regards to time and space are reflected in statements attributed to Otherworld beings about the lands from which they come. In one text, a man from the *síd* describes his country in the following manner: *Ní cían di shíu inid fail* ("Not far from here where it is"). In another tale, an Otherworld location is described as: *Atcíther di chéin ocus ní fagabair i n-ocus* ("It is seen from afar and is not found near"). A mortal returning from the Otherworld described it in the following manner: *bale ingnád cíarbo gnád* ("a place strange though it was familiar"). As Carey points out, in these tales it often seems "as if we are separated from the Otherworld by no barrier save concealment (*díchelt*)[174]:

> The Otherworld is nearby, perhaps indeed immediately present, but hidden and alien as well. It may be reached by way of the holy places, whether these lie beyond the lands settled by the *túath* or at the tribal center. The whole of the Otherworld may lie beneath a single well or hill; or a single Otherworld palace may be linked to points far distant from each other in the geography of mortals. All of these anomalies and contrasts point to the idea of a world which, although immanent everywhere and under certain circumstances accessible, nevertheless transcends and is incommensurate with our own.[175]

Another aspect of sacred time pertains to the measurement and marking of time, especially in relation to social activities and religious observances. In 2011, archaeologists re-examining an earlier excavation of a burial complex at Magdalenenberg, Germany, near the Black Forest, made a number of remarkable discoveries. They had previously excavated a large Iron Age mound and royal tomb, around which were a number of secondary burials, as well as timber structures and rows of wooden posts. They found that the placement of the secondary burials matched the constellations visible in the northern hemisphere at Midsummer 618 BCE, while the timber alignments marked the positions of the moon, most notably the lunar standstill.[176] If these conclusions are correct, this could support Julius Caesar's report that the Celts in Gaul measured time by nights rather than days. The importance of the moon in Celtic contexts is reflected in a number of textual and folkloric references.[177]

Another fascinating physical representation of temporal cycles and sacred points in time comes from a bronze tablet unearthed in a vineyard at Coligny, France (now known as the Coligny calendar). When the fragments were pieced together, they outlined a tablet containing a table of 62 consecutive months, including two separate "intercalary" months. The tablet was divided into 16 vertical columns, each of which contained the tables of four months (except for columns 1 and 9, each of which began with an intercalary month which occupied about half a column). The 62 months are roughly equivalent to five solar years.[178] Apart from the two intercalary months, the names of the months (which are in Gaulish) are: *Samonios, Dumann(i?os)*,

Rivros, Anagantios, Ogron(ios), Cutios, Giaman(ios), Simivisonna-, Equos, Elembiv-, Edrin(i?os), and *Cantlos* (whose names will be discussed below). Some of these months consisted of 30 days and some consisted of 29.[179]

The first intercalary month is preceded by the word *Matus* meaning "good." The word *antaran*, presumed to be an abbreviation of a word equivalent to *intercalaris*, is found at the start of the second intercalary month. In the rest of the monthly headings, the name of each month is followed by one of two abbreviations: *Mat* "good" (*matus*, Cf. Old Irish *maith*, "good") or *Anm* (*an-matus*, "not good"). Interestingly, the classification of months as either "good" (i.e. "generally auspicious") or "not good" ("generally inauspicious") is further reflected in the days of each month. The months are divided into two parts, with the days set out in a vertical alignment and marked with Roman numerals. In the first half of the month, the days are marked with the Roman numerals I to XV (1–15). Beneath the line of the 15th day, every month has the subheading *Atenoux* ("Returning Night"). Below this is the second half of the month, in which the days are numbered again from I to XIII or XV (1–14 or 15), depending on whether the month contained 29 or 30 days.

Generally speaking, in months categorized as "good," each day of that month is also categorized as a "good day" (with certain regular exceptions). In months categorized as "not good," most days are just notated as "day" (also with certain regularly occurring exceptions).[180] The notation *amb* is found at days 5 and 11 of each month, as well as at days 3, 5, 7, 9, 11, 13 and 15 of the second half of each month. *Amb* is regularly accompanied by the designation for "day," never by that denoting "good day." *Amb* may be a short form of *ambi-* denoting "lifeless, barren," which would fit the designation of these days as just "days" and not "good days."[181] At the end of months containing 29 days is the word *Diuertomu*. It is possible that the word comes from the verb *di-vert* ("pour, spill"), which may indicate a ceremonial act needed to avert misfortune, as this word is found in connection with "not-good" months.[182]

A further set of interesting notations occurs in the two intercalary months. The 60 days of which the two intercalary months are comprised are notated with the abbreviations for the twelve regular months, and this is repeated five times (12×5 being 60).[183] In each series of twelve months (beginning with and including an intercalary month), each month displays a notation associated with days 7, 8 and 9 in both the first and second halves of each month that derives from those same days in the month which follows it. The system is quite complex, but the important thing to note is that in each month—and in each half month—days 7, 8 and 9 were of special importance.[184]

It has been suggested that this time period may reflect something similar to that mentioned in Pliny's account (*Natural History* XXX, 13) where he says that the druids in Gaul ritually gathered mistletoe from oak trees to be used for healing purposes, and that this rite took place above all on the 6th day of the moon. The reason given is that the moon was already exerting great influence even though it was not yet halfway through its course. Prior to this statement, Pliny noted that the moon marked out the beginning of months and years and cycles of 30 years for the Gaulish Celts.[185] The idea that the healing properties of plants and herbs was on the increase during the waxing moon was still current in Irish and Scottish folk tradition in the last centuries.[186] If the month began on the new moon—at the first visible sign of the new crescent—then days 7, 8 and 9 directly follow the 6th day mentioned by Pliny. If, however, the lunar cycle was reckoned from the start of the three nights of the dark moon (which would make sense if the Gauls reckoned time by nights rather than days), then the sixth day of the moon, according to Pliny, could in fact be day 9 of the Coligny calendar.

Another fascinating aspect of the calendar concerns notations associated with the month of *Samonios*. In many of the yearly cycles, a notation is found in connection with that month: *MD Trinoxtion Samon Sindiu* ("Good day: the *trinux* "three nights" of *Samoni* [start?] today).There has been quite a bit of confusion regarding the meaning of the names of the months, particularly in regards to the word *Samonios*. This contains the root word *sam-* meaning "summer," and many early studies assumed this was a summer month with which the year began. However, as we will see in Chapter 3, the Celtic Year began in darkness, both at sundown and at a waning point of the year's light. The name for the New Year in Old Irish was *Samain*, denoting "summer's end" (< *sam* "summer" + *fuinn* "end"). In modern times it denotes the festival that begins on the evening of October 31st and runs into November 1st.

Prior to the adoption of the solar-based calendar, the start of the month (and the year) would have been at the new moon. Therefore, the word *Atenoux* ("returning night") marks the point at which the moon begins its return, back into the waning cycle and the three days of the dark moon from which the new lunar cycle would emerge. In terms of Samain, its reckoning would have originally been on a new moon that occurred between the autumn equinox and winter solstice. It may be that the Gaulish calendar operated in a similar way and began with a similarly named month. If so, we might envision a progression of month names and symbolism as follows. The name of the relevant month from the modern calendar is provided in parentheses, as it refers only approximately to the lunar month under discussion. While a number of the months have defied translation even by specialists, others are more amenable to translation.[187]

(**Nov**) *Samonios*: Potential analogue with Old Irish *Samain*, "summer's end" (< *sam* + *fuinn* < *fonn* "base, bottom, foundation"), with the first syllable deriving from the I.E. (Indo-European) root **sem-* meaning "summer."[188]

(Dec) *Dumann(i?os)*: Possible derivation from I.E. **dheub-*, "deep, hollow," with suffixed zero-grade form **dhub(h)-no-* in Celtic **dubno-*, "world (< "earth, ground" < "bottom") > Old Irish *domain* "deep; profound, intense; bottom, floor (of vat, sea); depth(s)." Another possibility is a derivation from the I.E. root **dheu-* (extended form **dheubh-*), with a range of meanings denoting "to rise in a cloud," such as smoke, vapor or dust, related to semantic notions of breath, and color adjectives denoting "dark, dusky."[189] Interestingly, in the Scottish Gaelic folk calendar, the name for December is *An Dúbhlachd* (< *dubh* "black, dark; sad, mournful"; *Cf. dùbhleachd,* "darkishness, dark blue; wintriness, tempestuousness.") In some sources it is spelled *Dùdlach,* which means "depth of winter, tempestuous weather, gloominess, dreariness, storm," and used in the phrase *dùdlachd a' gheamhraidh* "the depth of winter."

(Jan) *Rivros*: This has been theorized to derive from the intensive prefix *ro-* + *ivos* "feast"? < I.E. *dhēs-*, the root of a variety of words pertaining to religious concepts, and contracted from an earlier form meaning "to put, set," resulting in words meaning "festival, fair, holiday, feast, fest."[190] (*Cf.* OIr *feis,* verbal noun of *foaid* "spends the night; feasts.")

The Scottish Gaelic calendar contains a period known as *Am Faoilleach,* which begins on the Friday nearest to three weeks before the end of January, and ends on the Tuesday nearest to the end of the third week of February. It was proverbial for its variableness; stormy weather towards the end of January was prognostic of a fruitful season to follow, and vice versa. It was sometimes called "season of the wolf-ravage," reflecting the archaic term *faol* "patience or forbearance" but also meaning "wolf, wild dog."

However, in other Scottish folk sources it was spelled *Faoilteach,* and referred to the last fortnight of winter and the first fortnight of spring (Old Style). Sometimes the first half of this time period was called *Am Faoilteach Geamhraidh* (the Faoilteach of Winter) and the second half *Am Faoilteach Earraich* (The Faoilteach of Spring). This word appears to derive from *faoilte* "delight, cheerfulness; joyful salutation at meeting; welcome, welcoming; invitation to a feast, hospitality." This time period included (or immediately preceded) the time when the ewes gave birth, as the result of which there was a return of fresh food in the form of ewe's milk after a difficult period during which winter food stores were low. This was a great cause of celebration in the community and an integral part of the Irish and Scottish folk festival of Imbolc.[191]

(Feb) *Anagantios*: The -nt- in the month name suggests that it is a present participle, perhaps based on the root *anag-* "protect" (*Cf.* OIr *aingid*), or a compound formed from the negative prefix *an-* + *ag-* "go, drive."[192] An o-grade suffixed form of the latter resulted in **og-mo-*, "furrow, track" (metaphorically "an incised line"). In Celtic this gave the word *ogam,* from

Old Irish *Ogma* (*Cf.* Gaulish *Ogmios*), the name of a deity who was credited with inventing the ogham alphabet. The meaning of the word was literally "to incise, cut." In the Scottish Gaelic calendar, the general period of time pertaining to the month of February was known as *An Gearran,* from *gearr,* "cut, bite, gnaw; taunt, satirize; engrave; shear (as grass); geld an animal."

(Mar) *Ogron(ios):* Perhaps "cool, cold month?" deriving from I.E.*oug (which gave Gaulish *ogros*; *Cf.* Welsh *oer,* Irish *úar*). In Scottish Gaelic tradition March was *Am Màrt,* a loan-word which denoted the month of March (as well as Tuesday), and also referred to the time suitable for agricultural work which started in March but could extend into April depending upon the weather and sowing conditions; (*Cf.* the phrase *gaoth gheur nam Màrt,* "sharp wind of March").

(**Apr**) *Cutios:* Scholars simply do not have a solid idea about the meaning of this month name. It could derive from I.E. **keud-* "magical glory" (seen in the Greek word *kudos*), but this is far from certain.[193] A more promising possibility is a derivation from *gheu-* "to pour, pour a libation," with suffixed form **ghu-to,* "poured." This root occupied a prominent role in Indo-European religious terminology, and was used to refer to making a libation or pouring a liquid sacrifice, as well as the action of "pouring" or heaping earth to form a burial mound. Greek has the phrase *khutē gaia,* "poured earth" (which referred to a burial mound); *khutē* continues the Indo-European verbal adjective **ghu-to,* "poured."[194] This period of time directly preceded or included the pivotal point in the year when summer began, so perhaps libations were poured at this time.

(May) *Giaman(ios):* This word may contain the I.E. root **ghei-,* the theoretical base of *ghyem/ghiem* meaning "winter."[195] This has led to a great deal of confusion as to which season was considered the start of the year in the Gaulish calendar. However, if we attribute to this word the same type of formation that exists in *Samonios* ("end of summer"), then it may simply denote "end of winter." The suggestion that these two month denoted the start and end of the ritually significant dark/light or winter/summer seasons is supported by Old Irish *céitemain* ("start of summer") denoting May Day and *cét(h)-gaimrid* ("the start of winter") denoting "November," although in these two instances the beginning, rather than the end of the season is marked.[196]

(June) *Simivisonna-:* Because of its length, this word is suspected of being a compound word. However, the way to divide the word is unclear. *Simi-* could be connected to Latin *semi-* "half" (< I.E. **semi-*).[197] As **semi-* denotes "half-," as the first member of a compound, it is well placed in this word. Another possibility is I.E. **sem-* meaning "one, as one, together with." A suffixed form *som-o (from o-grade form **som-*) denotes "same," and a suffixed form *sōm-i (from lengthened o-grade **sōm-*) denotes "seemly, fitting, agreeable."[198] Some theorize segmenting away *-sonna.* I suggest the end of the word may represent the divine feminine ending -*ona* seen in a variety of sacred names, like that of the widely venerated goddess Epona, or the Gaulish goddess *Adsagsona*. The middle syllable, *uis*, could derive from a variety of words, such as **weis* "to flow"; **wes-* "to live, dwell, pass the night" (with derivatives meaning "to be"); *es-* "to be," or **(e)su* "good" (originally from **es-* "to be"). *Simi* + *uis* + *ona* could provide a variety of intriguing but indistinct meanings, such as "Divine feminine thing/Goddess [that is a] seemly or agreeable flow" (perhaps alluding to a river?), "Divine feminine thing/Goddess that is agreeable and good," "Divine feminine thing/Goddess [that is] half [of] being (i.e. life/living?)," or "Divine feminine thing/Goddess [with whom it is?] agreeable to live or dwell, or to pass the night." The last two interpretations could refer to the summer solstice, the halfway point in a solar cycle, and the divine being may be the sun in its longest hours at this time of the year. All of this is speculation, of course, but it does open up some possibilities for further discussion.

   (July) *Equos*: "Horse-month" (< I.E. **ekwo-* "horse"; *Cf.* Old Irish *ech* "horse"). This could refer to the horse races which were an important part of the Lugnasad celebrations that took place at the end of July/start of August in seasonal celebrations in a variety of Celtic countries.[199]

   (Aug) *Elembiv-*: This word is very difficult to interpret. Some wonder if *biu* could be connected to Old Irish *beo* "living."[200] If so, this word comes from the I.E. root **bheu-* "to be, exist, grow," with zero-grade form **bhu-* found in Welsh *bod* "to be" and Old Irish *both*, "a hut."[201] The I.E. root **el-* meant "red, brown," often forming animal and tree names (such as the extended form **elmo-* "elm"), while the root **ele-* means "to go." The root **em-* means "to take, distribute."[202] Perhaps there is some connection with the distribution of food at harvest time.

   (Sept) *Edrin(i?)os*: This word is also obscure. Some have speculated whether the start of the word could be connected with Old Irish a*ed* "fire." The I.E. root *ad-* means "to, near, at," with Celtic **ad-* "to, at" in compounds.[203] Another theory is a derivation from I.E. **eue-dh-r̥,* "udder" with suffixed O-grade **oudh-r̥,* "exuberant, exuberate," perhaps referring to the abundance of the land at this time. The root **reie-* means "to flow, run," with nasalized zero-grade form **ri-ne-ə*, remade as **ri-nu*, and suffixed form **rei-no*, Rhine, from Gaulish Rēnos "river." Or, we might consider the root **rendh-* "to tear up," used of things "torn off" (such as a rind), perhaps referring to deer antlers or the shell of nuts in the autumn.[204]

   (Oct) *Cantlos*: This could be related to Gaulish *cantalon* (*Cf.* OIr *cétal* "song "< I.E. **kan-* "to sing"). As this is the month leading up to and including the start of the Samhain assemblies, singing, chanting or reciting may have formed part of the festivities. In Scottish Gaelic, October was known as *An Dàmhair*, a word meaning "earnest, keen, eager, zealous; rutting of deer;

rutting time; noise, rutting riot," pertaining to the deer-rut and its distinctive sound.

While some of this is speculative, the translation of a number of the month names seems fairly clear. A working model of the Coligny calendar might be as follows (the months whose names are less clear are noted with an asterisk):

November—Summer's End
December—Dark Month
January—Great Feast
February—Cutting Month
March—Cold Month
April—Libation Month
May—Start of Summer
*June—Agreeable Goddess to dwell with/pass the Night
July—Horse Month
*August—Distribution Month
*September—Abundance Month
October—Month of Song

Literary sources depict the druids as advisors to chieftains on matters regarding omens and auguries, as well as lucky and unlucky days. Pliny wrote that the Gaulish Celts measured months and years and "ages" of thirty years by the moon. The Coligny calendar is lunar-based, and marks out lucky and unlucky days and months. Its basic construction represents an adjustment of the lunar year to the solar year by adding intercalary months of 30 days at 2½- and 3-year intervals alternately. Piggott points out that the calendar's scheme could relate to a 19-year cycle known in Greek and Babylonian mathematics, or might be related to the 30-year cycle mentioned by Pliny.[205] As it contains 60 primary months (2 × 30), this may affirm Pliny's report. While the calendar appears to be lunar rather than solar in nature, it is reasonable to conjecture that the Celts would have noted the passage of solar and lunar cycles, and also paid attention to the stars (which would have formed part of their own system of astronomy including constellations). Undoubtedly these heavenly bodies formed part of native origin myths as well.[206]

Sacred Origins and Knowledge of the Past

All of these sources—whether archaeological, historical or literary—contain fascinating glimpses into concepts associated with creation and the origin of things. In the tale of Fintan, the king must locate the oldest man in order to obtain information about historical precedents associated with various aspects of society and religion. The legitimacy, power and stability of sovereignty (and by extension, that of society) depended upon knowledge of first beginnings. The knowledge of the past (and of the origin of things) provided the basis for many important socio-religious precedents. These were used in legal proceedings, the administration of regal duties, and religious rituals (from pagan ceremonies to folk charms). In many of these settings, certain words or actions are described as a repetition of what others once did (deities, ancestors, saints, etc.). This re-enactment of "what the gods did in the beginning" is an important feature of many religious traditions and derives in part from elements of origin myths.[207]

Themes which originated in the pagan era may well have been recorded in the early historical period. As with Tomás Ó Cathasaigh's quote at the start of this chapter, John Carey also maintains that Irish literature "preserves various ideas which are probably at least to some extent reflections of pre–Christian doctrine." A good example is the early tale *DeGabail in tSída* ("The Taking of the Fairy Mounds"), which states that the first Gaels in Ireland "made peace with the gods of the land" in order to successfully raise their crops and herds.[208] The story recounts that before humans came to Ireland there was a famous king of the Túatha Dé Danann named *Dagán* (the Dagda). His power was great, for when human beings came to Ireland he destroyed their grain and milk "until they had made the friendship of the Dagda." After this was done, he saved their grain and milk. His power was apparently vast, for it was he who apportioned out the *síd* mounds to the members of the Túatha Dé Danann.[209] A later important partitioning was made by the legendary poet and judge Amairgen. In the tale *Mesca Ulaid,* it states that the land was divided into an upper and a lower half. The Gaels inhabited the upper half, and the half of the earth below the surface belonged to the Túatha Dé Danann, "who went into hills and supernatural dwellings, and dug *síd*-domains underground" (*Do-chuatar Túatha Dé Danann i cnoccaib ocus sídbrugaib cu ra accalset sída fo thalmain dóib).*[210]

The information presented in this chapter may be seen to constitute a considerable body of knowledge pertaining to the shape, at least, of certain elements of native belief regarding cosmology and sacred origins. We have encountered numerous references to perceptions of a three-fold cosmos; special attributes, colors, winds and objects associated with the four directions; the importance of the sacred center (which was in some cases associated with the World Tree); beliefs about the concept of *síd,* which included the importance of a reciprocal and respectful relationship between the worlds; stories associated with local flood myths and the eruption of waters (many of which are connected with Otherworldly women); references to ancient sages who shape-shifted throughout the ages and preserved important socio-religious knowledge; and concepts regarding Otherworld time and sacred cycles.

In light of this body of information, we cannot reasonably maintain the stance that we know nothing at all about Celtic cosmology and belief. It is both true and highly regrettable that we cannot always know how old these concepts may be, or in what state of integrity they were recorded. However, data from historical sources, archaeology, Classical accounts, Indo-European studies, and the study of comparative religion and the frequency and tenacity with which these elements appear and re-appear over many centuries, in both literary contexts and folklore sources support the possibility that they may in fact reflect aspects of native tradition.

While not all aspects of indigenous origin legends are likely to have survived the advent of Christianity intact, it is not inconceivable that some elements of native belief pertaining to sacred origins were preserved in certain tales or accounts. Carey notes that while we do not necessarily have *direct* knowledge of the beliefs of the pagan Irish concerning the origins of the land or its people, "there can scarcely be any doubt that legends addressing these questions were important to them."[211] In this chapter we have explored some intriguing and engaging aspects of native cosmogonic perceptions. In Chapter 2 we will explore how origin stories were perceived during the medieval era in Ireland, as the old religion and the new stood shoulder-to-shoulder with each other, co-existing during a fruitful period of creativity and growth for many centuries.

2

Creation, Cosmogony
and the Ancestry of the Gods

In a number of Indo-European mythologies, the creation of the world or cosmos often results in the coming-into-existence of two groups of divine beings. The first group may consist of giants or primal deities associated with creation, the cosmos and the elements. From these are descended a second order of gods connected with the earth, society and culture, and the lives of mortal beings. It is this second group who figure most prominently in mythological tales, and they are associated with the land, subsistence, war, magic, wisdom, skill, and a variety of other roles and functions.

In this chapter, we will explore aspects of early Irish literature to see if any trace of these early divine figures may be discerned amidst the blend of native Celtic, Medieval, Christian, and Classical elements that influenced the formation of early Irish literary sources. Information concerning Irish divine figures may be gleaned from a number of sources, including *Lebor Gabála Érenn, Táin Bó Cuailgne, Cath Maige Tuired, Acallam na Senórach* and the *Dindshenchas.* This exploration, however, will focus on sections of *Lebor Gabála* which profess to set forth the genealogy of the Túatha Dé Danann, the pre–Christian deities of Ireland.[1]

Many scholars have commented on the apparent lack of a native Irish creation myth. This is not entirely surprising in that the incoming religion had its own myth of origins to promote. It is quite remarkable (as well as fortuitous) that any literary evidence concerning the nature of native Irish pagan beliefs has survived at all. The preservation of components of Irish pre–Christian religion reflects the efforts of the church to combine native and Christian elements into a hybrid "tradition" which embodied facets of both.

What constitutes a creation myth? How might we recognize elements of native Irish cosmology in this hybridized literature? An examination of elements associated with creation mythology in other Indo-European traditions may help us recognize these cosmogonic structures, as well as their two attendant groups of divine beings.

Representations of Creation in Indo-European Mythology

Three types of primary creation scenarios tend to occur in Indo-European mythological settings:

(a) Duality (represented by two halves of the cosmos from which the Earth and Sky are created)

(b) Life from Death (the sacrifice and dismemberment of a primal being from whose body the elements of creation are formed), and

(c) Cyclical Creation (often depicted as a struggle between order and chaos in a perpetual cycle of creation and destruction).[2]

All three types of creation myths are present, to varying degrees, in Hindu, Greek and Norse mythology, and in many of these accounts we can perceive the existence of two different classes of divine beings.

In Norse creation myths, both Duality, and Life from Death are evident. Two opposing regions come together (one of heat and one of cold), which results in the appearance of a primal being (*Ymir*) from whom a race of giants is produced. *Ymir* meets his death at the hands of his three grandsons, Odin, Vile and Ve, and from his dismembered body the earth and the cosmos are created.[3] Odin is the chief Deity of the Norse Gods, a group of sacred figures associated with the land, society, and the world of human beings. These gods differ from earlier divine beings connected with creation, and it is this second group who figure most prominently in the myths (Odin, Thor, Balder, Freyr, Tyr, Loki, Frigg, Freyja, etc.).[4]

In an early Greek account of the creation of the world, various elements of the cosmos emerge from *Chaos* ("gaping void"). These in turn create other elements, and a union between Heaven and Earth produces the first beings, a race of giants known as the Titans. The Titans *Kronos* and *Rhea* (his sister and consort) have a son whose birth heralds an important change.[5]

This shift occurs in numerous mythological systems, and is frequently the result of mythological incest or some other unusual or significant union. After the birth of a father-/warrior-god or king (who often overthrows his father or grandfather, or an early race of gods or giants), a new class of deities comes into existence.[6] In Greek tradition, the pivotal figure in question is Zeus, whose amorous liaisons result in the creation of numerous divine progeny. These are the familiar deities of Greek myth (Apollo, Artemis, Hermes,

Ares, Dionysus, Hephaestus, Athena, Aphrodite, and so forth) who differ from the earlier primal beings and are associated with the land, society and the world of men.

Hindu mythology has preserved a prodigious number of accounts concerning the creation of the earth and the cosmos.[7] In some of these accounts, the world exists for a great span of time before dissolving into chaos, from which a new universe emerges. Every cosmogonic cycle consists of four successive ages, each one considered inferior to the previous one. In Greek tradition this same idea manifests as a cycle or progression of five ages (rather than four). These cycles do not involve destruction, but are each associated with a different race of men.[8] *Lebor Gabála Érenn* (hereinafter LG), a medieval Irish text concerned with the origin of things, also records five successive races of "men." Each race inhabits the primordial land of Ireland for a period of time, ultimately perishing from disease, flood, war, or other misfortune, making way for the next "age" or "race."[9] Before commencing our exploration of LG to see if two classes of divine beings may have formed part of Irish pre–Christian tradition, we will first need to discuss the composition and nature of the text itself.

Origins and the Creation of Lebor Gabála Érenn

A great deal of scholarly discussion has taken place over the years in an effort to ascertain what *Lebor Gabála Érenn* represents and of what materials it was comprised. Some scholars feel that most elements in LG can be traced to Christian sources, while others suggest it is a vast repository of pagan tradition. Both of these extreme views, however, are likely to miss the mark. There is a third school of thought which maintains that *Lebor Gabála* is a blend of some native traditions (including local histories, genealogies, and socioreligious information of various types) and some foreign traditions (which have their origin in Classical, Christian and Medieval sources).[10] It is this more balanced and widely accepted school of thought which we will follow.

In two comprehensive articles on *Lebor Gabála*, R. Mark Scowcroft describes the text as an "anonymous, scholarly composition designed to provide Ireland and her inhabitants with a continuous and comprehensive history from Noah to the Norman conquest."[11] He points out that its primary purpose was not to collect native traditions, but to find a place for Ireland in the biblical history of the world and provide an appropriate ancestry for her inhabitants as descendants of Noah. In the process, origin legends and other mythical or pseudo-historical narratives (older than or independent of LG) which had been preserved in native Irish tradition were interpolated into the text.[12] Dáibhi Ó Cróinín describes the process as follows:

Christian historians made no effort to compete with the pagans, but preferred to adapt and integrate what they could into their own writing. Thus biography became hagiography and the lists of kings and emperors of the various races were joined to form the synchronistic history of universal man.[13]

The Irish literati worked hard to integrate their country into contemporary medieval schemes of historiography, geography and ethnography. In the process, they created an "ancient history" of the Gaels which corresponded in many aspects to that of the Israelites. However, certain elements and variants in the text suggest that rather than reflecting a deliberate analogy with Biblical tradition, they may derive from other sources as well. These sources include medieval perceptions of European and Near-Eastern history, medieval Irish politics, traditions concerning conflicts between medieval Irish tribes or *túatha*, elements of Indo-European cultures and mythologies, and elements of early Irish traditions and cosmology.[14]

Alwyn and Brinley Rees characterize the process through which LG was formed as "a laborious attempt to combine parts of native teaching with Hebrew mythology embellished with medieval legend."[15] Rather than labeling the text as a medieval work of fiction (due to the insertion of Biblical elements and the artificiality of certain aspects of the pedigrees), they point out that the scribes who compiled the text lived much closer to the pre–Christian world than we do.[16] It is not unreasonable to think that some pagan traditions may have remained in circulation, whether or not their significance was completely understood by those who recorded or recited them over the course of time.[17] In addition, the brothers Rees point out that *Lebor Gabála* retains a number of features which the study of other mythologies would lead us to expect in myths about the beginnings of things.[18] They are referring to the condition of Ireland at the time of the alleged five invasions, when the land had not yet been completely formed, divided into provinces or named:

> From a mythological point of view, nothing really exists until it has been "formed," "defined" and "named," and in as much as *Lebor Gabála* is concerned with the origin of physical features, boundaries and names, it retains some of the essentials of a cosmogonic myth.[19]

The Pseudo-Historical Invasions of Ireland

Before we proceed, it would be helpful to have an understanding of the basic elements of the creation narrative found in in the text. Here is a summary of the main events associated with each of the "invasions" of Ireland, as set forth in the First Recension of the pseudo-historical narrative *Lebor Gabála Érenn*[20]:

(1) *Cessair*, the daughter of *Bith* ("World"), a "son of Noah," enters Ireland, accompanied by three men and three companies of women. All die in the Flood except *Fintan*, son of *Bochna* ("Ocean").

(2) After the flood came *Partholon* (Irish for Bartholomew), who was descended from *Aithech* ("peasant; boor; giant or monster"), a son of Magog, son of Japheth, son of Noah. During Partholon's time, lakes burst forth, plains are cleared by him, and ploughing, building, churning and brewing first take place in Ireland. The chthonic *Fomoire* ("Fomorians") harass Partholon and his people. Later, all of Partholon's party die of plague on Beltaine (May 1st), except *Tuan*, who, like Fintan, survives to document these pre-historical happenings for later ages.

(3) *Nemed* is also descended from Aithech. His name means "sacred" and contains the same root seen in the word *nemeton* "sacred place." Those of *nemed* status in Irish society were in good standing with the tribe, and therefore allowed to attend religious assemblies. Nemed's wife was *Macha*, and her presence in LG marks the first of three stories associated with this important goddess. During Nemed's time, more lakes and plains arise. He too is besieged by the Fomorians, and when he dies of plague in Ard Nemed ("The Height of Nemed" or simply "Sacred Mound/Hill"), his people continue to be oppressed. They are required to pay a huge tribute of grain, milk and progeny to the Fomorians every Samhain (November 1st). Eventually they fight off the Fomorians, and the three surviving chieftains of Nemed's people divide the land between them. Later they leave the island. Semeon goes to Greece, Fergus and his son Britan cross over to the Isle of Britain, and Bethach goes to the northern islands of the world.

(4) The *Fir Bolg* arrive in Ireland on another pagan Irish holiday, Lugnasad (August 1st). Although this was considered one single invasion, these descendants of Nemed were divided into three groups—the *Fir Bolg*, the *Fir Dhomhnann*, and the *Gailioin*. They have five chieftains, all sons of *Dela*, and they divide themselves into three landing parties. *Slanga* arrives in Leinster, *Gann* and *Sengann* enter the two Munsters, and *Genann* and *Rudraige* land in Connaught and Ulster. Nine different members of the Fir Bolg become kings of Ireland, an office or function which they were said to institute. The reigns of the last five kings were characterized by periodic slayings, at intervals of about five years. The last of these kings, *Eochu mac Eirc* (whose first name derives from Old Irish *ech* meaning "horse") is the ideal king, a perfect model of sovereignty. It is he who is on the throne when the Túatha Dé Danann arrive.

He is also the first king of Ireland to be slain by a spear, the weapon sacred to sovereignty.

(5) In this pseudo-historical narrative, the Túatha Dé Danann were also considered to be descendants of Nemed, and are thus related to the Fir Bolg. This, of course, was an attempt to reduce their status from that of divinities to just another group of mortals. It was said that the Túatha Dé Danann had previously been in the northern islands of Greece, learning *druidhecht* ("the arts of druidry"), a story element that is found in a slightly different form at the beginning of *Cath Maige Tuired*. It was also said that they considered their men of learning to be gods, but their husbandmen (farmers and herders) to be non-gods. The Túatha Dé Danann arrive in Ireland on Beltaine (May 1st), and they bring with them their most sacred treasures: the sword of Nuadu, the spear of Lug, the cauldron of the Dagda, and the stone of Fál (which also appear in the early part of *Cath Maige Tuired*). They engage in battle with the Fir Bolg, who are defeated and retreat to the outermost islands in the sea. The Sons of *Míl* are the next invasion, and this invasion represents the arrival of the Gaels in Ireland.

The Descent of the Gods

In Scowcroft's masterful articles on *Lebor Gabála*, he points out that despite its relative age, LG preserves some very old traditions—historical, legendary and mythological.[21] In addition to the formation of the land and its features (the bursting forth of rivers and lakes, and the clearing of plains), a more detailed reading of the text shows that LG appears to preserve information about the origin of things associated with human society: cultivation, grinding, churning, building, trading, horse-racing, arts, crafts, poetry, knowledge, the origin of kingship, the administration of justice, and the holding of assemblies.[22]

In light of the cosmogonic nature of the native elements that occur in LG, one might also expect to encounter information pertaining to the gods in such a setting (particularly primal deities associated with creation). With this is mind, we can now examine those portions of the text which refer to the Túatha Dé Danann in some detail.

The second tract of *Lebor Gabála* (*De Gabálaib Érenn*) is of particular interest, as it presents a great deal of information pertaining to the Túatha Dé Danan, including what is purported to be their genealogy.[23] Prehistoric genealogies were culturally important because they legitimized the seat or lineage of kingship, thus preserving the status quo in society and maintaining custom and order. They were often recited at important social or religious events. Divine, semi-divine (or noble or heroic) ancestors provided a foundation upon whose reputation, status, or divinity one might attain or maintain power and position. These ancestral figures also provided their descendants with a certain mystique (in some cases derived from their descent from or connection with Otherworld beings).

During the medieval era, historians and genealogists in Ireland maintained this type of tradition by preserving or supplying eponymous ancestors for population groups on a national, territorial, and familial level. Providing Biblical ancestors for all the peoples of Ireland was considered to be very important, as it included them in the new Christian schema. It also gave all population groups a common origin, a method used to legitimize everyone no matter what their position in society, thereby reducing conflict (whether physical or ideological). The authors of Ireland's literary corpus of toponymic legends known as the *Dindsenchas* performed a similar task in recording or positing eponymous founders, many with divine or semi-divine ancestry, for the place-names of Ireland.[24]

Why should a genealogy of the Túatha Dé Danann have been preserved in a text whose goal was to provide Biblical ancestry for the people of Ireland? One reason is that by providing the pagan deities with human ancestry, their status could be diminished, demonstrating that they were no longer gods. Without a divine pedigree, they could be passed off as just another invasion of mortals who were conquered or subdued by the next incoming population group.

In addition to these practical concerns, however, Scowcroft makes the important observation that "the mythographers of Christian Ireland were too interested in the old gods to leave them alone."[25] In LG, the Túatha Dé Danann are said to be the descendants of *Nemed* ("Sacred"). However, they were not apparently included in the earliest accounts of these invasions, and it seems that originally only Partholón, Nemed and the Milesians appeared in the story (with the Fir Bolg and the Túatha Dé Dannan added later).[26]

The earliest summary of Irish pseudo-history is actually found in a British source, the *Historia Brittonum* (hereinafter referred to as HB), written in Wales in CE 829–30. This text appears to embody a number of earlier strands of tradition (of oral and Welsh derivation, as well as literary and Latin provenance) and also contains some Old Irish material resembling an early version of *Lebor Gabála*. It is likely that at least some of these sources originally existed as separate texts in Wales, North Britain and Ireland.[27] In HB, the invaders are Partholomus (Partholón), Nimeth (Nemed), the three sons of Míl, and a "company of eight"; here the Túatha Dé Danann are not listed as one of the groups of invaders.

The scheme recorded in *Historia Brittonum* had been evolving over generations. The conceptual framework of successive occupations of Ireland was explored in increasing detail in the ninth, tenth and eleventh centuries. By the time of the writing of *Lebor Gabála*, around the year 1050, the history of Ireland's inhabitants reflected a wide variety of Biblical, native and medieval traditions, as well as newly created adaptations.[28] These alterations resulted in the generation of an invasion myth which fused elements of pagan theology with the politics of medieval Ireland.[29] In addition to socio-religious motivations for providing a common ancestry for the peoples of Ireland, it is reasonable to suppose that for the proponents of the new religion, the pagan gods of the Irish were a problem to be handled (and perhaps also a force to be reckoned with). John Carey writes:

> It was an audacious move to weave the divinities of their pagan ancestors into the framework of their history, and this "explanation" of the immortals seems never to have sat entirely easily in the minds of the medieval Irish.[30]

The claim that the Túatha Dé Danann had human ancestry is not made prior to the poems of the 10th century and never fully ousted an earlier theory that they were destructive or uncanny spirits.[31] Carey points out the artificiality of accounts that describe how the gods "came to Ireland" with the attendant need to fit them into a series of settlements:

> Surely they were always there, an ineradicable part of the land whose powers they are: they do not come "from" anywhere—any more than the *Fomoiri* seem to do...[32]

He also points out that while we may never be able to confidently reconstruct the processes through which native and learned traditions came together, one element of the account is likely to be an old one: however they got there, it is the gods who rule Ireland when the Gaels first arrive.

> The new land belongs to these immortals ... whose weapons are magic and illusion. Ireland, before the Gaels can win it for themselves, is itself a kind of Otherworld.[33]

The arrival of the Túatha Dé Dannan is described in *Lebor Gabála* as follows:

> The descendants of *Bethach mac Iarbonél Fáith mac Nemed* were in the northern islands of the world learning druidism and knowledge and sorcery and cunning until they were pre-eminent in the arts of the heathen sages. They are the *Túatha Dé Donann* who came to Ireland. It is thus that they came: in dark clouds.[34]

The gods land in the west and cast a darkness upon the sun for three days and nights. This is a significant and often ritualistic period of time in Celtic tradition, frequently associated with journeys to the Otherworld, important adventures or ordeals, and changes of state or status. After three days and nights of darkness, the Túatha Dé Danann are able to vanquish the Fir Bolg in battle, thus experiencing a change of status as they take possession of the land and its sovereignty.[35]

The Ancestry of the Ancient Gods

In *Lebor Gabála,* a Biblical origin for the Irish was provided through one of the three sons of Noah (Japheth) from whom the peoples of Europe were said to descend. In LG, the Sons of Mil are said to be descended from Japheth's son Gomer, while the peoples who came to Ireland before the Gaels (the Gaileóin, the Fir Domnann, the Fir Bolg, and the Túatha Dé Danann) are alleged to descend from Magog, another son of Japheth.[36] This arrangement differs from that of the Old Testament. A number of other additions and alterations appear in LG which constitute departures from Old Testament tradition, as well as an expansion of the Biblical model in which known population groups attributed their origin to one of the sons or grandsons of Noah.[37]

In the Bible, Japheth's descendants occupy Asia Minor and the Mediterranean. In LG they inhabit a similar area, but also occupy all of Europe. In Biblical tradition, the offspring of Japheth's son Gomer are listed as Ashkenaz, Riphath and Togormah. In LG, Gomer has two sons: Emoth (from whom come the "northern peoples of the world") and Ibath. Ibath is said to have two children, Bodb and Baath, figures who do not appear in Genesis and whose names are of Irish origin.

Several names from the pedigree of the Túatha Dé Danann in LG also appear in *Historia Brittonum* as well as in the genealogies of the Leinstermen from Rawlinson B.502 (hereinafter RawlB502).[38] A few of these names are similar to those of persons in the Bible, but it is also possible that the author(s) of these pseudo-historical texts, when encountering unusual or unfamiliar Irish words, may have felt they recognized in those names the names of figures familiar to them from Christian tradition.

However the genealogies in *Lebor Gabála* were formed, it is clear that at some point native Irish lore, and Biblical and medieval traditions were stitched together into a pseudo-history which served a variety of purposes. In spite of these goals, the artificiality of the pseudo-historical genealogical arrangement in LG is obvious: the pagan Irish gods cannot, of course, be descended from Noah, supporting the theory that their genealogy is a hybrid of native and non-native traditions.

With this in mind, we can proceed in our exploration of the ancestry of the Túatha Dé Danann as described in *Lebor Gabála.*[39] Sections 12, 13, and 75 of the text provide us with useful data from which a genealogy of the Túatha Dé Danann may be reconstructed. In mapping out the relationships described in the text, I found that the data in these sections was remarkably internally consistent.[40]

The names of the first three people who are said to be the ancestors of the Túatha Dé Danann are biblical in origin: Noah, Japheth and Magog.

However, most of the names which follow after these three figures are likely Irish in origin: *Faithecht, Braimin(d), Esrú, Srú, Sera, Tat/Tait, Paimp, Agnoman, Nemed, Iardan/Iarbonél, Bethach, Ebath/Ibath, Baath, Eno/Éna, Tabarn and Tat/Tait.* Let's take a look at the meaning of each of these names, in order of appearance in *Lebor Gabála.*

(1) **Faithecht** seems to appear in HB as *Aurthoch.*[41] Similar names appear in RawlB502: *Ethecht, Aurtacht, Aurthecht.*[42] In a genealogy given by Keating in *Foras Feasa ar Éirinn* (which he attributes to the lost *Cín Dromma Snechta*) a figure called *Fáthach* is mentioned, the ancestor of Partholón and Nemed, and brother of Baath and Ibath. I have been unable to locate a Biblical figure whose name is similar to that of Faithecht.[43] The name likely derives from Old Irish *fáith* "seer, prophet" and may mean "One who is Skilled in the Art of Prophecy" (*cf.* its derivative *fáthach* "possessed of knowledge or skill; wise"; note also the suffix of *dánacht* "poetry, art of poetry"). Prophecy was a highly revered (and divinely derived) skill which figures prominently in the literature, ascribed to poets, druids and other figures with high socio-religious status. A Divine Seer would be an appropriate ancestor for the Túatha Dé Danann.

(2) **Braimin(d)**. Again, I was not able to locate any Biblical figure with a similar name. It may bear some relation with the Old Irish word *brithem* "judge" (pl. form *brithemon*), another highly revered role in early Irish society. The second syllable may be the common adjectival ending *–ind*, reflecting the lenited form of *find* "white, bright, blessed," seen in a number of divine and personal names. Like the Divine Seer above, a "Blessed/Sacred Judge" would also be an appropriate ancestor for the gods.

(3) **Esrú** is also mentioned in RawlB502. Two similar names appear in HB (Ezra and his father Izrau). Ezra the scribe is a well-known Biblical character, where he is the son of Serai'ah (a figure whose name may be reflected in that of Esrú's grandson Sera below). Ezra does not appear in Genesis, however, nor is he associated with Noah and his offspring. Other possibilities exist that may support a native origin for Esrú's name.

The word may derive from *esruth* "scattering, bursting forth," perhaps denoting the propagation of divine progeny or the dissemination of divine knowledge or power. This word is sometimes used in phrases pertaining to cosmogonic elements: *esruth sin, esruth gáith,* and *esruth rind*—the scattering or bursting forth of storms, wind and stars. A figure called *Esras* appears in *Cath Maige Tuired*, one of the four sages with whom the Túatha Dé Danann studied occult lore and magic. A derivation from *esrais/esrus* "out-let, passage; means, way, opportunity" has been suggested.[44]

If the name reflects a compound word, perhaps it is comprised of *es(s)* "cataract, rapid; rapidly flowing stream; waterfall," and *sruth* "stream, river, current; stream of the sea." The second element might also reflect *sruith*, "old, senior, venerable, revered, hon-oured," used as a substantive to denote an "elder, ancestor, reverend person, sage." This might suggest a meaning in the range of "Waterfall of the River/Stream" or "Waterfall/Stream of the Sage/Ancestor." While this derivation may admittedly be a bit forced, watery sources (including rivers and waterfalls) are often associated with knowledge in early Irish literature (see Chapter 7). In some cases, sages and their activities are connected with these locations. An important site of Otherworld-related activity was *Ess Ruaid* "the Red/Noble Waterfall," whose name might also be reflected in that of the figure *Esrú*.[45] Overall, this word seems to reflect imagery associated the possession or dissemination of divine wisdom.

(4) **Srú** appears in RawlB502 as *Srú* or *Zrú*, but does not appear in HB. If the name is Irish, it might derive from *sruth* or *sruith* ("River/Stream" or "Sage/Ancestor"), reflecting imagery similar to the figure described above.

(5) **Sera** is not listed in HB, but may appear in RawlB502 (spelled *Sara*). Biblical tradition provides several possible candidates: *Seraiah* (the father of Ezra), *Serug* (a descendant of Shem) and the female name *Sarai/Serah*. However, a person by the name of Sera appears in another Irish source as the grandfather of Tuan, a figure associated with primal floods and cosmogonic elements. In one version of Irish pseudohistorical legend, *Tuan* was the sole sur-vivor of the people of Partholón, and lives to tell the story of *Lebor Gabála* to Saint Finnian. He somehow survives the plague that killed the rest of Partholón's group, and lives through many gener-ations in the form of a stag, a boar and an eagle. Finally he is changed into a salmon who is caught and eaten by the wife of *Cair-ill*, who gives birth to him in human form so that he can recite to others the early mythic history of Ireland.[46]

(6) The name of the next figure, **Tat/Tait,** is most instantly recognizable as a Welsh word meaning "father," appearing in the name of figures like *Tad Awen*, "Father of Inspiration." However, an Irish origin for the name is also possible, through words denoting "join-ing" or "union": *táth* "joining, welding, binding" (*cf. táthaid*, "joins, welds, unites," as well as "welder, smith, artificer"). "One who

Joins/Unites," perhaps a Divine Artisan or Artificer, is an appealing possibility. However, the name could also be the result of reduplication, a reflex of the word *aite* "foster-father; tutor, teacher."

(7) **Paimp** is a word whose meaning is unclear, although the inclusion of the letter "p" (which does not occur in Irish) may indicate alteration through Welsh channels. It is likely that the form *Boib* (seen in HB) or *Banb/Bainb* (RawlB502) are more reflective of the original form. If so, the latter may reflect an element seen in the name of one of the three eponymous goddesses of Ireland, Banba (perhaps from *banb* "a young pig," used in the phrase *in banb samna*, "the pig eaten at Samhain"). If the form *boib* in HB is more accurate, this could reflect the word *badb* "raven, scald-crow," seen in a number of divine names and an important mythological symbol.

(8) **Agnoman** appears in RawlB502, as does the possibly related name *Ogamuin* (spelled *Ougumun* in HB). Its meaning and origin are uncertain. One possibility is that it might be an Irish rendering of the name *Agamemnon*, a name potentially known to the compilers through their familiarity with Classical texts.[47] Alternately, it may be related somehow to the word *ogam* (or the name of its inventor, Ogma mac Elathan).

(9) **Nemed** is a word of native origin whose original sense was probably that of a sacred or consecrated place, with secondary meanings (from the special qualities attributed to sacred space) of privilege, status and dignity. As an adjective it means "holy" or "sacred" and as a noun "privilege, sanctity or sanctuary." In the earliest law tracts it signified all persons of free status. Freemen were considered "holy" (*nemed*) in that they were qualified to participate in public religious rites. In early Ireland, the upper classes of society (*neimid*) included secular and ecclesiastical lords (*saerneimid*) and professionals (*daerneimid*), as distinguished from rent-paying vassals (*aithig*). A similar distinction existed among the gods between skilled deities (*áes dána*) and farmers (*áes trebtha*).[48]

The concept of *nemed* also finds expression in the word *nemeton*, which refers to a sacred place (possibly originally a clearing in the wood). A *nemeton* could exist at, nearby, or in connection with groves, hills, lakes, wells, tumuli and royal sites, which often formed the symbolic center of the *túath*. These were points of access to the Otherworld as well as places of cult and sanctuary for the pagan Celts. It is reasonable to suggest that the descent of the gods from a figure called Nemed, who was associated with sacred sites and ritual events, might have formed part of native Irish tradition.

(10) *Iardan/Iardanais* or *Iarbonél* (the third form designated as
"Faith" "Seer") is a figure whose name variants suggest a number
of intriguing possibilities. *Iardan* could be a compound from *íar*
"after, across; end; dark, black" (a word sometimes used in formations have the sense of "west" or "western") plus *dán* "gift, skill,
especially of poetry." This would suggest a meaning along the
lines of "Dark Skill" or "Skill which Originates in the West." The
West was often associated with the Otherworld, and was also the
direction associated with learning in the cosmological scheme
outlined in "The Settling of the Manor of Tara."

A name relating to "dark" or obscure skill which originates in
the west (or in the Otherworld) would be appropriate for a divine
seer. Medieval Irish poets and judges were sometimes said to possess the skill of "dark speech," a purposeful use of obscure or
archaic language, which not only preserved their status as part of
the elite learned classes, but may have been used to keep certain
information from the non-learned of the tribe.[49]

One variant form of this name was *Iardanais*. *Danais* is the
equivalent of *Tanais*, the ancient name of the River Don in Rus-
sia. This river designation (and that of numerous others in
Britain and on the Continent) is thought to derive from the IE
root *danu-* "river."[50] The seer's name may be a descriptive term
("Dark River") or may reflect movement "across" a river. Travel
over or across a body of water frequently signifies a change of
state, or a journey to the Otherworld.[51]

The third variant is *Iarbonél*. The initial element may derive
from *íarmúa/íarmó* "great-grandson/child" (sometimes used with
the meaning "descendant") with the second element denoting *nél*
"cloud." In an Indo-European system of mythic analogy in which
the elements of the cosmos are compared to the body parts of the
primal being, clouds are associated with the brain or thoughts.[52]
Grigory Bondarenko has written about Indo-European poetic and
narrative sources in which poets or sages attribute their wisdom
to a connection with or journey to the clouds, or to having access
to the power of the clouds.[53]

An epithet "Descendant of Cloud" may allude to the seer's ability to obtain knowledge from the heavens or the unseen world. In
addition, as we saw above, in some versions of the LG narrative,
the Túatha Dé Danann were said to arrive "in dark clouds."

The confusion which seems to surround the name of this
divine personage may derive from (or have been influenced by)
references to sages and poets who appear in *Auraiceipt na n-Éces*,

a medieval Irish poetic primer associated with the training of the *filid* or poet-seers.[54] One of the personages who figures in the *Auraiceipt* is *Iar mac Nema*, a name very similar to that of our seer, *Iardan mac Nemed*. *Iar mac Nema* was said to have discovered *íarmbélra*, "The Obscure Language of the Poets."[55] The *Auraiceipt* also mentions *Nél*, the son of *Fenius Farsaid*. Both *Iar mac Nema* and *Fenius* were sages associated with poetic lore, learning, and traditions pertaining to "common" and "poetic" languages. We can see certain similarities (as well as possible sources of confusion) between the names of *Iardan mac Nemed* and *Iar mac Nema*, *Iarbonél* and *Nél* (son of *Iar mac Nema's* fellow sage Fenius), and *Iarbonél* and *íarmbélra* (the poetic language discovered by *Iar mac Nema*). However these variants came about, they all seem to be associated with poetry, prophecy, or the acquisition of divine wisdom, "dark" or "obscure" skills which are associated with, and often derived from, the Otherworld.

(11) *Bethach*'s name appears only in *Lebor Gabála*. It may reflect the word *bethach* "nourishing," or some form of *betha/bethu* "life, existence; food, nourishment; sustenance, maintenance." This would suggest a meaning along the lines of "One Who Provides Nourishment" or "One Who Sustains Life." Interestingly, *Bethach* (whose name is associated with life) is one of the survivors of the people of *Nemed*.[56]

(12) *Ebath/Ibath* appears in HB as *Iobaath* and in RawlB502 as *Enbath*. These names reflect native words which refer to the aspen or yew tree and may also be associated with imagery pertaining to sacred trees or *bile*, ritual sites, and divine wisdom. This particular name will require additional discussion, which is presented in the following section.[57]

(13) *Baath* is found in RawlB502 (spelled *Boath* or *Baoth*) and in HB, as stated above (*Baath* son of *Iobaath*). The name may reflect an Irish word, perhaps *bath* "death" or *bath*, explained as "sea" (*muir*). As it is our contention that some of the names in LG may reflect primal figures or elements associated with creation, the second interpretation may be most suitable. Interestingly, *Baath* ("Sea") is one of those who survive the deluge of Nemed's time (along with his father *Ebath* and grandfather *Bethach*).

(14) *Eno/Éna* appears in RawlB502 as *Énna* (and perhaps also as *Énoc*). This second name may suggest that of the Biblical figure Enoch, the great grandfather of Noah (and the only character mentioned thus far who is actually associated with Genesis).[58] It may also be that a similar Irish word was thought to be a variant

or reflection of Enoch. A derivation from the word *én* "bird" is possible (*cf. éonu,* acc.pl. of *én,* and *énach,* a collective form, "birds"). Due to the fact that the names of *Éna*'s father and son both mean "sea," it is also possible that the name may reflect a form of the word *en* "water" (gs. *ena,* as in the phrase *sruaim ena*). Or, perhaps it is a form of the verb *enaid;* in *Bérla na filed,* an obscure poetic language associated with *Éna*'s great-great-grandfather *Iardan Iarbonél,* the word *enaid* means "shows, makes known."

(15) ***Tabarn*** does not seem to appear in sources other than LG. The grandchild of *Baath* ("Sea"), his name reflects the Irish word *tabairn,* which also means "sea."

(16) A second figure by the name of ***Tat/Tait*** appears in Section 97 of *Lebor Gabála,* which states: "It is at Tait son of Tabarn that the testimonies concerning the Túatha Dé Donann converge." Indeed, after mapping out the family tree of the Túatha Dé, we can see that *Tait/Tat* is the common ancestor of all the subsequent members of the Túatha Dé Danann. As we saw before, it is possible that the name reflects a word relating to concepts such as "joining" or "union" (perhaps the joining or uniting point of the old gods and the new). Or, as an important ancestor figure of the rest of the Túatha Dé Danann, it may reflect the Welsh word *tat/tad* "father" or a reduplicated form of Old Irish *aite/aiti,* "foster father," "teacher." It is with this common ancestor or father-deity that we encounter the Indo-European mythological shift in focus from deities associated with creation to those associated with the land and the world of human beings. The descendants of the primal deities listed above constitute the well-known divine figures of early Irish myth and legend: the Dagda, the Mórrígan, Oengus, Boand, Bríg, Ogma, Macha, Lugh, Manannán, Goibniu, and others.

The Yew, the Ash and the Salmon

There is one figure among the primal Irish deities whose name requires additional discussion. This is *Ebath,* son of Bethach ("He Who Promotes Life"), and great-grandson of Nemed ("Sacred/Place"). In the Ogam alphabet, *ebath/ebad* is said to represent "ea" or diphthongs beginning with "e." It is associated with the aspen in some cases (but elsewhere with the herb elecampane). The spelling of the name is erratic, and there is considerable fluctuation and confusion between the forms *ebad* and *edad* throughout *Auraceipt na n-Éces,* where the ogam alphabet is discussed at some length.

Some of this irregularity is the result of confusion with the word *idad* (the letter "i"), which is connected with the yew tree. The trees associated with the ogam alphabet are grouped into four classifications: chieftain trees, peasant trees, herb trees, and shrub trees. The aspen is listed as a peasant tree and does not figure prominently in early Irish tree lore.[59] The yew, on the other hand, is included among the chieftain trees and, along with the oak and the ash, was considered a *bile*, a sacred tree under which assemblies might be held. These trees were associated with sacred sites like wells, hills and burial grounds.[60]

The *Dindshenchas* tradition records the name of five particularly sacred trees: The Tree of Tortu, the Tree of Dathí, the Tree of Uisnech (all ash trees), Éo Rosa (a yew) and Éo Mugna (an oak or yew). The last tree, Éo Mugna, was said to bear apples, nuts and acorns. In one *Dindsenchas* account it is described as an oak (*dair*), while in two others it is said to be a yew (*éo*). In at least one of the poems it is explicitly referred to as a *bile*.[61]

Two of the five trees are yew trees, while the other three are ash. Here we might recall that the world tree of the Norse was an ash. This symbol of the *axis mundi* played an important role in ancient Norse ritual and continued to do so in the folklore tradition. The gods were said to dispense justice from an assembly beneath the world tree, reminiscent of tribal assemblies of the Celts which took place in the presence of the *bile*.[62] Hilda Ellis Davidson makes this important observation about the world tree:

> As the center of the cosmos, the sacred tree was linked with creation legends.... It was appropriate that the sacred center should be the place where kings are chosen and proclaimed, and where the law was recited.[63]

Many have speculated on a possible connection between the symbolism of the world tree and the widespread veneration for trees found in Celtic tradition. The nature of sacred locations as described in both literature and folklore, and archaeological evidence concerning the structure of Celtic sacred sites (both natural and manmade), seem to support such a connection. It may be that sacred trees or *bile*, as well as wooden posts or stone pillars mentioned in literary sources and found at Celtic ritual sites, may have served as symbols of the world tree in the community in which they were located.

How can we account for (or clarify) the confusion between *ebad/edad* and *idad*, words which refer to either the yew or the aspen? Damian MacManus has discussed at length the work of the composers of the *Bríatharogam*, the oldest, least contaminated and most trustworthy source of information on the types of *ogam* and their associations.[64] He points out that the recorded name of the ogam characters for E (*ebad/edad*) and I (*idad*) pose considerable problems of interpretation and etymology, and that this confusion is found as early as Cormac's Glossary.[65] Perhaps the kennings (sets of cryptic associations) associated with these letters may shed some light on the problem.

Edad is associated with the aspen or poplar tree. It represents the letter é and words which begin with é. It is connected with the salmon in the kenning "é—the crafty one of the water, i.e., salmon."[66] An alternate spelling, *ébad*, was also mentioned in connection with the salmon in the kenning: "fair swimming letter—a kenning for the great salmon … *é/éo* is a name/ word for the salmon and it is written [with the character] *ébad* as [in] the "Alphabet of the World," i.e., three stags, i.e., deer, salmon, three salmon, a snipe, i.e., a blackbird" (notably, the three animals in "Finn and the Man in the Tree").[67]

The kennings for "I" pose fewer problems than those for "E," and refer primarily to the yew tree (*ibar* in the glosses).[68] Fergus Kelly mentions that apart from *ibar*, another Old Irish word for "yew" was *éo* (cognate with Welsh, Breton and OHG words for yew).[69] MacManus states that *ibar* cannot have been the old name of "I," but that Old Irish *éo* could have been (<PI *iwas; Cf. Welsh *yw* "yew-tree" and Gaulish *Ivo*).[70]

The yew tree, then, was associated with both the letter "I" (*ibar*, "yew") and the letter "E" (é). The kennings connected with these letters display associations with both the salmon (*é/éo*, as in the phrase *éo fis*, "salmon of knowledge") and with an older word for yew (also *éo*). There is clearly a measure of overlap between the E and I kennings, the former pointing to *éo* "yew" or *éo/é* "salmon" and the latter to "yew" (glossed *ibar*). The kennings seem to have been composed at a time when the names of these letters were known to mean (E) "yew" or "salmon," and (I) "yew," both of which are important mythological symbols in early Irish tradition.[71]

The World Tree of the Irish

The word *ebath*, then, was associated with the diphthong *éo* with its early attendant meanings of either "yew" or "salmon." We have seen that the yew tree was considered sacred and was one of the chieftain trees. As a *bile,* it was connected with religious assemblies and sacred sites. I suggest that the yew may have served as a symbol or representative of the world tree in early Irish tradition. As such, it would reasonably appear in association with creation myths and scenarios and their attendant divine figures.

In many cultures, the world tree is referred to as the "Tree of Life." The father of *Ebath* ("Yew") was *Bethach* ("He who Promotes or Sustains Life"), who survived the deluge of Nemed's time. The *axis mundi* is also frequently referred to as the "Tree of Wisdom." The word *ebath* was associated with the kenning *érnaid fid/fer* ("discerning letter, wood or tree" or "discerning man"). This may refer to the use of rods of yew in divination rites as well as the connection of *ebad* (é) with the legendary *éo fis* ("the salmon of knowledge").[72]

In addition, the world tree is often associated with longevity or immortality. The Tree of Mugna (a yew) may well have been perceived as such, as it is evergreen.[73] The yew tree is glossed as "oldest of woods" (*siniu fedaib*) and "oldest tree," probably referring to its well-attested longevity.[74] Indeed, in Britain and other regions, the yews are the oldest intact trees.[75]

Earthly representatives of the world tree are often found in connection with sacred or holy sites. In Ireland, ash and yew trees were often planted near churches. These trees symbolized immortality well into the Christian era. Various socio-religious rites were held near the site of the world tree (or its localized symbolic representative). In Scotland, the gathering place of the Stratherick Frasers was known as *Tom na h-Iúbhraich*, "The Hill of the Yew." This important site contained a yew tree as well as an ancient burial ground. An important parallel is the site known as *Taigh nan Teud*, which was considered to be the center-point of all Scotland. It was located near the yew tree of Fortingall, the oldest living tree in Europe, and was undoubtedly a sacred site in ancient times.[76]

While the word *éo* connotes a yew tree, it had an earlier meaning of "stem" or "shaft," and can refer to a tree in a more general sense. Perhaps this reflects the symbolic central pillar or shaft which connects the three worlds (Upper, Middle and Lower Worlds) in a number of world cosmologies, and helped facilitate communication between them.[77] Interestingly, as yew trees grow to an extreme age they rot in the middle, existing for many centuries with a hollow space in their center (sometimes filled with earth in which other plants may thrive).[78] A large, ancient tree with a hollow center would be a fitting symbol of the world tree and its role as a conduit between the worlds.

An Early Irish Cosmogonic Tale

We have seen that the name of the divine figure known as *Ebath* ("yew tree") may signify the world tree. If so, this lends support to the theory that the names of the ancestors of the Túatha Dé Danann reflect elements of a native creation scenario. These primal deities do appear to be associated with concepts one would expect to encounter in a myth of origins, including the primordial sacred site with its focus on the World Tree. If, perchance, any of the information that has come down to us through the admittedly distorted lens of medieval Irish pseudo-history is reflective of native belief, we may be able to discern or propose a hypothetical prototype of an Irish cosmological narrative:

In ancient times, before the creation of Ireland, there was *Fáithecht,* the Divine Seer, who saw all that was to be. Next was *Braimind* the Judge, who laid down the laws by which all should live. The offspring of Braimind was *Esrú,* who was responsible for disseminating this sacred knowledge. Then came *Srú,* who created the Waters from which the world was formed. The offspring of *Srú* was *Sera,* grandfather of *Túan,* who lived through many ages in the form of a stag, a boar, an eagle and a salmon. From *Sera* there came *Tait,* the Divine Artisan, who joined together all the elements of the cosmos.

Next were *Badb,* the Raven, and *Ogamuin,* whose wisdom generated the *ogam* for preserving and communicating knowledge. After them was *Nemed,* who created the Sacred Place where the gods might communicate with those on earth. *Nemed's* offspring was a great Seer, who was called by many names and who possessed dark skills. This Seer created the obscure language known only to the learned, and was sometimes called the Descendant of the Clouds. From the Seer came *Bethach,* "The One who Sustains Life," and then *Ebad,* the Yew, who is the Tree of Life, the sacred ceremonial tree or *bile.*

The offspring of *Ebad* was *Baath,* the great Sea which surrounds the World Tree. Next came *Éna,* a being of the waters, who gave birth to *Tabarn,* creator of the vast oceans of the earthly realms. Finally there was *Tat,* the Great Father, who is the common ancestor of all the divine beings who came next. Those divine offspring are the gods who live in the *síd* mounds and who have dealings with the people of the Middle Realm. They are called the Túatha Dé Danann, the Tribes of the Goddess Danu, and are reknowned for their great power and skill.

As speculative and undoubtedly inaccurate as this narrative may be, the elements embodied in the names of the primal divinities are along the lines of what we would expect when dealing with an early class of divine beings associated with creation. In addition, the offspring of these deities follow the mythic pattern and constitute the second class of deities associated with society, the land and the world of human beings.

In *Native Elements in Irish Pseudohistory,* John Carey remarks that *Lebor Gabála* "reflects a deep (and for its time remarkable) reverence for and interest in native traditions concerning bygone times." He states that this blending of pagan and Christian lore demonstrates the redactors' commitment to both traditions, for they were convinced that both were true and both were important, and thus worked very hard to reconcile one with the other.[79] This effort to reconcile the traditions is apparent in the words of a scribe who worked on the Second Redaction of *Lebor Gabála,* as he struggles to understand and faithfully transmit the names, attributes and characteristics of the divine figures whose legends and traditions he records:

> …Some say that the Túatha Dé Danann were demons, seeing that they came unperceived (and they say themselves it was in dark clouds that they came, after burning their ships) and for the obscurity of their knowledge and adventures, and for the

uncertainty of their genealogy as carried backwards; But that is not true, for their genealogies carried backward are sound; howbeit they learnt knowledge and poetry; for every obscurity of art and every cleverness of reading, and every subtlety of crafts, for that reason, derive their origin from the Túatha Dé Danann. And though the Faith came, those arts were not put away, for they are good, and no demon ever did good.[80]

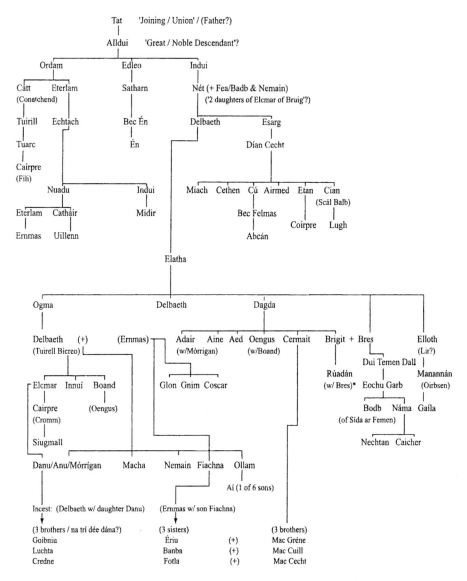

Ancestry of the Túatha Dé Danann from Lebor Gabála Érenn.

3

Sacred Cycles and
the Mythic Symbolism of Time

In traditional cultures, cosmological narratives provide culturally important information about how the cosmos and the earth come into being, and
the origins of important things (including those associated with nature and
culture). These narratives also describe how each culture symbolically per-
ceives the features and inhabitants of the landscape and the environment,
and their perceived place in an animate and meaningful cosmos. In addition
to perceptions and beliefs about sacred space, another important component
of cosmology is that of sacred time, which in traditional cultures is frequently
conceived of as cyclical, rather than linear. In this chapter, we will discuss
the seasonal activities of early Ireland and explore the overlapping cycles of
work patterns, folklore beliefs, and mythological parallels which were interwoven into the sacred cycles of time.[1]

In early Ireland, a yearly cycle of work activities existed which had a
strong seasonal basis, and was originally based on the movement and herding
of livestock.[2] From this cycle, cultural patterns emerged pertaining to a variety
of social activities, including courtship, marriage, raiding, and holding seasonal assemblies.[3] Evidence pertaining to work and gender roles, and folk
traditions associated with seasonal festivals, suggest that one half of the year
may have been regarded as the "male" half and the other the "female" half.
These gender-specific patterns may have also manifested in the veneration
of male or female deities, in accordance with the season or quarter of the
year.

The yearly cycle seems to have been originally divided into two halves,
a warm summer period (*sam*) and a cold winter period (*gam*). After the adoption of the Gregorian calendar, summer began on May 1st when livestock
were moved away from the settlement, towards higher ground and summer
pasture, and away from the young, growing crops. Winter began on November 1st when the herds had returned from summer grazing.[4] It seems that at

some point the seasons were divided into two once again, resulting in a total of four seasonal holidays or festivals: *Beltene* on May 1st, *Samain* on November 1st, *Imbolc* on February 1st, and *Lugnasad* on August 1st. While early information pertaining to the spring festival is scarce, in the folklore record Imbolc appears to have been associated with the birth of animals and the return of a fresh supply of milk. Lugnasad, which marked the beginning of autumn, seems to have been primarily a harvest festival.[5] Let us examine each of these festivals in turn, exploring their connections with agricultural and pastoral cycles, before going on to explore their connections with gender roles, folklore and the veneration of male and female deities.

The Symbolism of Agricultural Cycles

Beltene, which marked the beginning of the summer half of the year, was also known as *Cétshamain* ("the first of summer"). On this day the herds were moved away from settlement areas to new grazing areas and summer pastures.[6] There were a number of advantages to this practice. By moving the herds up to higher pastures, fresh food could be obtained for the animals at a time when supplies of stored fodder would have been reduced or exhausted.[7] In addition, it was extremely important to move the animals away from the emerging crops and grain.[8] For these reasons, the community divided itself on Beltene. Women and children left with the flocks and herds, taking with them equipment for cooking, dairying and spinning. It was important that everyone left simultaneously so that no one's cattle remained near the growing crops.

Men stayed behind to weed the fields and protect the crops (and in some cases, to prepare for warfare or raiding). It is believed that a few women would have also remained in the settlement to garden, cook, take care of the sick and elderly, and provide for the working men.[9] Because of the separation of men and women at this time, Beltene was the end of the marriage season (and therefore, traditionally an unlucky day to wed).[10]

As the summer progressed, previous stores of vegetables and grain would have run out; July was often regarded as a period of scarcity.[11] *Lugnasad*, which took place on August 1st, marked the beginning of the grain harvest (primarily wheat and barley).[12] While the reaping of grain seems to have been primarily considered men's work, some women may have come down from the hills to help with the harvest. Their ability to leave the summer pastures or "sheilings" was facilitated by the fact that less milking and dairying were required during this part of the summer.[13]

The summer months (May through September) were considered the prime season for raiding (another area of male concern), but little warfare took place in August due to the important work of the harvest. Early accounts of assemblies associated with Lugnasad cite the importance of maintaining peace at this time.[14] Early sources also mention that marriage contracts were formed during the Lugnasad assemblies.[15] Some women would have been present at the great harvest assemblies, and marriageable women may have left the summer pastures to be present at this important social event when many marriages were arranged.[16] These early accounts also provide evidence that ancestral figures were remembered and mourned at Lugnasad, not at Samain, as has popularly been supposed (this association only came into being when in the early centuries of the last millennium, the Church instituted the Feast of All Souls at that time of year).[17]

While the other three seasonal festivals were primarily associated with the herding and care of animals, Lugnasad seems to have been predominantly a harvest festival. However, during the month of August, lambs were weaned from their mothers, which would then cause the ewes to ovulate. Breeding at this time of year would result in the birth of lambs five months later around the time of Imbolc, when fresh milk was most needed.[18] Quite a number of human babies may also have been born around Imbolc, the product of sexual unions which took place nine months earlier at Beltaine (prior to the departure of women to the summer pastures).[19] This may have resulted in Beltaine folk traditions associated with joyful fertility celebrations and sexual unions.[20]

Samain (which means "summer's end") marked the start of the winter season. It was also the end of the old year and the beginning of the new. Just as the Celtic day was reckoned from dusk to dusk (thus originating in darkness), so too did the year originate in a dark period.[21] By Samain all the animals and their caretakers had returned from the summer pasture. The harvest had to be gathered in by this date, and supplies of cultivated vegetables and wild fruit and nuts also gathered and stored.[22] Many sheep and cattle were expecting next spring's young, and with fresh milk no longer available, people turned to provisions of cheese produced from the abundant milking and churning activities of the summer.[23] Some older and surplus animals (the latter primarily young males) were culled, but most were grazed on crop stubble and stores of grains and grasses throughout the winter.[24]

Samain also marked the end of season for hunting deer and wild boar.[25] This was the beginning of the boar's breeding season, during which time the animals would be left alone. Earthly (and legendary) boar hunts took place in preparation for this festival, and wild or domestic pigs (fattened on acorns and crop stubble during the autumn) seem to have been the symbolic "sacrificial animal" of the season.[26] After Samain, some outdoor work was still required (feeding and tending animals, property maintenance and various household tasks), but at this time of year the emphasis shifted from outdoor concerns towards indoor activities (such as preserving meat and food stores, spinning and weaving).[27]

The bounty of food stores after the harvest, and the shift in social emphasis from outdoor to indoor, resulted in the guesting and feasting season. Nobles and clients met each other at rounds of feasts where relationships might be fostered or tested, and marriages arranged.[28] Informal courtships which began during visits to the hills and mountains during the summer (or at the August gatherings) sometimes led to more formal marriage negotiations or alliances during the winter months when the entire community was back together again.[29] Samain also marked the end of the official season of warfare. However, events that took place during feasts could sometimes lead to political tensions, as well as competition.[30] These events may have been expressed through tales of mythical hunts and adventures, feasts and arguments, and battles and contests.[31] Storytelling formed an important part of the social activities associated with the dark half of the year, and music, poetry and tales would have been recited during the feasts.[32]

A great deal of pressure must have been involved in the period leading up to Samain. Crops and wild foods had to be harvested and stored, and sufficient grain, root vegetables, cheese, honey and salted meat and fish preserved to last throughout the winter. The herds had returned, including pregnant animals that had to be maintained throughout the cold months. Deer and boar hunting had taken place, as well as other general preparations for the winter season. Creditors and debtors often settled their accounts at this time, and many lords now expected their winter tribute (partially consuming it during the lavish feasting).[33] Although it was often a time of plenty and relative leisure, there were numerous tensions and anxieties associated with the season. These may have led to rituals of propitiation and protection (as at Beltaine, the other most important liminal point of the year) as well as rites and offerings of thanksgiving.

In addition to the tangible pressures of the season, the beginning of winter was also a time of impending darkness and difficulty, with overtones of possible misfortune, illness, or death. Samain was a particularly liminal time, when many interactions between the seen and unseen worlds took place. It is easy to see how imagery associated with danger, death and the spirit world became associated with this time of year. Important rites of propitiation and divination (which are common in New Year's celebrations around the world) probably also took place at Samain, a time of endings, darkness and completion, as well as new beginnings, creation and the unknown.

Imbolc took place on February 1st and was the symbolic beginning of spring. Animals which had been bred during the summer months gave birth around this time, and the return of fresh milk would have been welcomed. Cow's milk had long since run out and stores of food largely consumed during the guesting and feasting (as well as by the family itself during the winter months). At this time, old food supplies were depleted and the new supplies had not yet come.[34] Farmers anxious to replenish their dwindling store of milk worked to ensure that their sheep gave birth before the cows, as sheep are able to graze lower for grass and survive better on the meager vegetation of late winter.[35] In addition, ewe's milk is extremely delicious and nutritious and has a higher fat content than cow's milk, making it all the more valuable during the cold weather and the almost inevitable food shortages which took place at the end of winter.[36]

The festival of Imbolc seems to have had a predominantly female focus. In addition to assisting with or supervising the birth and care of smaller animals, women were responsible for resuming milking, churning and dairying.[37] During the winter months they were in charge of providing hospitality to guests and supervising the use of food stores for domestic and social consumption. In Irish folk tradition, women opened up the cupboards on February 1st to take stock of their food supplies. The birth of lambs at Imbolc was a time of great happiness, as it provided new food stores and a renewed sense of plenty, and ensured the continuation of life.

The name of the festival of Imbolc may derive from its associations with ewe's milk (supporting, on various and often differing grounds, the false etymology in Cormac's Glossary). Some have suggested a connection with purification and lustration rituals. A simple derivation from an Old Irish word denoting "belly or womb" (*bolg*) with the intensifying prefix *imm*- is quite possible. Whatever the origin of the name, the emphasis of the holiday is on female activities, birth, and the production of milk.[38] In Christian times, the holiday was associated with Saint Brigid, who many scholars feel was originally connected in some way with the early Irish goddess *Bríg*, a divinity associated with poetry, healing and smithcraft. As a Saint, Brigid was primarily credited with the protection of women and animals in childbirth, and was associated with fertility and domestic concerns. While the Christian feast of Candlemas (which is near Imbolc) was instituted only in the 11th c., there are indications that prior to Christianity the ritual focus of the season was on motherhood, both animal and human.[39]

For men this was a season of relative inactivity. It was not yet time to plow or plant seeds, but the observation of weather omens in preparation for these activities took place at Imbolc. Men's work with the land would resume sometime after Imbolc; sowing often did not take place until March.[40] As the weather warmed and the days grew longer, in addition to agricultural concerns, spring was a time of resumed raiding. Spring warfare was less profitable than summer raiding due to the weakened condition of the cattle. Therefore it was often a useful time to settle disputes and rivalry among allies and vassals, eliminate rivals, and align forces prior to the larger outings of spring and full-fledged raids or warfare.[41] It is interesting to note that while clients were obliged to provide military service during the hostings of spring and autumn, in some cases they could only be raised in a tribal "hosting" between mid–January and early March (the period of time surrounding Imbolc).[42] This may be connected with a secondary manifestation of Saint Brigid: *Bríg ambue*, "Bridget of the cowless warrior."[43]

If we look at the patterns that emerge from the activities associated with the agricultural year in early Ireland, it seems reasonable to suggest that the bright half of the year (Beltaine to Samain) was associated with male energies or concerns, and the dark half of the year (Samain to Beltaine) with female concerns.[44] The male half began on May 1st when women left to tend the herds, the men remaining in the settlement to tend the crops. This was the end of the marriage season (due to the separation of the sexes after Beltaine), and the beginning of the primary season for warfare and hunting (both of which are male concerns). At Lugnasad, male activities were still the main focus, as reaping and other harvest activities were primarily the work of men. However, there would have been some female presence to assist with the harvest, a presence supported by the prevalent marriage customs associated with Lugnasad assemblies.

The female half of the year began at Samain, the end of the old year and the beginning of the new cycle. Women and the herds had returned from summer pasture, and many of the animals were pregnant from summer breeding. It was the end of the hunting and warfare seasons, and the work focus shifted from outdoor to more domestic activities (many of which were presided over by women, including feasting and hospitality). This was the start of the dark half of the year, a liminal period associated with the unknown (the supernatural) and creation (often linked with female energies). Imbolc, the other festival that took place during this half of the year, was associated with birth, lactation, female concerns and the continuation of life. Men would have been relatively inactive, waiting to plow and sow, and planning raids and hunting in the warmer months to come.

Seasonal Beliefs and Gender:
The Symbolism of Folklore

Folk customs and beliefs associated with the Quarter Days formed a strong part of Irish culture even into the present era. A great deal of energy went into the observation of these holidays and their associated symbolism. Because of their connection with important agricultural practices, the church could not efface these indigenous calendar customs. As a result, while some holidays received a measure of Christian overlay, many of the practices associated with the pre–Christian feast days reflect age-old rhythms and beliefs. Folk traditions recorded as early as the 16th and 17th centuries (as well as the larger body of tradition documented in the last century in Ireland and Scotland) seem to reflect a pattern of male and female symbolism which parallels that seen in the patterns of the yearly work cycle.

Prior to the seasonal movement of people and flocks on Beltene, important assemblies and festivals took place. In some cases, new chiefs or leaders were inaugurated and installed.[45] The festivals may have involved large assemblies of people and the ritual use of bonfires (as well as offerings or sacrifices) to encourage abundance and fertility, and ensure the protection of livestock and produce.[46] Early texts and folk traditions mention the running of cattle between two fires to protect them against disease. Although there was a joyous and life-affirming aspect to these celebrations, Beltene was also a time of potential danger. It was important to ensure that the crops, animals and the community maintained good health and survived during this important growing season (a time when the community was divided).[47] In Ireland, Scotland and Wales, folk records from a variety of eras indicate that the Beltene fires were created by men (who also presided over the attendant rituals of propitiation and protection).[48]

A number of rituals associated with protection and propitiation were recorded in 18th century Scotland, which feature men in the central role. At Beltene, groups of men gathered to create a caudle of eggs, butter, oatmeal and milk, which was then poured onto the ground as an offering. Special cakes were created by the men as well, which were offered to various animals as an entreaty to them not to harm the flocks.[49] In Ireland, the male head of the household sometimes walked around the boundaries of the farm in a protective rite. He was often accompanied by others who carried implements and tools associated with animal husbandry, as well as seed grain, well water and the herb vervain. The procession started in the east and stopped at each of the four cardinal directions, where a small ceremony was enacted by the father of the household.[50] In both Scotland and Ireland, the father of the house often recited a blessing and performed certain rites to protect the family, the house and farmstead, and the herds and crops.[51]

Another folk rite from Scotland involved the baking of a Beltaine cake by groups of men or boys who had gathered for that purpose. The cake was broken into pieces and distributed to the group. One of the pieces was blackened with ash, and whoever received that piece was known as the Hag (*Cailleach*) of Beltaine. This person was treated as a symbolic victim of sorts, and was even sometimes picked up and tossed "into" (over) the fire.[52] It has been suggested that these "victims" originally represented male heads of households who had failed to pay their debts or obligations, and were thus excluded from rituals. Martin Martin records that in 17th century Scotland all fires in the community were extinguished on the Eve of Beltaine, and brands from a fire ritually kindled by nine groups of nine men were then distributed to each household (except those who were penalized or sanctioned).[53] There were also folk traditions in which fire or coals were not given out of the house at Beltaine, for fear of the household's "luck" leaving with the fire. This custom may originate in earlier times when only those who were castigated or deviant in some way would need to ask for fire on Beltaine (all others having duly received the new fire).[54]

There may have been a predilection for male energies or authority at Beltaine, or a fear or superstition of female energies. Natives in one Scottish village maintained an ancient custom of sending a man to cross a salmon stream early on May morning, and preventing any female from doing so in the belief that this would hinder the salmon from coming into the river.[55] We saw above that the mock "sacrificial" victim was called the Hag of Beltaine, a name with derogatory connotations. In many folklore contexts, witches or witch-like figures are referred to as *cailleachs*. Indeed, in some areas of Scotland, cattle were driven around the fire to protect them from witches, and piles of straw, furze or broom thrown into the fire by the cowherds who cried out "Fire, Fire—Burn the Witches."[56] The separation of the sexes may have also manifested in May Day festivities in which men dressed as women or played female roles (including the May Queen).[57] This may have been a symbolic way of prolonging the period of male energies, as women do not seem to have played a large part in these traditions.[58] The act of guising (a part of the festivities at Samain as well) may indicate the liminal nature of the holiday and symbolize the upcoming crossover of gender roles or associations.[59]

Lugnasad was a favorite time for the holding of fairs, and early medieval sources record the Lugnasad gatherings or *oenachs* of Carmun and Tailtiu. The Annals of the Four Masters record that the line of horses, carts and people thronging to the Lugnasad fair at Tailtiu in 1168 was six miles long. This gathering continued into the 1700's, while that at Carmun disappeared in the Middle Ages. Numerous fairs are still held, including many Lammas Fairs or Gooseberry/Bilberry Fairs.[60] On the Eve of Lugnasad, great bonfires were lit in Scotland, and "saining" rites or charms were performed to ensure that the milk of the cattle retained its virtue and substance.[61] A special cake was made of sun-dried grain (usually barley) which was toasted on a fire of rowan or other sacred wood. Pieces of this ritual cake were distributed by the male head of household to the members of the family, who then walked around the hearth fire in a sunwise direction.[62]

On Lugnasad, it was hoped that the first crops were ready for harvesting, and it was considered improper to cut any grain before this time. If the crop was not yet completely ripe, a symbolic portion was cut on this day by the male head of the household (and the remainder harvested when it was fully ready). The newly gathered grain was used to prepare a festive meal.[63] While many women were still away tending the herds, some women would have returned to assist with the flax harvest (which was often considered women's work) as well as the harvesting of grain.[64] Their presence at Lugnasad assemblies led to the arrangement of both temporary and permanent marriages; August was a good time for entering into such alliances prior to the busy period of the harvest and the heavy work-load of the pre-winter season.[65]

In Scotland, an important custom associated with the harvest was the cutting of the last sheaf. This was sometimes referred to as the Hag or *Cailleach*, and the privilege of cutting it was often given to a young woman. However, a male reaper held the sheaf while the woman cut it with a scythe. In many cases, the sheaf was considered an undesirable object which was passed onto other farmers who had not yet completed their reaping. For the last one to receive the Cailleach, this could be a symbol of upcoming need or want. In other cases, though, the sheaf was dressed and decorated and hung up at the harvest supper (and referred to either as the Harvest Maiden or the Cailleach). She was often toasted at the supper with the phrase: "Here's to the one who helped us with the harvest."[66] We can note symbolism pertaining to the mixing of the sexes (in preparation for the shift to female energies at Samain) in the custom where the male reaper holds the stalk while the female cuts it, as well as in the return of some women at harvest time and the arrangements of marriages.

November Day and Eve were regarded by old people as one of the leading festivals of the year in modern Irish folk tradition. It was believed that all crops and livestock had to be in by Samain and that spirits and fairies were abroad on this night. Offerings of food were left near the doors of houses for the fairies in order to ensure their favor in the coming year.[67] The belief that the fairies "flitted" or moved residence at Samain and Beltaine may reflect the seasonal movement of parts of the community. Divination was common at Samain, and was usually associated with love, fertility and marriage. Some of these rites were performed using apples and hazelnuts, the produce of trees associated with the Otherworld.[68] Guising, processions and pranks also took place, and many activities that were not normally acceptable were overlooked or tolerated.[69]

At dusk on Samain great fires were lit. It is interesting to note that Beltaine fires were lit at dawn on May morning, while Samain bonfires were often lit at dusk.[70] Torches were lit from these fires and used by the men to circle the farms and the fields in a sunwise direction for protection.[71] Rites of propitiation took place in many areas, such as the traditional offerings of ale made to a sea-deity in the Isle of Lewis.[72] Feasting also took place (even in the poorest households) and apples and hazelnuts were often included in this ritual meal.[73] One folklore account describes a Samain cake that was traditionally made by groups of women who gathered together for this special purpose. They began their work after sundown, marking out a large space in the house by a line (which was then considered to be consecrated ground). The women sat on the ground in a circle and took turns preparing and toasting the sacred cake, working in a sunwise direction.[74] It should be noted that while women often prepared festal food (including special oatcakes or bannocks for certain holidays), the Samain cake involved a particular ritualized ceremony (and contrasts with the ritual creation of Beltaine foods by groups of men).

An interesting Samain custom in Irish tradition was the procession associated with the *Láir Bhán* ("White Mare"). A group of youths blowing on cow horns were led by a person in a white robe or sheet holding a decorated horse skull in a procession from house to house, where a long string of verses was recited.[75] In the literature, the white mare could be a symbol of the Goddess of Sovereignty (who, as we shall see, was associated with Samain). Similar imagery may also underlie the *Mari Lwyd* tradition of Wales. This also involved a procession with a decorated horse skull that went from house to house to engage in poetic contests. While the *Mari Lwyd* customs take place between Christmas and New Year, the nature of some Yuletide customs suggests that some Samain customs (associated with the pre–Christian New Year) were transferred to the Gregorian New Year (or the period between Christmas and New Year).[76]

In the folklore traditions, Samain has a pronounced association with spirits, fairies and the forces of the unseen world. Numerous legends and folktales describe interactions between the inhabitants of this world and the Otherworld. In many cases these tales describe the appearance of ominous or mysterious men and women, whether in the form of deities, spirits, fairies or witches (the latter of which re-appear in modern Halloween customs and imagery). Samain guising, pranks and divination attest to the liminal nature of the holiday, a time "outside of time" when interactions between the worlds could take place. It was a time of darkness, mystery and the unknown, but also a time of creation. The Celtic New Year was born out of darkness, just as the Celtic day started at dusk. The shift from male to female energies was symbolized by the creation of Samain cakes by groups of women working after sundown, processions associated with the white or grey mare (symbolic of the Sovereignty Goddess), and imagery associated with witches or hags (as well as other spirits) whose powers were honored but also feared.

Imbolc folklore has a pronounced female energy, with its focus on birth and lactation. In later times, the holiday was associated with Saint Brigid, and numerous rites took place which honored this beloved figure. In Ireland it was believed that Brigid traveled around the countryside on this night, blessing people and livestock. Cakes or butter were put outside on the windowsill as an offering, and then checked in the morning to see if she had come. Sometimes a sheaf of corn was placed beside the cake for the saint's beloved white cow.[77] A ribbon or piece of cloth known as a *brat Bríde* ("Brigid's Mantle") could also be left outside to be touched by the saint. Her blessing imbued the object with healing and protective properties, including assistance in childbirth.[78] Brigid's crosses were made of straw or rushes (in the form of three- or four-armed crosses, as well as diamonds and lozenge shapes) and hung in the home and barn. The ritualized creation of the crosses often involved the impersonation of Brigid by a member of the family (in many cases, the eldest daughter).[79] A sheaf of straw was sometimes made into the shape of a human figure (representing Brigid) and then dressed and decorated. In some areas, unmarried girls carried the figure around the community from door to door, thus bringing the blessing of Brigid to each house.[80]

In 18th century Scotland a sheaf of oats was dressed in women's garments and placed in a large basket called "Brigid's Bed." A wooden stick or club was placed next to the figure. Then the women of the house and her assistants cried out three times: "Brigid is come, Brigid is welcome." This was done just prior to going to bed. Upon arising in the morning, the women looked among the ashes of the fire to see if the impression of Brigid's club was there (an omen of good crops and a prosperous year to come).[81] Folklore accounts from 19th century Scotland describe the Brigid figure being decorated with shells, crystals, flowers and greenery. A wand of sacred wood such as birch, broom, bramble or willow was placed next to the figure, and the track of this object was sought in the morning in the ashes of the hearth.[82] As in Ireland, groups of girls carried the figure in a solemn procession. They visited every house, and everyone was expected to give a gift and honor Brigid. Afterwards, the girls retired to a particular house and feasted on the food that had been given out during the procession. The door was barred and the windows secured, but the figure of Brigid was placed where she could be seen by all. Later on, groups of young men arrived and humbly asked permission to honor Brigid. After some parleying they were admitted, and dancing and singing took place throughout the night.[83]

At this time of year, men waited for the appropriate time for spring ploughing. They sometimes turned a sod or two symbolically at Imbolc, and engaged in weather divination. To see a hedgehog come out of his hole was a good sign. If he stayed out, it indicated the return of good weather. If he returned to his hole, more bad weather was to come.[84] In Scotland the revelatory animal was a serpent (the hibernating adder). On Imbolc it was supposed to emerge from its hollow and a hymn was sung to it:

> Today is the day of Brigid,
> the serpent shall come from the hole
> I will not molest the serpent,
> nor will the serpent molest me.[85]

The serpent was sometimes referred to as "The Daughter of Ivor" or "The Queen" (indicating its female identity) and its hole was often referred to as its "knoll or mound" (reminiscent of the significance attached to fairy mounds or hills in Celtic tradition). We can see that the folklore traditions connected with the four Quarter Days reflect the patterns and alternation of gender roles seen in the annual work cycle.

Mythological Patterns and Divine Figures

In addition to gender-related patterns associated with the work cycle and folk customs, we may also be able to discern a parallel pattern of male and female deities associated with the seasonal alternation of gender roles. Not surprisingly, the deities in question are among the most well-documented divinities in early Irish sources: The Dagda, Lug, The Mórrigan, Macha, and Bríg (Brigid).

Geoffrey Keating associated Beltaine ceremonies with the hill of Uisnech, a site in the east central lowlands which was traditionally regarded as the sacred center of Ireland. He describes how a bonfire was lit there in the midst of a large assembly, on whose behalf sacrifices were made. While no other extant literary source corroborates his report, archaeological excavations on the summit of Uisnech have in fact revealed a large area of scorched earth containing the charred bones of many animals.[86] That sacral fires were associated with the holiday in fairly early times is evident from a reference to Beltaine in Cormac's Glossary. He states that at Beltaine a "lucky" fire was created—two fires made by Druids "with great incantations"–through which cattle were driven to safeguard them from disease.[87]

There is also a reference to Uisnech in the early Irish tale "The Wooing of Étain." The tale mentions a famous king of the Túatha Dé Danann called *Echu Ollathir,* who was also known as the *Dagdae* (literally the "Good or Best God"):

> for it was he who performed miracles and saw to the weather and the harvest, and that is why he was called the Good God.[88]

Later in the tale, the Dagda's dwelling is said to have been at Uisnech, "the center of Ireland."[89] In various literary sources the Dagda appears as a warrior and protector of his people. He was said to have expertise in druidic magic and to own a magical club with powers of life and death. He had fertility associations and possessed a cauldron of inexhaustible abundance.[90] The sources depict a beneficent and powerful figure associated with abundance and fertility, magic and protection, the weather and the harvest, and the powers of life and death (all concepts associated with Beltaine) who lived at the very site where Beltaine rituals for abundance and protection are recorded as having taken place.[91]

The origin of the Festival of Lugnasad was attributed to the god Lug, the Irish version of a widespread, multi-skilled pan-Celtic deity (variously appearing as Lug(h), Lugos, and Lleu). One of the most important tales associated with Lug states that he instituted the festival to honor his foster-mother Tailtiu who had died from the exertion of clearing many plains (presumably in preparation for agriculture).[92] Other versions of this origin myth state that Lug set up the assembly to honor two of his wives (who had also "died").[93] These stories are interesting in light of the social arrangement at this time of year, when some women are returning to help with the harvest, but when many men's wives were absent from them. The legends appear to reflect the male focus of the holiday, while honoring the secondary (but very important) female contribution.

Lug's association with agriculture is further explained in *Cath Maige Tuired* as the gods are freed the oppression of the Fomoire (to whom they must pay an exorbitant tribute). The Túatha Dé Dannan king at the time was Bres, who proves to be an ungenerous and unfit ruler.[94] Bres is finally captured by the Túatha Dé Danann. However, Lug spares his life in return for agricultural information concerning the proper times to plow, sow and reap.[95] Lug not only arranges for a beneficial outcome (which results in a successful harvest) but also institutes a festival to commemorate this victory.

Just as women begin to "infringe" upon the male half of the year in a beneficial and helpful capacity in the annual work cycle, so too do various divine women manifest and enact a helpful symbolic role in the myths and legends associated with Lugnasad. Most of these divine women are said to have "died" and been buried in certain hills, much as mortal women are remembered, but are not physically present, residing up in the hills or mountains at this time of year.[96] Tailtiu is recorded as having reclaimed meadowland from woodland with an axe, after which it became a blossoming plain known as Bregmag. She then perished on the new moon nearest the Feast of Lug, and from that time the "chief Fair of Erin" was held around her grave.[97] The site of the Oenach of "Teltown" (an Anglicization of the name Tailtiu) was marked by a mound, and the site may still be visited today. After the death of Lug's two wives, they were also buried at sacred hills: *Nas* at the site named for her (modern Naas) and her sister *Bui* at *Cnogba* (the Hill of Knowth).[98] After their death, it was said that the Gaels came "with Lug" from the site of Tailtiu where he raised a fire to mourn his wives, an event which then grew into the assembly of Tailtiu.[99]

Another legendary woman associated with Lugnasad was Carmun. The Dindsenchas account of Carmun mentions the assembly mounds at the site, which was named for her, and the great gathering that took place at harvest time. Carmun is described as an experienced battle leader who (out of distress or want) ventured westward into Ireland and tried to use magic to destroy the sap of "all swelling fruit." One female member of the Túatha Dé Danann (*Bé Chuille*, "Woman of Hazel") and three male deities go to confront Carmun and her three sons, who are subsequently defeated. Carmun is captured and later dies "among the oaks of the strong graves." The Túatha Dé come to mourn her ("for the delight of her beauty") and raise the first wailing over her. This was said to be the "first true fair of Carmun." It is interesting to note that Carmun's grave was dug by Bres, according to the judgment of the elders.[100] The festivities associated with the assembly continued for seven days. The first day of the assembly was the fair of the saints, the second for high kings and the third day for the women of Leinster, described as: "womenkind not small in esteem abroad; this is their gathering, the third day."[101]

Although direct evidence has not yet been established to my knowledge, it is believed that a Lugnasad assembly was also held at Emain Macha (or Ard Macha) and associated with the goddess Macha. In the Dindshenchas of *Ard Macha*, the goddess appears as the wife of Nemed, a figure credited with the clearing of twelve plains (including one which bore her name). She was buried on that plain, and to mourn her, the men of Ulster held the Assembly of Macha at that site. The account goes on to tell the story of her subsequent pairing with *Cruinn mac Agnoman*. She appears mysteriously (i.e. from the Otherworld), tends to Cruinn's house and sleeps with him. After that, he became a man "rich in herds." Despite her warning not to mention her, Cruinn goes to an assembly and boasts that his wife, although pregnant, can run faster than two horses belonging to King Conchobar. She wins the race, but dies from the effort, after giving birth to twins (*emain*). While the date of the festival is not mentioned in these accounts, horse races are known to have been a prominent feature of many Lugnasad assemblies.[102]

While a male figure arranged and instituted the harvest festival, a variety of female divine figures associated with agriculture or fertility are connected with the myths of Lugnasad. This appears to reflect men's roles as caretakers of the crops and harvest, and women's roles assisting with the harvest, returning from the hills to perform this act. Tailtiu, Carmun and Macha were associated with sacred hills, mounds or plains, and were honored at a Lugnasad assembly. All three demonstrate some connection with agriculture or abundance: Tailtiu cleared the land, Carmun used magic to try and destroy the "sap of fruit," and Macha brought great abundance to her husband. After bestowing their blessing or contribution, the women "die" and "disappear" into features of the landscape, no longer physically present, but symbolically present and highly venerated.

If the mythological cycle follows the work and folklore cycles, we would expect to see a predominance of female symbolism at the time of Samain.

One of the most interesting mythological episodes associated with Samain is found in *Cath Maige Tuired*.[103] Here it states that the Dagda had arranged to meet a woman about a week before Samain. He encounters her at the river *Unshin* in Connacht, and finds her with nine loosened tresses on her head, with one foot to the north of the river and one foot to the south. The "woman" in question is the multi-aspected goddess known as the Mórrígan (whose name either means "Great Queen," if spelled as shown here, or "Nightmare Queen," if spelled without a mark of length on the first syllable: *Morrígan*).

After their union, she provides assistance to the Dagda and the Túatha Dé Danann in the form of strategic planning, magic, physical support and prophetic information. She tells the Dagda to summon the *aés dána* ("People of Arts/Skill") to her to receive her counsel. She also provides magical intervention and together they chant spells against the enemy. The Mórrígan herself will destroy the Fomorian king. Magical weapons made by the "the three gods of skill" (a trio of craftsmen deities who are brothers), provide an especially powerful boon. These events take place the week before Samain, after which the Túatha Dé Danann disperse, arranging to reconvene on Samain Eve for the battle.[104]

Before continuing with the narrative found in *Cath Maige Tuired*, we should note a remarkable detail pertaining to the Mórrígan's involvement in this event. When she unites with the Dagda, she stands astride a river whose name (*uinnius*) signifies an ash-tree. The ash was a sacred tree in early Irish tradition (as well as in Norse mythology, where the World Tree was an ash). In Ireland, spear shafts were often made of ash. The union of the Dagda and the Mórrígan at this site just prior to Samain is clearly of great significance. Once she has united with the Dagda, she bestows her blessings and assistance upon the gods, and they begin to gain strength and power in their fight.

The narrative mentions a number of deities who assist with the battle, including Lug, Ogma, Goibniu and Dian Cecht. Significantly, it is after the strengthening of the host by the Mórrígan and her poetic chanting that the battle turns in favor of the Túatha Dé Danann. The text states that immediately after The Mórrígan chants a powerful magical incantation, the battle broke and the Fomoire were routed. She then ritually announces the victory to various heights and *síd* mounds, rivers and waters."[105] Here we might recall the various folklore traditions associated with Samain which included the symbolism of the white or grey mare (symbol of the Sovereignty Goddess) as well as the power and skill associated with poetic craft. The union of the divine couple results in the bestowal of the goddess's blessing and assistance, which eventually guarantees the success of the venture (and the prosperity of the tribe). The Mórrígan's actions are consistent with her role as a Goddess of Sovereignty.

Another attribute of The Mórrigan which may connect her with Samain is her magical skill. In *Lebor Gabála Érenn* her mother Ernmas ("Death by Iron") was said to be a witch, and her daughters Macha and Mórrígan display skill in magic, shapeshifting and prophecy. Witches or hags were associated with Samain in numerous folklore sources. In *Táin Bó Cuailgne* the Mórrígan appears before the hero Cú Chulainn as a beautiful young woman and an old hag, a feat which various divine women associated with Sovereignty also perform.[106] The concept of a trio of witches or warrior-goddesses (like the Mórrígan and her sisters Macha and Nemain, all three of whom are referred to as *Badb*, "scald-crow") may have been known throughout various parts of the Celtic world. This is suggested by a Gallo-Roman inscription to the *Cathobodua* ("Battle-Raven") as well as a British inscription to the "three *lamia* or witches."[107] The imagery associated with these figures is still manifest in the connection between Hallowe'en or Samain and the magic, powers (and fear of) witches.

Two other divine women associated with magic and witchcraft were also connected with Samain in early Irish tradition. *Tlachtga* is a legendary female figure and daughter of the arch-druid *Mug Roith,* from whom she was said to have learned "the world's magic." She was evidently well-versed in magic and portrayed as a powerful and independent female figure. Tlachtga is said to have directed the druids to gather and create fires at Samain, at a site named for her (*Cnoc Tlachtga*, now the Hill of Ward in County Meath).[108] Another supernatural figure associated with Samain was known as *Mongfind* ("Bright/White Mane"). She was the wife of Eochu Muigmédon and stepmother of Niall of the Nine Hostages. Mongfind was well known as a sorceress, and died on the eve of Samain by taking poison (which she had actually prepared for her royal brother). After her death, the people are said to have referred to Samain as "The Festival of Mongfind":

> …so long as she was in the flesh, had powers and was a witch: wherefore it is that on Samain Eve women and the rabble address their petitions to her.[109]

The symbolism of Mongfind's name ("Bright/White Mane") brings to mind the light colored horses associated with the Goddess of Sovereignty (and associated Samain folk processions). One tale states that Mongfind was the wife of a king, as well as the mother of a king. The story tells how she tests Niall and his four stepbrothers to determine which would be king. The young men have an encounter with an old hag who turns out to be the Goddess of Sovereignty, a multi-aspected and powerful figure associated with the land, fertility, and the powers of life and death.[110] The imagery connected with these female figures (and the festival itself) demonstrate a pronounced association with darkness and creation, life and death, magic and transformation, and female power and authority.

Finally, the association of Imbolc with the Irish goddess Bríg, a goddess of poetry, smithcraft and healing, and her later incarnation Saint Brigid (associated with healing, childbirth, and domestic concerns) are well-documented. It is interesting to note that Bríg's husband was Bres, a figure associated with the festival that is located directly opposite Imbolc in the seasonal calendar. Perhaps an early myth placed the couple on opposite sides of the year wheel and elaborated in detail the conflict between Bres and Lug, the victor and patron of the harvest.

We can see that the annual cycle of symbolism associated with work activities, folk traditions, and mythology all point to the distinct possibility that the summer half of the year (Beltaine to Samain) was associated with male concerns and the winter half (Samain to Beltaine) with female concerns. The original two-fold division of the year was marked by great festivals with a pronounced liminal character, overseen by and perhaps dedicated to the great tribal-god of the Túatha Dé Danann (The Dagda) and the Sovereignty Goddess and female namesake of the gods (The Mórrígan, epithet of the great Irish goddess also known as Danu or Anu, as we will discover in an upcoming chapter). The further division of the yearly cycle marked the great celebrations of the harvest (instituted by Lug, who is depicted as a newcomer to the Túatha Dé Danann) and the late winter/early spring traditions (probably enacted locally or in the home) associated with Bríg/Brigid and Imbolc.[111] The overlapping and co-existing cycles of work on the land, folklore beliefs and practices, and mythic and legendary events, help demonstrate the cyclical nature of time in an Irish cultural context, and perhaps in other Celtic contexts as well.

4

Divining the Divinities

The Mórrígan, Danu and Anu

Searching for the Goddess Danu

Early Irish literature contains numerous references to a group of super-natural figures known as the *Túatha Dé Danann* (the "People or Tribes of the Goddess Danu"), the pre–Christian deities of the Gaels in Ireland. Strangely, the figure of Danu does not play an active role in the tales, and is known to us only through a limited number of references. Through a careful examination of these early Irish sources, the identity and alternate epithets of Danu become apparent—an identity which has profound implications for our understanding of the title *Túatha Dé Danann*, as well as the mythological corpus and some of its most notable figures.[1]

The word *Danu* (gen. *Danann*) was seen as a proper name,[2] a personage from whom the God-tribe apparently took their name.[3] In *Lebor Gabála Érenn* (hereinafter LG), she is the daughter of *Delbaith*,[4] whose name may derive from the Old Irish verb *delbaid* "to shape, form, ordain or design." In the Dindshenchas poem on *Codal,* she appears as *Danainn,* wife of Ganann, a man whose daughter Eachrad was pursued by *Aed,* son of the Dagda. Danainn is here said to have a daughter named *Gorm* (blue, or green as of vegetation; dark or black, used figuratively as "illustrious, splendid"). In another source she is said to have born three sons to her own father, who were referred to as *na trí dée dána.*[5] While this phrase has been interpreted as "the three gods of Danu," a meaning of "the three gods of *dána*' (gpl. of *dán* "gift, endowment, skill, especially the art of poetry") may be more appropriate (due to the mark of length in the word *dán*). In some sources, the three brothers are said to be Brian, Iuchar and Iucharba, a trio who were responsible for the murder of Cian, the father of the god Lug (an ignominious act on the part of offspring of such an eminent figure as Danu).[6] However, a more suitable threesome exists in the form of three craftsmen deities, the brothers

Goibniu, Luchta and *Crédne*, whose skills play an important role in the out-come of *Cath Maige Tuired*. This skilled trio seems more deserving of Danu's parentage or patronage, and a closer examination of the evidence helps show that these three skilled deities are more likely to be her sons. In *Cath Maige Tuired* we encounter the following:

> ...*luid Lucc ocus Dagdae ocus Ogma go trí déo Danonn, ocus doberat-side grésa an cathae do Lugh; ocus roboth sect mblíadnai oca foichill ocus ag dénom a [n-]arm.*
>
> ...Lug and the Dagda and Ogma went to the three gods of Danu, and they gave Lug equipment for the battle; and for seven years they had been preparing for them and making their weapons.[7]

While the three gods are not explicitly named in this passage, shortly thereafter the Dagda asks various members of the *Túatha Dé Danann* what skills or pow-ers they will wield in an upcoming battle. Goibniu (the smith), Crédne (the bra-zier) and Luchta (the carpenter) reply by describing the weapons they will construct. It seems reasonable to assume that these three, the makers of weapons, are the "three gods of Danu" whom Lug, Ogma and the Dagda consult to obtain equipment for battle, and that these three craftsmen are the three gods in question. Due to a perceived connection between the name *Danu* and the words *dán(u)/dán(a)*, one of the goddess's offspring (*na trí dée dána*, whoever they were) was credited with having a son called *Écna* "wisdom, knowledge or enlightenment," who in turn had a son called *Érgna* "understanding."[8] While the members of the *Túatha Dé Danann* were known for their many skills, this "wisdom lineage" may be a learned conceit arising from the lin-guistic confusion mentioned above (a possibility we will explore further on).

What of Danu's union with her own father? In attempting to understand the role of mythological incest, it must be remembered that it functions in a symbolic manner, and may be portrayed in the religious systems of cultures that do not condone it within their society. In Hindu tradition, its significance is as a potent yet dangerous creation act, where the father, representing the Sky, unites with the Earth, in the person of the daughter.[9] Danu, who will be shown to have an aspect as a goddess associated with the land, unites with her father, whose name might reflect his identity as a creator deity (a being who in some traditions represents or inhabits the celestial realms).[10]

In various source materials, Danu is referred to as a *bantúathach* ("witch, female magician"), is listed as a sorceress of the *Túatha Dé Danann*, and is also called a *bandrúi* "female druid."[11] The word *túathach* (< 1 *túath* "people, tribe, nation; country, territory") means "populous or lordly." Used as a sub-stantive, it denotes a "lord or chief" (in this case, a female lord or chief, a fit-ting title for the female namesake of the God-tribe). However, *túathach* (< 2 *túath*, used in compounds to denote "northern, left, on the left; wicked, evil") is glossed as meaning "witch or magician."[12] As we will see, Danu's mother is also described as a witch, so it may be that the second interpretation should receive more emphasis (although both may be applicable).[13]

One of the most notable references to Danu occurs in *Lebor Gabála* and reads: *Donand Mathair na ndea* "Donann, Mother of the Gods."[14] A number of scholars have posited a possible connection between Danu/Donu and Dôn, the mother of a number of divine figures from the Mabinogi who may have originally constituted part of a "Welsh Pantheon."[15] This may suggest parallel roles as ancestresses or "mothers of the gods" (a concept we will explore in more detail below). Dôn's divine offspring includes *Gofannon*, the Divine Smith, apparently the Welsh equivalent of the Irish smith god Goibhniu.[16] This fact may reinforce the suggestion that Goibhniu and his two brothers are *na trí dée dána*. The concept of Danu as a Mother goddess seems to have found expression in the land itself. She is commemorated in a feature of the Irish landscape known as the "Paps [Breasts] of Danu," from which one might infer a connection with fertility or abundance.[17] Indeed, in *Lebor Gabála* she is described as "fair, generous Donann," perhaps symbolic of abundance or prosperity.[18]

At this point we can list a number of attributes associated with the figure of Danu: divine ancestress, mother (or leader) of the gods, progenitor of wisdom, goddess of the land, magician or druid, and goddess of prosperity or abundance. In order to further clarify the significance of these disparate references, we must examine a number of popular theories concerning the origin of Danu's name. One theory proposes a derivation from Old Irish *dán*.[19] A second theory suggests a connection with a widespread group of river names. A third theory sees the name as a late formation arising from confusion arising from the phrase *na trí dée dána* and other linguistic factors. There is also the potential connection (linguistically or thematically) between *Danu/Donu* and the Welsh figure of Dôn, as well as the possibility of confusion or conflation with another divine figure known as *Anu*. Let's examine each of these theories in turn.

Danu, Goddess of Skill

As we have seen, the Old Irish word *dán* (gsg. *dánu/dána*, n/gp. *dána*) means "a gift, endowment; skill, craft, science, artistic faculty, the art or faculty of poetry." In early Irish society, the term *aes dána* ("people of skill") referred to skilled persons or artists, and especially to poets. These revered artisans were divided into two groups: the *prímdanae/dagdanae* ("prime or best artisans") and *fodánae* ("under" or "lesser" artisans). Highest among the *aes dána* were the *sáir* "carpenters," *gobainn* "smiths," *umaide* "braziers," *cerda* "goldsmiths," *legi* "doctors," *breithemain* "brehons" and *druid* "druids." Other listed professions included the *senchaidi* or historians, *selgairi* "hunters" and *deogbairi* "cupbearers," as well as chessplayers, grammarians, and *lucht cumachtai* "folk of might or power." This last group consisted primarily of magical practitioners and included *corrguinig, tuathaig* "sorcerers," and *ammaiti* "wizards."[20]

These same professions are found amongst the ranks of the Túatha Dé Danann, and include divine smiths, druids, physicians, cupbearers, and so forth—as well as the three craftsman deities Goibniu, Luchta and Credne. There appears to have been a distinction noted among the Túatha Dé Danann in which their people of learning were considered gods, while their farmers and herders were considered non-gods (perhaps akin to the distinction between *prímdanae* and *fodanae*).[21] This emphasis on skill (*dán*) in society, as well as among the gods, is noteworthy, and a word which reflects this emphasis would seem to be an appropriate root from which the name of the mother of the gods might be formed.

The word *dán* was sometimes used synonymously with *cerdd* and *eladu*, especially when referring to the pursuit of a skilled nature or profession. The term *aes cerdd* referred to practitioners of a profession, as well as people of any trade or art (other than farmers of land). The term *aes eladan* was used in a similar way. The word *elada/elatha* denotes an art, science, or acquired craft or skill, especially of literary or poetic art. Its underlying meaning is "skill," whether in an art or craft, an exhibition of skill or craftsmanship, or skill in deception, craft, cunning or wile. *Elatha* is the name of a Fomorian king who was the lover of Ériu and father of Bres. If the concept of *elada* was personified, the concept of *dán* may have been as well.

As we saw above, *Écna* "wisdom, knowledge or enlightenment," and his son *Érgna* "understanding" were depicted as descendants of *na trí dée dána*. *Éicse* "divination, wisdom, the profession of a seer, revelation, lore, learning, poetic composition, skill or profession" was also personified as the "well-loved daughter of Dána" (*Eicsi ilgradhach inghen Dána*).[22] However, the term *ingen dána* also means "a poetess," much as the term *fer dána* referred to a male member of the *aes dána* (a man of skill, or a male poet). Some of these references may reflect confusion between the name *Danu* and words *dána/dánu*. They may also contain purposefully crafted layers of poetic metaphor and figurative speech. In either case, there appears to be an emphasis on the concept of *dán* among the learned members of society, as well as among some members of the god-tribe (of whom *Danu* was portrayed as leader, mother or ancestress).

Danu, Goddess of Rivers

Another popular theory suggests that Danu's name derives from the Indo-European root **dánu-* meaning "river."[23] The ancient and widespread association of Celtic female divinities with bodies of water (including rivers) is well-attested. A group of river names found throughout the region inhabited by the Celts derives from this Indo-European root. The root *dánu-* is found in the name of a number of notable confluences: the Danube (< *Danuvius,* Celtic **Dánouios*), the Rhône (<*Rodanus,* Celtic **Rodános,* with *ro-*intensive prefix), the Russian river Don (anciently *Tanais*), the Dniester (< **danu nazdya,* "river to the front"), the Dnieper (< **danu apara* "river to the rear") and the River Don in Yorkshire. It may also be origin of the British river Don in County Durham, the Doon in Ayrshire, Scotland, and the River Donwy in Wales.[24]

In considering the connection between female deities and bodies of water, it is interesting to note a second widespread group of river names. These derive from the root *deva,* "goddess." A related British form **déuá,* "goddess" (perhaps "the goddess" par excellence?), as well as an older Celtic form **Deiuos* "god," and Indo-European **deiuós* are postulated (cf. Latin *divus* "divine, god," with cognates in many languages). Celtic derivatives include Old Welsh *duiu* and Welsh *dwy* (as in *Dubridiu* and *Dyfrdwy* "water of Dwy"). The name was apparently widespread in Britain: British *Deva* (> The River Dee in Kirkcudbright and River Dee in Aberdeenshire), *Devionissum, Devona,* other British *Dee* rivers, *Afon Dwyfawr* and *Afon Dwyfach* in Wales, and numerous *Deva* rivers in Ireland, Gaul and Spain.[25]

Another group of hydronyms derives from this root, giving *Devona* (< *deva* "goddess," with the feminine divine suffix **-ona* = "Divine Goddess"). These river-names were often transferred to camps or settlements located on the banks of rivers. Ptolemy, circa 150 CE, provides us with an extremely early attestation of the name of the River Don (*Devana*). In Scotland, this is attested in a river name (*Devana*) and its associated place-name *Devoni* (*Devana*), a polis of the Pictish *Taexali Ravenna.* On the continent, it occurs in *Devona* (> Dewangen in Wurtemburg), *Divona Cadurcorum* (*Cadurcus* > Cahors, Lot, France), a river *Divona* (> Divonne, Ain, France), a goddess *Divona* (*Dibona,* in a Gaulish Roman text), and two similarly named springs.[26] In Scotland there are two closely situated rivers whose names derive from both roots: the River Dee (< *Deva* "goddess") and the River Don (< *Devona* "divine goddess"), located near Aberdeen (Gaelic *Obar-dheathan* "mouth of the Don"). The belief among Celtic peoples in the presence of a divinity in the water is attested by both groups of names.[27] Nicolaisen had some interesting comments on the practical importance of these concepts:

> If the lexical meaning of the river name Don (< *Devana* or *Devona*) is "goddess," just as the neighbouring Dee (< *Deva*) implies divine qualities, the Don, like the Dee, was therefore, from a Pictish perspective, not just a river in which people might fish, on which they might travel by boat, which might provide water for washing and other household purposes, and so on, but at one and the same time a divine being

which demanded some form of worship and adoration, perhaps even placation in times of flooding and other threats. This dual nature of certain water courses, if not all of them, may not be easily understood in our own times but may have not troubled the Pictish perception at all. If this was so, there are likely to have been particular locations where the worship of flowing water provided special cultic significance...[28]

More recent folklore traditions appear to preserve the idea of a river (or the deity or spirit thereof) demanding placation or sacrifice. The river was a living and divine being, both beneficent (bringing fertility, water and food) and dangerous (capable of destruction, flooding and drowning). In some areas, when a person drowned it was believed s/he had been taken by the spirits who dwelt in the water. These spirits could not be deprived of their victim without great peril. To rescue such a person was considered highly dangerous, for the water would not be cheated of its due. If it lost one victim, it would take another. This tradition was noted in Ireland, Scotland and England. Certain rivers required a particular number of lives each year (or every three or seven years), and would take them without fail. A relevant saying was recorded in Aberdeenshire pertaining to the Rivers Dee and Don:

> Bloodthirsty Dee, each year needs three,
> But bonny Don, she needs none [or but one].[29]

Rivers whose names derive from the I.E. root *danu- make an appearance in *Lebor Gabála*. Tract One of LG describes the pseudo-historical origins of the Gaels and their alleged wanderings prior to arriving in Ireland. After passing the singing sirens of the Caspian Sea they reach the Riphaean mountains, where their druid Caicher prophesies their advent to Ireland.[30] These mountains were conceived of as the source of the river Tanais or Don, which flows into the Sea of Azov.[31] There, at the source of a river named Don, the entry of the Gaels into their new homeland is prophesied. By following the river, they eventually arrive at their destination (according to the pseudo-historical narrative embodied in LG).[32]

This portion of Lebor Gabála contains a possible parallel with historical theories pertaining to the dispersion of Indo-European culture and languages. J.P. Mallory states that Proto-Indo-European may have evolved from languages spoken by hunter-fishing communities in the Pontic-Caspian region. He points out that settlements may have been originally confined to the major river valleys and their tributaries, and this may have resulted in considerable linguistic ramifications.[33] It is in this area that we find a proliferation of river names which derive from the root *danu (including the rivers Don, Donets, Dnieper, Dniester and Danube).[34] Areas in which *danu- derived river names are found continued to play an important role in the development of Celtic language and culture.[35] The Danube valley in particular served as a corridor for the development or dissemination of key elements pertaining to Celtic cultures and languages (whether such cultures developed as a result of waves of migration coupled with trade, conquest, or a more gradual process of "cumulative Celticity").[36]

These *danu-* river names are found on the Continent and in Britain, while *Deva* river-names occur in Spain, Gaul, Britain, Scotland and Ireland, and *Devona* names in Germany, France and Scotland. The concept of a goddess known as *Danu* "river" (or perhaps more simply, *Deva* "goddess") who presided over or lived in the waters, may have followed the expansion or diffusion of Celtic peoples or cultures from Eastern Europe through the Danube valley and into western Europe. If Indo-European *danu-* is the root word underlying Danu's name (and this is far from certain), these concepts may underlie some aspect of her origins or attributes.

Donu and Dôn: Divine Ancestresses

We have examined several theories pertaining to the origin of Danu's name, including a derivation from the Old Irish word *dán,* or the Indo-European root *danu-*. One of the difficulties with the first theory is the mark of length over the vowel in the noun *dán,* which to my knowledge only appears in connection with the name of the goddess once (in the phrase *Eicsi ilgradhach inghen Dána,* noted above). Linguistic considerations pertaining to the Indo-European root *danu-* are intriguing but inconclusive, for as we have seen, the root *danu-* may produce river names with a spelling of either *don(u)* or *don*.

It has also been suggested that Danu may be connected with the Welsh ancestress or mother goddess figure known as *Dôn*. The possibility that both the Irish and Welsh recognized a mother goddess or ancestress figure is supported by other cognate pairs which occur in Irish and Welsh sources, including: Lir and Llyr, Lugh and Lleu, Goibniu and Gofannon, and Nuadu and Nudd. A possible connection between the two female figures is strengthened by the fact that the earliest extant example of Danu's name is spelled *Donu,* which is cognate with Welsh *Dôn*.[37]

If this earliest attestation is in fact the original spelling of Danu's name, then we could at least rule out a derivation from Old Irish *dán*. We might still consider the possibility of a derivation from I.E. *danu-* (which can result in names containing "a" or "o"). The Brothers Rees suggest that Dôn's name may be a bye-form of *Donwy,* which occurs in *Dyfrdonwy* (< *dyfr-* "water") and perhaps also in *Trydonwy,* both being names of rivers in Wales (*cf.* the Modern Welsh term for the Dee, *Dyfrdwy*). *Dyfrdonwy* is described in a late text as "coming through the veins of the mountains" (somewhat evocative of the connection between the source of the Tanais or Don, and the Riphaean Mountains). *Dyfrdonwy* is also said to be the name of one of "the three wells of the ocean."[38] Like *Dyfrdonwy*, the source of the River Shannon in Ireland is also described as a well which existed beneath the ocean:

> Connla's well, loud was its sound, was beneath the blue-skirted ocean; six streams ... run from it, the seventh was Sinann ... a spring ... under the pleasant sea...[39]

This well, located at the river's source, was conceived of as a source of *imbas* ("Great Knowledge") or wisdom, as was the source of the River Boyne. The quest for *imbas* is described in a poem from the *Dindshenchas* pertaining to the well at the source of the Shannon:

> The nine hazels of Crimall the sage drop their fruits under the well...
>   from the juice of the nuts they form the mystic bubbles,
>   thence come ... the bubbles down the green-flowing river.
>   There was a maiden of the Túatha De Danann [*Sinann*]...
>   every sort of fame was at her command,
>   save the mystic art (*imbas*) alone.
> [She] came ... to the river and saw ... the lovely mystic bubbles.
>   [She] goes on a ... venture after them
>   into the green-flowing river and is drowned...[40]

Like the Irish Otherworld, the Welsh Otherworld *Annwfn* (later shortened to *Annwn*), was generally said to lie beneath the earth or in bodies of water. Certain descriptions found in The Book of Taliesin seem to indicate some association with the sea as well. In one poem, *Annwfn* is referred to as *Annwfyn llifereint* "Annwfn of floods." In another poem (*Preideu Annwn* "The Spoils of Annwn") the otherworldly fort *Caer Sidi* is attacked by three shiploads of Arthur's men. A third poem states that "the streams of the sea" are around *Caer Sidi's* corners, bringing to mind the streams that flowed from Connla's well. The poem goes on to state: "and the fruitful fountain is above it"–perhaps suggesting that Caer Sidi is at the bottom of a spring (or is a well at the bottom of the ocean, like *Dyfrdonwy* or Connla's well).[41]

If the cognate names *Donu* and *Dôn* are derived from a root word meaning "river," then these aquatic associations would add greatly to our portrait of Danu. Not all are in agreement about this, however. Eric P. Hamp rejects these traditional arguments (derivations pertaining to water, etc) and proposes that *Danu is rather derived from the same root as Latin *bonus* (Old Latin *duenos*), from Proto-Indo-European *dueno- "good," via a Proto-Celtic nominative singular n-stem *Duonú* meaning "aristocrat."[42] There is another important derivation which must be considered, one which may take pride of place. Linguistically, there is good chance that the names *Donu* and *Dôn* belong to a root word meaning "earth"–Indo-European *gdon- "earth" (which is continued in Old Irish by the uncommon word *du* "place, spot"). A derivative from *ˣgdonios* gives Old Irish *duine* "man, person,"–literally, "belonging to the earth," "earthling."[43] If this is indeed the case, as seems likely, then we must jettison a derivation from the I.E. root *ˣdanu-* "river" as well as a derivation from *dán* "skill." If the cognate names of these two goddesses, who are both portrayed as "Mothers of the Gods," comes from a root word meaning "earth," this will have important ramifications as we continue our exploration. For now, there are other derivations for the name that we must delve into.

The Eleventh-Century Birth of a Pagan Goddess?

There is another important argument pertaining to the origin and development of Danu's name that must be considered. This theory has been discussed, in part or in full, by a number of scholars, who see the name *Danu/Danann* (earlier *Donann*) as late and artificial, possibly arising from conflation with the goddess name *Anu/Anann* (who is discussed below), as well as confusion relating to the phrase *na trí dée dána* and the theonym *Túath Dé*. What follows is a summary of ideas presented by John Carey (some of which reference the position of Stern), as well as the work of Elizabeth Gray, T.F. O'Rahilly and Gerard Murphy.[44]

Prior to *Lebor Gabála*, in earlier texts such as the ninth century *Sanas Cormaic*, as well as those thought to derive from the lost eight century text *Cín Dromma Snechta*, the old gods are not referred to as *Túatha Dé Danann*, but simply as the *Áes Síde* ("People of the Síd mounds") or as the *Túath(a) Dé(a)* ("People(s) of the God/dess"). In some cases they were referred to as *Fer Déa* ("The Men of the Goddess"), as in the older ninth century version of *De Gabail in tSída*.[45] Carey points out that the name *Donann/Danann* does not seem to appear in any source prior to the poems in LG (approximately 11th c.).[46] In the pseudo-historical movement it became necessary to distinguish between the Old Gods and the Israelites, both of which might be referred to as *Túath Dé*. It may be at this time that the pagan gods were distinguished from the tribes of Israel by the designation *Túath(a) Déa*; such forms are common in *Cath Maige Tuired*. In *Cóir Anmann*, the new god-tribe designation is further glossed: *Túatha Dea .i. Donand*.

Adding to the confusion is the name *Domnann*, which appears in place-names in Connacht, and in the names of tribal groups referred to in *Lebor Gabála* and the sagas, such as *Fir Domnann, Domnannaig,* and *Túath Domnann*. Note the similarity between the phrases *Fer Déa/Fir Domnann,* and *Túath Domnann/Túath Dé Donann*. By the ninth century, *Domnann* is already shown in a corrupted form as *Donann* (as in *Táin Bó Regamna*). The name *Domnann* also appears in connection with a Fomorian king, *Indech mac Dé*

Domnann (although no earlier than LG). In *Cath Maige Tuired*, the confusion is evident, as there are examples of both *Túatha nDea Domnonn* and *Indech mac Dei Donann*. It has been suggested that these place- and population names which contain -*o*- rather than -*a*- may account for the -*o*- of the earliest attested form of the deity name (*Donann/Donu*, in later sources *Danann/ Danu*).

Another influence may be the '*trí dée dána*' to whom Lug appeals for assistance in making weapons for a battle against the Fomoire. The meaning of the phrase *trí dee dána* seems to have been misunderstood and reinterpreted over time, later appearing as *trí dee Donann/Danann*. In addition, the alliterative quality of the phrase *trí dee dána* may have influenced the phrase *Túatha Dé Donann/Danann* (from the simpler *Túatha Déa*). That the name of the god-tribe appears in this longer form for the first time (in what evidence we possess) during the pseudo-historical movement may be significant. By the time of *Lebor Gabála,* poems contain references to *Túathe De Donand* and *Donand mathair na ndea*. The second phrase may have been influenced by a reference in *Sanas Chormaic* to the divine female figure *Anu*, who is glossed in the following manner: *mater deorum Hibernensium* ("mother of the gods of Ireland").[47]

Simple phonetics may have further confounded the problem. Murphy points out that the Old Irish for "Peoples of the Gods of Donu" would be *Túatha Dé nDonann*, rather than *Túatha Dé Donann*. If an earlier phrase *Túatha Dé nAnann* was in existence, the identical sound of the nasalized words *nAnann* and *nDannann* may well have created this confusion. It may also have influenced the name of the hills described by Cormac as *Dá Cích nAnann*, but given by Keating as *Dá Chích Dhannan* (both situated in County Kerry).

To summarize the process suggested above, we begin with the need to distinguish between the pagan Irish gods (*Áes Síde/Fer Dea/Túath Dé*) and the Israelites (also *Túath Dé*), resulting in the phrase *Túath(a) Déa*. As *Donann/Donu* appears to be earlier than *Danann/Danu*, it may be that place and tribal names containing the word *Domnann* (later appearing corrupted as *Donann*) were an early influence. Additional confusion may have ensued from references to a trio of deities known as *na trí dée dána,* who over time are referred to as *trí dee Donann/Danann* (and whose alleged offspring included *Ecna mac na trí nDea nDána, dán* being confused or equated with the name *Danu*). The alliterative effect of *trí dée dána* may have also influenced the formation of the name *Túatha De Danann.* Cormac mentions *Anu, mater deorum Hibernensium,* while a gloss in *Cóir Anmann* reads *Túatha Dea .i. Donand*. Other references reflect the perceived genitive/nominative pairing *Anann/Anu,* and *Donann/Donu* or *Danann/Danu* (possibly influencing the associated place-names, earlier *Dá Cích nAnann*, later *Dá Chích Dhanann*). By the time of *Lebor Gabála,* we encounter poems containing references to

Túathe De Donand/Túatha Dé Danann, and the descriptive phrase *Donand mathair na ndea.*

Anu, the Enduring One

Another line of inquiry pertains to the figure of Anu. Gerard Murphy suggested that Danu's characteristics were transferred to Anu, or that they were the same deity.[48] It is also possible that Anu was the original deity, her attributes becoming attached to the developing figure of Danu. It is difficult to say with absolute certainty which deity (or deity name) came first, in spite of the earlier attested reference to Anu and the apparent early absence of the name Danu, for we are still left to contend with the cognate names Donu and Dôn, among other matters. It is possible, of course, that additional references pertaining to Anu or Danu once existed but have not survived, the dating or content of which could help clarify the situation. Perhaps some light may be shed on the matter by examining references to the goddess Anu, the figure with whom Danu is often equated or confused. As with Danu, research into the figure of Anu provides us with references which, while not great in terms of quantity, also contain potent imagery. The earliest extant information we have about Anu is recorded in *Sanas Chormaic:*

> Ána, i.e., mater deorum hibernensium. It was well she nursed *deos,* i.e., the gods: de cujus nomine dicitur *ana,* i.e., plenty [and the] *Da chích Anaine* "Two Paps of Ana" west of Luachair nominantur, et fabulaverunt. Vel *ana* quod est *annio* vel *aniud Graece* [?] quod interpretatur "dapes" [.i. biad "food"][49]

Certain elements in Cormac's account may reflect native traditions, such as Anu's role as "mother of the gods," symbolism pertaining to nourishment and plenty, and a connection with a feature of the landscape. However, given the propensity of members of the learned classes to conflate or combine native elements with elements from other sources (including Biblical, Classical, and wider Medieval learned sources of the time), the account may also contain non-native elements. One possibility is that the description was influenced by the figure of Cybele from Virgil's *Aeneid,* where this "mother of the Classical gods" makes a brief appearance in Book 7 (as well as in other sources). The commentaries of Servius pertaining to Virgil's work, and the Etymologies of Isidore, are two texts known to have influenced the compilers of the Irish glossaries. Servius notes that Cybele of Mount Ida is the same as Earth, which he says is "the mother of the gods" (*mater deorum*). He goes on to quote Isidore, where Cybele is described as follows:

> They imagine the same one as both Earth and Great Mother…. She is called Mother, because she gives birth to many things; Great, because she generates food; Kindly, because she nourishes all living things through her fruits.[50]

We can note some similarities between the description of Cybele and Cormac's account of Anu. However, they are not identical, which may suggest that Isidore's description provided a framework for presenting or interpreting native Irish materials.

The name Ána/Ana is a Latinization of a name that would have been spelled *Anu* in Old Irish (genitive form *Anann*). It is possible that *Anu* may derive from *ana/anae* "wealth, riches or prosperity" (used figuratively to denote "treasure"). Cormac notes that twin hills near Killarney in County Kerry were regarded as Anu's breasts ("as they say in story"). Anu was connected with the south of Ireland as a goddess of prosperity, known even in recent times. She was revered in the province of Munster, which was said to owe its fertility to her.[51] *Sanas Chormaic* glosses her name as meaning "plenty," and mentions a feature of the land, *Da Chích Anainne*, "The Two Paps of Ana," that were named after her. *Cóir Anman* also mentions this locale, and says that in Munster she was revered as *bandía in tsónusa*, "goddess of good fortune or prosperity."[52] These notable mountains in County Kerry are still referred to as the Paps of Anu.

In later texts, Anu's name was used synonymously as a designation for the land of Ireland: *íath Anann*, "land or territory of Anann."[53] In one example, *Anann* (.i. imbith) .i. Eire, we encounter the word *imbith*, perhaps from *imbed* (variants *imbid, imbeith*), "large quantity or number, abundance, excess," used especially of an abundance of wealth, riches or food. An interpretation of *imbith* as "abundance of wealth" is compatible with the proposed meaning of the name *Anu* "wealth, riches, prosperity." Another interpretation of *imbith* might derive from 2 *imm* (intensifying prefix, sometimes adding little to the meaning of the word) and *bith* "world," "land, territory, soil," or "existence, life." Both meanings of *bith* would be apposite in terms of a possible connection with land or territory (the Paps of Anu) and the perpetuation of life.

When used in compounds, *bith* may have the meaning "lasting, permanent, perpetual," perhaps providing an epithet "(Great) Lasting or Perpetual One." Another word meaning "lasting or enduring" is *buan*, found in the name of several legendary figures. It occurs in the name *Buanan(d)* (perhaps from *buan* "lasting or perpetual" and *finn* "white, bright, blessed"). Such a name may suggest a title "Bright or Blessed Enduring One." In *Sanas Chormaic*, a figure by this name is associated or compared with Anu/Anand: *Búanand ... i. bé nAnand* (although this could be a false etymology). In one Dindshenchas poem she appears as *Anand finn*, "Anand the fair," wife of Furudran, one of Finn mac Cumhall's favorite soldiers. The other favored soldier was Lethluachra. Each man had a stronghold, and in a stronghold in between these lived Anand, "from whom it was called *Dún Anainne Finne*." Anand slept with Lethluachair, but their tryst become known and Furudran killed Lethluachair, who was buried in that plain, *Mag Lethluachra*.

Gwynn felt that the collocation of Anann and Lethluachair suggested a connection with the Kerry hills known as *Dá Chích Anainne iar Luachair*. This connection with the Fiana is seen in *Sanas Chormaic* as well, where Anu is compared with *Buan mumi na fian* "fostermother of the *Fian*," and also referred to as *daghmat[h]air*, "good mother" (*dag* ["good"] when used in compounds may take on the meaning of "good or noble," sometimes with an intensive significance).[54]

> Buanan, nurse of the heroes, i.e., *bé n-Anann* (a) from their similarity to each other, for as *Ánu* was mother of the gods, sic Buanann erat mother of the heroes, i.e., a good mother. Aliter Buan-ann [.i. daghmatair "good mother"] the *buan*, i.e., is *bón* from *bonum*, as is said *genither buan ó ambuan* "*buan* is born from *ambuan*" i.e., good from evil. The *ann* that is in *Buanann* denotes mater. It is this that is in *Ana* [*Anand* B] i.e., mater deorum. Buanann then (means) a good mother for teaching feats of arms to the heroes.[55]

John Carey has suggested that Anu's name may have been involved in the formation of the name of another female figure of the Túatha Dé Danann. This is the divine woman *Dianand* or *Dinand* (*Danand* in later manuscripts), a witch figure (*ban-tuathach*) of the Túatha Dé Danann. In *Cath Maige Tuired*, Lugh consults "his two witches," Díanann and Bé Chuille, regarding the assistance they will provide in an upcoming battle. The two women reply that they will enchant the trees and stones and sods of the earth so that they become a terrifying host.[56] Díanann's name could derive from *dían* "swift" and *find* "white, bright, blessed." Bé Chuille's name could mean "Woman of Hazel," a type of wood associated with magic or wisdom, or it could reflect 2 *coll* "destruction, spoiling, injury." Carey suggests that *Dianand*'s name is contracted from **Día Anann*.[57] A further association with witchcraft or magic is implied in a passage from *Lebor Gabála* in which Ana is said to be the seventh daughter of Ernmas the witch.[58] In Irish and Scottish folk traditions, certain characteristics were believed to be passed down to the seventh son of a seventh son, or seventh daughter of a seventh daughter, including the gifts of music, healing or prophecy.[59]

Another reference to Anu occurs in *Acallam na Senórach*.[60] Cáel, a warrior of Finn's retinue, wishes to pursue Créde, a woman of the *síd*, who is the daughter of "a king of the uplands of Kerry."[61] Créde demands that her suitors woo her with poetry, and Cáel is ready at the door of the *síd* mound with a poem he received from his foster-mother Muirenn from the *Bruig*:

> Travel I must on Friday,
> as a true and welcome guest,
> The long way to Créde's house,
> on the mountain's north-east slope.
>
> Fate brings me there,
> to Créde at Anu's Breasts,

There to be well tested,
four days, and four again.

Her pleasant house is crowded,
With women, men, and boys,
Druids and musicians,
A guardian of doors and ale.

Her bower by the Lake of Hosts,
of silver and yellow gold,
A thatched roof made of feathers,
dark purple and brown…

She who possesses all of this,
from ebb-tide to the flood,
Créde of the three-peaked hills,
unrivalled in the land.[62]

Later in the poem the wonders and treasures found inside the *síd* mound are also described. Is this perhaps a description of the inner realms of the Paps of Anu?

The thatching of her roof,
bird feathers, yellow and blue,
Of carbuncle and glass,
the space close by the well.

About each bed four pillars,
of well-wrought silver and gold,
Topped with a ball of crystal,
a pleasure to the eye.

A vat of red enamel,
a source of pleasing malt,
Shaded by an apple tree,
replete with heavy fruit.

Whenever Créde's horn is filled,
with mead from this fine vat,
Four of the apples, all at once,
fall into her cup…[63]

Proinsius McCana proposed that legends associated with Anu may have become attached to the figure of St. Ann. He writes: "It is significant that so many pagan traditions and cults survived and flourished almost to our day in consequence of the fact that they were accommodated under the capacious mantle of the Church and thereby acquired a rather spurious seal of respectability." He cites Brighid as a primary example, as well as a group of three holy sisters who "cannot easily be dissociated from the trio of goddesses who figure so often and so prominently in the early mythological legends."[64] We will shortly meet this trio of sisters.

Danu, Goddess of Wisdom

At this point, we can discern a number of parallels between descriptions of Danu and Anu. Both Danu and Anu are referred to as "mother of the gods," a role Danu appears to share with the Welsh figure of Dôn. Danu is said to have united with her father in an episode which may reflect a cosmogonic act of creation, and which resulted in the birth of three skilled deities. One of these deities may have been Goibniu, the Smith God. Dôn is likewise credited as being the mother of various deities, including a Divine Smith, Gofannon. Anu may have had epithets meaning "Noble Mother," "Lasting or Perpetual One," and perhaps "The Good Mother." Both Danu and Anu are associated with attributes of abundance or prosperity (Anu, via her name and several descriptive passages, and Danu, described as "fair and generous"). Both are associated with a pair of hills which were perceived of as the breasts of a goddess. If the names Donu and Dôn derive from an Indo European root meaning "earth," this would tie in well with these attributes of abundance and prosperity, as well as the associated place-names.

If we still entertain that a linguistic derivation from I.E. *danu-* ("river") is possible, we are left to contend with the fact that apart from this possible (but uncertain) derivation, references to Danu do not mention any connection with water (a situation that also applies to Anu). Dôn may have had some aquatic symbolism (including two possible river names), but these are primarily connected with Otherworld locations and sources of wisdom. Perhaps this is related in some way to Danu's perceived associations with poetry, and with Danu and Anu's connection with magic. While Danu's name does not derive linguistically from the word *dán*, there may have been a conceptual link, resulting in the personification of Dán and poetic offspring.

It is difficult at this stage to discern which goddess is the original. The persuasive linguistic argument regarding the formation of the phrase *Túatha Dé Danann,* and the early reference in *Sanas Chormaic,* would suggest that Anu is the earlier figure. While the surviving remnants of what would once have been a much more extensive body of literature do appear to mention Danu only in later sources, we must confess that through the extant manuscript sources we do not currently have access to the entirety of the learned (or folk) traditions of early Ireland. There may have been more pieces in play, some of which could lend clarity to the situation.

Also, we are left to contend with two pieces of information that might suggest an earlier origin for Danu. The first piece of data is the important linguistic connection between the names *Donu* and *Dôn*, both likely reflecting a root word meaning "earth," and both figures serving as "Mother of the Gods." In medieval Welsh literary tradition, Dôn and her divine offspring are mentioned in a number of sources. Are these attributions detritus left over from the attributes of Cybele in Isidore or some other borrowed Medieval source? Or could they represent an earlier stratum of religious symbolism that was preserved in both Ireland and Wales? Numerous studies have pointed to earlier Celtic symbolism that was preserved in both cultures. We must also consider the possibility of a later literary or cultural borrowing between Ireland and Wales (like the Irish word *síd* appearing in the Welsh Otherworld locale *Caer Siddi*, among other examples).

The second piece of data is the statement that Danu engaged in mythological incest with her father, Delbaeth. If Danu/Donu does represent a goddess associated with the Earth (which her name linguistically supports), and if her father represents a creator god associated with the sky, then this episode may represent the Indo-European creation scenario described earlier in this chapter. In other mythologies, the offspring of such a cosmogonic union might consist of cosmic elements, features of the land, or other important deities.

What is interesting in this context is that the "offspring" of this mythic union are forms of poetic art, wisdom or skill. Whether this represents an early reflection of the Irish preoccupation with wisdom, poetry, and skill, or whether it is a later learned fabrication, it is still a fascinating cultural artefact. We could interpret the mythic scenario of Danu, daughter of Delbaeth ("One who Shapes, Forms, Ordains, Designs"), uniting with her father and giving birth to the "three gods of skill" as a cosmogonic fragment, one that has parallels in other Indo-European cultures. But what if Delbaeth is not a god, but a poetic concept personified?

A poetic metaphor in which aspects of wisdom and skill are portrayed in personified form is expressed in a number of medieval Irish sources. For example, there are several poems in which *aí* (earlier form *aui*, a monosyllable) "poetic inspiration, learning; metrical composition" is personified.[65] As a noun it was originally masculine, but later feminine, thus accounting for its depiction as a woman in these poems. In this excerpt, note the personification of *aí* and other forms of wisdom and skill (my translation):

> *Fo chen aí*
> *Ingen sois*
> *Siur chéile*
> *Ingen menman...*[66]

> Welcome, Inspiration
> Daughter of Great Knowledge
> Sister of Reason
> Daughter of Thought...

A longer example occurs in *Immacalam in Dá Thuarad*, when the poet Ferchertne asks the aspiring student Néde whose son he is. Néde replies (my translation):

Ni ansa: macsa Dana,
Dán mac Osmenta
Osmenad mac Imráiti
Imradud mac Rofìs
Rofis mac Fochmairc
Fochmorc mac Rochmairc
Rochmorc mac Rofessa
Rofìs mac Rochuind
Rochond mac Ergnai
Ergna mac Ecnai
Ecna mac na trí ñDea ñDána.[67]

Not difficult [to tell]: I am (a) son of Poetry
Poetry son of Meditation
Meditation son of Thought
Thought son of Great Inquiry
Great Inquiry son of Seeking
Seeking son of Discovery
Discovery son of Great Knowledge
Great Knowledge son of Great Intelligence
Great Intelligence son of Understanding
Understanding son of Enlightenment
Enlightenment, son of the three gods of Skill.

In this poem, the nouns are either masculine or neuter. While the word *mac* most commonly denotes "son, male descendant" (as well as "boy, young person in general"), when followed by the genitive in various figurative and technical expressions, it can express a calling or function. This is seen in phrases such as *mac eclaise*, "son of (the) church" (i.e. a cleric or churchman) or *mac foglama* "a student." There are numerous interesting cultural examples of this usage, including *mac alla* "son of a cliff" ("an echo") and *mac tire* "son of (the) land/country," ("a wolf"). In regards to the previously mentioned reference *Eicsi ilgradhach inghen Dána* ("Éicse the well-loved daughter of Dána"), the noun *éicse* is accordingly feminine. It denotes a variety of meanings associated with poetry, learning, and divination ("divination, faculty of divination, wisdom, profession of a seer; revelation, lore, learning; especially poetry, poetic composition; poetic art, skill or faculty, calling of a poet").

Interestingly, the one instance where the gender of a personified concept does not match that of a noun is in relation to the mention of Dána, "daughter" of Delbaeth; the Old Irish noun *dán* is masculine. However, if we remember the figurative phrase *ingen dána*, "a poetess," the phrase may make more sense. But what of the figure of Delbaeth? If he is not a deity, but a poetic concept personified, this may be an example of the well-known concept of the Poet as Shaper, Former and Creator. William Gillies has written about this widespread phenomenon:

It seems most natural to think of the poet as an artisan, and the tradition as supplying a blueprint, on the basis of which he creates an artefact which may be more or less aesthetically exciting, depending upon the genius and devotion of its maker, but which must ... be capable of doing the job it was made for, like a finely-wrought weapon or utensil. I have no doubt that this is why "fashioning," "making," "crafting" and "shaping" are the terms which the bardic poets most frequently apply to the act of poetic composition.[68]

Caerwyn Williams also refers to the vocabulary of the poets' "power over things" in both Irish and Welsh traditions, as reflected in Old Irish *creth* "poetry" and *cruth* "form," and Welsh *prydydd* (cf. *pryd* "shape, form").[69] Poets not only crafted poetry, but their words were believed to have a potential physical effect upon their listeners (not to mention upon the reputation and status of kings or patrons). Perhaps the concept of the "Poet as One who Shapes or Forms" had a daughter (*ingen dána,* "a poetess,") from whom it was naturally envisioned that the three gods of skill were given form (or "birthed"), followed by the rest of the lineage. Whether or not Delbaeth and Danu were originally deities with a role in a cosmogonic myth, the perceived "roots" of their names may have found expression in a poem (and other literary expressions) in which various types of wisdom and skill were described or depicted in personified form.

However, also in the *Immacallam* is a statement that the three gods of dána were the offspring of a goddess—but in this case, Brigit: "Three sons of Brigit the poetess, namely, Brian and Iuchar and Úar, three sons of Bres son of Elathu; and Brigit the poetess, daughter of the Dagda Mór, king of Ireland, was their mother."[70] As discussed above, while these three sons, who have no known connection to wisdom or skill, are not likely to be the divine trio involved, it is possible that Brigid, as patron goddess of the poets, may have played some role. As the reference is late, and the connection with Danu/dán had likely become more obscured, Brigid may have been seen as a reasonable progenitor for the gods of poetic skill. Without access to the "originals," in whatever form, the traditions seem to have become hopelessly entangled.

But perhaps there is a way through the labyrinth. Let us return to our discussion of the similarities (and possible confusion) between the figures of Danu and Anu. As noted above, if we note the early reference to Anu in *Sanas Chormaic*, and the linguistic argument pertaining to the possible later development of the name of the god-tribe, an argument could be made for Anu as the original deity and Danu as a later conflation. However, it would be quite remarkable if medieval Irish clerics or scribes managed to invent a new pagan goddess (Danu) in the process of trying to suppress the pagan traditions with which their new faith had to compete! But if Donu and Dôn represent Divine Ancestresses, and their names are derived from a root meaning "earth," this could represent a reasonable piece of evidence for Donu as the original form (with the names of the two goddesses becoming confused through the *nDanann/nAnann* phonetic scenario, amongst other things). The arguments seem to becoming circular—or are they?

Both Danu and Anu are directly styled "Mother of the Gods." One potentially very fruitful explanation is that these are not separate goddesses (or goddess names), but are in fact titles or epithets of the same deity (Danu, who is also known as Anu; and Anu, who is also known as Danu). Further, both names may be epithets for another deity altogether. Numerous Celtic deities have a primary "name" and several titles or epithets by which they are known. The gods may be referred to by these various names in different stories or poems, something that would not have caused confusion in earlier periods when these names were remembered and the traditions were current. For example, the Dagda (Mór) was also known as *Eochu Ollathair* and *Ruad Rofhessa*. The actual name of *Manannan mac Lir* is given as *Oirbsen*, Oengus is called the *Mac Óc*, and Lugh was referred to by the epithets *Lámfada*, *Samildánach*, and *Mac Eithne*. The propensity of the Irish for the symbolism of "three" in cultural and religious contexts is well-attested. Here we might remember the Gaulish inscription *Tarvos Trigaranus*, for example. In the literature we encounter Brigid and her two sisters (also named Brigid), the three harpers (and offspring of Boand) who created the three strains of music, and numerous other examples.

If we posit that the information contained in these scattered references to Danu and Anu refer to the same deity (whether that deity is Danu, Anu, or a third goddess), we possess quite a bit of intriguing detail with which to round out our picture of this once elusive divinity: This goddess is known as the "Mother of the Gods," and displays attributes and epithets associated with that title and role. She is associated with the land and its fertility, and with abundance, wealth and plenty. She has associations with magic and witchcraft, and may have also had a conceptual connection with wisdom and skill. If this theory is correct—that at least some of the attributes associated with Danu and Anu reflect those of a single goddess—our initial condition of not possessing much detail shifts to having a potentially fuller picture of this divine figure.

There is one final and significant observation we must consider, which is that neither Anu nor Danu figure actively in the literature.[71] Considering all of these significant attributes, why would such an important figure not have had a more active role in the narrative materials? The same could be asked in regards to the Welsh *Dôn* and the elusive *Modron*. As we saw in Chapter 2, sometimes primal mythological figures function in this manner, appearing early on in origin tales and the like, but not playing an active part in later accounts. Despite their noble titles and attributes, the figures of Danu and Anu seem to lurk in the shadows, as if their descriptive epithets are merely hinting at—or pointing towards—something else entirely. Let us step out of the shadows and see what (or who) that "something else" might be.

Finding the Great Queen

In the literature, certain Irish divinities play a larger role in the narratives than others, such as the gods Lug, The Dagda, Ogma, Midir, Manannán, Oengus, Dian Cecht and Goibniu, and the goddesses Macha, Boand, Sinann, Flidais, and Bríg. Danu and Anu, however, only appear in short passages. By way of contrast, one cannot help but note a prominent, powerful and independent female character who seems to dominate the scene, taking an extremely active role in a number of tales (including the *Táin, Cath Maige Tuired* and others). This is the figure known as *An Mórrígan*.

Her name has been interpreted as meaning either "Phantom/Nightmare Queen," or "Great Queen." The first meaning derives from the spelling *Morrígan*, without a mark of length on the first vowel (the root behind that syllable is also found in the English word "nightmare"). This is the earliest *attested* spelling of the goddess' name. However, without access to the entire corpus of written materials (and in light of scribal errors and the propensity of some scribes to take a fairly casual attitude in regards to accent marks), we cannot be absolutely certain this is the original meaning or spelling. In other written sources, there is a mark of length on the first syllable, giving a meaning of "Great Queen" (a meaning which may be suggested by her prominent role, and by her numerous impressive attributes). Whichever spelling is the original, both forms are likely to be epithets or titles, rather than denoting a proper name.[72]

In various narrative contexts, this goddess is commonly portrayed as a goddess of war with magical and sexual overtones, a battle fury who stirs up fear or strife, sometimes with little obvious motive. However, additional inquiry reveals a far more complex and potentially well-rounded figure. While some sources focus on her well-documented attributes of battle, conflict and death, a careful and more comprehensive exploration of all the sources shows that she was also associated with leadership and strategy, shape-shifting and prophecy, sovereignty and kingship, victory and prosperity, animals (including ravens and cattle) and features of the land.

The Mórrígan has two sisters, *Macha* and *Nemain*, and the three were known collectively as *na Mórrígna* "the Great Queens."[73] *Nemain* was sometimes referred to by the epithet *Badb* "raven, scald-crow," as were The Mórrígan and Macha in certain contexts.[74] Proinsius MacCana sees this trio of war goddesses or witches as a widespread phenomenon in Celtic religion:

…that they were known throughout the Celtic world is virtually certain; the Catho-bodua, "crow/raven of battle" attested in Haute-Savoie corresponds to the Irish *Badbh Chatha,* and the notion of the trio of furies recurs in Britain in the Benwell inscription *Lamiis Tribus,* "To the Three Lamiae [Witches]."[75]

The three sisters were daughters of *Ernmas,* whose name appears to mean "death by iron," potentially referring to a deed of slaughter or violence.[76] While this explanation may suggest a malevolent war-like figure, it must be remembered that as with the Mórrígan's role as a war-goddess, the protection of the people required the use of warfare and weapons in order to secure victory, ensure their survival and well-being, and ultimately establish peace. Like her daughter, Ernmas was associated with witchcraft and magic, and was referred to as *bantuathach* "witch."[77]

In addition to these frequently highlighted attributes, The Mórrígan was associated with a number of place-names and features of the land, which may suggest a connection with fertility and abundance. These include *Gort na Morrígna* "the Morrígan's field" in County Louth; ancient cooking sites known as *Fulacht na Morrígna* "the Morrígan's hearth"; the "Bed of the Couple" (a location connected with Brúg na Bóinne, modern Newgrange), the site where the union between the Dagda and the Mórrígan took place in *Cath Maige Tuired*; the "Comb and Casket of the Dagda's wife" (a place-name associated with two hills), and *Dá Chích na Morrígan* "The Two Paps of the Mórrígan" (also located near Newgrange).[78]

The Mórrígan's connection with features of the land which were associated with nourishment, and sexual union (particularly hills whose name may symbolize the life-sustaining breasts of a goddess) strongly suggest connections with fertility and plenty, powers not usually attributed to her. And, although "motherhood" in the traditional sense is not often thought to be one of The Mórrígan's strong suits, literary references indicate that she was in fact the mother of numerous offspring, including fifty-two warrior-children (twenty-six male children and twenty-six female children), as well as an ill-fated son Meche, and a daughter Adair (whom she has with the Dagda).[79]

In *Táin Bó Cuailgne*, a figure (who is later identified as the Mórrígan) presents herself to the hero Cú Chulainn in the form of a beautiful young woman, "wrapped in garments of many colours."[80] She says she has brought him treasure and cattle, and that she loves him as a result of remarkable tales she has heard about him (a common Celtic narrative motif). Cú says she has come at a bad time, when his people "no longer flourish here, but famish," and indicates that he cannot attend to a woman at such a difficult time. She replies that she may be a help to him, but he states that it "wasn't for a woman's backside" that he took on his ordeal. Rejected, she vows to hinder him.[81]

While some interpret this episode as further evidence of her vindictive, martial quality, it is more likely to represent her identity as a Goddess of Sovereignty. In numerous tales, women from the Otherworld who represent or embody Sovereignty appear before a male figure to test their worth. In many of these episodes, the woman offers them assistance, wealth or abundance, or sexual union. The goddess's appearance is often a test to see if the male figure recognizes in whose presence he stands. If he does, and if he undertakes certain worthy (or challenging) deeds, her power and blessings are bestowed upon him. The goddess may then ensure that he achieves success and/or obtains the kingship. If he does not recognize her, or is otherwise deemed unworthy, he is rejected by the Goddess and misfortune often ensues.

Even in this short survey of the Mórrígan's various appearances and attributes, we can see that in addition to a connection with battle and conflict, she had well-attested associations with the land and rulership, abundance and fertility, magic and witchcraft, and wisdom and skill, attributes that were also prominent in descriptions of Anu and Danu. However, the most telling point—and the key to our inquiry—is found among the references to the three daughters of Ernmas. In several of these references, the Mórrígan is directly identified as Anann, which is said to be her proper name. A representative example comes from Lebor Gabála:

> *Badb ocus Macha ocus Anann .i. in Morrígan, díatat Da Chich Anann i Luachair,*
>
> Badb [Nemain] and Macha and Anann (that is, the Mórrígan) after whom the Two Paps of Anu in Luachair are called.[82]

Another passage in LG further equates the Mórrígan with Danu, as well as Anu:

> *in Mor-rigu ... is dia forainm Danand o builead Da Chich Anann ... ocus o builed Túatha De Danann,*
>
> The Morrigu ... it is from her additional name Danand that the Paps of Anu are called ... as well as the Túatha De Danann.[83]

The significance of these findings is evident. The god-tribe of the Irish was not named for an imperceptible progenitor about whom little is known, but held as their figurehead the Great Queen herself, an individual about whom we know a great deal. The number of stories which feature the Mórrígan is not a chance survival. Her identification with the figure of Danu suggests a revision in how we view and respond to the term Túatha Dé Danann, in light of the numerous powerful and well-documented aspects of the Mórrígan. The Mórrígan, in turn, acquires additional layers of definition and distinction as her attributes are taken in combination with those of Danu and Anu. While the references to these divine figures initially seemed like a tangled ball of thread, they are actually more akin to the intertwining images in a knotwork design, each one connected to and leading towards the other.

A Cosmogonic Tryst at the World Tree

In order to fully understand the complex nature of the Mórrígan, one additional concept should be explored—that of dualism. While modern materialist-reductionist society tends to view duality in terms of opposing forces or ideas, traditional cultures embrace this concept as expressing two differing yet complementary parts of a sacred whole. Winter and summer, male and female, light and dark (to name just a few examples) were regarded as necessary elements of creation, existence and the perpetuation of life, not conflicts to be solved or avoided. Death was viewed as part of a sacred cycle, a natural part of life's experiences. In Hindu and Celtic traditions, this concept was expressed in numerous ways, including the veneration of great goddesses of battle and death whose powers and influence also ensured the continuity of life. The fusion of these symbolic dualities may be perceived in the character of the Mórrígan, and in the names of her parents: Delbaeth, "He who Shapes or Forms," and Ernmas, "Death by Iron," bringing together these cosmic dualities in the figures of a Creator God and Destructive Goddess.

The primal concept of the whole, the sacred, the earth, and life itself, as emerging from such a union is found in a number of mythologies. In Irish tradition, this duality (as unified within the whole) was expressed in several ways. The land was symbolically divided into North and South (which was echoed in later times by a similar division of parishes). The year was originally divided into two halves, light and dark. In "The Wooing of Etain," the young god Oengus obtains his father's dwelling place for himself by asserting that a pledge he had received, which permitted him to dwell there for a day and a night, actually constituted eternity: "for it is clear … that night and day are the entire world."[84]

The joining of Delbaeth and Ernmas is mirrored in the union of their daughter, a goddess often connected with battle and death, with the Dagda, a deity frequently associated with life and prosperity.[85] Of course, The Mórrígan is also associated with life and abundance, and The Dagda possesses a club which yields the power of life or death. In *Cath Maige Tuired*, the union of these two important deities takes place at Samain, the end of the old year and the beginning of the new, a sacred portal when creation arises from destruction. The Dagda comes upon the Mórrígan as she stands with one foot to the north and one foot to the south of a river, a place of liminality and possibility. Once she has joined with him, she begins to take charge of the conflict between the Túatha Dé Danann and the Fomoire, providing guidance, advice, leadership, and magical assistance. As a result, the fortunes of the Túatha Dé Danann improve and they achieve victory.[86] As a Goddess of Sovereignty, The Mórrígan's assistance, skill, magic, blessings and protection were required to ensure the victory and continuation of the tribe, and the prosperity of the land and its people, whether mortal or immortal.

The union of The Dagda and The Mórrígan takes place at the River Unius in Connaught. Acts of creation, or of great mythical or cosmological import, often take place in or near bodies of water. An inquiry into the name of the river provides another clue as to the significance of this event. In Old Irish, the word *uinius* means "ash tree." The ash was considered one of the respected "chieftain trees" in early Irish tradition, and could serve as a *bile*— ancient, sacred or venerated trees which formed part of early ritual sites. Two very important legendary trees were said to be ash (the Tree of Tortu and the Tree of Dath-í). In addition, a specific ash-tree is noted as having been located at Uisneach, a site considered to be the cosmological center of Ireland. In various cultures, including those in parts of Europe, the ash tree was a symbol of the *axis mundi* or World Tree which vertically connected the earth with the Otherworld realms (both Upper/Celestial and Lower/Chthonic). The *Dagda* and The *Dagmathair* (an epithet of Anu) unite at the sacred portal of Samain, over a river known as the Ash-tree, perhaps the symbolic center of the world or cosmos, underscoring the significance of these events and the divine beings involved in these narratives.

If, as the evidence suggests, The Mórrígan was an epithet for the goddess Anu, who was also equated with the figure of Danu (whether that derives from earlier primal attributes or later learned perceptions), it is The Great Queen herself who is the "Mother of the Gods of Ireland." As the daughter of Delbaeth ("He who Shapes or Forms") and Ernmas ("Death by Iron"), she combines within herself a wide range of attributes encompassing life and death, battle and protection, sovereignty and prosperity, sexuality and fertility, magic and skill, and prophecy and shape-shifting. She is a goddess who presides over the battlefield and may cause strife or death, as well as one who bestows victory and protection, and ensures prosperity and peace. It is she who unites at Samain with a god associated with life and prosperity, perhaps at the site of the *axis mundi* itself. These insights illuminate additional layers of meaning in the tales in which the Mórrígan appears, and inform our perceptions of her mythological, cosmological and societal significance—as well as those of the Túatha Dé Danann, the divinities of the ancient Irish over whom she presided, and from whom the god-tribe ultimately derived its name.

5

Restoring the Rightful Goddess

Sovereignty in the Tales of Findabair and Gwenhwyfar

As we saw in the last chapter, one of the most important elements of Celtic polytheistic religion was the veneration of the Goddess of Sovereignty. This multi-aspected divinity was associated with leadership, the land, fertility, battle, magic, and many other attributes. In early Irish and medieval Welsh literature (as well as Celtic folklore sources), this divine figure may appear in either human or animal form, and is identified under a variety of names and titles. Regardless of variances in appearance or nomenclature, the underlying archetype is the same. The importance and identity of this deity would have been recognized and understood during the pagan era, but over the centuries the shape-shifting Sovereignty Goddess began to be misunderstood. As a result, a goddess associated with battle is depicted as a vicious harpy rather than a Divine Protectress, and a goddess whose blessings ensure the success of the kingship and the fertility of the land is interpreted as a sexually wanton woman.

In some of the narratives and poems that have survived, the presence of the Sovereignty Goddess is fairly easy to discern. In other cases, one must peel away layers of projection and misrepresentation in order to recognize her. In this chapter we will explore themes from the early Irish tale *Táin Bó Fróech* ("The Cattle Raid of Fróech") and episodes from Arthurian materials pertaining to the character of Gwenhwyfar (the Middle Welsh spelling of Guinevere) to see how these images of sovereignty were preserved, adapted or distorted in the literary corpus.[1]

Táin Bó Fróech begins with a description of a young warrior named *Fróech* (whose name means "heather"), a figure whose father is *Idath* of the

Connachta and whose mother is the divine woman *Bé Find* of the *Áes Síde*. *Findabair,* the daughter of *Ailill* and *Medb,* falls in love with Fróech through reports of his fame and character. The young man is advised to visit his mother's sister, the goddess *Boand,* who provides him with many gifts. Armed with treasures and finery, he proceeds to Crúachu, the royal fortress of Ailill and Medb, where he is warmly welcomed.

After he has been in Cruachu for some time, Fróech encounters Findabair at dawn at a river where he has come to bathe. He asks her if she will come away with him, but she refuses, reminding him that she is the daughter of a king and queen. While she demands her proper bride price, she also states that it will be her choice to go with Fróech because of her love for him. Unaware of their dialogue, Ailill confides to Medb that he fears Findabair will run off with Fróech. The verb he uses is *élúd,* "depart, escape, elope; secret or stealthy departure," or (as a legal term) "evasion of rightful claims, neglect to comply with legal customs or duties." In spite of Ailill's worries, Fróech does the right thing and formally asks for Findabair's hand. Ailill agrees to the match, provided that a bride price is met. However, the bride-price is outrageously extravagant, and Fróech storms off.

Ailill then voices his concern that if Fróech takes Findabair away, "a multitude of the kings of Érin" will besiege and destroy them. Medb points out that they will also be dishonored. However, she reassures Ailill that she will arrange matters so these misfortunes do not occur. The couple deceitfully asks Fróech to demonstrate his swimming abilities in a pool of water. While he is in the water, they ask him to procure a particular rowan branch for them from the far side of the pool. While in the water, Fróech secretly catches and hides a salmon that has swallowed a ring, a token given to him by Findabair. Unbeknownst to him, however, the pool is also inhabited by a monster. The beast seizes Fróech, who cries out for his sword. No one dares to respond out of fear of Ailill and Medb. Findabair leaps into the water and brings Fróech a sword with which he kills the monster.

Afterwards, Ailill and Medb speak to each other regretfully of the evil they have done to the young man, but also say that Findabair must die for bringing him a sword. Fróech is taken to the Otherworld realms by his mother's people. Upon his return, the king and queen make peace with him and prepare a great feast. At the feast, Ailill demands that Findabair produce the ring, which was originally a gift from father to daughter, but she is unable to produce the ring. Fróech steps forward and states that there is no treasure he would not give for the girl, "for she brought the sword that saved my life." He then produces the ring inside the cooked salmon.

This would seem like a fitting point of conclusion to the tale, as well as a happy ending. Findabair promises herself to Fróech, but he is not permitted to sleep with her until he accompanies Ailill and Medb on the great Cattle

Raid of Cooley. The divine woman Bé Find appears before her son and tells him that a herd of white red-eared cattle that she had given to him have been stolen. Rather inexplicably, she also tells him that his wife and three sons have likewise been stolen and taken to the Alps. She counsels him against setting out on the cattle raid, but he has sworn to go.

Before setting out, however, Fróech attends to the theft of his family and cattle. He enlists the help of the great hero *Conall Cernach* and the two travel to the Alps. There they encounter a woman herding sheep who tell them that Fróech's cattle and family are nearby, and that Findabair is with the king. She asks Fróech if he trusts his wife. He replies, "We trusted her before she came, but perhaps we do not trust her now." The two men are told that a serpent guards the king's courtyard. Fróech passes this task off to Conall Cernach saying, "I will not go to my wife, for I do not trust her." He says that he does trust Conall, however, and knows that he will not betray them. When Conall encounters the serpent, it leaps into his belt, enabling the two heroes to storm the fort and free Findabair and her time-traveling offspring. The warriors, wife and children return to Ireland after a brief stopover in Scotland to retrieve three of Fróech's cows. At this point, Fróech leaves to undertake the Cattle Raid of Cooley with Ailill and Medb as he had promised.[2]

Two of the most intriguing themes in this tale have to do with abduction of a woman: Ailill and Medb's fear of their daughter's abduction by Fróech (and the consequences of such an action), and Fróech's sudden mistrust of Findabair when she has been abducted by another man. Information about abduction and the repercussions which result from it are mentioned in the eighth century Irish law text *Cáin Lánamna* (CL) and elaborated upon in various contemporary and ensuing commentaries and glosses.[3] CL describes a variety of sexual and marital relationships (many of which were far from canonical), and categorizes them in descending order. Nine types of sexual union are enumerated in the text, from a union of joint property (*lánamnas comthincuir*) to unions in which the man (or the woman) contribute the majority of goods or wealth to the marriage. The sixth type of union, *lánamnas foxail* (< *fochsal/foxal*, verbal noun of *fo-coisle,* "taking away, removing, carrying off; abduction"), is one in which the woman allows herself to be abducted without her kin's consent.[4]

The law tracts also provide information about the responsibilities of rearing any offspring that may result from union by abduction. One source states that if a child was born from a union forbidden by the girl's father, the man was responsible for rearing it. This law applied if the man abducted a woman in defiance of her father or kin, as in the case of *lánamnas foxail*.[5] Another source states that if a child was begotten within one month of the abduction it belonged to the mother's tribe, who could sell it if they so desired. However, the father could purchase the child, which was then considered to be the child of a woman "taken by abduction" (whether she had been a chief wife, *cétmuinter foxail*, or a secondary wife, *adaltrach foxail,* prior to the abduction). A child begotten after the first month (but before the man and woman entered into any regular connection), was similarly considered. However, once a regular connection was established between the couple, the offspring that resulted from this connection were considered to be the children of a lawful partner, whether the woman was a *cétmuinter* or *adaltrach*.[6]

One legal commentary stated that if the abducted woman was a *cétmuinter*, she was exempt from the obligation of sharing the cost and responsibility of rearing a child born from this type of union (in cases where the woman returned to her husband). The abductor was obliged to pay body-fine and honor-price to the man whose wife she already was, and if the woman was a chief wife, full *eric*-fine was also due on account of her abduction. If the woman consented to the abduction, however, she had no personal claim to honor-price. Honor-price was payable to her family, as well as *corpdire* (if for some reason she died within one month).

The amount of an atonement fine, either payable to (or by) the woman, depended upon the question of her consent. It was also dependent upon whether or not she had accepted a bride-price (*coibche*), which was given by the husband to the bride's father.[7] The bride was entitled to a portion of the bride-price, but forfeited her share if she attempted to conceal from her father the fact that she had received it. If the marriage broke up through the fault of the husband, the *coibche* was retained by the bride's father.[8] *Cáin Lánamna* also stipulates the specifics of the division of goods, should a couple involved in union by abduction separate.[9]

We can now see why Ailill might be concerned about the consequences of his daughter being abducted, in regards to bride-price, honor-price, or being financially responsible for the rearing of children. Regardless of these legal considerations (and the potential dishonor of the daughter of a king and queen being abducted), the laws do not seem to support Ailill's anxiety that he and Medb would be attacked by other Irish rulers if Findabair was abducted. In order to understand the story in more depth, we may need to move away from the world of early Irish law to that of native mythological symbolism. Perhaps there is something afoot here that goes beyond finances and saving face. If we start by examining the figure who is central to all of this action (and the attendant concerns), some light may be shed upon the more confusing aspects of the narrative.

Findabair's name derives from the words *finn* "white, bright, blessed" and *síabair* "a spectre, phantom, supernatural being."[10] That being the case, perhaps she was originally a divine being, rather than a noble personage. It is quite commonplace in medieval Irish literature for former deities or supernatural characters to be euhemerized into kings and queens, heroes and heroines, noble ancestors, and the like. Fróech himself is the result of a mixed worldly-Otherworldly union, which is perhaps one of the reasons why he is portrayed so favorably (and why Findabair is so taken with him). In spite of his many fine qualities, Findabair is keenly aware of her position and importance, and it is she who decides the terms of their relationship. In spite of the gifts and wealth Fróech brings to the table, she clearly states that it is her own decision to go with him. This is one of the hallmark traits of the Sovereignty Goddess, for it is she who chooses her mortal consort.

Another unusual aspect of *Táin Bó Fróech* is the abrupt change in the tone of the story after Fróech and Findabair have been "cleared" to marry. This is the point at which we would expect the couple to unite, but due to Otherworldly intervention (the message from Fróech's divine mother regarding the theft of his supernatural cattle), Fróech and Findabair do not have the opportunity to sleep together. Fróech's mother tells him that his wife has been abducted, and a quest must be undertaken in order to retrieve her. This act changes the course and tone of the narrative dramatically. Prior to the abduction, Fróech states that there was no treasure he would not give to obtain Findabair. After the abduction, he says several times that he is not sure he trusts her. Why should the abduction of the woman (who is the victim of the act) cast a shadow on her trustworthiness? Is Fróech concerned that she will sleep with another king? The answers to these and other puzzling questions can be answered by looking at stories associated with themes of betrayal and distrust in medieval Welsh literature.

A well-known female figure from the Celtic literary corpus who was associated with abduction and mistrust is *Guinevere*. In Middle Welsh her name was spelled *Gwenhwyfar*, which in early Welsh was written *Guinhuiuar* (denoting the name or title *Guenhuibar*). This name also means "white/ blessed" "phantom/supernatural being," and is cognate with the Irish name Findabair.[11] Both women were sometimes portrayed as paragons of beauty, intelligence and dignity, and at other times associated with mistrust, betrayal and the possible downfall of a king (Ailill, in the case of Findabair, and Arthur, in the case of Guinevere). Like Findabair, assertions about Gwenhwyfar's character degenerate as her story progresses.

In the earliest sources, Gwenhwyfar is generally portrayed in positive terms. In the 11th century Welsh tale *Culhwch ac Olwen* (one of our earliest sources of information concerning native perceptions about Arthur), Gwenhwyfar heads a list of the "leading ladies" of the island of Britain. She is also counted amongst the things that Arthur valued most.[12] Gwenhwyfar is mentioned several times in the *Triads of Britain*, a collection of traditional lore presented in "triads" or groups of three. Although preserved in manuscripts from the 13th century onwards, Rachel Bromwich states that the contents of the triads "bear marks of a high antiquity; and those in the oldest collections must be regarded as embodying much genuine early tradition, in however mutilated and fragmentary a manner."[13] Triad No. 56 records the names of "Arthur's Three Great Queens," three women all named Gwenhwyfar.[14] Mythological characters with three names or aspects abound in Celtic tradition. In some cases (as with the Irish goddess *Bríg*), this triplism manifests as three persons or siblings all with the same name.[15]

Gwenhwyfar is also mentioned in a story embedded in Triad No. 53 ("The Three Harmful Blows of the Island of Britain"). In this episode, a figure named *Gwenhwyfach* was said to have struck Gwenhwyfar, an action that resulted in the famous Battle of Camlan.[16] In *Culhwch and Olwen*, Gwenhwyfach is said to be Gwenhwyfar's sister, and she is listed after her more famous sister in an enumeration of the "leading ladies" of the island.[17] The battle of Camlan is referred to in Triad No. 84 as one of the "Three Futile Battles of the Island of Britain" (and here noted as the worst of these futile conflicts). In this triad the cause of the battle was said to be a quarrel between the two sisters Gwenhwyfar and Gwenhwyfach. Gwenhwyfach does not appear elsewhere, to my knowledge, and it is possible that she is a fictional doublet of Gwenhwyfar, and that the story as it appears in these triads may be artificial.[18]

Following Ifor Williams, Bromwich mentions the possibility that *Medrawt* (later known as Mordred) might be the figure intended here, as the person who struck Gwenhwyfar (a story found elsewhere). However, she points out that there is no evidence that Medrawd's treachery formed any part of Welsh tradition prior to the publication of Geoffrey of Monmouth's *Historia Regum Brittaniae* ("The History of the Kings of Britain") in 1136, a popular work which was compiled from some native Welsh elements with a great deal of foreign, borrowed and fabricated material. While Mordred is depicted as a disloyal and unlikeable character in later sources, earlier Welsh bardic references to him seem to indicate that the contrary was the case in earlier times.[19]

Another attack on Gwenhwyfar is mentioned in Triad No. 54, the "Three Unrestrained Ravagings of the Island of Britain." The first ravaging occurred when Arthur's nephew Medrawd entered his uncle's court in Cornwall and left no food or drink unconsumed. Following this affront, he dragged Gwenhwyfar from her royal chair and struck a blow upon her. The second ravaging consisted of Arthur's response: going to Medrawd's court and consuming all of his food and drink. Strangely, no mention is made of a reprisal specifically pertaining to the affronts to Gwenhwyfar.[20]

Up to this point, the only negative associations pertaining to Gwenhwyfar consist of affronts to her royal person (which of course may also be read as challenges to Arthur and his sovereignty). However, in another triad we encounter a reference to the story that Gwenhwyfar betrayed Arthur. This occurs in Triad No. 80, where three women (*Essylt, Penarwen* and *Bun*) are listed as the "Three Faithless Wives of the Isle of Britain." Unusually, this "triad" has been appended with a fourth component at the end: "and one was more faithless than those three: Gwenhwyfar, wife of Arthur, since she shamed a better man than any of them."[21] This fourth statement may be an artificial and later addition, perhaps influenced by the work of Geoffrey of Monmouth.[22]

In the Triads of Britain, traditions pertaining to women are featured in Triads No. 55–58, 66, and 78–80, which are grouped together in *Peniarth* 47 as *Trioedd y Gwragedd,* "Triads of the Women."[23] *Peniarth* 47 and 50, although preserved in manuscripts dating to the 15th c., derive from a source closer to *Peniarth* 16 (the oldest collection of triads) than the *Red Book of Hergest* (c. 1400).[24] Certain linguistic considerations suggest that Triads No. 56–58 are the oldest of the group, and these triads (which relate to famous or noteworthy women) contain the names of Arthur's three mistresses, the three Amazons of the Island of Britain, and the reference to the Three Great Queens of Arthur.[25] Triads No. 53 and 54 (which refer to Gwenhwyfar's mistreatment by her sister and Mordred) and Triad No. 80 (which appends Gwenhwyfar in a rather artificial manner to the list of the Three Faithless Wives of Britain) may therefore represent a later tradition than Triad No. 56 (the "Three Great Queens of Arthur").

It is important to recognize that the theme of Gwenhwyfar's betrayal first takes on its full and most familiar form in Geoffrey of Monmouth's work. He has Arthur marry Guinevere, "the loveliest woman in the whole island" (echoing a similar tradition from the Triads). Arthur then leaves on a great campaign, entrusting the security of Britain to his nephew Mordred and his queen. Later Arthur is informed that his nephew was wearing his crown "in tyranny and treachery" and that the queen had broken her marriage vows and joined Mordred in "unconscionable lust." Geoffrey writes that he would not speak on this "deplorable topic" but for its alleged inclusion in a mysterious "British book" he often alludes to (but whose existence may well be fictional), as well as from reportedly having heard the tale from Walter of Oxford.[26]

This tale of adultery has all the earmarks of hearsay, if not outright invention, and amongst his many fabrications, Geoffrey seems to go to special efforts to justify this particular story. Not surprisingly, this tale of intrigue proved immensely popular, and the new themes of adultery and betrayal were taken up by later authors, including Wace, Layamon, Chrétien de Troyes and Malory. Although Guinevere was still portrayed as a worthy queen in these sources, each author (to varying degrees) takes up the theme of adultery and continues to elaborate upon it. However, the possibility that Guinevere was originally considered a positive character in native Welsh tradition is supported by the fact that the name Gwenhwyfar was not an uncommon name in late Medieval Wales.[27]

In order to ascertain the original identity and character of Gwenhwyfar, it may be useful to revisit the earliest sources in which she is mentioned, which include *Culhwch and Olwen* and *The Triads of Britain*. In the Triads, Gwenhwyfar is referred to as one of Arthur's Three Great Queens (*Teir Prif Rhiain Arthur*). She is similarly referred to as a queen (*penn rhianed yr ynys hon,* "Chief Queen in this island") in *Culhwch and Olwen*, as well as in the later Romances of *Owein, Peredur* and *Gereint*.[28] However, Guinevere is not referred to as Arthur's queen *per se* by the 12th. c. *Gogynfeirdd* (medieval poets who sang the praises of Welsh princes). This may be explained by the fact that although in Modern Welsh the meaning of *rhiain* is no longer "queen," but "maiden" or "lady," there are a few examples in Middle Welsh in which the word retained its original meaning.[29] Another anomaly is the fact that Gwenhwyfar is not mentioned at all in *Peniarth* 16, which contains the oldest collection of triads. However, as we have seen above, *Peniarth* 47 and 50 (in which she does figure) derive from a source closer to *Peniarth* 16 than does the *Red Book of Hergest*.[30]

Evidence to support a pre–Geoffrey tradition that Gwenhwyfar was Arthur's consort comes from a well-known passage in the *Vita Gildae* by *Caradog* of *Llancarfan*. The story relates how Gildas arrived in Glastonbury at a time when a certain King *Melwas* was reigning "in the summer country" (probably an allusion to Somerset, the county in which Glastonbury is situated). Gwenhwyfar had been violated and carried off by the "wicked king." Arthur and his host searched for her for a year, after which they prepared to besiege Glastonbury. Gildas stepped between the contending hosts of the two rivals and advised Melwas to return the "ravished lady."[31]

The tradition that Gwenhwyfar was abducted by Melwas was known to the famous Welsh poet *Dafydd ap Gwilym* and other bardic sources of a similar date.[32] In Geoffrey's hands the abductor is given as Modred (or Medrawd in the *Bruts*). Other writers freely altered the identity of the transgressor. He appears as *Valerin* in Ulrich's *Lanzelet, Gasozein* in *Diu Crone*, and *Lancelot* in the Vulgate cycles. There are also episodes in *Peredur* and various *Perceval* romances in which a figure referred to as the "Red Knight" insults Gwenhwyfar by splashing wine in her face.[33]

As we can see, abduction tales are found in both Irish and Welsh sources. Scholars have noted similarities between certain themes in the Arthurian and Fenian cycles of tales. One well-known and relevant exemplar is the abduction of Finn's wife Grainne by his nephew Diarmid (a story which also features a salmon and a rowan branch). This may support the possibility that the abduction of Arthur's wife by his nephew is a Welsh version of a well-known (or well-traveled) narrative motif.[34]

However, early sources do not claim that Mordred was Arthur's enemy (or his nephew). In fact, a number of bardic references refer to him as a paragon of courtesy and valour.[35] Be that as it may, a natural rivalry may have existed between Arthur (a king with no living heir, in some tales) and his sister's sons (Mordred is said to be the son of Arthur's sister in Geoffrey's work).[36]

The role of the "sister's son" is very important in Celtic culture. In one common pattern of descent, the descendants of a grandfather—which include his sons and their sons, as well as the sons of his daughters—may have a claim to his title or position. Therefore Arthur's nephews—in this case, his sister's sons—could be his supporters or his rivals. The reason for the inclusion of the sister's sons is actually very practical. A king's offspring may be sired by him, with his queen. However, if his wife is secretly unfaithful, her offspring could be fathered by someone else, perhaps someone not of noble birth or not of an appropriate lineage. But, the sons of the king's sister (who is also a member of the royal or noble lineage) are clearly *her* offspring, regardless of who the father might be. Therefore, they are counted as part of the family lineage, and later may vie for the throne or other position held by their uncle.[37]

With a variety of possible rivals and/or heirs, there are numerous scenarios which might be played out. A nephew could ally himself with his uncle and hope for a position in his entourage. Or, he might set himself up as a rival to his uncle. Another of Arthur's nephews in the medieval literature was Gawain. He is listed before Mordred in Geoffrey's work, which may suggest that he was the older brother. If so, he may have been considered first, before his younger brother, for a future position of power. Gawain is almost invariably described in very positive terms in the narratives. If this suggested scenario is correct, this could have set the scene for desperate or aggressive actions on the part of Mordred. This aggression plays out in Triad No. 51, where Medrawd is listed as one of (and the worst of) the "Three Dishonoured Men in the Island of Britain." In this triad, Arthur is involved in a military struggle with the emperor of Rome, leaving Medrawd in charge of his realm. Interestingly, the text says that Arthur's army traveled beyond the mountains of Mynneu (the Alps). This is the same boundary that Fróech had to traverse in order to retrieve his wife.[38]

One additional abduction tale associated with Arthur must also be considered. This is a well-known episode from *Culhwch and Olwen* in which *Creiddylad*, daughter of *Lludd Llawereint* ("Lludd Silver-Hand") goes off with one suitor (*Gwythyr* son of *Greidawl*), but is abducted by another (the supernatural figure *Gwynn ap Nudd*). The two rivals engage in battle, with Gwynn emerging as the victor. Arthur summons Gwynn to him, and (like Gildas) makes peace between the two rivals. Arthur further makes a judgment that the woman is to be left unmolested in her father's house, and that the two suitors must battle for her hand every year on the first of May, from that day until Judgment Day. The suitor who prevailed on Judgment Day would win the woman's hand.[39]

Here we should note that the names *Gwynn* and *Finn* are cognate, and that in one source Finn was said to be a descendant of a figure by the name of *Nuadu*, a name cognate with that of *Nudd*. Additionally, Nuadu's epithet *Argetlám* ("Silver-Hand") is cognate with the name of Creiddylad's father, *Llawereint*.[40] It is also interesting to note the ritualistic time period of one year mentioned in the tale, as well as in the story of Gwenhwyfar's abduction by Melwas, perhaps suggesting some sort of seasonal myth. This time period also figures in the First Branch of the Mabinogi, where the woman *Rhiannon* complains to *Pwyll* that she is being given to a man against her will. The man's name is *Gwawl,* which is cognate with Old Irish *fál* (seen in the name of the *Lia Fáil,* a stone used to determine kingship). In the story Rhiannon states that she prefers to be with Pwyll, and instructs him to meet with her in one year's time.[41]

Who are these women, and why are they being abducted? In most sources, Gwenhwyfar is described as Arthur's queen (*rhiain*), a word which also appears in the name of the Welsh figure of *Rhiannon* ("Divine Queen") and which is cognate with Old Irish *ríga(i)n* "queen, noble lady."[42] The confusion about the identity of these women is perhaps best illuminated by noting the reference in the Triads to the "Three Great Queens" of Arthur, and similar references to "Three Great Queens" from early Irish tradition. Irish sources refer to a trio of divine sisters (*An Mórrígan, Macha* and *Nemain*) who were collectively known as *na Mórrígna,* "The Great Queens." All three sisters were, in various sources, referred to by the same epithet: *Badb,* "scald-crow."[43] These Irish women are manifestations of the Goddess of Sovereignty, a figure whom the king must successfully recognize, woo or impress, and unite with, in order for his reign to be successful and for the land and the people to prosper.[44] It can be no mere coincidence that these Irish divinities, like the three women all named Gwenhwyfar, were referred to as "The Three Great Queens" of their respective islands.

When the Goddess of Sovereignty enters into relationship with a mortal king, she is not his queen, but a self-appointed lover and supporter. The confusion in literary sources concerning these women's roles as queen or consort (a confusion which only increases with time) demonstrates that the original identity of these figures had become increasingly obscured. Far from being a consenting adultress, a hapless victim, or weak-willed partner, Gwenhwyfar instead represents a Brythonic manifestation of the Goddess of Sovereignty. Over time, the sexual aspects of the Goddess of Sovereignty's role as empowering benefactor became confused and transmuted into tales of promiscuity, adultery and betrayal. Originally it was understood that the Goddess had many partners, that she considered, judged, chose, blessed and empowered many men. Thus it was said of Queen *Medb* (who many perceive as a reflex of the Sovereignty Goddess, albeit in altered form), that she was never with one man without another one waiting in the wings. This is an acknowledgment of power, not promiscuity. Edel Bhreathnach writes about the alteration from goddess to queen:

> Such a radical change to perceptions of kingship might have led to the complete purging of the *banfheis,* the physical mating of the land goddess and the king, and the belief system that accompanied this ceremony. However, as with much of early Irish culture, goddess and ritual were transformed but not obliterated. Old and Middle Irish literature is replete with allusions to sovereignty goddesses and strong elements of their cultic and fecund, often promiscuous, nature. These goddesses are often relegated to women subject to kings as their spouses or lovers, or are attested as historic queens who retain the personification of sovereignty in personal names such as Eithne, Gormfhlaith or even Temair.[45]

In early written sources, men intentionally sought union with (and the empowerment of) the Goddess of Sovereignty. Like Fróech, the men may seek her blessings, but it is she who decides which man is worthy of her attentions and empowerment (as well as with which man she will unite). In later tales, the female figure becomes something to attain in a purely physical way. But to try and abduct or control the Goddess of Sovereignty is folly, for any connection with her will be her decision alone. Indeed, in *Táin Bó Fróech* this is precisely what is stated by Findabair. When Fróech asks her to run off with him she refuses, citing her lineage and the importance of receiving proper tribute from him. She says, "You are not so poor that you cannot get me from my people, and it will be my choice to go with you, for it is you I have loved."[46] Here we should also recall that it was Rhiannon's choice to visit Pwyll on account of the love she bore him.[47]

One of the most prominent elements associated with the Goddess of Sovereignty is the theme of her sexual union with the rightful king. So prevalent was this imagery that the word *feis* ("spending the night, sleeping") was used in connection with a ritual used to elect a king (*tarbfeis*), as well as other festivals held by or presided over by kings (such as the *Feis Temra*). Likewise, the king's inauguration was referred to by the term *banais ríg* (< *ban* "woman" + *feis*).[48] No *feis* with Findabair was permitted for Fróech, however, until he had proven himself. This too is a common theme in stories pertaining to the Sovereignty Goddess. The candidate is chosen by the Goddess and tested prior to being installed. Findabair's independent decision-making and actions, and her rescue of Fróech, must certainly be interpreted as her intention to support him.

The gift of a sword, presented to the man by a female figure, is also noteworthy, for it is with this gift that the male figure can defend and ultimately empower himself. This theme is reflected in tales associated with Arthur's famous sword, which is known as *Caladfwlch* in *Culhwch and Olwen,* later referred to as *Caliburn,* and finally *Excalibur.*[49] It is undoubtedly of great significance that Fróech was rescued with a sword given to him by a noble/divine woman in a body of water. Votive offerings into bodies of water were widespread throughout Celtic territories and frequently included offerings of weapons. These bodies of water were almost invariably perceived of as the abode of female divinities. Offerings of swords were extremely common, especially in Britain, suggesting a viable and ancient origin for the motif.[50] The connection between sacred or empowered weapons, and divine or legendary female figures, also played out in later Arthurian tales. In Malory's work, the sword Excalibur is returned to the Lady of the Lake by being thrown into a body of water.[51]

The candidate elect for the position of king or ruler is also associated with immersion in liquids in a more ritualized setting. In *Táin Bó Fróech,* after the young man has rescued himself from the pool with the sword, Ailill and Medb order a special bath to be made for him. The bath consisted of a broth of fresh bacon with the flesh of a heifer chopped up in it. An adze and an axe were also added to the bath.[52] In the 12th c., Giraldus Cambrensis (Gerald of Wales) mentions a ritual bath associated with an inauguration ritual in northern Ireland. In the ceremony, the king allegedly had intercourse with a white mare, which was then killed and prepared as a ritual meal. A bath was prepared for the king in the same water, and he sat in the bath and also drank the broth.[53] Fróech's bath takes place after Ailill and Medb have accepted him as their daughter's consort (and potentially as the future king). Fróech's meat-infused bath is reminiscent of the Irish inauguration rite, which is associated with Dumézil's first function in Indo-European cultural settings: kingship. Fróech's bath also included an axe and an adze, symbolic of the second and third functions (warriorship and fertility). It is interesting to note that a cup, an axe and an adze also feature in a Scythian origin myth associated with kingship, as recorded by Herodotus.[54]

Taking all of this into consideration, I suggest that *Findabair* and *Gwenhwyfar,* both of whose names mean "Bright or Blessed Supernatural Being," are figures whose original identity and significance as manifestations of the Sovereignty Goddess were transmuted into representations of mortal women associated with kingship.[55] Their confusing literary nature—worthy consort and untrustworthy queen—can be more easily understood in light of this alteration of character and identity. These divine women do sleep with men other than their husbands, but not because they are disloyal or victims of abduction. Originally respected and sought after as divine figures who could empower a king, over time the women become objects to acquire or control. What all of the abductors and contenders fail to realize is that it is the choice of the woman/Goddess which man she will support and bless with her presence and power. She cannot be obtained by force, and the only way to win her favor is through honorable deeds and nobleness of character. It is not the men who choose the woman, but the Sovereignty Goddess who chooses them.

6

Mistress of the Wild Things:
Abundance and Feminine Power in Early Irish Sources

A number of early Irish literary sources refer to a female figure by the name of Flidais, an intriguing but relatively under-explored character who received some attention in early German academic sources,[1] but less so in recent studies.[2] Flidais is perhaps most well-known from *Táin Bó Flidais* (TBF), an early Irish tale which has survived in two versions, a short version found in *Lebor na hUidri* (LU), The Book of Leinster (LL) and Egerton 1782, and a longer, more detailed (but incomplete) account in the Yellow Book of Lecan.[3] The tale is considered to be a preliminary tale (*remscéla*) to *Táin Bó Cuailgne* (TBC), perhaps due to Flidais' connection with the hero Fergus mac Róich, as well as the tradition that she was the owner of supernatural cattle.[4] A later variant of the tale, probably somewhat politically motivated, occurs in the 16th century Glenmasan manuscript and a 17th century manuscript of the Royal Irish Academy (B. IV.1).[5]

Fergus was one of the greatest of the Ulster heroes, and his exploits are detailed in a number of early Irish tales. In addition to these, he was credited with rising from his grave, as mighty as he was in life, to recite the story of *Táin Bó Cuailgne* in its entirety to the poet Senchán Torpeist. Originally a king of Ulster and resident at Emain Macha, he fell in love with Ness, the daughter of Eochaid Sálbuide. She agreed to marry him only on condition that her son from a previous encounter, Conchobar mac Nessa, was allowed to sit on the throne for one year. Fergus agreed and became Conchobar's foster-father. However, Ness connived with the nobles to prevent Fergus' return to the throne. In another story, Fergus encouraged the sons of Uisnech to return with Deirdre from Scotland, where she had fled from Conchobar who desired her. In spite of his having given a pledge for their safety, Conchobar murders the three brothers and takes Deirdre for himself. Outraged,

Fergus returns and burns Emain Macha to the ground. He and his warriors set out for Cruachan, where they join forces with Queen Medb and her husband Ailill in Connacht. In stories outside of TBC, Fergus and Medb are sometimes depicted in an amorous affair. However, his most frequently cited consort is Flidais.[6]

The Irish texts of *Táin Bó Flidais* from LL, LU and Egerton 1782, as well as a translation of the LU version of the tale, were provided by Windisch in *Irische Texte* II.[7] These were used as source materials in Leahy's early 20th century *Heroic Romances of Ireland*. Leahy's notes state that he followed Windisch's translation fairly closely, providing a literal translation of the text, with occasional insertions from LL (including the first part of the story, which is missing in LU) and a few passages from the other manuscripts (which he perceived to be generally in agreement with LU).[8]

In spite of his clumsy attempts to set the story into verse form, and numerous English archaisms, prior to the publication of this book, Leahy's translation (which is over a century old) was the only accessible published English translation of TBF.[9] While it is beyond the scope of this chapter to provide a new annotated edition of TBF, in the version which follows I have made modifications to Leahy's translations and modernized numerous archaisms, many of which obscured the meaning of the text. I have also differentiated between two primary characters, Ailill Finn (husband of Flidais) and Ailill mac Mata (husband of Medb), by spelling Ailill Finn's name "Oilill," in order to remedy the confusion of two kings both named Ailill. Here, then, is the story of Táin Bó Flidais.

Táin Bó Flidais

Flidais was the wife of Oilill Finn in the territory of Kerry. She loved Fergus mac Róich on account of the glorious tales about him, and messengers always went from her to him at the end of each week. When Fergus went to Connacht, he brought this matter before Ailill mac Mata. "What shall I do in this matter?" said Fergus. "It is hard for me to lay bare your land, as there would be a loss of honour and reknown to you as a result."

"Yes, what shall we do in this matter?" said Ailill. "We will consider this in counsel with Medb."

"One of us should go to Oilill Finn, so that he may help us," said Medb. "And as this involves a meeting of someone with him, there is no reason why it should not be yourself that goes to him, Fergus: the gift will be all the better for that."

Fergus set out then, with thirty men, including the two Ferguses (Fergus mac Róg and Fergus mac Oen-lama) and Dubhtach, until they arrived at the

Ford of Fenna in the north of the lands of Kerry. They go to the stronghold and welcome is brought to them.

"What brings you here?" said Oilill Finn. "We ourselves had the intention of staying with you on a visit, for we have a quarrel with Aillill mac Mata. If it was one of your people who had the quarrel, that person would stay with me until they had made their peace. However, you shall not stay with me," said Oilill Finn, "for it has been told to me that my wife loves you."

"If we shall not stay with you, we must have a gift of cows," said Fergus, "for a great need lies upon us: the sustenance of the troop of men who have gone with me into exile from Ulster."

"You will carry off no such gift from me," said Oilill, "because you are not staying with me on a visit. People will say that it is to keep my wife that I gave you what you asked. I will, however, give your company one ox and some bacon to help them, if such is your pleasure."

"I will not eat your food," said Fergus, "because I can get no gift of honour from you."

"Out of my house with you all, then," said Oilill.

"That shall be," said Fergus. "We will not begin to lay siege to you." They all take themselves outside.

"Let a man come at once to fight me beside a ford at the gate of this stronghold," said Fergus.

"For the sake of my honour, that will not be refused," said Oilill. "I will not hand the strife over to another; I will go myself." So Oilill went up against Fergus at the ford.

"Which of us, O Dubhtach, shall encounter this man?" said Fergus.

"I will go," said Dubhtach, "for I am younger and keener than you are." Dubhtach went against Oilill. He thrust a spear through Oilill Finn so that it went through his two thighs. Oilill hurled a javelin at Dubhtach, so that he drove the spear right through him and out the other side. Fergus threw his shield over Dubhtach. Oilill thrust his spear at Fergus' shield so that he drove the shaft right through it.

Then Fergus mac Oen-Lama comes by. He holds a shield in front of Fergus. Oilill struck his spear upon the shield so that it was forced right through it. Fergus leapt so that he lay there on top of his companions. Flidais comes by from the stronghold and throws her cloak over the three.

Fergus' people take flight, and Oilill pursues them. There remained behind twenty men slain by him. However, seven escape to Cruachan Aí, where they tell the whole story to Ailill and Medb. Ailill and Medb arise, and the nobles of Connacht and the exiles from Ulster with them. They march into the territory of Kerry Aí with their troops, as far as the Ford of Fenna.

Meanwhile the wounded men were being cared for by Flidais in the stronghold, and their healing was undertaken by her. Then the troops arrive at the stronghold. Oilill Finn is summoned to Ailill mac Mata, to come to a conference with him outside of the stronghold.

"I will not go," said Oilill, "the pride and arrogance of that man there is great."

However, it was for a peaceful meeting that Ailill had come to Oilill Finn, both so that he might save Fergus (as it was right he should), and so that he might afterwards make peace with Oilill Finn, according to the will of the nobles of Connacht.

The wounded men were brought out of the castle on handbarrows so that they might be cared for by their own people. Then the men attack Oilill Finn. While they are storming the stronghold, they could not get hold of him. For a full week it was thus with them. Seven times twenty heroes from among the nobles of Connacht fell during the time that they tried to storm the stronghold of Oilill Finn.

"It was with no good omen that you came to this fortress," said Bricriu.

"True indeed, is the word that is spoken," said Ailill. "The expedition is bad for the honour of the Ulstermen, in that their three heroes fall, and they do not take vengeance for them. Each one of the three was a pillar of war, yet not a single man has fallen at the hands of one of those three. Truly these heroes are great to be under such "wisps of straw" as attack the men of this stronghold. It is most worthy of scorn that one man has wounded you three!"

"Woe is me," said Bricriu. "Long is the length upon the ground of my "popa" Fergus, since one man in single combat laid him low."

And so the champions of Ulster arise, naked as they were, and make a strong and obstinate attack in their rage and the might of their violence, so that they forced the outer gateway until it was in the middle of the stronghold. The men of Connacht go in beside them. They storm the stronghold with great might against the valiant warriors who were there. A wild, pitiless battle is fought between them, and each man began to strike out against the other and destroy him.

Then, after they were weary from wounding and overcoming one another, the people of the castle were overthrown. The Ulstermen slew seven hundred warriors there in the stronghold, including Oilill Finn and thirty of his sons, Amalgaid the Good, Núado, Fiacho Muinmethan, Corpre Cromm, Ailill from Brefne, the three Oengus Bodbgnai, the three Eochaid of Irross Donann, the seven Breslene from Aí, and the fifty Domnall.

For the assembly of the Gamanrad were with Oilill, as well as each of the men of Domnan who had bidden himself to come to him to aid him. They were in the same place, assembled in the stronghold, for they knew that the exiles from Ulster and Ailill and Medb with their army would come to demand the surrender of Fergus, for Fergus was under their protection. This was the third group of heroes in Ireland, namely the Clan Gamanrad of Irross

Donnan, the peninsula of Donnann. The other two were the Clan Dédad in Temair Luachra and the Clan Rudraige in Emain Macha. But the other two clans were destroyed by the Clan Rudraige.

The men of Ulster arise, and with them the people of Ailill and Medb, and they laid waste to the stronghold. They take Flidais out of the fortress with them, and carry off the women of the stronghold as captives. They take with them all the costly things and treasures that were there: gold and silver, horns and drinking cups, keys and vats, and garments of every color. And they take what there was of cattle, including one hundred milk-cows, one hundred and forty oxen, and three thousand small cattle.

And after these things had been done, Flidais went to Fergus mac Róich, according to the decree of Ailill and Medb, so that they might have sustenance [from her herds] on the occasion of the Raid of the Cows of Cuailgne. As a result of this, Flidais used to support the men of Ireland from the produce of her cows each seventh day, in order that during the raid she might provide them with the means of life. This then was the Herd of Flidais.

As a result of all this, Flidais went with Fergus to his home, and he received the lordship of a part of Ulster, Mag Muirthemne, along with lands that had been in the possession of Cú Chulainn son of Sualtam. After some time, Flidais died at Trag Bali, and the state of Fergus' household was none the better for that. For she used to provide for all of his needs, whatsoever they might be.

Fergus himself died some time later, in the land of Connacht, after the death of his wife. He had gone there to obtain knowledge of a story. For in order to cheer himself, and to fetch home a grant of cows from Ailill and Medb, he had gone westwards to Cruachan. So it was in consequence of his journey that he found his death in the west, through the jealousy of Ailill. This, then, is the story of the Táin Bó Flidais, which is among the preludes of the Táin Bó Cuailgne.

The Independent Goddess

Early Irish literature is full of tales in which somebody wants something that is in the possession of someone else—be it land, cattle, a woman, magical objects or weapons, power or kingship—and they engage in battle, deception, magic or cunning in order to obtain it. At first glance, Oilill Finn seems like just another casualty in the long list of those who were on the losing end of things. Was his only crime having a wife that loved another? Why was this enormous assault visited upon him and his people?

If we look back at Oilill's words (and words matter a great deal in these stories), he states that the normal procedure for resolving a dispute is that the aggrieved party visits the other party, who allows them to stay "for a visit" (i.e., receive hospitality) until they had made peace. In other words, if someone has a quarrel with you, they come to you to peacefully resolve the issue, and you in turn allow them to stay with you during the process of resolving that dispute. After all, the aggrieved party may have travelled some distance to meet with you and may be suffering from some loss or injury as well.

The process described by Oilill seems to outline his understanding of how social relations should be conducted (at least according to this story). What does early Irish law have to say about these matters? Fergus Kelly writes that a great deal of importance is attached to the duty of hospitality in the laws, the wisdom-texts and the sagas. The *briugu* or "hospitaller" attained high status through his capacity to provide hospitality to all free members of society. Even base clients were under obligation to provide a feast for their lord and his retinue during the winter circuiting and hosting season.[10]

To some extent, the obligation to provide hospitality fell upon all householders. To refuse food and shelter to those to whom it was due was to be guilty of the offense of *esáin*, literally "driving away" (also referred to as *etech* "refusal"). This offense required compensation appropriate to the rank of the offended person. One source stated that the house from which everybody is refused hospitality forfeits its *dire*, the payment which would otherwise be made in the event of its destruction. While there were some limits on the amount of hospitality that could be expected to be provided by certain grades of person (based on their ability to do so), Heptad 13 states that a king is obliged to provide hospitality to a law-abiding person, but not to his retinue. In some circumstances, hospitality had to be refused. For example, a criminal could not be fed or protected.[11]

By refusing to allow Fergus to stay with him, Oilill was guilty of *esáin*, which would require compensation to be paid appropriate to Fergus' rank. Since no hospitality or compensation was given, Fergus attacked Oilill's stronghold and took things of value. Oilill may have also forfeited his *dire* by refusing hospitality to everybody in Fergus' party, although we do not know if that was his usual behavior. While a king was obliged to provide hospitality to a law-abiding person, but not to his retinue, Oilill does the exact opposite: Fergus was refused, but a token subsidy of an ox and some bacon was offered to Fergus' men (an action which may have been intended as an insult).

Another possibility is that Oilill considered Fergus to be a criminal, someone who by law he must not feed or protect. However, as far as we can tell, Fergus' only crime was to have received messages of amorous intent from Oilill's wife. The story does not say if Fergus reciprocated those messages. In fact, he seems not to know what to do about the whole affair and goes to confer with Ailill and Medb. At this stage, nothing overt has taken place, as far as we can tell. Fergus heeds Medb's advice to go in person to speak with Oilill. We do not know if means to simply clear the air, or whether he has come to ask for Flidais. His actions at the beginning of the story certainly seem non-aggressive.

Fergus is at first welcomed at Oilill's stronghold, but he is never given a chance to speak and explain the purpose of his visit. Oilill does ask him why he has come, but immediately outlines the usual method for resolving disputes and bluntly refuses that process to Fergus, due to rumors he has heard. Whatever Fergus' original intentions were, he is never given an opportunity to voice them or discuss potential options. Later in the story, Oilill also refuses an invitation to engage in a peaceful discussion with Ailill mac Mata. The insults to Fergus lead to violence, and Oilill eventually loses all.

What if Fergus' intention had in fact been to ask for Flidais, to come to some arrangement with Oilill? If the marriage was a loveless one, and/or if Fergus offered a substantial bride-price, perhaps they would have come to a peaceful agreement. If this was Fergus' intention, he never had a chance to explain. As a result of the conflict that ensues, Flidais is taken from Oilill's stronghold. Since she had already expressed her romantic interest in Fergus, we can't really say she that was taken away by force. As we saw in the previous chapter, there were many types of sexual union recognized in early Irish law, including those resulting from abduction.

In one type of union, the woman allows herself to be abducted without her kin's consent. In another type, the woman goes away openly with the man but is not given by her kin.[12] While these two types of legally recognized forms of union may have originally been conceived of as pertaining to unmarried women, it seems they could also apply to married women. Some law-texts seem to hold a hard line towards women who leave their husband without justification (and there were many legal reasons why she could do so). If there was no just cause for a woman to leave her husband, Heptad 51 considers her "an absconder from the law of marriage." Such a woman would have no rank in society and could not be harbored or protected by anyone.[13] This would have been a heavy penalty for Flidais had she simply left Oilill, and had he not been guilty of refusing hospitality.

Flidais makes only a few short appearances in the tale, but her actions are highly significant. It is she who sets the tale in motion by sending love messages to Fergus. When the three Ulstermen are struggling in single combat against her husband, Flidais emerges from the stronghold and throws her cloak over them. By this simple action, she independently leaves the protection of her husband's domain and makes a symbolic statement. Later in the tale Flidais cares for the wounded and undertakes their healing. Near the end of the story we find out that she owns an enormous number of cattle. She leaves with Fergus and supports the men of Ireland with the produce of her herds so that during the Cattle Raid of Cooley she could provide them with the means of life.

It is interesting to see a female figure who owns so much cattle, which were the basis of wealth in early Irish society. In early Irish law, a woman's ability to own property was somewhat limited. There were situations in which a woman could inherit valuables from her father if he had no sons, but she could not usually inherit land (other than a life-interest in it). Also, normally she could not pass land on to her husband or sons, for it reverted back to her kin-group upon her death. However, if her husband was an alien (such as a Briton), someone who would have no land in the túath, she could pass a specified amount of land on to her son. By virtue of owning land, a female heir had more legal rights than other women. And if her inherited land was occupied by somebody else in defiance of her lawful claim, she could undertake a set of procedures known as *tellach* (or in this case, *ban-tellach*) in order to legally assert her claim and take over the land.[14]

A woman's rights were somewhat different in relation to moveable property like cattle, the most common form of "currency." A woman was not typically capable of sale, purchase, contract or transaction without the authorization of her father, husband or other legal guardian. She did have the right to give away items of her own personal property as a pledge on behalf of another, including her embroidery needle, workbag or dress. However, she could not give cattle, horses, silver, gold, copper or bronze without her husband's permission. In a marriage of equal ("joint") property, either partner could dissolve a contract made by the other, except in the case of certain essential or beneficial contracts. However, if a woman married a landless man or a stranger from another túath, or if it was she who brought the majority of wealth to the marriage, the normal roles of husband and wife were reversed and the woman made the decisions in the marriage.[15]

A woman's social role and rights were increased if she was wealthy (through land or cattle) or if she possessed certain skills. Additional rights and honor were afforded to a female wright, a female physician of the túath, women who helped make peace or negotiated for hostages in conflict situations, women who were "abundant in miracles," and "the woman revered by the túath." These women might count themselves as not being dependent upon a husband. Her award in cases of legal injury was assessed by the judge of the túath in relation to the woman's dignity (*míad*) and her possessions.[16] We have seen that Flidais possessed skills as a healer. The ownership of an enormous herd of cattle would have given her additional legal rights and social standing, and she might therefore be able to consider herself not dependent upon a husband. Perhaps these issues came into play in Flidais' choice to send messages of love to another man—because she was powerful and independent enough to do so.

In this text, Flidais appears to have associations with kingship, battle, protection, healing, wealth and abundance. There is another attribute that must be noted as well: fertility and sexuality. Flidais is often said to be most well-known from her connection with Fergus, a hero whose legendary attributes of strength and virility are mentioned in *Taín Bó Cuailgne* and other texts.[17] Fergus' virility was such that it was said he required seven women to satisfy him in the absence of his supernatural wife Flidais.[18] While this is generally regarded as evidence of Fergus' sexual potency, it could just as well be interpreted as a testimony to the sexual powers of Flidais.

Fergus had three well-known consorts, all of whom were associated with kingship. Ness was the wife of a king and mother of a king. Medb was daughter of a king and wife of a king. Nevertheless, Fergus' actual wife appears to be Flidais. Although wedded to one king, she takes the initiative and chooses another due to his reputation. She walks out of her husband's stronghold unimpeded and throws her cloak over Fergus and his comrades with no apparent repercussions. When Fergus and his entourage finally manage to storm the fortress of her husband, they are not actually rescuing her. When she is taken out of the stronghold she is not a captive, nor has she been abducted. Although the story states that she "went to Fergus" by decree of Ailill and Medb, in truth this was Flidais' own choice and her original intention.

Indeed, some of Flidais' actions and attributes seem to fit those of the well-attested archetype of the Sovereignty Goddess. She is married to one king but is able to choose her next consort. She acts independently of her husband in showing favor to Fergus, and when her husband has been removed from the scene, she leaves with the man she herself has chosen. In addition, Flidais seems to be associated with all three Dumézilian functions: Kingship (First function); Battle (Second function), and Fertility (Third function). Like Gwenhwyfar and Findabair, Flidais may be a manifestation of the Goddess of Sovereignty. As we will see, she exhibits other attributes which associate her with wild creatures and the natural world, that which is beyond the confines of the túath, as well as unique manifestations of feminine power and independence.

The Otherworldly Herds of Flidais

In some texts, Flidais is described as the owner of numerous or remarkable cows or bulls. Elsewhere, she is associated with herds of wild or supernatural cattle or deer. Flidais and her herds are mentioned in the *Túatha Dé Miscellany* (TDM), a brief collection of lore pertaining to the Túatha Dé Danann composed somewhere between 900 and 1100 CE. John Carey suggests that in the form in which the text has survived, it probably belongs to the second half of that period (c. 1000–1100 CE).[19] In TDM, Flidais is mentioned in a significant passage:

> *Flidais dia tá buar Flidais. A cethri ingena: Airden agus Bé Chuille agus Dinann agus Bé Théite.*
>
> Flidais, from whom are [named] the cattle of Flidais. Her four daughters: Airden, Bé Chuille, Dinann and Bé Théite.[20]

Carey writes that the meaning of the phrase *buar Flidais* in TDM is "deer, wild animals," which he states is apparent from a pedigree of the Éoganacht Caisil which mentions both cattle and deer (a reference we will examine below).[21] He also states that this entry accounts for the kenning *buar Flidais* as denoting "deer."[22] Carey concludes that as a result of the references to Flidais which allude to her supernatural character "it seems likely that Flidais was a goddess of wild creatures." He also points out that "it was presumably her animal associations which led L [one of the versions of TDM, contained in The Book of Leinster] to place her at the head of its version of the TDM list (LL 1116–1117)," a position held by Bríg in other versions.[23]

One of the principal concepts expressed in the Túatha Dé Miscellany pertained to two categories which existed within the Túatha Dé Danann: the *áes dána* ("gods of skill") and the *áes trebtha* (those associated with farming, herding and house-holding). Many of the members of the Túatha Dé Danann were associated with skills that were revered in Celtic society. In the text, Lug, Brigid and the divine druid Matha are included in the first group (the *aes dána*), while Flidais and her cattle (as well as various "kings of the animals") are listed in the second category (the *aes trebtha*).[24] In addition to social status, this duality may also reflect a distinction between that which is "inside" and that which exists "outside" of the túath or beyond social norms and conventions. As a figure associated with wild animals (and perhaps the wilderness in general), Flidais may thus be connected with that which is outside the bounds of society.[25]

Another reference to Flidais and her cattle appears in the 11th century Metrical *Dindshenchas,* in a poem pertaining to *Benn Boguine.* In the poem, a valuable supernatural cow has strayed across the River Bann from the divine woman who owns it:

> Flidais was the woman's name,
> daughter of Garb son of Gréssach
> that well-attended generous woman,
> wife of Ailell the Bearded.[26]

The wandering cow gives birth to two calves (a cow and a bull), from whose union a herd of Otherworld cattle are produced. A brindled bull stood at the head of the herd "to face danger for their sake," protecting them from the attack of wolves, tame beasts and hunters. It also apparently defended the herd from the attentions of over-zealous milkmaids, for it was said that "no milk-maid milked them." This may refer to a belief that the produce of supernatural cattle was considered to be unobtainable or taboo, belonging solely to denizens of the Otherworld (not to mention dangerous to obtain).[27]

The poem goes on to say that when the great bull bellowed, the cows of Ireland died from hearing its call, as they were irresistibly drawn towards the Otherworld herd. When a cow belonging to Fiachra mac Niall's foster mother is lured away, he searches all of Ireland for it. He eventually arrives at *Benn Boguine* where he "smote throngs of the chiefest herds," thereby protecting the cows of Ireland from this supernatural threat. Here we can see the potentially dangerous aspects of Flidais' Otherworldly herds.

Cattle belonging to Flidais are referred to in a version of the first recension of *Lebor Gabála*, where Flidais' name is glossed *Flidais, diata buar Flidais,* ("Flidais, from whom are [named] the cattle of Flidais").[28] An association with both cattle and deer occurs in the late Middle Irish source *Cóir Anman*. Here Flidais is said to be the wife of a mortal king named Adamair. Interestingly, the king is identified by the name of his female consort and referred to as *Adamhair Flidais* (perhaps a testament to her power or authority). Carey suggests that the king's name came about due to a reinterpretation or misunderstanding of the phrase *a mathair Flidais* "his mother Flidais."[29]

> Adammair Flidaise Foltcháin, that is, Flidais the queen, (one) of the Túatha Dé Danann, 'tis she was wife of Adammair, son of Fer Cuirp; and from her *Buar Flidaise* ("Flidais" kine") is said, and from her Adammair *Flidaise Foltcháin* ("Flidais Fairhair's Adammair) is said of the king.[30]

Adamair and Flidais were said to have a son, Nia Seaghamain, whose name is fancifully explained as "warrior of deer-treasure." During his reign, "cows and does were milked together," a benefit that his mother bestowed upon him. Elsewhere it states that it was Nia himself by whom "two kinds of cattle were milked: cows and does. Flidais Foltchain was his mother, whose cows were does (*elti*)."[31] However, as milking was typically women's work (and certainly not the work of a king or prince), we should probably take this passage to reflect the concept that Nia's kingship bestowed upon the people the bounty of both domestic and wild animals:

> *Nia Ségamain, .i. is ségh a main, ar is cuma nóblighthea bai ocus eillti fon aenchumai cach día ré linn, ar bá mór in main dó na neiche sin sech na righu aili. Ocus is sí in Flidhais sin máthair Níadh Ségamain maic Adamair, ocus do bhlightheá a flaith Niadh Ségamain, ocus issí a máthair tuc in cumhachta tsidhamail sin dó.*
>
> Nia *Ségamain*, that is, *ség* "deer" is *a máin* "his treasure"; for during his time cows and does were milked in the same way every day, so to him beyond the other monarchs great was the treasure of these things. And it is that Flidais who was mother of

Nia Ségamain son of Adammair; and in Nia Ségamain's reign those dual cattle were milked and it was his mother that gave him that fairy power.[32]

The passage continues: "Of him, the poet sang: Good was the chief with the greatness of his treasures, which old Nia Ségamain made. 'Tis for him that does were cows, for Nia Ségamain the *siabra*; that is, 'enchanted' or 'streamy' was he. Or, it is the fairy-folk that constrained the does to be milked in his reign."[33]

The Wild Banquet

Flidais' name is believed to derive from *fled* "a feast or banquet" (with a secondary or related meaning of "a beverage") + *os(s)*, a word which may have originally referred to any kind of bovine animal but which later signified "a wild ox, deer or stag."[34] Taken together, *fled* and *os* may suggest a meaning somewhere along the lines of "cattle/deer-feast or banquet" or "cattle/deer-beverage," possibilities which are supported by other references to Flidais. In TBF, as the owner of large herds of cattle, Flidais distributes a veritable feast of milk for the men of Ireland. In somewhat later sources Flidais bestows upon her son Nia an abundance of milk of both cattle and wild deer. Perhaps the range of meaning of the word *os* ("bovine animal" and later "wild ox, deer or stag") contributed to this attribution. Flidais is associated with domestic herds in TBF and with Otherworldly herds in the Dindshenchas. This additional association may have extended to (or been derived from) an association with wild animals. It is interesting to note that folklore accounts relating to the "fairy banquet" describe the feast as consisting of silverweed, heather, barley meal and the milk of goats and red deer.[35]

In the earliest studies of Flidais, Thurneysen described her as an archetype of the woodland goddess and guardian of the forests and wild animals, somewhat comparable to Classical goddesses like Diana or Artemis. He proposed relating the name Flidais to the word *os* signifying "faun," implying that the name was comprised of two words, *flid* + *os*, which he suggested meant something along the lines of "wetness of faun" (with the significance of "untamed").[36]

In a thesis from 2009, Noémie Beck wrote that such a derivation would give a genitive form (*buar*) *Flid Ois,* a form she notes does not appear in the texts, as the name is always written as one word and not spelled with the letter "o." For some reason, she takes this as proof that the name Flidais cannot be connected with the word *os.*[37] There is, of course, no reason to expect that the words would appear separately; many deity names derive from two separate word elements (Dagda, Mórrígan, Boand, etc). In addition, the second word element in some names undergoes a spelling change: *Cf. Dagda (< dag* "good, best" + *dé/dia* "god") and *Boand* (< *bó* "cow" + *find* "white, bright, blessed"). There are many examples of compound words in which the vowel(s) in unstressed syllables may contain variant spellings. One well-known example is the compound word *imbas/immus* which actually derives from *imm* + *fius*.

Beck then cites Ó hÓgain in questioning the antiquity and genuineness of Flidais as a deity figure, based on the assertion that her name is never declined in the texts, whereas "all other divine names are declined."[38] This is in relation to the phrase *buar Flidaise* (rather than *buar Flidais*), a form Beck says is never encountered in the texts and "which must be indicative of a medieval invention." She states: "In view of this, it must be acknowledged that Flidais is highly likely not to be a genuine goddess"[39] The genitive form *Flidaise* is in fact found in the passage from *Cóir Anman: Buar Flidaise* "Flidais' kine." Even if this were not the case, a spelling variation of this nature would not be proof of any such wide-ranging assertion.

In addition, in several sources Flidais is clearly stated to be a member of the Túatha Dé Danann. She was also said to own or inhabit her own "fairy mound." In *Lebor Gabála*, three male characters (*Oengus Mac Óc, Cerman* and *Cermaid*) are described as being the first people "whom speech-messengers summoned" to go into the mounds of *Flidais*.[40] Flidais' connection with the Otherworld was still present in the 16th century version of TBF from the Glenmasan manuscript. In one poem her herds are described as "Flidais' red cows," perhaps denoting their supernatural nature (Otherworld animals are often white and/or red in color). In this story, Oilill Find sends messengers to Flidais' dwelling to announce the arrival of the poet Bricne with a song of praise for her. Flidais' association with the *síd*-mounds is suggested by a line in a poem to one of her cows:

> Rise, marvelous cow, Maol Flidais whose milk is sweet …
> Remain no longer on these cold hills, but accompany us on our royal road…
> For the wife of Oilill also comes with us on this journey,
> And if report be true, you and she came together out of fairy dwellings.[41]

In later sources, Flidais' abode is described as a "castle" or "fortress." In the Glenmasan version of TBF, *Dún Flidais* (also called *Rath Morgan*) was located to the west of Carrowmore Lake.[42] In another source, her sanctuary was said to be located on a hill above Loch Letriach.[43]

Regardless of assertions about Flidais' divine nature (or lack thereof), Beck does make the useful observation that later medieval glossators seem to have interpreted the element *seg-* in Nia Segamain's name as relating to obscure glossary words like *seg* "milk" or *segamail* "milk-producing." She points out that the element likely reflects the Celtic root word *sego-* meaning "force, vigour" (*Cf.* OIr *sed/seg*, "strength, vigour"), a form also seen in the deity name *Segomo(ni)* known from dedications in Gaul. She also notes two relevant and intriguing Ogam inscriptions from Waterford: *Neta Segamonas* and *Netta Segomanus.*[44] I would add that there is another word that may have influenced the passage: OIr *séd/ség* meaning "deer" (vowel quality uncertain), with many examples referring specifically to "wild deer."[45]

We have seen that Flidais' name may mean "deer/cattle feast or beverage." Ó hOgain supports an interpretation of her name as demonstrating a connection with liquid (particularly milk).[46] However, there are references to another liquid associated with Flidais, in this excerpt from a reference to her daughters (to be explored further below):

> *Fuil chon, fuil hilchon, fuil fletha Flithais.*
> "Blood of a wolf, blood of many wolves, and the blood of the feast of Flidais."[47]

As a figure associated with wild animals and wild places, Flidais may be connected with hunting (or the protection of animals from hunters), activities connected with the shedding of blood. Another possible inference is that the "blood of her feast" referred to blood that was spilled as the result of the battle that took place in TBF.[48] A clear connection with battle is mentioned in the *Bansenchus*:

> Flidais was the consort of Ailill Find.
> Fergus was the too active lover.
> Though slender she destroyed young men.
> She decreed hard close fighting.[49]

Though not a warrior herself, Flidais' actions cause the destruction of men and the spilling of blood.

Flidais' name may refer to an Otherworld feast associated with the milk of cattle and/or deer, as well as the fertility and abundance of domestic animals, wild herds and supernatural creatures. It may also reflect an association with hunting, protection and warfare. This dual nature is exhibited by a number of female divine figures in Celtic sources and other Indo-European contexts. The goddess may provide abundance, healing or blessings, but may also display a potentially destructive side through her connection with warfare (which of course may ultimately provide protection and survival for her people). In this case, "the blood of the feast of Flidais' may symbolize her vigilance in protecting the wilderness and its creatures, her herds of cattle and deer, as well as her independence, sovereignty, and feminine power.

The Daughters of Flidais

In various sources, Flidais is credited with a number of supernatural offspring, all of whom are female.[50] TDM mentions a group of four daughters:

Arden, Bé Chuille, Dianann and *Bé Tete*. Let's examine each of these women in turn.

As John Carey points out, it is tempting to associate *A(i)rden* with the figure *dea Arduinna* known from Continental dedications.[51] The name of this goddess, *Arduinna*, has survived in the names of the forests *Arden* and *Ardennes*, and the tutelary goddess of these regions may have been a figure resembling Flidais.[52] *Arduinna* was a local goddess of the Ardennes forest, often associated with boars. A bronze statuette portrays her riding upon a boar and carrying a dagger in her hand. It is unclear if she is a huntress or an avenger who protects the animals of the forest.[53]

Two of Flidais' four daughters listed in TDM are also known from other sources. *Bé Chuille* and *Di(a)nann* appear in *Cath Maige Tuired* (CMT) as two sorceresses (*dí bantuathaig*) who have the ability to transform trees and stones and sods into armed men. They appear in this same capacity in *Lebor Gabála* and later sources.[54] In CMT, Lug calls upon various members of the Túatha Dé Danann and asks what skills they will offer in the upcoming battle.[55] Flidais' daughters magically assist the Túatha Dé and contribute to the success of this important endeavor. *Bé Chuille*'s name may signify "Woman of Hazel" (*coll*), a tree often associated with magic and divine wisdom.[56] *Dianann/Dianand* may derive from *dían* "rapid, swift" and *find* "white, bright, blessed," perhaps giving "Bright Swift One," an auspicious name for a sorceress. Other possible interpretations are that *Bé Chuille*'s name could derive from OIr *coll* "destruction, spoiling, injury" ("Woman of Destruction") and that *Dianann*'s name may derive from the phrase *dia anann*, "the goddess Anu," or reflects some confusion with the deity name *Danu/Danann*.

The name of Flidais' fourth daughter in TDM, *Bé Théte*, has often been interpreted as "Wanton Woman" (< 1 *téite* "warmth, comfort; luxury, wantonness"). However, it probably derives from 2 *téite* "assembly, fair, gathering, assembly hill," giving "Woman of the Assembly/Gathering." Indeed, an "Assembly of Teite" (*Oenach Teite*) is mentioned in the *Dindshenchas*. A prose account pertaining to *Lumman Tige Srafáin* contains the following story (as well as a fanciful explanation of *lumman*):

> Lumman of Tech Srafain, whence is it so named? Not hard to say. *Lumman* is the name for any shield, that is, "lion," for there was no shield without the image of a lion on it ... for the lion is fierce ... and these images were made by means of spells and magic lore...

Now Corbb mac Cinain had a shield such that seven of the kings of Ireland dared not face battle or duel with him. There was at that time a warrior, who was also a seer and poet, namely Fer Bern mac Regamna, brother of Find mac Regamna who had a wife Teite, daughter of Mac Nia, from whom Oenach Teite has its name.[57]

In this account, Teite's father is *Mac Nia*, a name which may reflect confusion with Flidais' son (*mac*) *Nia*. Teite's mother in this text, however, is *Fainche Tré-Chichech* ("The Three-Breasted"). Unless Flidais possesses an epithet, or an unusual attribute of which we are unaware, we may be dealing with different strands of tradition. However, the obvious attribute one might associate with Teite's mother Fainche is an over-abundance of milk, something also widely attributed to Flidais.[58] The story goes on to tell how Fer Bern mac Regamna took a poem to ask for the shield from Corbb, which he received. He was glad of this, for a battle was brewing between Art mac Cuinn and the men of Ireland with the Picts of Dal Araide. Fer Bern fights bravely with his trusty shield but is gravely wounded and returns home to seek healing. He reaches *Tech Strafain* and succumbs to his wounds. His grave was dug with his spear on one side of him, his sword on the other, and his shield of red yew across him.

The narrative is followed by a poem which describes how Fer Bern was seeking a special mantle of grey which did not endure folding; which neither spike of holly or branch of tree would catch upon; that guarded one as a brooch guards a cloak; that needle or thread did not run through; that bore no imprint of having been woven; which was not white, grey or dun, red, blue or purple, tartan, striped or checked; a mantle which guarded the head and hid the scars underneath; which was lodging for the night and a shelter against winds; a cover for the breast through the dark night; that lasted as well when it was thread-bare as when it is new; a cloak such had not been cast over seers. He says the cloak which he demands is worthy of a request at the assembly, perhaps referring to the Assembly of his sister-in-law Teite.[59]

In another source, *Acallam in Senórach*, a tale is told in which the noble chief sage to the god Manannán mac Lir was *Libra Primlíaig*, the "Chief Physician." He had three daughters, Clidna, Aífe and Etáin Fholtfinn, of the Túatha Dé Danann. They fell in love with three young men and went to elope with them. The girls went to the port to meet with the three warriors, and got into boats with them. They raised the sail to the top of the mast and sailed from there to the Shore of Téite, daughter of Ragamnach, in the south of Ireland. The shore received its name because *Téite Brecc* ("The Freckled") went to the shore with a hundred and fifty women to play in the waves, and all were drowned there. On account of that, the place is called the Shore of Téite. This anecdote is immediately followed by an account of Clidna's death by drowning and the subsequent naming of the Wave of Clidna. A poem follows which mentions both the Fort of Téite and the Grave of Téite.[60]

A fifth daughter of Flidais is mentioned in *Acallam na Senórach*. This is the divine woman *Fland/Flann*, whose name means "red, blood-red."[61] In the tale, the divine woman Bé Binn, daughter of Elcmar, has administered a purging healing ritual to Cailte, after which he complains of a terrible headache. Bé Binn says to Cailte:

Flann, daughter of Flidais, will wash your head for you…
Every head she washes suffers no pain afterwards nor balding.
One who has had his head washed seven times by her
Can see equally well by day or night.[62]

Here we might note the Romano-Celtic goddess Damona, *"Divine Deer/Ox,"* a healing goddess venerated at a number of shrines and springs. Her imagery included snakes (representing healing or regeneration) and ears of grain (indicating fertility or abundance). Her name suggests a connection with cattle or deer, and perhaps also dairy produce. Suppliants who visited Damona's sanctuary could stay overnight to experience a heeling sleep.[63]

Healing goddesses were also mentioned in an early Irish spell originally edited by Kuno Meyer over a century ago.[64] The spell refers to three daughters of Flidais (*teora ingena Flithais*) who were invoked to heal various kinds of injuries. Perhaps Flann is one of the three healers called upon in the charm. Flidais herself has a connection with healing, as we saw in TBF.[65] In the spell, the first two compound words contain elements of an attested dvanda compound, *fuilfeóil* (denoting "flesh and blood") and one wonders whether this might reflect the actual origin of the first line of the first two stanzas. It certainly flows more easily than the word *béoil* in recitation, and also preserves the alliteration (especially in the second stanza).

Another possibility is that if the second word is a form of *bél* "lips, mouth; edge, rim; opening of wounds; cavity, orifice," it could also refer to extended meanings of "speech, talk." Indo-European healing charms and spells mention three types of healing: the medicine of plants, the medicine of the knife, and the medicine of formulas.[66] In a discussion of Indo-European sagas and formulae, Calvert Watkins notes numerous examples in which the hero kills a dragon or serpent-like creature.[67] He points out that in healing charms, the dragon-slaying formula is transposed into a worm, real or figurative, which is perceived as the cause of illness.[68] In these spells the enemy to be conquered in order for healing to take place is a snake or worm that must be killed or expelled.[69]

Watkins also states: "The roster would be incomplete, though, without the predictable examples where the serpent of myth has become a real live snake."[70] In this charm, the venom of snakebites is mentioned as one of the wounds the charm is meant to heal. It is fascinating to note that directly after the invocation of the three daughters of Flidais, the serpent itself is actually called upon to heal the wound. The following is an updated version of the *éle* or charm/spell (my translation):

> *Trëéle trebéoil:*
> *A neim hi naithir*
> *A chontan hi coin*
> *A daig hi n-umae*

Nip on hi nduiniu.
Trëéle trebéoil:
Fuil chon, fuil ilchon,
Fuil flede Flithais.

Níp loch, níp chrú
Nip att, níp aillsiu
Ani frisi-cuirither mo éle.

Admuiniur teora ingena Flithais!

A naithir, hicc a n-att!
Benaim galar
Benaim crécht
Suidim att
Fris-benaim galar.
Ar choin gabes
Ar dhelg goines
Ar iarn benas.

Bennacht forin ngalar-sa
Bennacht forin corp hí-ta
Bennacht for in n-éle-sa
Bendacht forin cách rod-lá.[71]

three-fold charm, three-fold speech
Its venom in a snake
Its strife in wolves
Its flame in copper
May it not be a blemish in a person.
three-fold charm, three-fold speech
The blood of a wolf,
the blood of many wolves
The blood of the feast of Flidais.

No blackness, no serious wound
No sore, no abcess
The thing on which my incantation is cast.

I invoke the three daughters of Flidais!

O Serpent, heal the swelling!

I strike disease
I incise an ulcer
I settle a tumour
I heal suffering.
From wolves that attack
From a pointed implement that wounds
From an iron weapon that strikes

A blessing on the sickness
A blessing on the body in which it is
A blessing on the charm
A blessing on each person who casts it.

Perhaps the most famous of Flidais' daughters (who now number six) is *Fand*, the fairy lover of Cú Chulainn from *Serglige Con Chulainn*. Fand is also mentioned in the Dindshenchas of *Loch Léin*. The poem describes "bright vessels" belonging to her which were created by fairy craftsmen. These may be drinking vessels (*cf.* the "cup" of Conor mac Nessa mentioned later in the account), and could suggest some connection with the liquids associated with her mother Flidais:

> Lén Linfiaclach…
> was the craftsman of *Síd Buidb*, "Bodb's Fairymound."
> Tis he that lived in the lake,
> making the bright vessels of Fand, daughter of Flidais.
> Every night after leaving off work,
> he would cast his anvil away eastwards
> to "The Anvil of the Decies" as far as the grave mound;
> And three showers it used to cast (to the holy grave)…
> a shower of water and a shower of fire
> and a shower of purple gems.
> The same thing (i.e. the casting away of his anvil)
> Nemannach practiced
> when beating out the cup of Conor mac Nessa….
> Whence *Loch Léin* is named.[72]

Fand plays a more active role in "The Wasting Sickness of Cú Chulainn." In the story, Cú Chulainn is angry at himself for missing a cast at some birds with his sling. He sits with his back against a pillar stone and Fand (in a purple mantle) and her sister *Lí Ban* (in a green mantle) appear to him in a vision and whip him to the point of death. This results in Cú undergoing an extended illness.[73] At one point in the story, Cú is not healed even after a year, and returns to the same stone where he originally encountered the two sisters. Lí Ban appears to him and says that they did not intend to do any injury to him but to seek his friendship.

She has come to him now on behalf of Fand, whose husband Manannán mac Lir has abandoned her. Fand has set her romantic sights on Cú Chulainn, and Lí Ban's husband Labraid will promise Fand to Cú if he comes to the Otherworld for one day to provide service in battle.[74] Cú says that he is in no fit state to do so, but Lí Ban assures him that his sickness will last but a little while, and that her husband will restore all of his strength. Cú sends his charioteer Loeg to learn about the land from which the woman has come. Loeg is presented to Fand, daughter of Áed Abrat:

> Aed means fire, and he is the fire of the eye; that is, of the eye's pupil: Fand moreover is the name of the tear that runs from the eye; it was on account of the clearness of her beauty that she was so named, for there is nothing else in the world except a tear to which her beauty could be likened.[75]

Loeg returns and describes the Otherworld to Cú Chulainn in glowing terms in some exceedingly beautiful poetry. One of the poems contains references to Fand and her sister (and the dangers of fairy music):

> They are beautiful women, victorious,
> Never knowing the sorrow of the vanquished…
> The beauty of Fand deserves glittering reknown;
> No king or queen is her equal…
>
> In the house I heard musicians
> Playing for Fand.
> If I had not made haste to go away
> I would have got my hurt from that music…[76]

Cú helps Labraid with the battle, and then sleeps with Fand and stays with her for a month in the Otherworld. As he prepares to return to Ireland, they arrange to make a tryst at the yew tree by the strand known as *Iubar Cinn Trachta* (Newry). Cú's mortal wife Emer finds out about the tryst and comes to the trysting place with fifty armed women to slay Fand. Emer expresses her unhappiness and feelings of dishonor to Cú Chulainn. He in turn asks if he should not stay with the fairy woman, who he says was "fair, pure, bright and well-skilled, a fit mate for a monarch, filled with beauty, can ride the waves of the ocean, and has a mind that can guide with firmness." Emer answers him with this well-known reply:

> "Truly," said Emer, "the woman to whom you cling is in no way better than I am myself! All that's red seems fair, what's new seems glittering; what is set above is bright, while things well-known are sour. Men worship what they lack, and what they have seems weak…. Once we dwelt in honour together, and we would so dwell again, if only I could find favour in your sight."[77]

Cú is moved by Emer's words. The two women each offer to walk away and be the deserted party. Fand was seized with an urge for lamentation, "and her soul was great within her, for it was shame to her to be deserted and return to her home; moreover, the love she bore to Cú Chulainn was tumultuous in her, and in this fashion she lamented, and lamenting sang this song." Here are excerpts from Fand's lament:

> It is I that will go on the journey
> I give assent with great affliction…
> I would rather be here … than to go
> To the sunny palace of Aed Abrat.
>
> O Emer! The man is yours
> Well may you wear him, good woman
> What my arm cannot reach
> That I am forced to wish well.
>
> Many were the men that were asking for me
> Both in the court and in the wilderness…

It is better for a person to turn away
Unless he is loved as he loves...[78]

Manannán mac Lir discerns that Fand was in danger in the situation, due to the unequal warfare with the women of Ulster (and also likely to be left by Cú Chulainn). He comes from the east to find Fand and was perceived by her, although no one else was conscious of his presence. When she saw Manannán, Fand was seized by a great grief and bitterness of mind, and she recited a song (of which the following are excerpts):

Behold the valiant son of Lir...
There was a time when he was dear to me
Even if today he were nobly constant
My mind loves not jealousy...

One day I was with the son of Lir
In the sunny palace of Dun Inber
We then thought, without doubt
That we should never be separated.

When Manannan, the great one, espoused me,
I was a worthy wife for him
For his life he could not win from me
The odd game at board-games

I see coming over the sea...
The horseman of the cresting wave...
At thy coming, no one yet sees,
Anyone but a dweller in the fairy-mound...

I bid thee farewell, O beautiful Cú
We depart from thee with a good heart
Though we return not, be thy good will with us
Everything is good, compared with going away...[79]

Cú sees Fand leave with Manannán, and in his grief he makes great leaps into the air and goes to live in the mountains for a long time with neither food nor drink. Emer goes to Emain Macha and tells the people of Cú Chulainn's state. Conchobar sends his learned people, his people of skill and his druids to find Cú. The hero is so wild that he tries to kill them all, but they chant spells and bind him fast. Cú then begs for a drink, and the druids give him a drink of forgetfulness so that he would have no remembrance of Fand or anything he experienced. They also give the drink to Emer so she could forget her jealousy, for her state of mind was no better than that of her husband. Manannán shakes his cloak between Cú and Fand, so that they might never meet together again.[80]

From these accounts we can see that Flidais' six supernatural daughters were associated with a wide range of attributes: the wilderness and wild animals, hunting and protection, magic and spells, warfare and destruction, assemblies, healing, magical vessels, visionary states, Otherworldly lovers, beauty, skill, and guidance.

Deer-Goddesses and Antlered Gods

As we have seen, Flidais appears to have a connection with deer through her supernatural herds and the meaning of her name. Deer play a prominent role in Celtic narratives and legends, and often appear at liminal times or places to entice or lead people into an Otherworld encounter.[81] Both mortals and supernatural figures may be changed into deer form. However, this type of transformation most often affects female characters. In folktales, women may be transformed into deer, and the fairy figures who are seen with deer are almost invariably women.[82]

One of the most well known female figures associated with deer is *Sadb*, the mother of Finn's famous son *Oisín*. Sadb appears before Finn in the form of a doe, having been enchanted by *Fer Doirich* the druid. Although Finn's hounds chase her, he gives her protection. He is surprised and delighted when she turns into a beautiful woman the next morning. They are soon married and Sadb becomes pregnant. For a while, Finn abandons fighting and hunting, but he eventually returns to his old ways. Sadb is again under the magical influence of Fer Doirich and abandons the newborn Oisín in order to follow Finn. Seven years later, Finn finds a naked boy under a rowan tree on Ben Bulben. Oisín ("Little Deer") becomes a great warrior and poet of the Fianna, and the subject and source of many Fenian tales.[83]

The literature also contains tales in which women in the form of deer are actually shape-shifting manifestations of the Goddess of Sovereignty. The Dindshenchas poem about *Carn Máil* tells the story of the seven sons of the warrior Daire, who were all named Lugaid on account of a prophecy. Daire owns an enchanted fawn, "shaped like wild deer." Four of his sons let their hounds loose after it. The fawn flees swiftly before them as far as the Sinann, where it fell prey to them. The sons of Daire cast lots to find out which share of the enchanted fawn was theirs. While they were in the house sitting by the fire, a hideous hag enters who was tall as a mast, with a black face and misshapen features. As Gwynn translates: "Dire the dazzlement she cast upon them from her eyes."

The sons felt that they would rather be buried alive than look upon her. She addresses them and says that one of them must sleep with her that night or she will devour them all. Perceiving the danger they are in, Lugaid Laigde agrees to sleep with her. Then, as the firelight grows dim, she transforms into a wondrously beautiful woman. Her eyes were such that three shafts of sunlight were in them, and wherever her gaze fell, all was bright. A crimson mantle slid down from her fair breasts. Lugaid asks her where she had come from, and she replies, "I will tell you, gentle youth; with me sleep the High Kings. I, the tall slender maiden, am the Kingship of Alba and Erin. To you I have revealed myself this night, yet nothing more will come of our meeting. The son you will have, it is he that I will sleep with." She says his son's name will be Lugaid mac Con, and declaims that he will be a druid and a seer and a poet.[84]

A connection between women and deer is also present in earlier non-literary sources. Horned or antlered male deities are known to have been venerated in Britain and on the Continent.[85] They appear to be associated with the forest or the wilderness, wild animals, hunting, abundance and fertility.[86] It is not widely known that images of antlered goddesses also exist.[87] An image of a native pre–Roman British horned goddess from Richborough, Kent (*Rutupiae*) dating to the second century CE shows a horned female bust in low relief on a fragment of pottery. This somewhat rudimentary depiction portrays a head with antlers, which surmounts a torso with a pair of breasts indicated by small mounds of clay.[88]

A bronze statue of an antlered goddess in Romano-Celtic style was found at Besançon and is now in the British Museum in London. She holds a dish in her right hand and a cornucopia in her left, perhaps symbolizing the fertility and abundance of the wilderness.[89] A second bronze statue of an antlered goddess (also in Romano-Celtic style) was found at Puy-de-Dôme and is in the Musée de Clermont-Ferrand. Both of these antlered goddesses are depicted cross-legged, similar to the position of some of the horned gods (a position which may reflect that of the hunter at rest).[90]

Male and female horned or antlered deities appear to share a number of common attributes, and are most often depicted alone (though there are exceptions).[91] A female deity portrayed on a carving at Sommerécourt (Haute Marne) was depicted sitting in a cross-legged position with a large cauldron of food and fruit in her lap. She is encircled by a large ram-headed snake (a frequent attribute of the horned or antlered god) which eats from the great bowl on her knees. The carving was found with a companion-piece which depicts a male antlered deity who feeds two similar snakes from a large dish.[92]

There are several other images which may be connected. A horned figure from the La Tène era, with hands in *orans* position (a posture assumed to be that of invocation or blessing), was depicted on a metal object from Waldalgesheim, Germany. This figure bears either large curling horns (perhaps those of a ram or supernatural creature) or two large leaf ornaments in the vegetal style and is depicted in a squatting position. Most scholars have assumed the figure is male, and no mention has been made of two clearly delineated circles on the torso which appear to depict the breasts of a woman.[93] There is also the suggestive imagery from a Gaulish ritual pit at St.

Bernard, Vendée, which contained a votive offering of a cypress tree, deer antlers and the figurine of a goddess.[94]

A less certain example is an image depicted on a stone altar dedicated to the god *Maponus* from Ribchester, Lancashire (*Bremmatennacum*). On the back of the altar are two goddesses who are thought to represent either huntresses or personifications of the state. The first theory may be supported by the fact that the goddess on the left has an object on her head which has been interpreted as a pair of horns, a horned headdress, a small crown or upturned lunar crescent. In addition, the cognate figure of *Mabon* was associated with the hunt in medieval Welsh tradition.[95]

A quite convincing piece of evidence was noted by Beck, and comes from an inscription engraved on a column discovered at Dobrtešavas, near Šempeter in the territory of Celeia (Croatia). The inscription was dedicated to the goddess *Carvonia*, "Divine Deer/Doe Goddess" (< Indo-European *ker-*, extended e-grade **keru-*, suffixed form **kerw o* "having horns"; *Cf.* Welsh *carw*).[96] The inscription reads: *[Ca]rvoniae Aug(ustae) sacr(um) p[r]o salute C[n.] Atili Iuliani,* "Sacred to the August (Goddess) Carvonia for the safety of C[n.] Atilius Julianus." As the dedication was made for the safety of a man who bears the *tria nomina* of Roman citizens, Beck suggests that Carvonia may have been a protective and salutary goddess.[97]

Horned female figures appear in literary sources as well. Horned sorceresses were said to have opposed St. Samson.[98] In *Macgnimartha Finn*, the hero encounters three supernatural women who are described in the following manner: *co ongnaib ban sidha* ("having horns of fairy women"). John Carey suggests an alternate reading of the phrase as *co ngnaib ban sidha* "with the beauty of women of the *síd.*"[99] In one Irish folktale, a group of supernatural women assist a mortal woman with her spinning. Versions of the tale from Tipperary state that these fairy women had horns on their heads.[100] This detail could perhaps denote their dangerous or Otherworldly attributes (or their "Otherness").

It is possible that Flidais is an Irish reflex of one of the early antlered goddesses. Horned or antlered deities appear to be associated with animals (particularly the deer, bull or ram), the forest or wilderness, hunting (or the protection of animals), fertility and abundance, regeneration and healing, and battle and protection.[101] These are all attributes associated with Flidais as well. The dish or vessel of the antlered goddesses may represent nourishment or abundance, or may be a parallel with the vessels connected with Flidais' daughter in the Dindshenchas (or with the liquids associated with Flidais herself). If one aspect of the god Cernunnos is "Lord of the Animals," perhaps the antlered goddess (or Flidais) may be perceived as "Mistress of the Animals" (a role she appears to be connected with in the Túath Dé Miscellany).

A number of scholars (and popular writers) have described Flidais as a "goddess of wild creatures," a "divine forest woman" or "woman of the woods," and a "goddess of venery and wild things."[102] A number of native Celtic deities were associated with the forest or the wilderness, and appear to rule over or protect wild creatures. In addition to Arduinna, the goddess of the forest of the Ardennes, the deities *Abnoba* and *Artio* were also worshipped on the Continent. *Abnoba* was venerated in the area of the Black Forest and described by Miranda Green as "a divine huntress, associated with the goddess Diana" and "a mistress of the forest" who may have had maternal or fertility associations. Artio, a divine figure whose name means "Bear," was worshipped in Gaul and Switzerland. A figurine represents her seated in front of a bear which stretches its head towards her. In her lap is a basket of fruit, perhaps symbolic of abundance or fertility. The bear does not appear subservient to her, nor is it threatening. Artio may be a divine protector of bears or other creatures of the forest.[103] Like Flidais, these deities are associated with the forest, wild animals, hunting, protection, and fertility or abundance.

The Chariot of the Goddess

In addition to the above mentioned roles, some scholars have stated that Flidais was drawn along in a chariot pulled by deer. I have been unable to identify any primary source that confirms this concept. Thurneysen described Flidais as a "wild woman of the forest," but does not appear to mention a chariot.[104] In *Celtic Gods and Heroes*, however, Sjoestedt states: "Flidais is a woodland deity and travels in a chariot drawn by deer."[105] Ross follows Thurneysen, describing Flidais as "a goddess of wild things" and "a goddess of the wilds ... owner of supernatural cattle and protectress of deer herds."[106] However, she also states that Flidais is represented as ruler of the beasts of the forest and was portrayed as being drawn along in a chariot pulled by deer.[107] She cites Thurneysen for this reference, but I suspect that the idea may have come from Sjoestedt, whose work Ross lists in her bibliography.

There are two potential sources for this idea. The Greek goddess Artemis and her Roman counterpart Diana are depicted as divine huntresses, and Artemis, at least, was said to travel in a chariot led by four horned deer. It is possible that Greco-Roman imagery influenced the description of Flidais. Flidais, as well as Artemis/Diana, were associated with the fertility and abundance of the wilderness, as well as the protection of deer and other wild animals. Both the Celtic and Classical goddesses display the dual nature of some Indo-European deities, exhibiting an association with life, healing or blessings, as well as death, illness or destruction. Of particular note is the fact that they exhibit an independent nature, and seem to represent feminine power which does not rely upon the authority of men. Both Artemis and Flidais make conscious, independent decisions about their sexuality (chastity in the case of Artemis, and sexual choice in the case of Flidais), decisions which they defend vigorously.[108] Anne Ross writes:

> Portrayals of Diana do occur in various parts of Roman Britain, and the evidence suggests that, in some cases at least, some native goddess was invoked in this classical guise. Although there is no goddess in the vernacular tradition who can be considered to be exclusively a divine huntress, several of the goddesses are concerned to a marked degree with venery and wild things. Perhaps the most likely Irish claimant to the title of goddess of venery and wild things is Flidais, wife of Adammair, owner of supernatural cattle and mistress of stags.[109]

Diana generally appears in Classical guise in Roman Britain and Gaul, but there is some evidence for her association with indigenous cults. One of the Gaulish "hammer-gods" is pictured with a consort who carries a bow and arrow. Whether this is a native huntress or a version of Diana is unknown. Other Celtic female deities, such as Abnoba of the Black Forest and Arduinna of the Ardennes, were also sometimes conflated with Diana, demonstrating that this type of fusion was not unknown in the Celtic world.[110]

There is also the possibility that the concept of Flidais being carried in a chariot drawn by deer derives from native Celtic imagery. Model or votive wagons, chariots or carriages are quite common in early Celtic contexts. These wagons are most often drawn by oxen, stags or swans.[111] One of the most intriguing examples is a seventh century BCE ritual wagon from Strettweg, Austria. The wheeled platform is dominated by a central female who carries a bowl above her head and is surrounded by male soldiers. Stags with prominent antlers stand at each end of the wagon, and are flanked by pairs of women who grasp their antlers.[112] These carriages are thought to be models of real vehicles in which the image of a deity was placed.[113] Deer, female figures, warriors and a vessel figure prominently in the imagery of this cult-wagon, and are also found in connection with Flidais. In light of this, it is possible that Flidais was associated with a wagon or chariot in native tradition.[114] Anne Ross discusses these artefacts and their possible association with Flidais:

> Numerous votive models of carriages, drawn by stags, oxen or swans, are still in existence, on which aquatic birds of various kinds are set, bird and horned beast sometimes united to form a composite cult animal. It is clear that on occasion the image of the deity would be set in the carriage…. These small chariots are most probably votive models for real vehicles in which the image of the god or the divine priest-king would be placed, and live birds, reared for this purpose, used to accompany the procession. The descriptions of the woodland goddess Flidais, who was reputed to drive in a chariot pulled by deer, are reminiscent of this cult motif…[115]

There are other well-known examples of figures riding in chariots drawn by animals. In one famous account from TBC, Cú Chulainn achieves a sort of mastery over various types of wild animals. In one adventure, his horses become uncontrollable and he gathers deer and swans to help pull his chariot. He returns to Emain Macha with his chariot drawn by horses as well as wild deer, to which he has affixed a number of swans he also captured live.[116] As noted above, both deer and water birds were commonly depicted on votive models of chariots.

There are other examples of Indo-European divinities associated with the wilderness and with sacred carts or wagons. In addition to Artemis and her chariot drawn by horned deer (perhaps the closest analogue to Flidais' chariot, if not the source itself), the Norse goddess Freya was said to ride in a chariot drawn by cats.[117] We have already seen that Abnoba of the Black Forest and Arduinna of the Ardennes were sometimes conflated with Diana, and that Arduinna was depicted riding on a boar. In Hindu tradition, the word *vahana* (lit. "that which carries, that which pulls") denotes the being (typically an animal or mythical creature), that a Hindu deity is said to use as a vehicle. Deities might be depicted riding or mounted upon the vahana, or it may be depicted at the deity's side or symbolically represented as a divine attribute.[118]

Another possible analogue is the Norse goddess Skadi, who was also associated with hunting. She left her mountain habitat to marry the sea god Njord. However, the marriage was unsuccessful as neither party was happy living away from home. Skadi returned to the hills where she went about on skis and hunted with her bow.[119] Like Flidais and Artemis, she functions independently and appears to be "in her element" when roaming alone in the wilderness. Interestingly, the name of Skadi's husband Njord is the Old Norse equivalent of Nerthus, the Germanic earth goddess described by Tacitus in his *Germania*. These names may have originally constituted a divine pair, as there are traces of other male/female pairs in Norse mythology with similar or related names.[120]

Nerthus represented "Mother Earth" and was believed to have the power to intervene in the affairs of men. Her image, which only the priest could view or touch, was carried in a sacred wagon drawn by oxen. Nerthus was warmly welcomed everywhere she went, and during her sacral time no weapons were taken up, no hostilities took place, and peace prevailed. When Nerthus was returned to her sanctuary (a grove located on an island), the wagon, the cloth with which it was covered, and a symbol contained inside the wagon, were cleansed in a sacred lake by slaves who were then drowned.[121] The concept of a deity in a cart or wagon venerated in a ritual procession is supported by the discovery of two elaborately decorated wagons in a peat-bog in Denmark dating to about 200 CE. With them was a small stool of alder, which may have served as a seat for the occupant. Clay vessels and loom pieces were also found with the wagons, suggesting an association with women.[122]

Literary and iconographic portrayals of Flidais, Artemis/Diana, Skadi and Nerthus, as well as archaeological evidence of Celtic and Germanic provenance, suggest a prototypical goddess figure whose image was carried in a chariot or wagon pulled by deer or oxen. This divine personage seems to have been associated with the abundance of the land and/or the wilderness (as well as certain sacred animals). A ceremonial procession and the sacrifice of a bull may have formed part of her rite of worship.

The Feast of the Deer-Goddess

Another figure with whom Flidais may share symbolic attributes is the *Cailleach* (literally "Veiled One") or "Hag" of Scottish and Irish folklore tradition. In Ireland, the *Cailleach Bhéarach* ("The Old Woman of Beare") is a somewhat chthonic character who was credited with great antiquity and longevity. She was associated with the creation of the landscape, (particularly cairns and rock formations, islands in the sea, and lakes in the mountains) as well as the power of thunder, storm, tides, winds and waves.[123] She is also connected with an island off the coast of Cork which was sometimes associated with the land of the dead.[124] In one Irish folktale associated with Finn mac Cumhall, the Cailleach assumes the shape of a deer in order to lure him into a trap.[125]

The *Cailleach Bheurr* of the Highlands of Scotland is also said to be very old and has borne witness to many great natural events. She too is said to have arranged the geography of various districts. In addition to a single great Cailleach, there were also a multitude of local cailleachs. They are portrayed as supernatural hags or witches associated with the wilderness, who haunted various mountains, rivers or districts, and bestowed benefits or misfortune on humanity as they saw fit.[126] These may be folklore reflexes of local goddesses of the wild, some of whom were propitiated at wells which the cailleachs were still said to guard in the early 20th century.[127]

Interestingly, in Scotland, the Cailleach Bheurr is associated with deer and was said to own a magical cow.[128] A number of folktales and folk accounts mention a connection between the cailleachs and wild deer. The Isle of Jura was home to a local group of seven giant cailleachs as well as the *Cailleach Mhór nam Fiadh* ("The Great Hag of the Deer"). The *Cailleach* of Ben Breck was said to frequently assume the form of a gray deer. Many local *cailleachs* were said to own, herd and milk the deer of their district, of which they were very fond.[129] These wild deer were said to be the "cattle" of the *cailleachs*, which is precisely how the deer belonging to Flidais were described.

The *cailleachs'* role as protectors of deer appears in a number of stories pertaining to hunters. Most *cailleachs* were reputed to dislike hunters, even to the point of trying to attack or kill them. It was considered a bad omen for a hunter to see one of them.[130] Protection of their deer was so important to the *cailleachs* that they sometimes used magic to charm their deer herds so that the animals could avoid pursuit.[131] In some cases, instead of killing hunters, the *cailleachs* ask for a large share of their catch.[132] This motif occurs in stories in which both hunters and fishermen visit a witch to ask for her blessing so that their hunt will be successful. If her blessing was obtained, upon their return the hunters share their catch with her.[133]

These tales may reflect earlier traditions in which the goddess of the forest or the waters had to be entreated and propitiated. In some Scottish folk tales hunters are said to meet or encounter the witch "in her own hut." There are no chairs in the dwelling, so both parties were required to squat upon the floor (a position reminiscent of the posture assumed by the horned god and antlered goddess). In two versions of this tale, the witch is specifically referred to as a *Cailleach*. Some stories state that some of the *cailleachs* had a reputation as a seer. A song about the old, gray *Cailleach* of Raasay mentions that "hundreds resorted to her." One of these divining witches was the *Iorosglach-Urlair* ("of the floor"), whose favorite position was sitting upon the floor.[134]

We have seen that Flidais possesses a number of symbolic attributes similar to those of the *Cailleach*. Both are associated with the wilderness and "that which exists outside of society." They both own herds of wild deer which they cherish and protect, and which they are sometimes said to milk. Both are associated with magical bulls or cattle, as well as bodies of water or liquids. They are capable of bestowing blessings (fertility, abundance, healing) or misfortune (illness, destruction, death). Both are powerful in their own right, and do not seem to be dependent upon the world of men. The image of the Cailleach, who squats on the floor in her "hut," may reflect the earlier posture of antlered gods and goddesses, as well as the veneration of woodland goddesses in local shrines. Flidais' chariot may be a reflex of earlier rites in which the image of a female deity was carried in a ceremonial procession, and the sharing of the hunter's catch with the local *Cailleach* may represent that which was once offered to propitiate the divine huntress.

There is one final piece of evidence that may help support a connection between early hunter goddesses, antlered goddesses, women associated with deer, the *Cailleach* and Flidais. In a number of Scottish folktales, a hunter takes aim at a deer only to perceive that she is a woman. The two fall in love and arrange to marry. However, due to the meddling of a witch, they become separated. After numerous adventures, the hunter finds his love on a distant island and they are happily married.

In one variant of the tale, the couple is able to marry early on without any hindrance from the witch. However as time goes by, problems arise (a common occurrence in tales concerning human/supernatural unions). In this instance the hunter finds himself facing economic ruin because his Otherworldly bride consumes an entire ox every day. This is a widespread motif connected with the *Cailleach*. Traditional accounts state that innumerable ox-bones are found in the loft of the hag's house. These numerous bones (from oxen which she has apparently consumed) are meant to demonstrate her great longevity and antiquity.[135]

In an Irish folklore account, the *Cailleach*'s father was said to slaughter an ox for her benefit every year on her birthday.[136] This brings to mind a report by the 2nd century CE Greek writer Arrian commenting on the hunting practices of the Celts. He mentions a Celtic hunter-goddess to whom sacrifice was made in order to neutralize the theft from the natural world engendered by the act of hunting. The sacrifice is stated to have taken place on the goddess's birthday.[137] Although Arrian refers to the goddess as Diana, this is clearly an example of the Greco-Roman habit of referring to Celtic gods by the name of a deity who was most similar from their own pantheon. Here is Arrian's account:

> Some of the Celts have a custom of annually sacrificing to Diana, while others institute a treasury for the goddess, into which they pay two oboli for every hare caught, and a drachma for every fox (because he is a crafty animal and destroys hares), and four drachmae for a roe-deer, in consideration of his size, and greater value as game. When the year comes round to the return of the birth of Diana, the treasury is opened and a victim purchased out of the money collected, either a sheep, or kid, or heifer, according to the amount of the sum … after having sacrificed and presented the first-offerings of their victims to the Goddess of the chase, according to their respective rites, they give themselves, with their hounds, to indulgence and reaction, crowning the latter on this day with garlands, as an indication of the festival being celebrated on their account.[138]

Although the sacrifice given to the Celtic woodland goddess in this account is not specifically an ox, various types of animals (a heifer, sheep or goat) could be offered depending upon the resources that were available. The important detail is that the hunter-Goddess received a sacrifice on her birthday, like the Cailleach whose father slaughtered an ox on her birthday.

Sovereign Mistress of the Wild

Flidais appears to be a goddess of the wilds, the owner of supernatural cattle and divine protectress of deer. She displays affinities with the archetypal roles and forms of the Sovereignty Goddess. Flidais also shares attributes of form and function with other Indo-European goddesses of the wilderness and the hunt, and may be an Irish manifestation of an early type of deer-goddess or antlered divinity. She may also be connected with female divinities of abundance and prosperity who were venerated at local shrines or in ritualized processions. There may be traces of continuity in the figure of the *Cailleach*, who roams the land while herding, milking and protecting her deer.[139] As we can see, the figure of Flidais is a great deal more complex than previously assumed, and her attributes may be summarized as follows:

(1) Flidais *Foltcháin* ("of the beautiful hair"), a member of *Túatha Dé Danann*

(2) Owns or lives in her own *síd*-mound (perhaps the same as *Dún Flidais*)

(3) Her name may mean "feast/beverage associated with deer"

(4) Own or protects herds of wild deer and cattle

(5) Possesses an Otherworld cow/bull whose wild offspring are a threat to mortal cattle

(6) She is counted among the *áes trebtha* (rather than the *áes dana*), those of the gods who were associated with land, farming, herding and fertility

(7) Connection with milk of wild deer and cattle (the abundance of the wild)

(8) The milk of her domestic cows can provide unlimited sustenance

(9) Lover and wife of Fergus (associated with sexual potency/fertility/protection)

(10) Wife of several mortal kings, association with Sovereignty

(11) An association with blood which results from warfare/hunting/protection

(12) Has numerous divine female offspring with multiple wide-ranging attributes

These attributes create quite an image of female power, associated with the three Dumézilian functions: (1) Sovereignty, (2) Warfare and (3) Abundance. Flidais is a beautiful Otherworld woman who owns her own *síd* mound and operates outside of the confines of society. She is sexually independent and chooses her own lovers. Her sexual power is equal to that of seven mortal women and she is not beyond plotting or warfare to fulfill those needs and desires. She owns huge herds of wild deer and cattle, and a supernatural cow and bull. We might envision Flidais presiding at an Otherworld banquet inside her sacred mound, serving forth vessels of deer milk or blood (depending on her desire) and sleeping with divine or mortal men as she pleases. Far from being simply the consort of Fergus, Flidais is a complex and powerful figure who both embodies and protects the abundance of the wild and that which is outside of society. She is an empowered sovereign woman who lives in her own sanctuary, chooses her own sexual partners, and appears to live by her own rules.

7

The Circle of Nine
Priestesses, Islands and Magical Rites

In this third and final section of the book we will begin to explore the concept of liminality, a word which refers to things which are "neither this nor that" (or which may be "both this *and* that"). One aspect of this concept pertains to boundaries between this world and the Otherworld, and those who were reputed to have the ability to transverse those boundaries. In this chapter we will discuss the theme of the "nine Otherworldly women," tracing it through a variety of medieval sources and into the ancient past as well. We will examine variations in form and function of the "circle of nine," as well as connections with the cauldron or vessel, and associations with Otherworld locations and islands.

Cauldrons and Nine-fold Symbolism

In a well-known passage from the 12th or 13th century medieval Welsh poem *Preideu Annwfn* ("The Spoils of Annwn"), King Arthur and his retinue travel to the Otherworld to free a prisoner named *Gwair* who is being held captive there.[1] The poem is attributed to the legendary Welsh poet-seer Taliesin, who appears to derive from a historical figure known from sixth century praise poems and later became a legendary figure, the ultimate archetype of the poet-seer.[2] In the poem, Arthur's retinue undertakes a journey to *Annwfn* (later contracted as *Annwn*), a word which means something along the lines of "Not-World" or "Under-World." This appears to be the name used by the Welsh (and perhaps the early Britons) to refer to Otherworld realm(s).[3] During the expedition, Arthur also hopes to acquire a magical cauldron owned by *Pen Annwn* ("The Chief of Annwn"). The cauldron would not boil food for a coward, and was said to be kindled by the breath of nine maidens.[4] It is a perilous journey, for at the end of each stanza the poet states that although three shiploads of men set out, except for seven, none returned."[5]

The Otherworld is referred to by a number of descriptive terms through-out the poem. The prison where Gwair is being kept is said to be located in *Caer Siddi* ("Fairy/Otherworld Fortress"?), a word clearly based on the Irish word *síd(h)*.[6] Other terms used to refer to the Otherworld include *Caer Vedwit* ("Mead-Feast Fort"), *Caer Golud* ("Fort of Impediment"), *Caer Rigor* ("Pet-rification Fort"), *Caer Vandwy* ("Mand(d)wy Fort"), and *Caer Ochren* ("Angu-lar Fort"). The phrase *Caer Pedryfan* ("Four-Cornered Fort"), which may simply allude to "the four corners of the fort" in relation to *Caer Siddi* is mentioned twice in the poem.[7] One passage refers to *Caer Wydr* ("Fortress of Glass"), a location where six thousand men stood on top of the wall and where communication with their watchmen was very difficult. This site appears to echo a passage describing a glass tower in the middle of the sea mentioned in the *Historia Brittonum*.[8] It may have also led to associations or confusion with the site of Glastonbury in Somerset, which became associated with Arthurian legends.[9]

The cauldron of the Chief of Annwn is mentioned in lines 11–17 of the poem. Here the poet speaks of the cauldron and a group of nine Otherworldly maidens:

> I am splendid of fame—a song was heard
> In the four quarters of the fort, revolving [to face] the four directions
> My first utterance was spoken concerning the cauldron
> My eulogy, from the cauldron it was spoken.
> Kindled by the breath of nine maidens
> The cauldron of the Head of Annwn,
> What is its disposition [with its] dark trim, and pearls?
> It does not boil a coward's food; it has not been destined to do so.[10]

The importance of the symbol of the cauldron is well-documented in numerous Celtic cultures. Archaeological evidence shows that the cauldron was an important cultural and religious artefact in Celtic cultural contexts since earliest times. Numerous sheet-bronze vessels have been excavated at Celtic sites on the Continent as well as in Britain and Ireland. Some of these objects were used for cooking or other household purposes, and some appear to have had more esoteric or religious functions, including use as votive offer-ings, in funerary deposits, and other religious or magical functions.[11]

In Irish and Welsh literary sources, cauldrons appear with some frequency and seem to represent or embody three types of functions or characteristics:

(1) Nourishment and abundance
(2) Healing and transformation
(3) Wisdom and inspiration

The Irish deity known as *An Dagda* was said to own a cauldron of abun-dant nourishment from which no company ever went away unsatisfied.[12] In the medieval Welsh tale *Branwen Daughter of Llyr*, the Irish king Matholwch is given a magical cauldron of rebirth which could re-animate slain warriors, though they would no longer have the ability to speak.[13] In another medieval Welsh story, *The Tale of Gwion Bach*, a magician and diviner named Cerridwen creates a magical herbal elixir in a cauldron which would confer the gift of foresight upon her son. The three magical drops which leapt from the vessel at the end of a year and a day fell instead upon a young lad named Gwion Bach, who was tending the fire. As a result he obtained the ability to shape-shift into different forms, as well as the gifts of poetry and prophecy. The lad would eventually be transformed into the legendary poet-seer Taliesin ("Radiant Brow").[14]

In *Preideu Annwfn*, the cauldron would not provide nourishment for the cowardly. Courage was an important personal and cultural attribute in a number of Celtic cultures. Celtic warriors were noted for their strength, skill, loyalty and courage, as well as their ability to determine and undertake right action. Early ethnographic sources frequently mention the bravery of Celtic warriors. When Alexander the Great encountered the Celts and asked them what things they feared most (hoping they would say they feared him), they surprised him by saying that they feared only that the sky might fall on them.[15] Diodorus Siculus mentions that the Celts in Gaul did not fear death, believing that the human spirit was immortal and would enter another body after a certain number of years. Their courage in the face of battle (and apparent lack of fear of death) was such that they sometimes fought wearing little or no clothing or protective armour.[16]

Another well-attested theme in Celtic tradition was the sacrality of the number three, and the related number nine as well. Nine hazel trees grew around the Well of Wisdom in *Cormac's Adventures in the Land of Promise*, and the "ninth wave" was a symbol of the powerful but invisible border between this world and the Otherworld. Nine was also a commonly used magical number in divination and folk cures.[17] In addition to being "three times the sacred number three," nine can also represent "eight plus one." This arrangement appears in the examples of Cathbad the druid and his eight disciples, and Cú Chulainn's eight smaller weapons and one larger one. In some cases, nine may have even symbolized an organized cosmogonic whole. This is exemplified in a description of Queen Medb traveling with nine chariots (two to each side, two in front and two behind her, with her own chariot in the center), and King Loegaire's injunction to join nine chariots together "according to the tradition of the gods."[18]

In *Preideu Annwfn*, a group of nine women was associated with an important Otherworld cauldron. Groups of nine women appear in other literary sources as well. Nine witches were encountered by Peredur in the medieval Welsh tale of the same name.[19] Nine supernatural women are also mentioned in the *Dindshenchas* poem pertaining to *Inber n-Ailbine.* In this poem, a young man named *Ruad mac Rígduind* ("Red or Noble One, son of the Royal Fortress") sets out on a journey across the sea with three boats (as did Arthur and his men in *Preiddau Annwn*). When his ship stops abruptly on the open sea and is unable to move, Ruad cuts it loose and swims to a "secret spot." There he encounters "nine female forms" who explained to him the reasons for his delay. (Sadly, this part of the manuscript is missing or illegible). The nine women are described as "fair and firm" and "excellent and strong," and it was apparently difficult to approach them (reminiscent of the description of *Caer Wydr*).[20]

Nevertheless, Ruad manages to sleep with the nine women under the sea, on beds made of bronze, for a period of nine nights. Although one of the women becomes pregnant, he is allowed to leave on condition that he would one day return. After seven years of adventure, Ruad returns to Ireland but fails to visit the spot where he first encountered the nine women. When he touches land, a "martial strain" was heard: the song of the "tuneful women in their pure mellow and sweet-sounding speech" who pursue Ruad at spear-point in a metal boat. The nine avenging women, "fierce, radiant and bright," catch up with the young man, and the wronged Otherworld woman kills both him and their son.[21] As in many accounts pertaining to the Otherworld, keeping one's word and showing respect appear to have been extremely important.

Later, the theme of the "nine Otherworldly women" was mentioned in Welsh and British sources as well. Geoffrey of Monmouth's late 12th century work, *The History of the Kings of Britain,* was immensely popular in its time. In spite of the fact that it was primarily a fictitious endeavor, it does appear to contain some native themes. At the end of his story, Arthur is mortally wounded and carried from the battlefield to the Isle of Avalon so that his wounds might be healed.[22] This place name derives from Welsh or British *Avallon,* "Divine Place of Apple Trees" or "Place of Divine Apple Trees." The same story was described in more detail in a work by Gerald of Wales (Giraldus Cambrensis), *On the Instruction of Princes (De instructione principum)*:

> The burial place is now known as Glastonbury, and in ancient times it was called the Island of Avalon. It is indeed almost an island, being surrounded by marshes, and so in the British language it was called *Inis Avallon* or Apple Island, since apples grow there in abundance. Then too Morgan, the noble matron and lady-ruler of those parts, who was closely related by blood to King Arthur, transported Arthur after the battle of Kemelen to this land … to heal his wounds.[23]

The story reappears in Geoffrey of Monmouth's *Vita Merlini,* written fifteen years after his first highly influential work:

> The island of apples, which men call "the Fortunate Isles," gets its name … because it produces all things of itself…. There nine sisters rule by a pleasing set of laws

those who come to them from our country. She who is first of them is more skilled in the healing art, and excels her sisters in the beauty of her person. Morgan is her name, and she has learned what useful properties all the herbs contain, so that she can cure sick bodies. She also knows an art by which to change her shape.... After the battle of Camlan.... Morgan received us with honour...[24]

It is probably significant that Morgan's name means "Sea-born." In these legends we encounter groups of nine supernatural women who are associated with voyages across the sea and/or Otherworldly islands. They are credited with skills that in some cases appear to originate in the Otherworld, such as healing, shape-shifting and inspiration, as well as courage and leadership, and passages between the worlds.

Cults and Sacred Islands

There is another intriguing example of a group of nine sacred women which comes from a very different setting. This description is found in a series of early Classical accounts which refer to islands inhabited by holy men or women during the pre–Christian era. The tradition that offshore islands were the abode or sanctuary of spirits and deities, as well as holy human inhabitants, was mentioned by Plutarch in his first century account *De Defectis Oraculorum* (18, 419C–420A):

> Demetrius then said that there were many desert islands scattered around *Brettania*, some of which were named from spirits and heroes. He said that he himself, having been sent by the Emperor to enquire into and inspect them, had sailed to the island nearest the desert ones; it did not have many inhabitants, but they were all held sacred and inviolate by the *Brettanoi*.
>
> Soon after he arrived, there occurred a great turbulence in the air and many portents, with rushing winds and raging thunderstorms. When these ceased, the islanders said that the passing of one of the great ones had taken place: for just as a lamp when it is lit shines without evil effect, but when it is extinguished is troublesome to many, so great souls are benign and mild, but their extinction and destruction often, as now, produces great winds and storms and often infects the air with pestilent effects.
>
> And there was one island there in which Cronos was held asleep under guard of Briareus, for that sleep had been contrived as his bonds and around him were many spirits, his attendants and servants.[25]

This fascinating account seems to suggest that there were many islands scattered around the coast of Britain during the pre–Christian era that were named for various gods or heroes. At least one of these islands was inhabited by a small community of religious persons who were held sacred and inviolate by the Britons. The islanders attributed a bout of raging winds and storms as evidence that "one of the great ones" (perhaps a divine or heroic being) had passed away, evidence perhaps of an aspect of British pagan belief.

Also of interest is the assertion that on another island near Britain, a figure likened to Cronus was reported to be held, bound in sleep. In Classical mythology, Cronus (whose name means "Time") was the offspring of Uranus (heaven) and Gaea (earth). On the advice of his mother he castrated his father, thus separating heaven from earth. Cronus was the father of Hestia, Demeter, Hera, Hades and Poseidon, as well as Zeus, who later overthrew him.[26] In various accounts, Cronus became either a prisoner in Tartarus (the Underworld), or a king in Elysium. This was a sort of afterlife reserved for mortals who were related to the gods and other heroes, but which later expanded to include those chosen by the gods, the righteous and the heroic. Homer locates the Elysian Fields on the western edge of the Earth, by the stream of Okeanos (a description which would fit the coast of Britain quite well). In the time of Hesiod, they were known as the Isles of the Blessed, or the Fortunate Isles (a term used by Geoffrey of Monmouth). In some Classical accounts, Cronus is the ruler of these islands.[27] It is difficult to say whether the account is purely Classical in origin, or whether it may reflect aspects of British tradition that were similar enough for Demetrius to equate the two traditions.

Another sacred island was described in the late first-century BCE/early first century CE *Geography* of Strabo, in which he mentions an island located near Britain on which sacrifices were performed. He likened these rites to the sacrifices in Samothrace associated with Demeter and Core.[28] The main site of Demeter's veneration took place at Eleusis, a town fourteen miles west of Athens, where the religion and ceremonies associated with the goddess and her daughter had their center. It was open to all who wished to become initiates, and grew to include participants from all over the Hellenic world and the Roman Empire. Devotees were sworn to absolute secrecy. Indeed, the mysteries at Eleusis were so successfully kept secret that scholars are not agreed on which aspects of the mysteries can be known with any certainty at all.[29]

That being the case, it is somewhat puzzling that Strabo knows enough about the sacrifices of Demeter and Core, and those of the British island, to make a comparison. However, there are allusions to potentially relevant activities in the *Homeric Hymn to Demeter*. The words of the hymn seems to suggest that ritual elements associated with her rites may have included the following: fasting, the wearing of special garments, the carrying of torches, a ritual period of nine days, the exchange of riddles or jests, and partaking of a sacred drink. While only a high priest known as the *Hierophant* could reveal to worshippers the ultimate mysteries, a priestess of Demeter who lived in a special house was also prominent in the cult.[30]

While it is unclear exactly what activities or sacrifices Strabo is referring to, his account may suggest that a highly developed Celtic religious center may have been active on an offshore island located near the coast of Britain whose rites were associated with a goddess (or goddesses).[31] It is possible that these divine women were associated with fertility of the earth and agricultural cycles, as was the case with Demeter. Another possibility is that the religion was associated with the cycles of the seasons, as in the myth of Core/Persephone. Core is the queen of the Underworld, but also associated with springtime and the fertility of vegetation.

Strabo also wrote about a small island "not far out to sea" that was located at the mouth of the river Loire, off the coast of Gaul. He mentions that the island was said to be inhabited by a group of women who were from a tribal group known as the *Samnitae*. Strabo writes that the women were "possessed by the god Dionysus," which likely means that they practiced rites in veneration of a Celtic deity who was likened in some way to Dionysus. This deity was propitiated with initiations and appeased with other sacred rites. Apparently no men set foot on the island, although the women could sail to the mainland to have sex with men, after which they returned to their island sanctuary. Strabo mentions the yearly re-thatching of the roof of their temple, and the penalty of death that befell any woman should she drop her load of thatch and allow it to touch the ground.[32]

These fascinating accounts reflect a belief in (and the potential existence of) offshore islands near Britain and Gaul on which communities of holy people resided who venerated various male and female deities. It is fascinating to reflect upon the possibility that a group of holy women lived on an island off the coast of Gaul who venerated a deity in some way akin to Dionysus, or whose potentially ecstatic activities (which included initiations and "other rites") may have been reminiscent of Dionysian cults. The reference to the women's independent status and choice to travel to have sex with men (who were not otherwise allowed on the island) may have been influenced to some degree by Classical accounts of the Amazons. However, the reference to the re-thatching of their temple may be accurate, as archaeological evidence from the Iron Age shows many examples of thatched temples in various Celtic territories.[33]

Another offshore island inhabited by women was recorded by Pomponius Mela in his first century BCE *De Situ Orbis* (3.6), in which he recounts an earlier report by Pytheas of Massilia. In this account the women are specifically said to be nine in number:

> In the Brittanic Sea, opposite the coast of the Ossismi, the Isle of Sena belongs to a Gallic divinity and is famous for its oracle, whose priestesses, sanctified by their perpetual virginity, are reportedly nine in number. They call the priestesses *Gallizenae* and think that because they have been endowed with unique powers, they stir up the seas and the winds by their magic charms, that they turn into whatever animals they want, that they cure what is incurable among other peoples, that they know and

predict the future, but that it is not revealed except to sea-voyagers and then only to those traveling to consult them.[34]

The reports of Strabo and Pomponius Mela bear a certain resemblance to each other, but also display a number of differences. Both refer to islands located off the coast of Gaul (or near Britain) which were inhabited by groups of holy women who performed certain rituals and were associated with the veneration of a particular deity. In one instance, the deity is likened to Dionysus; in the other, the deity is not named (nor is the gender of the deity given). One island is said to be located near the mouth of the Loire, while the other is near the region of the Ossismi. In both instances, the sexual status of the women is mentioned: perpetual virginity in one case, and independence from men (with the choice to travel to have sex with them) in the other.

As in the Welsh poem *Preideu Annwfn,* we might interpret the word "virgin" to reflect the unmarried and/or religious status of the women. From the ethnographic and literary materials we have at our disposal, it seems that virginity did not always have the same importance in native Celtic cultural contexts as it did in Classical contexts (or in later medieval Europe). In Pomponius Mela's account of the nine sacred women, they are specifically referred to as priestesses and are credited with magical abilities, healing, shapeshifting, prophecy, and control over the seas and winds. It is interesting to note that these are basically the same abilities credited to the various groups of nine women in the literary sources given above.

The Ancient Isle

The priestesses in Pomponius Mela's account are referred to as *Gallizenae,* a word which probably derives from the Greek term *galli* ("priests") plus a mutated form of the name of the island, *Sena.* The island's name appears to be derived from the Celtic adjective **seno* ("old"), giving a meaning of "Ancient One" or "Ancient Island." This root word occurs in a variety of personal and place-names, including *Seni* (the river Shannon in Ireland), *Abainn Sin* ("old river," a place-name in Sutherland), *Sena* (an unlocated river mentioned in the *Ravenna* 108.30), and *Sena* (a river in Umbria mentioned by Ptolemy, and a town constructed upon it in the land of the *Senones*).[35] The Senones ("Ancient Ones" or perhaps "[Devotees of?] the Ancient One") was a tribal designation used by Celts living in the Po Valley in Italy, as well as in Gaul.[36] In the first century BCE, the capital of the Gaulish tribe was located at Vellaunodunum, and along with the Carnutes, they occupied the territory between the Seine and the Loire.[37]

Where might the island of Sena with its nine priestesses have been located? If we look back at Pomponius Mela's reference to the island being located opposite the coast of the Ossismi, several possible answers emerge. Julius Caesar stated that the Ossismi were a Celtic tribe living in northwestern Gaul. Strabo, in his *Geography* (4.4.1) makes the same connection:

> They are the O[i]sismioi, whom Pytheas names <Os>timioi, dwelling near a certain promontory thrust out far enough into the Ocean…[38]

The promontory in question is believed to be the Armorican Peninsula.[39] Pytheas apparently named many of the promontories of Armorica, including the most southerly one, the Pointe du Raz. Just eight kilometers farther out to sea from the tip of this promontory is a very small island known as the Île de Sein (known in Breton as *Enez Sun*). The island is located in the sea routes travelling south from the English Channel, and is known for its dangerous waters, unexpected currents, and thirty miles of reefs (which later required the construction of numerous lighthouses and beacons). Due to harsh Atlantic winds no trees grow on the island. Early sailors attempting to navigate safely around the southwestern tip of Armorica would have sought passage between the headland and these islands. The Île de Sein is only 2.5 kilometers long and just six meters above the ocean. On several occasions it was completely submerged beneath the sea. The presence of several standing stones on the island show that it may have been inhabited (or at least visited) in ancient times.[40] The name of the island (Île de Sein) would suggest that this is the isle of Sena (and indeed, it may well be).

Pomponius Mela states that the island of the nine priestesses was located "opposite of" or "off the shore of" the territory of the Osissmi. He does not, however, give any indication what direction off the coast of Gaul it was located. The Channel Islands are located to the north-east of the Armorican Peninsula, in between Britain and France, and would perhaps better qualify as being located in "the Brittanic Sea." Strabo (*Geography* II, 5, 15) says that the northern side of Gaul was "washed by the whole *Prettanic Strait*."[41] Pliny the Elder, in his first century CE *Natural History* (IV, 109) states that the seas around the shores of Gaul included the *Oceanus Septentrionalis* (located at the Rhine), the *Oceanus Britannicus* (located between the Rhine and the Seine), and the *Oceanus Gallicus* (located between that region and the Pyrenees).[42] If his statement is accurate, the *Île de Sein* would be located in the *Oceanus Gallicus*, and the island of priestesses described by Pomponius Mela in the *Oceanus Britannicus* could be one of the Channel Islands. The islands are quite close to this region, just to the west of the Seine and to the north of the Gaulish coastline.[43]

The Île de Sein is extremely small and sparsely inhabited (often numbering just several hundred people in historical accounts) and may have been sparsely populated in earlier times as well. Its ability to support an isolated community of nine women might be in question, unless the religious community was assisted in some way by supporters on the mainland. While the island contains a number of attractive natural features, for a small group of religious women in the Iron Age it could also have been a bleak and inhospitable place, with high winds, no trees, and treacherous waters. We must also consider the statement that these priestesses only revealed prophetic information to sea-voyagers who had journeyed to the island to consult them. The island was very dangerous for sea-travelers to approach, due to dangerous waters, currents and reefs. This difficulty of approach might have served as a sort of test or ordeal that those wishing to consult the women had to overcome. It might also have kept travelers away from the island, which could be desirable in a spiritual sense, but not in terms of the practicalities of survival.

Taken together, these Classical accounts suggest that there were numerous islands off the coast of Britain and Gaul on which communities of holy people lived, or which were considered holy in and of themselves. Pytheas' travel records (as recorded by Pliny in his *Natural History*) mention the existence of no fewer than ninety-six islands located in what he calls the "Gallic Ocean." As Rivet and Smith point out, the word *Sena* may be an epithet, "the ancient one/place," rather than a name.[44] Both of these considerations open up the possibility that another island might have been known as "the Ancient Isle" (without necessarily ruling out a link between the priestesses of Sena and L'Île de Sein).

While the tiny, treeless island of Sena was sparsely inhabited, the Channel Islands (Guernsey, Jersey, Alderney and Sark) were settled since at least the Mesolithic period by bands foraging and hunting in the forests that then covered the land. From about 4,000 BCE onwards, agriculture and megalithic grave construction were introduced, followed by copper and bronze working in the mid first millennium BCE. The seaways around the Channel Islands were well-trafficked by travelers and traders dealing in pottery, amber, gold, bronze and tin. This was the case in spite of the waters around the islands which are shallow, with numerous rocks and reefs, and the presence of strong tidal currents which change direction several times daily (and are most formidable near Alderney). Most seagoers would have tried to avoid the reefs and shallows between Jersey and the Cotentin peninsula, easing along the west side of Alderney, before heading for the open sea. On such a route, Guernsey would have been a very desirable place to land.[45]

Interestingly, there are differences between the archaeological records of Guernsey and Jersey starting in the Late Bronze Age (c. 1300 BCE), differences which continued to be significant in the Iron Age and even up to the early fifth century CE. During the Bronze Age, Jersey shows more sign of maritime trade than Guernsey. This situation changes dramatically in the Early Iron Age (c. 700–400 BCE) when there is evidence for human occupation on Guernsey but little on Jersey. This is due to in part to the position of the islands and their potential for maritime interaction. In later periods, lowered sea levels made Jersey a difficult and dangerous place to land. Guernsey, however, was relatively free of reefs and shoals and made a better stopping place for sea travelers.[46] Evidence for Iron Age settlements have been found on Guernsey, including timber structures and a cemetery,[47] as well as pottery, cooking pots, spindle whorls and loom-weights.[48] Interestingly, during this period there do not seem to have been any fortifications on Guernsey. The current evidence for settlement (while not extensive) suggests a community which benefited from its position on a trade route, and which could provide safe harbors and fresh water for travelers and the inhabitants of the island.[49]

In terms of possible ritual sites, at Jerbourg Point a bank and ditch system was built across a narrow land bridge which joined the promontory with a set of naturally occurring cliffs. Pottery jars and bowls have been discovered on the eastern side dating to the Late Bronze or Early Iron Age.[50] This rampart was built along an outcropping of quartz which runs across the entire peninsula and would have formed a natural border or boundary.[51]Another promontory was purposely separated from the rest of the island by a rampart with banks and ditches on the south part of the island, at Pointe de le Moye. Sheer sea cliffs formed a natural barrier on either side of this promontory as well.[52]

It is also interesting to note that of the Channel Islands, it is only on Guernsey that Iron Age burials been found.[53] These contained grave goods such as swords, scabbards, spearheads, shields, knives, arrowheads, sickles, armor, copper bracelets and rings, iron rings, pottery and copper vessels, and beads of amber, jet and glass.[54] Four burials were even cut into the granite, one including a timber lining.[55] Most of the grave goods suggest that male warriors were interred within, although one grave at La Hougue au Comte may have been that of a woman.[56]

To what might these unique burial sites be attributed? One theory is that they represent noble elites who had prospered from maritime trade, a theory that makes a good deal of sense. Another possibility is that when the Romans conquered Gaul between 58 and 52 BCE (campaigning especially hard against the Armorican tribes in 56 BCE), widespread disruption ensued, interrupting traditional contact and trade between Armorica and Britain. Refugees from Gaul may have fled to the Channel Islands, which would account for the enormous coin hoards of the period found on Jersey, and the unusual warrior burials on Guernsey.[57] It is also within the realms of the possible that during the Iron Age, Guernsey may have contained a religious community of women who were responsible for the burial of kings or heroes, a theory supported by the two specialized areas set apart by banks and ditches, and the unusual burial sites.

Island of Souls, Isle of Apples

One interesting development of the Iron Age in Gaul was the setting up of stone stelae, some of which were connected with burials. These tall stone slabs or stones were associated with gravesites in the Paris Basin, Brittany and southern France. The stelae are carved with imagery that portrays a female figure, through the depiction of eyes and/or a face, necklaces, a pair of breasts, and sometimes arms as well. Two particularly fine examples of these statue menhirs were found on Guernsey, one called *Le Câtel* (at Câtel) and the other called *Le Gran' Mere* (at Saint Martin). The statue menhir from Câtel was discovered in 1873 beneath the floor of the parish church and was set up in the churchyard. It is a granite slab over two meters tall with indications of a U-shaped necklace and prominent breasts.[58]

The statue menhir from St. Martin was also set up in the churchyard, where there had once been a stone slab with two hollows placed at its base (presumably for votive offerings, healing water or other ritual activities). Offerings were still placed in front of the statue as late as the 19th century. A churchwarden, fearing a resurgence of idolatry, broke the statue in two. It has since been restored and now stands between the gates of the churchyard. This statue is more realistically carved than the one at Le Câtel, and has a stronger focus on the face than any other French Neolithic figure. This is due to the fact that the original Neolithic carving was actually reworked during the Iron Age.[59] It seems significant that the menhir at Câtel is situated near the center of the island, while that at St. Martin is situated near the approach to the earthworks on the Jerbourg Peninsula.

A number of legends pertaining to supernatural women have been preserved on Guernsey, which contain references to both fairies and witches. The tradition that both good and bad witches existed on the island was recorded in the folklore archives.[60] The region of Le Catioroc (where a number of the warrior graves were located), is close to the Neolithic passage grave known as Le Trepied, which was reputed to be a famous meeting-place for the witches of Guernsey.[61] Witch trials were actually held on Guernsey in the 16th and 17th century. Some witches were so dreaded that no one dared speak against them when the day of trial arrived. A total of 103 trials were held on Guernsey, quite a large number compared with the 1,000 that took place in all of England during the same period.[62] Black witches were said to cause illness, fly through the air, change shape and cause storms. White witches were said to be able to protect people against sorcery and perform healing and divination.[63] Taken together, the powers of the "witches" of Guernsey seem to include all of those attributed to the priestesses on Sena: stirring up the seas and the winds, turning into animals, healing cures and soothsaying.

Is it possible that Iron Age habitation and ritual activity on Guernsey, including female statue menhirs located at the center of the island and at the approach to the specially delineated area on Jerbourg Point, along with the unusual warrior's graves, somehow reflect practices associated with a community of women on Guernsey? The number and variety of Classical accounts which have survived that describe offshore islands and the religious activities that were said to have taken place on them, would support the possibility that a number of islands off the coast of Britain and Gaul served as religious sanctuaries and cult centers for groups of men or women (or both). The Île de Sein may well be the *Sena* of ancient report, and if so, Guernsey may have been representative of other sacred island sanctuaries.[64]

The tradition that divine or supernatural women presided over island sanctuaries where (amongst other activities) they transported and cared for ailing kings or warriors, is a theme that occurs in a number of Celtic contexts. This theme brings to mind a sixth-century account in Procopius' *Gothic Wars* (IV.20) in which he discusses the alleged location of an island, *Brittia,* which he says was not more than 200 stades from the mouth of the Rhine (at about 8 stades to the Roman mile, approximately 25 miles). It was said at that time to be inhabited by the Angles, the Britons and the Fresians (which seems to indicate that he is referring to the island of Britain). Procopius states that Brittia was divided by a wall that separated the temperate parts from the uninhabitable parts (presumably referring to Hadrian's Wall). However, elsewhere he also refers to a place called *Bretannia,* and it appears he has his terminology somewhat confused.[65]

Procopius recounts a "famous story" which he says he says he hesitates to believe himself, but which was attested by "countless people." Brittia, he records, was said to be the "home of dead souls." Numerous people told him that the inhabitants of an island off the coast of Brittia, instead of paying tribute to the Franks, acted as escorts of the dead. In their houses at nighttime they apparently heard a mysterious summons that caused them to go down to the beach, as a result of a strange compulsion which they did not understand. There they embarked on strange vessels and rowed to Brittia, where they were able to land with no difficulty (although in their own boats, it was next to impossible). On their return, their boats were lighter, although they never visibly saw any passengers within them.[66]

Because of the reference to the Franks, it is likely that in this portion of his account, Procopius is actually referring to France (and more specifically, Brittany). The inhabitants of an offshore island (which must have been considered to be the intended abode of the dead) would answer a mysterious summons, row to the mainland, collect their invisible passengers and row back to the island on which they lived. A more believable explanation than tax evasion for this type of activity is that a religious community lived on the island, and that this was part of their normal duties. Perhaps this is somehow connected with literary references to wounded kings and warriors being ferried by women to a supernatural island for healing or burial.

There are yet other fascinating references to offshore islands in the Classical sources. Pytheas apparently discussed a large number of islands in the "Northern Ocean," one of which he said had an abundance of amber. Diodorus Siculus also mentioned the island, referring to it as *Basileia* and saying that it was "above Galatia" (possibly referring to Gaul). He mentioned that the Rhine, the Rhone and the Danube passed through "Galatia," which would describe the region near modern Belgium and Holland.[67] Pliny referred to the island as *Balcia*, and says that Pytheas called it *Basilia*. (4.94–5). In Book 37, he says that according to Pytheas there was an island of amber located just one day's journey from an estuary of the ocean occupied by the Guiones, a Germanic people. In this passage, he also states that according to Pytheas the island's name was *Abalus*.[68]

There is clearly some confusion in these accounts. The name of the island of amber (*Basilia/Basileia/Balcia*) seems to reflect the Greek adjective *basileia* which means "royal." In Pliny's reference, however, he mentions there was an island (perhaps a different island?) called *Aballus*. This word appears to derive from Celtic *aball* meaning "apple."[69] In Irish literary sources, the apple tree, its fruit or its branch can symbolically serve as a token of passage or connection between this world and the Otherworld. There may have been an island known in ancient times as *Aballus*, which was later reflected in medieval British legends as *Avallach* or *Avalon*, and as *Emain Ablach* in Ireland.

We can see numerous parallels between medieval references to Arthur's journeys to Annwfn or Avalon, and historical (or pseudo-historical) references to sacred islands which served as sanctuaries to communities of holy people engaged in devotional practices and sacrificial rites. Some of these communities appear to have been comprised solely of women, credited with the ability to control the elements, cure disease, shape shift and predict the future. In *Preiddeu Annwn*, Arthur's retinue sets out for an Otherworld island, a dangerous expedition on which many set out but from which few returned. The cauldron they seek does not boil food for a coward; that is to say, it will only nourish or reward those brave enough to undertake and endure the adventure. The marine setting may be highlighted by the description of a cauldron ornamented with "dark trim and pearls."[70] Dark blue-black pearls are mentioned as being native to Britain in at least one Classical source.[71]

What of the nine maidens whose breath kindled the flame beneath the Cauldron of Annwfn? In a similar fashion, Taliesin (in his former incarnation as Gwion Bach) tended the flame beneath the Cauldron of Cerridwen.[72] The "breath" of the nine maidens which kindle the flame of the Otherworld cauldron may allude to the Welsh term *awen* meaning "poetic or divine inspiration." This word is cognate with Old Irish *aí* (older form **auí*) and means "blowing, breath, wind" as well as "inspiration." Patrick Ford writes that this same meaning underlies the Irish word *faith* ("seer") and its Welsh cognate *gwawd*, in what Indo-European specialist Calvert Watkins called "a metaphor of Indo-European date linking 'poetic art' with 'blowing, breath, wind,' a metaphor ultimately of pagan religious and cultic origin."[73]

Ford points out that Cerridwen brews up the "spirit" of prophesy in her cauldron, a vessel from which Taliesin claims to have gotten "his poetic inspiration" (*awen*). A similar idea is expressed in an Irish text which states that oral language or poetry (*aí*) poured forth from a particularly fine cauldron.[74] This "fire of inspiration" was also reflected in the "illuminating inspiration" of the poets of Ireland, a mantic ability known as *imbas forosnai*. Here the term *imbas* (< *imm*, an intensifying prefix + *fis* "knowledge") is combined with a form of the verb *for-osna*, "light ups, illumines," "shines," or "kindles." We will explore the concept of *awen/aí* in more detail in the final chapter of the book.

The Priestesses of Gaul

Previously we saw that the number nine could be considered sacred because it was the manifestation of three times the sacred number three. However, it could also reflect a sacred or cosmogonic whole, as in the concept of "eight plus one." Relevant to this is a group of eight or nine women mentioned in an inscription from ancient Gaul dating to about 90 CE. The inscription was engraved on a lead plaque and deposited in a woman's grave, and is known as the Larzac inscription. While an exact translation is difficult to render, the inscription seems to reflect a meaning along the following lines (my translation, with information in brackets providing helpful information for following the progression of ideas):

> In this [is] a magical spell of women,
> in their special Underworld names [or, their names are below]
> The charm of a seeress, a seer creates this
> for Adsagsona [the name of a goddess]
> Severa, daughter of Tertios,
> is the writing-magician and spell-weaver

> These two manifestations [skills?] are maintained below [in the Underworld]
> She sends down/releases this incantation.

> The names of this underworld magic group:

> Banona, daughter of Flatucia;
> Paulla, wife of Potiti…;
> Aiia, daughter of Adiega,

Poti … *atir* of Paulla
Severa, daughter of Valens
…wife Paulla
Adiega, mother of Aiia;
Potita wife of Primos … Abessa.[75]

This is a fascinating piece of historical evidence, even more tangible than reports about religious communities on offshore islands (although there is no specific reason to discount all the information in those reports).[76] The first eight lines of the tablet seem to indicate that a group of woman existed in first century CE Gaul who worked together for religious or magical purposes. Severa, daughter of Tertios, appears to be the head of the group of women. She is described as a seeress who created the charm tablet, as well as a scribe or "writing-magician" and a "spell-weaver." It is she who sends down to the Underworld the spell inscribed on the tablet. This description is followed by a list of the names of the other women.

There is some confusion as to how many people are actually listed in the inscription, due to places where letters or words are worn or missing. At first glance, it seems as though one or two of the names could possibly be those of men, depending upon the identity of missing letters or how the flow of the lines is interpreted. In line two we see that Paulla is the wife of a man whose name starts with "*Potiti-*". In line four there is a person whose name starts with "*Poti…*" and who is the "*…atir*" of Paulla. If this is a male person (*Potitius*), and even the same person mentioned in line two, then the man is both the husband of someone named Paulla and the father of someone named Paulla. The only explanation for this interpretation is that Potitus' wife Paulla has a daughter also named Paulla, and that Paulla's husband is somehow part of the group of women.

However, in line four we can see that the name *Poti-* … is incomplete, and could thus represent part of a male or a female name, depending upon the word ending (which is missing). In addition, the word "*…atir*" is incomplete, and could form part of either *matir* ("mother," as seen elsewhere in the inscription) or *patir* ("father," *Cf.* British form *pater*; although a form *atir* as in Old Irish *athair* could be possible).[77] I suggest the name is a female form, *Potita*, a woman who is the [m]*atir* of Paulla, which solves both the identity problem and the gender problem.

Another area of ambiguity occurs in line five. The phrase "Severa daughter of Valens" is followed by "*dona Paulliu….*" It is unclear if this means that Severa is the daughter of Valens and the daughter of *his* (i.e. Valens') wife Paulla, or if line six refers to a separate woman named Paulla who is *somebody's* wife. Somewhat similar confusion is found in the last line, where the phrase "Potita wife of Primus" is followed by the incomplete "*…Abesias.*" This could mean either that Potita is the wife of Primus and either the mother or daughter of Abessa. Alternately, the name Abessa may refer to a separate individual, and the missing letters or words in front of her name would clarify whether she is related to Potita and Primus, or is someone different altogether.

Finally, there is the question of whether Severa, daughter of Tertius (the seeress) is the same as "Severa daughter of Valens."[78] Both Valens ("Health") and Tertiu ("Third")/Tertius ("the Third") are fairly well-known Latin male names, which seems to indicate that these two women named Severa may be two separate individuals.

The first line of the inscription states explicitly that what is engraved on the plaque has to do with the "magic of women." If so, then taking into account the ambiguities mentioned above, the names of the woman could be (in alphabetical order):

Abessa (*line 8 of the name list; see notes below re: Potita wife of Primus*)

Adiega, mother of Aiia (*line 7 of the name list*) and

Aiia, daughter of Adiega (*line 3 of the name list; a mother-daughter pair*)

Banona, daughter of Flatucia (*line 1 of the name list*)

Paulla, wife of Potitius (*line 2 of the name list*)

Potita, mother of Paulla (*line 4 of the list; possibly mother of Paulla from line 2, Paulla from line 6, or another person named Paulla*)

Potita, wife of Primos (*line 8 of the list; while she could also be Potita mother of Paulla in line 4, this seems unlikely as it would mean she is mentioned in two separate lines; as regards the last name, Potita may be the mother or daughter of Abessa; or Abessa may be a separate and unrelated individual*)

Severa, daughter of Valens (*perhaps "and also daughter of his [i.e. Valens"] wife Paula"; or else Paulla is a separate unrelated person whose identifying markers are illegible or missing*)

The three names which seem clear and unambiguous are: Banona, Aiia and Adiega. Add to this Severa, daughter of Tertius (the seeress) and Severa, daughter of Valens, probably two separate people. There is Paulla (wife of Potitus) and Paulla (the wife of someone, perhaps Valens); as well as Potita (mother of Paulla) and Potita (wife of Primos, possibly mother or daughter of Abessa?). We are unclear about Abessa, whose identity and possible relationship to the others is obscured by missing data. It seems likely that the list identifies eight or nine women: Banona, Aiia, Adiega, Severa, one or two women named Paulla, one or two named Potita, and possibly Abessa. If there are eight, then with the addition of Severa, the seeress listed at the start of the inscription, this gives us the formula of "eight plus one"—the circle of nine. If so, we may be seeing a parallel with the imagery present in the description of Morgan and her eight sisters.

Severa seems to have been the primary magical practitioner, as well as the person who made or oversaw the creation of the tablet. She is a seeress, and the person who created the magical spell in honor or supplication of the

Gaulish goddess Adsagsona. Interestingly, the Gaulish word used in the text to refer to a "seeress" (*uidlua*) is the exact linguistic equivalent of the Old Irish name *Fedelm*, the seeress whom Queen Medb consults in *Táin Bó Cuailgne*. It has been suggested that the grave containing the tablet may in fact belong to Severa. If so, this would be physical evidence of an ancient Celtic seeress and priestess who worked with a group of eight female magical practitioners, performing rites and offerings associated with the realms that lay beneath our own.[79]

We have come full circle, from literary descriptions of the nine maidens of Annwfn whose breath kindled the flame beneath the Otherworld cauldron; the nine sensual and avenging sea-women of the *Dindshenchas*; and the nine supernatural sisters of the Isle of Avalon (chief of whom was Morgan le Fay); to Classical accounts of sacred offshore islands (including *Sena,* "The Ancient Island" and *Aballus,* "Isle of Apples") on which religious communities dwelt, including the nine priestesses or *Gallizena*. Taken together with the list of Gaulish magical practitioners from the Larzac inscription, these accounts and legends may contain memories of communities of holy people (including those whose members were exclusively women) who lived on islands off the coast of Britain and Gaul; who performed sacrificial, initiatory or devotional rites; and were credited with the skills of healing, prophecy, shape shifting and control of the elements.

We can catch just a glimpse of these independent groups of women who chose a highly specialized lifestyle (and perhaps also chose chastity or their sexual partners); whose powers and authority were widely respected; and whose rites were likened to those of Dionysus and Demeter. Like the women of Avalon, they may have served as psychopomps, ferrying wounded warriors to their island sanctuary for healing or for a final and honorable interment. Perhaps on Guernsey, with its unusual warrior's graves and ancient statues of female figures re-worked in the Iron Age, we may see a hint of the type of physical evidence that could uphold the testimony of the Classical authors. Whether or not Guernsey is the same as Pomponius Mela's *Sena* or Strabo's island of priestesses, there may be some truth behind these accounts. It is not beyond the realm of possibility that there were several (or numerous) such islands, as Plutarch's report mentions, holy islands whose inhabitants were held to be "sacred and inviolate."

Where were these islands and what rites were practiced there? That information may have been privileged, reserved only for the gods and their sanctioned representatives on earth. The priestesses of Sena were said to reveal their divinely-inspired knowledge only to those who made the perilous journey to consult them. In the medieval Welsh poem *Angar Kyfundawt,* Taliesin speaks of the many mysteries of the world, mysteries of which he also claims to have specialized knowledge:

I compose a song of impeccable degree …
the learned one gives instruction …
I know what's ranged between heaven and earth …
why a hollow echoes …
why silver gleams …
what transformation there is in the golden sea …
why ravens are iridescent….
The connected river which flows [around the world]:
I know its might, I know how it ebbs, I know how it flows….
I know how many creatures are under the sea …
how many divisions in a day …
how many drops in a shower …
[I know] which are the four sods of the earth, whose end is not known…[80]

8

Bird-Mask
and Rowing-Wheel

Mug Roith, Tlachtga
and Traditions of Druidic Power

In this chapter, we will discuss a unique figure from medieval Irish literature by the name of *Mug Roith* (variously spelled *Mog Ruith*, etc.) who was celebrated as an arch-druid in some texts and vilified in others. He was said to be an ancestor of the *Fir Maige Féne,* a population group from which modern County Fermoy takes its name. Mug Roith figures prominently in the Irish genealogies, and his role as the legendary protector and savior of the province of Munster from the aggression of king Cormac mac Airt was still remembered into the 17th century.[1]

Mug Roith is perhaps most well-known for his role in the late Middle Irish saga *Forbhais Dromma Damhgháire* ("The Siege of Knocklong"), which is found in the Book of Lismore.[2] A story with this title was mentioned in one of the Middle Irish tale lists.[3] It was first edited by Sjoestedt in 1926–1927, and accompanied by a French translation.[4] The saga was not translated into English until 1992 when Séan Ó Duinn published an English version of the text.[5] Mug Roith appears in a number of other medieval Irish texts (both prose and verse). In 1923, Käte Müller-Lisowski transcribed three poems pertaining to Mug Roith from The Book of Leinster, the Book of Ballymote and Rawlinson B 502, which have been translated for this exploration.[6]

In this chapter we will explore the saga, as well as a number of other literary sources pertaining to Mug Roith. Up to now, a comprehensive study of the figure of Mug Roith in his myriad appearances—as a figure both praised and denounced—had yet to be undertaken. Not every genealogical reference or apocryphal tale associated with him will be discussed here, but references will be provided concerning his later appearances. We will primarily focus on aspects of native belief concerning Mug Roith and his equally fascinating daughter *Tlachtga,* who was the subject of an excellent study by Kathryn Chadbourne.[7]

Possibly the earliest extant reference to Mug Roith is a genealogy, which was found on a slip of vellum inserted between two pages of a manuscript. Donnchadh Ó Corráin edited the passage and suggests a very early date for it—the middle third of the seventh century (c. 634–666).[8] Another early appearance is an Old Irish poem "Mug Ruith, rígfhili cen goi," noted solely by John Carey and subsequently edited and translated.[9] The poem occurs only in the Book of Lecan, where it follows an extensive prose section detailing the genealogy of Mug Roith.[10] The section of the text immediately preceding the poem is entitled *De fabulis Moga Ruith* ("Concerning the legends of Mug Roith"), which gives a short and sometimes confusing account of his career, including the siege of Druimm Damhgháire.[11]

The poem was written in a poetic meter that Carey describes as *cró cummaisc etir rannaigecht ocus lethrannaigecht móir.* In this type of meter, the first and third lines of each quatrain has seven syllables, while the second and fourth lines have five and end in rhyming monosyllabic words. The main ornament utilized in the poem is linking alliteration, with internal alliteration in many of the shorter lines (and some of the longer ones as well).[12] Carey feels the language of the poem suggests a date of composition in the ninth century, and that the poem, along with *De fabulis Moga Ruith,* constitute evidence that many of the details of Mug Roith's famous defense of Munster were known many centuries before the saga assumed written form.[13]

The poem begins with a well-known poetic formula: *Amal asbert an fili* ("As the poet said…"). It describes Mug Roith as a royal poet (*rígfhili*), judge (*breithem*), sage (*suí*) and druid (*druí*). His father is said to be *Cuinnesc mac Fir Glan,* a royal poet (*rígéices*) of the *Ulaid* (the people of Ulster). His mother was *Cacht,* daughter of *Cathmann,* and he was fostered by *Roth mac Ríguill* (after whom he was also named).[14] The poem states that Mug Roith studied poetry throughout Ireland for so long that there was no poet among the Gaels who was superior to him. After that study, he went to study martial arts of some kind with *Buanann,* a woman from the *Áes Síde.* After he was a sage in those arts as well, he went to learn "druidry" from Simon Magus. The poem claims that he and Simon waged a struggle against Peter, "for the sake of a blessing on [his] wisdom and weapons." As a result, "The Irish made him a god of druidry" (*Do-génsat ind Érennaig dia ndruídechtae dé*).[15] The statements concerning Simon and Peter are part of non-native legendary material that accrued to Mug Roith, which we will discuss further on.

The poem tells how Mug Roith was summoned from his home in *Dairbre* (Valentia Island, County Kerry) to help the people of Munster in a conflict against the *Uí Neill* in the north. In exchange for his magical assistance, he would be rewarded with his choice of territories in the province. Mug Roith, the "royal druid" (*rígdruäd*), was then lifted onto his chariot, which was surrounded by one hundred and forty spearmen. After they had set up camp on the slope of a mountain, Mug Roith planted his spear in the ground and the spring of *Cennmair* burst forth. The druids of the *Dál Cuinn* (the Ulstermen) enchanted the mountain, but Mug Roith, using his "precious magic" (*druídecht dil*) used his breath to strip away the enchantment. The rest of the poem outlines details of the ensuing battle, at the end of which Mug Roith is given possession of *Mag Mac nEirc* for himself and his descendants forever.[16]

In most sources, Mug Roith is depicted as a powerful druid. Interestingly, in this poem he is also depicted as a poet and a judge. In *Acallam na Senórach,* which dates to the late twelfth or early 13th c., Mug Roith was said to be one of the five best druids in Ireland, as well as one of the five best poets in Ireland (in the passage, six poets are actually listed).

> *Cuícír druad, ba dám duilig,*
> *is ferr taraill iath fuinid,*
> *is mebair limsa co becht*
> *a n-aisnéis is a ndráidecht.*
> *Ba díb Ba[d]gna a Síd Ba[d]gna,*
> *díb Cathbad drái degamra,*
> *Stocán mac Cuirc chrechtaig cháim,*
> *Mog Ruith is Find a Formail...*
>
> *Cuicer fili, uasal drem,*
> *is ferr thairaill iath nEirenn,*
> *is mebair liumsa co becht,*
> *a faisneis, a filidecht.*
> *Cairbri fili fuair dar ler.*
> *Amairgin indsi Gaeidel,*
> *Feircheirtne re Labraid Lorc,*
> *Mogh-Ruith is Find faeburnocht.*[17]

Dooley and Roe translate the poetic passages as follows:

> Five crafty druids, the best of our land,
> Their tales and their magic abide with me still.
> Badbgna of *Síd Badbgna,*
> Cathbad, famous druid, Stocán,
> Mug Ruith, and Finn from Formael...
>
> Five noble poets, the best of our land.
> I remember them well, their tales and their verse.
> Cairbre from afar, Amairgen,
> Labraid Lorc, Ferchertne,
> Mug Ruith, and Finn Fáebarnocht.[18]

Forbhais Droma Dámhgháire

Mug Roith's magical power and druidic deeds feature prominently in
Forbhais Droma Dámhgháire ("The Siege of the Ridge of the Assembly-
Calls"). Most scholarly references to the saga merely state that Mug Roith
appears as a sort of "arch-druid" and uses magic to defend the people of Munster from the aggressive actions of Cormac mac Art. In addition to its focus
on the wisdom and magical power attributed to Mug Roith and other druidic
figures, the tale is unusual in its negative portrayal of Cormac mac Art, who
is almost always depicted as the ideal king—wise, truthful and generous. The
saga is well worth reading in its entirety, but a recounting of the main aspects
of the tale (which is fairly long) is provided here, as a useful resource with
which to compare other references associated with Mug Roith.

The story begins with two men, *Fiacha Moilleathan Mac Eoin* and *Cormac Mac Airt*, son of Conn. They were both conceived on the same night,
prior to a battle in which both of their fathers were killed. Cormac became
king of Ireland and reigned for a long period of time, while Fiacha became
king of Munster. The narrative begins with an intriguing passage:

> Everybody was bent on describing to Cormac the house of Oengus ind Mac Óc [a
> deity]. "Nothing of this is true," said Cormac. "Why not?" said they. "If it were true,"
> said Cormac, "I would not be here all alone in my house of Wisdom-Studies as I
> usually am, without a visit from somebody from Oengus' house or indeed from
> Oengus himself." For Cormac was accustomed to be in his secret chamber giving
> judgments, for he himself was a judge as well as king. It was Cormac himself and
> Cairbre Lifechair and Fithil who were the first to draw up the correct procedures in
> matters of law and tradition.[19]

All of this became known to Oengus. He collected all of his knowledge
and wisdom, for it was revealed to him that Cormac wished to question him.
Oengus goes to Cormac's house and the king says he wants to know about
his future, if Oengus has knowledge of it. Oengus states that he does, and
Cormac asks the deity if disaster will overtake him.[20] Oengus says that it will,
but that Cormac can choose if it will take place at the beginning, middle or
end of his reign. Cormac asks to be given prosperity at the start and end of
his reign, but to let misfortune fall at the middle, the high point of his career
in middle age. He asks what sort of misfortune it will be, and Oengus says
that a devastating cattle disease will come to pass. Cormac asks why this
event will happen, but Oengus says he will not tell him. He does provide
counsel, however, and tells Cormac to be guided by his own decisions and
not to accept the advice of a steward, a woman or a slave in this particular
matter. Oengus says goodbye to Cormac and returns to his abode at *Brúg na
Boinne* (Newgrange). Cormac then recites a poem to his people describing
Oengus and their meeting together:

There appeared to me on the mound of Tara a beautiful, colourful young man. Surpassing [is] his beauty, handsome in appearance, his garments embroidered in gold. In his hand he held a silver tympan [a stringed instrument], its strings of red gold: sweeter than any music under heaven the sound of those strings. A bow of hide, making a hundred sounds of sweet melody, [and] over it were two birds. And these birds were able to play the tympan (and not incompetently either). He [Oengus] sat close to me in friendly fashion as he played the tympan to inebriate my spirit.[21]

Cormac then tells his people about the events Oengus said would happen. In spite of the dire prediction, Cormac laments Oengus' departure, saying, "This is what has made me impatient with every other type of company; so brief his visit, sorrowful for me his leaving. Joyful for me [was] the period of his appearance." Cormac continued to rule until the cattle disease arrived. Cunning though he was, he failed to heed its advance until it had already come, for fate decreed that this would be the turning point in his reign. He collected rents due to him from the five provinces, 180 cows from each. He divided these among the seven chief districts of Tara, as the cattle disease had decimated their herds and he was not one to withhold generosity.[22]

Cormac's steward arrives and tells him that there are not enough provisions for even one night's entertainment, as all of their cows have died. Cormac wishes he still had the cows he had distributed to the people. He retires to his study to pursue wisdom all alone for three days and nights. His steward informs him that he has found a way to obtain revenue. There were five provinces in Ireland, but two of them were in Munster. Cormac had only been drawing taxes from one of those. In addition, it was these same Munstermen who had killed his father; the murderer was the brother of Fiacha, who was now king of Munster.[23]

Messengers are sent to them asking for tribute, as well as compensation for the murder of Cormac's father, according to legal tradition. The people of Munster say they will not pay the tribute, but due to the decimation of Cormac's herds they will donate a cow from every farm to help him. However, they warn that this should not serve as a precedent for the future. Cormac says he prefers to have his rights upheld and receive a single, large donation. The Munstermen say they will not submit to his demands, and send their women, children, herds and belongings to islands and places of refuge. All those who could bear arms assembled around Fiacha.[24]

Cormac was angered, but also horrified, as he realizes that this was an omen of great calamity; he had never before made any illegal claim in his role as high king. He summoned his chief druids to him: *Cith Mór* ("Great Hardship/Battle"), *Céacht* ("Power"), *Crotha* ("Creates/Forms?"), *Cith Rua* ("Red/Noble Battle"), and *Ceathach* ("Hundredfold" or "Mantle," or "Smiting"?), who had never been at fault when predicting the future. Cormac asks them for a prediction concerning the outcome of the situation. They embark on their "secret arts of knowledge" and it was revealed that Cormac's expedition to Munster would be disastrous. Each druid recites a short rhetoric outlining the misfortune that will come. Cormac is angered, but they remind him that he has never found them to be wrong, "nor will he ever."[25]

Cormac goes out hunting by himself. A dense fog descends and he falls asleep at a *síd* mound. He is awoken by a radiant woman who welcomes him. She is *Báirinn Bhláith* ("Headdress of Flowers"?), daughter of the king of *Síd Bhairche* in Leinster. She says she has fallen in love with him, but until that moment has had no opportunity to speak with him. She invites him into the mound so she can obtain him as her husband, with the blessing of her tutor and her nurse. Cormac refuses to go unless he gets a reward of some kind. Báirinn says she knows what is on his mind; that he needs reinforcements for his expedition. She says she will give him a company of druids whose powers surpass those of any of his predecessors and whom no stranger can resist. They are the three daughters of *Maol Mhisceadach*: *Eirge* ["Rising/Taking up Arms"], *Eang* ["Tracks/Pursues"] and *Eangin*. The women will assume the form of three brown sheep with heads of bone and beaks of iron, equal in prowess to a hundred warriors. They will be swift as a swallow, agile as a weasel, and impervious to weapons. Báirinn also says she will give him two male druids, *Colpa* and *Lorga*, who can kill anyone in single combat as long as Cormac accepts nobody's advice but theirs. Cormac is delighted and his sadness leaves him. He follows Báirinn into the *síd* mound and sleeps with her, staying in the mound for three days and nights. He returns to Tara with the five Otherworld druids and pays no attention to his former druids. He tells his people of the help he has received in the *síd* mound and everyone is overjoyed.[26]

Cormac and his troops march south towards Munster. After they have set up camp, one of Cormac's former druids, Cith Rua, meets with the chief druid from Leinster, *Fios Mac Athfhis Mac Fhíoreolais* ["Knowledge, Son of Great Knowledge, Son of True Guidance"]. Cith Rua tells Fios where Cormac's troops are camped; Fios tells him that Cormac's warriors will be destroyed. Cith Rua says that nothing bad will happen to him for a month and a quarter and a year from that night, until "the sage of sages," Mug Roith, arrives. Their conversation is overheard and reported to Cormac, who orders his men to kill one of the druids and beat the other. The druids part ways and Cith Rua returns to camp in disguise. Fios travels southward and three times turns his face towards Cormac's army, using his occult power to direct a magical breath on them so that every man of Cormac's troops had the appearance of Fios himself. Cormac's men wildly attack each other until they realize that magic is afoot. Cormac complains to his new druids, who direct a magical breath at the army and "through intense magic" return each man to his own form.[27]

The next day Cormac and his men travel westward. Their seers examine the clouds for portents. Crotha, one of Cormac's former druids, encounters a druid from the neighboring territory whose name is *Fear Fátha* ("Man of Prophecy"). He tells Crotha that Cormac's demand for compensation may not be justified until Fiacha claims compensation for the death of his own father. Their conversation is overheard and Fear Fátha is pursued. He finds a stream and gives it three blows of a magic wand, so that it rises up in a deluge. Cormac's druids are able to restore the stream to its original form, and the army travels onward. The druid Céacht was out watching the sky when he encounters a druid named Art. They converse and subsequently argue. Céacht tells Art that his army cannot stand against three provinces. Art is pursued, but he turns his face towards the men, and "placing his confidence in his gods," directs a druidic breath into the sky which forms a dark cloud. The cloud descends upon his pursuers and confuses them, allowing Art to slip away. Cormac sends out some scouts, but Art's magic leads them astray. Cormac complains to his druids, who say that a sleep-spell has been put upon the men for a week. They counteract the spell with their "hidden arts and knowledge."[28]

Once again, the army proceeds forward. The druid Ceathach goes out to examine the sky and meets a man named Dubhfhios Mac Dofhis ["Dark Knowledge, Son of Bad Knowledge"]. They converse and Dubhfhios predicts a cloud of slaughter. Cormac orders that the conversation not be talked about openly, for fear of disheartening the troops. Cith Mór next emerges from the camp to examine the clouds and sky, to discern a way forward for the army. He meets another druid, Meadhrán, who predicts their defeat. Cormac's army proceeds onwards nonetheless, until they arrive at *Cnoc na gCeann* ["Hill of the Head"]. The troops gather, and talk and clamor amongst themselves. As a result of their noisy calls, it is decided that the hill will be called *Droim Dámhgháire*, "The Ridge of the Assembly Calls." Cormac asks Cith Rua to set up his tent. The druid tries to drive an alder post into the ground, but neither grass nor earth would receive it. Cith Rua tells Cormac it is not because he does not have the strength, but because of the king's attempted injustice. Cith Rua says to Colpa the new druid that he could have prevented Cormac from setting out because he knew of the consequences, except Colpa had encouraged him.[29]

Cormac asks his druids to raise the hill, as the ground occupied by Fiacha and the men of Munster was higher than the land on which they were encamped. The druids achieve the feat. Cormac sends a summons to the men of Munster challenging them to single combat. Colpa is able to defeat all challengers. Cormac then asks his druids to cause a drought in the area, except for the water and streams he needs for his own army. The men of Munster still refuse to pay the tribute, even though the drought is creating a shortage of milk from their cattle. They even resort to bloodletting the cattle and mixing the blood with dew as a sort of watery drink to be taken up through a straw or pipe. Finally, they become so weak that Fiacha agrees to the tribute.[30]

Cormac's nobles encourage him to punish the Munster men, for they feel he should not have had to travel away from Tara to collect the tribute. As a result, a very heavy tribute is demanded: the best of foods, a ninth part of all crops grown, and a son or daughter from each household as hostage. The men of Munster accept the conditions. Later, Fiacha asks his grandfather *Dil* for advice. Dil says that the only person who might be able to help them is his own teacher and foster-father, Mug Roith. Mug Roith had spent his first seven years training in the Otherworld, in *Síd Charn Breachnatan,* under the direction of an supernatural druidess named *Banbhuana* (< *ban* "woman" + *búan* "lasting, enduring"). Dil tells Fiacha that neither inside nor outside of a *síd* dwelling, nor in any other place, is to be found a form of magic which Mug Roith has not practiced. Also, among all the people of Ireland, Mug Roith is the only one who ever learned the magic arts within a *síd* mound. Fiacha asks Dil what price Mug Roith might require. Dil says it will be land and territory, for the place where Mug Roith currently lives is too remote and narrow.[31]

Dil is sent forth to speak with Mug Roith, who asks for the following fee: 100 cows with shining white hides, 100 pigs, 100 oxen, 100 racehorses, 50 cloaks of crisscross weave, and a wife. In addition, a man of counsel and wisdom is to be appointed by him to the king of Munster; if Fiacha follows his counsel, fortune will smile upon him. Mug Roith also asks that his descendants be given the right to convene meetings, with three men in attendance on the king and one at his right hand. Finally, he asks for the territory of his choice in Munster, over which the king cannot exercise authority. Dil informs Fiacha of Mug Roith's requests, and guarantors are set forth to formalize the contract. Mug Roith tells them he will leave the next morning. He asks Mogh Corb ("Devotee of the Ship/Vessel") about the battles that had been fought thus far. He says he regrets those who have fallen, and will avenge them with greater numbers from the other side.[32]

Mug Roith calls upon his student Ceann Mór to bring him his traveling equipment: two noble oxen from Sliab Mis, a beautiful warlike chariot made of mountain ash [rowan] with axle-trees of white bronze and gleaming decoration, the hide of a brown hornless bull covering the seats and sides of the chariot. Of that chariot it was said: "Day and night were equally bright in it." Mug Roith also had a sword, a bronze dagger, and two five-forked spears. He sets forth with 130 people in his company. When he arrives, he takes some time to choose his territory and has his five students measure the land. The students are named *Ceann Mór* ("Great Head/Leader"), *Búireach* ("Shouting/Bellowing"), *Dil Mór Mac Da Creiche* ("Great Destruction," son of the two

Boundaries or Territories), *Beant,* and *Muichead* ("Sadness" or "Smoke" + *cét* "first" or "hundred"). Mug Roith also chooses a wife, *Eimhne,* daughter of Oengus, Mogh Corb's student.[33]

Now it was time for Mug Roith to help the people of Munster, and they ask him for water. He casts his magic spear into the air, and at the place where it fell a well sprang forth. He asks Ceann Mór to find the place and says the stream that issues forth there will be named after him. The student goes off to search for the stream, and while he is gone Mug Roith recites a magical poem in which he invokes "a special stream … a cool waterfall … whose water is pleasant for all to drink." When he finishes the poem, a great rushing of water bursts forth. His student Ceann Mór recites a poem which contains the following images:

> A full vessel, a healthy vessel … a vessel of rest, a vessel of contentment…
> A vessel of health … a vessel of silver, and of gold, and of enamel.
> A vessel of peace…. Joy to you, and from you to Mug Roith…
> Strength will revive, it will bring back peace.

The water is distributed to people and animals alike, and dispersed into the land. With that, the magical exhaustion that had oppressed the men of Munster was lifted.[34]

The next day the people request that Mug Roith lower the hill on which Cormac's troops are encamped. Mug Roith asks them to turn his face towards the hill, for he is blind. Then, as he "concentrated on his god and his power," Mug Roith made himself as tall as the hill, with his head as large as a tall hill crowned with an oak forest. The people became terrified of him. Just then, a friend of Mug Roith's arrives to assist him: *Gadhra,* the son of the sister of his Otherworldly teacher Banbhuana. To the people of Munster Gadhra seemed beautiful, but to Cormac's army he seemed monstrous. Gadhra carried a large iron fork in his hands and wore a grey-brown mantle, hung all about with talons, bones and horns. He walks around the hill three times and utters a deafening roar. Then he assumes his proper form. Next, Mog Ruith begins to breathe against the hill. None of Cormac's people were able to remain in their tents due to the force of the wind that arose. Mug Roith recites a poem and the hill disappears from view, all covered in a dark cloud and a misty whirlpool. Cormac's retinue was in despair; some were even on the verge of death.[35]

Cormac's people feel their own magic arts have been turned against them, and Cormac begins to blame his druids. Colpa gets up and assumes a huge, grotesque shape, and Mug Roith tells Ceann Mór to engage in battle with him. Ceann Mór says he has never before done such a thing, but Mug Roith says he will accompany his student. It appeared as if he himself intended to fight, for he carried his speckled starry shield with rim of white silver, with a sword hung on his left side, and in his hands were two gleaming venomous spears. Mug Roith asks Ceann Mór to bring him his "poison-stone," "my hand-stone, my hundred-fighter, my destruction of my enemies." It was brought to him, and the great druid began to praise it. He put a spell upon it by reciting a magical rhetoric beseeching the hand-stone—his "fiery hard stone"—to become "a red water-snake that coils around its victims … a sea eel … a vulture among vultures that separates body from soul, an adder of nine coils around the body of Colpa." He gives the stone to Ceann Mór and says when Colpa meets him at the ford he should throw the stone into the water.[36]

As Colpa sets forth, Mug Roith sends a magic breath against him so that the stones and sands of the earth become furious balls of fire. Mug Roith then assumes a huge and imposing form. Colpa is amazed to find Mug Roith bearing arms, for he knew Mug Roith was blind. Colpa recites a magic rhetoric, to which Mug Roith responds in kind. Ceann Mór throws the stone in the water and it becomes a great water-eel. Ceann Mór decides to take on the form of a large stone standing by the side of the water. A storm arises over the ford and the river rises up in enormous waves. Ceann Mór strikes off Colpa's head with Mug Roith's weapon. However, he is seized by a great weakness and Mogh Corb runs off with the head. The next day, Lorga comes to fight against Mogh Corb and Ceann Mór, who had Mug Roith's hand-stone and magic spear in his hand. Ceann Mór stands by the ford and praises the hand-stone, beseeching it and predicting the destruction it will cause. Then he "put his confidence in his god and in the chief druid of the world, Mug Roith," and recites a magical poem. Lorga is trapped by the eel that arises from the magic of the *Lia Láimhe* ("hand-stone"). Ceann Mór strikes off Lorga's head with a flaming axe and this time he catches it before it even hits the ground.[37]

Meanwhile, crowds had gathered to watch the fight. Every person was saying, "O god whom we adore, reduce for us the strength of the storm and the amount of water in the ford, so that we may see the fiery dragon (the eel) that is doing the fighting." After the fight, the creature runs off to the north in pursuit of Cairbre Lifechair, but Ceann Mór pursues her and tells her to hold back, as it was not lawful for her to do that. He is able to quiet her down, and she resumes her shape as the hand-stone. The next day, Cormac's three female druids set forth in the shape of brown sheep with iron beaks. Mug Roith uses magical kindling wood, tinder and flint to create supernatural dogs that pursue the sheep. The sheep go underground, but the dogs find and devour them. Mug Roith then exhales a magic breath into the sky, which falls upon Cormac's camp in the form of a black cloud. He uses his breath to turn aside the magic of Cormac's druids, and Fiacha's people celebrate.[38]

Cormac asks one of his former druids, Cith Rua, to make a prediction for him, saying that he had been chief druid to Cormac's father and grandfather and had never told a lie. He tells Cith Rua that he regrets the insult he had given him. Nevertheless, Cith Rua says there is no favorable prediction to be had. Cormac asks him to talk to Mug Roith and offer him the kingdom of Ulster, as well as cows, horses, horns, cloaks and a place at his right hand at a drinking session. Mug Roith refuses the offer, leaving Cormac and his camp sad and depressed. Mug Roith leaves and goes to visit his teacher, Banbhuana, to seek her help and ask how the people of Munster would fare in the battle. He is warmly welcomed by her and stays overnight in the *síd* mound. She tells him to arise early the next morning, for she had seen that Munster would be victorious. As Mug Roith is about to leave, his son Buan says he has experienced a vision and wants Mug Roith to make a judgment on it. "Speak," said Mug Roith. It was then that Buan "had recourse to the venerable ancient speech, as he described his vision aloud." Mug Roith returns to Fiacha.[39]

Meanwhile, Cormac asks Cith Rua if there is anything that can be done to help his troops. Cith Rua said the only thing that can be done is to make a druidic fire. The people are to gather the best possible rowan wood available and create a fire. Once it is seen, those in the south (the men of Munster) will respond with their own fire. If the fires turn southwards, it is a good omen and Cormac should go in pursuit of the Munster men. But if the fires turn northward, Cormac should leave, for he will be defeated. Fiacha and his men see the druidic fire. Mug Roith says that every man should bring an armload of firewood (except for Fiacha). The wood should be from a hard tree where the birds of spring rest, and from a mountainside where the three shelters meet (the shelter from the March wind, the shelter from the wind from the sea, and the shelter from the wind of flame). Once their fire is kindled, it will be an inferno.[40]

Mug Roith asks Ceann Mór to prepare kindling for the fire. He tells the men to cut off shavings from the shafts of their spears. Mug Roith mixes the shavings together into a large bundle and sets fire to it. It bursts into flame as he chants a spell that begins: "I knead a fire, powerful, strong … an angry flame, great its speed…." He sets the firewood alight and it bursts into a great flame, as he chants a poem to encourage the fire:

> God of druids, My god above every god,
> He is god of the ancient druids.
> It will blow [the wind], may it blow,
> a low flame (to burn) the young vegetation,
> a high flame for the old (vegetation),
> a quick burning of the old,
> a quick burning of the new,
> sharp smoke of the rowan-tree,
> gentle smoke of the rowan-tree,

> I practice druidic arts,
> I subdue Cormac's power,
> Cécht, Crotha, Cith Rua–
> I turn them into stones.[41]

Mug Roith then shoots a druidic breath into the air so that a dark cloud arises, from which comes a shower of blood. He chants a spell that makes the cloud position itself above Cormac's camp. He asks his students how the fires are behaving and is told that each fire is threatening to attack the other, that they have flown up into the sky where they are like ferocious warriors or animals attacking each other. Mug Roith proceeds to adorn himself with garments of power:

> The bull-hide from a hornless brown bull belonging to Mug Roith was now brought to him along with his speckled bird-mask with its billowing wings and the rest of his druidic gear. He proceeded to fly up into the sky … along with the fire, and he continued to … beat the fire towards the north as he chanted a rhetoric: "I fashion druid's arrows…"[42]

Mug Roith continues to beat the fire towards the north, while Cith Rua tries to turn it southwards. Mug Roith succeeds, and Cith Rua is defeated along with his druids and *sluag síd* [host from the *síd* mounds]. Cormac's followers begin the march of evacuation. Mug Roith descends from the sky and gets into his beautifully ornamented chariot drawn by "fast and furious oxen having the speed of the wind of March and the agility of birds." With his bull-hide from a brown hornless bull with him, he advances to the head of the troops and a great destruction follows. Mug Roith asks what people are nearest to him, "though he knew the answer even as he put the question." The people nearest to him are Céacht, Crotha and Cith Rua. Mug Roith says his gods promised him that they would make stones out of the three as he caught them, provided he casts his breath upon them. He does so, and the druids are transformed into stones that are known as Leaca Roighne today.[43]

Mug Roith insists that the men of Munster travel forward until they reached Sliab Fuait. Fiacha's tent is set up. Cormac's men offer to give every tribute or tax that the men of Munster wanted. Mug Roith, Fiacha and the Munstermen say they will not accept the offer until they were in the north for two years and two quarter-years and two months, and even then Cormac himself must bring the tax and tribute. Connla, son of Tadhg son of Cian, the son of Fiacha's father's brother, is given to Cormac to be fostered by him. Cormac undertakes the lad's upbringing as part of his obligation. They remain in this way for a long time, observing the peace treaty between them. Mug Roith recites to the men of Munster all the casualties and deeds of the conflict. They return to their homes, and Cormac returns to Tara. Connla is brought up by Cormac and becomes accomplished and noble-minded; it was said that "his excellence was without compare in Ireland."[44]

However, Connla becomes infatuated with a woman from the *Síd* of Loch Gabhar, and forces her to have sex with him. She requests that he accompany her into the fairy realm, but he refuses to go. She asks that he at least turn his face in the direction of the fairy fortress so that the residents of the *síd* might see him. He does so, and she tells her people of the injustice done to her. Connla refuses their requests to make reparation, and they say that since he has violated their honor, they will violate his. They cast their breath at him and he becomes covered with scabs from head to foot. After that, he experiences a change of heart. Connla returns to Cormac, disfigured and disgraced. Cormac is sorry to see the young man in that condition, for he has great affection for him. Unfortunately, the only cure is to bathe in the blood of a king: Fiacha. Cormac points out that this would be the murder of a kinsman, but Connla says he would prefer that a friend of his dies than to remain in that condition. Cormac says he "swears by the gods his tribe swears by" that the cure is a true one—if it can be accomplished.[45]

Connla visits Fiacha, who is distressed to see him in that condition. He sympathizes with the lad and makes him welcome. Fiacha undertakes efforts to cure him. He gives Connla a bed as tall as his own, as well as control over a third of his judicial affairs. They continue in this way for a long time. One day, though, Fiacha goes for a swim and leaves his spear on the bank. Connla grabs Fiacha's spear and strikes him with it. The wounded Fiacha remarks upon the seriousness of his deed, and tells Connla that bathing in his blood will not do him any good. Connla dies from starvation and the skin condition, for no one will harbor him. No one bothered to inflict any other form of vengeance upon him, for it was not considered worthwhile to do so.[46]

Mug Roith Remembered

Mug Roith seems to have been quite a popular figure in Ireland, as evidenced by the wide range of witnesses: from a mid-seventh century genealogy to the ninth century Old Irish poem, and from *Acallam na Senórach* to the saga itself. A reference from the Book of Leinster (second half of the 12th c.) alludes to the extraordinarily long life attributed to Mug Roith, as well as some events pertaining to Simon.[47] It states that Mug Roith's lifetime spanned the reign of nineteen kings, up to Coirpre Lifechair; the rest of the poem is somewhat obscure.[48] References to Mug Roith's magical abilities and his prestige as a powerful druidic figure were still circulating in Ireland in the 17th century. Geoffrey Keating's *Forus Feasa ar Éirinn* ("Foundation of Knowledge of Ireland"), a narrative history of Ireland which drew from many sources (including *Lebor Gabála,* the *Dindshenchas,* royal genealogies and stories of heroic kings) was completed in 1634. Here is a passage from the work that mentions Mug Roith:

> This is how Cormac was at that time: the druids of Scotland were with him there practicing a great amount of druidry upon the king of Munster and upon his people ... not a drop of water was left beside the camp of the king of Munster, so that the people and cattle were in danger from death from want of water ... it was necessary for the king of Munster to send for Mogh Ruith, a druid who was in Ciarraidhe Luachra. And this Mogh Ruith lived during the period of the nineteen kings ... and when Mogh Ruith came the king was obliged to give him two cantreds of Fermoy ... when that was done, Mogh Ruith released the lock that was on the water keeping it from the host of the king of Munster by throwing a magic spear which he had up in the air, and in the place in which the spear fell, there sprung forth a well of pure water from it by which the men of Munster were relieved from the distress of thirst in which they were. And with that, the king of Munster with his host made an onset upon Cormac and his people, so that they drove them out of Munster without giving battle and without carrying off plunder from them.[49]

A somewhat similar account occurs in a manuscript written in 1701–1702 by the scribe *Uilliam mic Cairteáin* ("*Liam an Dúna*"):

> The Scottish druids were in the company of Cormac there, and were inflicting a great amount of enchantment upon Munster, so that they sealed with magic the waters of all of Munster, so that people and cattle were in danger of death for want of water. It is then that Fiacha Muilleathan, King of Munster, sent a message to Mogh Ruith ... the best druid who was in Ireland, and the place in which Mogh Ruith was at that time was Valencia Island, and he was at the end of his age, for he was aged and blind at that time, for he lived at the time of the nineteen kings ruling over Ireland; Mogh Ruith came to Fiacha Muilleathan and to the nobles of Ireland, and they complained to him greatly about what the druids of Cormac had done to them. Mogh Ruith promised to help them to victory and his choice of two cantreds in Munster was given to him by the men of Munster in order to prevent the enchantment of the druids.... Mogh Ruith hurled a magical spear which he had up into the air, and the place in which the spear fell, a well of pure water burst forth there, by which the men of Munster were saved from the excessive thirst which afflicted them, and he released a lock that was on the waters, and Fiacha with his host attacked Cormac with his host, so that he defeated them, and so that he pursued them to Tara, and brought a great slaughter upon them, and he did not accept a covenant with *Leth Cuinn* ["Conn's half—the north of Ireland] without homage and submission from Cormac...[50]

The two passages are quite similar, except that in the first passage the people of Munster are able to drive Cormac away simply by the release of the water (i.e. by a superior display of magic). The second passage refers to the battle and subsequent submission by Cormac, which also appears in the saga version. A third version dated to 1773 is similar to the first two, but includes this charming passage:

...the men of Munster were in great distress from the magical lock which the druids of Leth Cuinn put upon the rivers and waters of Munster ... this is what Mugh Roith said: "O High King," says he, "as much as the intellect and high knowledge of the experts of Leth Cuinn and all their means have bound together to oppress Munster at this time, I shall alone release it in spite of them to free the Munstermen." And as he was saying it, he took hold of his spear, and he sang a certain chant which is not known to anyone (and which is not known to me either) into the point of the spear, and he cast it on his right above his head ... where the javelin would fall ... the place would give forth water...[51]

The Hill and Assembly of Tlachtga

In addition to two sons, *Buan* and *Fercorb*, Mug Roith also had a daughter whose fame far outshone that of her brothers. Her name was *Tlachtga*, which appears to derive from Old Irish *tlacht,* "covering, protection; ornament, finish, beauty (hence "skin, hide"); garment, clothing." The second element could reflect Old Irish *gae* "spear, javelin, used especially of a spear blade or head," but this is far from certain. Chadbourne points out that Tlachtga is one of several women whose name became attached through Dindshenchas tradition to an important place of assembly:

She stands in the company of Tea, namesake of Tara, Macha of Emain Macha, Ériu of Uisneach, and Tailtiu of Tailtiu, but unlike her more famous counterparts, her name and legend have not adhered to the site originally named for her. Situated near Athboy in County Meath, Tlachtga is now known as the Hill of Ward.[52]

Keating wrote the following about the site, describing *Cnoc Tlachtga* ("The Hill of Tlachtga") as the place where certain rites were held:

...the fire of Tlachtga was ordained to be kindled. The use of this sacred fire was to summon the priests, augurs and druids of Ireland, to repair thither, and assemble upon the eve of All Saints [Samhain], in order to consume the sacrifices that were offered to their pagan gods.[53]

The modern name for *Cnoc Tlachtga* is the Hill of Ward, located in the archaeologically rich Boyne Valley. Just 30 miles north of Dublin, it is home to a number of important prehistoric sites, including the well-known passage tombs of Newgrange, Knowth and Dowth. Nearby is the Hill of Tara, which was associated with the kingship of Ireland. The sites are about 5,500 years old and predate the pyramids of Egypt. This dating, of course, places them several thousand years prior to the advent of Celtic language and culture in Ireland. The Hill of Ward is located on privately owned farmland, and unlike other sites was not excavated in any detail until very recently. Some work was done at the site in the 1930's, but after that it was virtually untouched until 2014, when a team from University College Dublin began archaeological work at *Cnoc Tlachtga*. The site contains four concentric earthworks measuring 150 meters in diameter with a central enclosed area about 500 feet in diameter. Archaeologists determined that the earthworks were constructed in three distinct phases over many centuries. There is some evidence that there may have once been a Neolithic tomb at the site, and that the location continued to be a focus for ceremonies after the tomb was abandoned or collapsed (or incorporated into a later stage of construction).[54]

The first phase of the earthworks was constructed during the Bronze Age (1200–800 BCE), while the final phase dates to the Iron Age (c. 400–520 CE). The middle phase, which coincides with the physical center of the monument, was built in several stages and is proving to be the "most mysterious," according to team leader Stephen Davis. Much of the work has focused on this middle phase and is providing clues about the ritual roles it may have played over the centuries. Excavations almost immediately revealed evidence of large-scale burning activity that could be related to ritual fires, or to metalwork, pottery, or glass manufacturing (activities of which they also found evidence). However, much of the other evidence at the site does point towards ritual activity. Large quantities of animal bones—a sign of large-scale feasting—have been found throughout all three phases. In addition, there is no evidence of residences or the activities associated with such, which strengthens the idea that the site was most likely set aside for purely ritual or celebratory activities.[55]

Work done at the site in 2014 showed that there were several very large three- or four- walled monuments that underlie the present monument, as well as a small enclosure to the south, which partially overlaps the current site. Excavations of the outermost ring provided evidence of how the site was built and included such finds as a piece of cattle bone dated to the fourth century BCE, a bone pin, and a fox tooth dated to the fifth century CE. The innermost ring contained three post-holes filled with deposits of clay, stones and charcoal. Hazel charcoal from one of the holes was dated to between the twelfth and tenth centuries BCE (attesting to the continued use of the site). In the northeast corner of an exposed section of the ditch was the burial of a child three to five months old, dating to the fifth century CE (the end of the Iron Age period). A large pit in the center of the site contained abundant amounts of animal bones, beneath which were hearth deposits consisting of layers of burnt clay, charcoal, and the remains of a timber post made of oak. The timber was dated to between the 11th and 13th century CE.[56]

Additional excavations took place in 2015 and showed that since the outermost ditch was fairly shallow, it is unlikely to have been used for defensive purposes, perhaps constructed for display (or, I would add, for ritual purposes). One of the objects found inside the ditch was a fragment of a human mandible and pieces of worked bone. In another ditch were pieces of shattered limestone with occasional flecks of charcoal and pieces of animal bone, as well as a spindle whorl. The inner ditch had very steep sides, and finds included pieces of shattered stone, worked flint and animal bone and a human molar. As with the other ditches between the raised circular banks of earth, these finds were probably re-deposited bank material. Nevertheless, the presence of a human mandible and molar from the outer and inner ditches may indicate that there was a votive aspect to the deposits, something that is seen in Iron Age ditches at other ritual sites. In addition, animal bones were placed at the base of the ditches as a deliberate act of deposition. A line of regularly spaced stake-holes cut into the bedrock, along the inner edge of the outer ditch, suggests the presence of a wattle wall.[57]

Archaeological tests showed that the rings were probably created first, possibly about 500 years earlier than the central part of the monument. The great enclosure was then backfilled, probably around 400 BCE. The two outer ditches date to about 400–500 CE (the end of the Iron Age), a date that also applies to the infant burial and a number of large cattle bones. The intense burning and oak timbers date to around 1100–1200 CE, and are probably the remains of a timber-framed building of some kind. Interestingly, the central mound produced very little archaeological material. I would note that this may be because the central point (as we learned in Chapter 1) was considered the most sacred, and there may have been restrictions on what took place in the central area. An on-line three-dimensional model has been created of the site, which can be viewed through a link provided in the endnote.[58] The UCD team puts forth this timeline regarding the creation and use of the site:

c. 3500 BCE: Neolithic activity on the hilltop; stone axes and globular bowl pottery

c. 1600 BCE: Early Bronze Age activity; finds include projectile points; possible era of construction of the central mound barrow (although this could be earlier)

c. 1200 BCE: Construction of the Great Enclosure

c. 800 BCE: Great Enclosure still in use; mandible of adult male deposited in outer ditch

c. 400 BCE: The Great Enclosure was filled in, probably deliberately

c. 100 BCE: Corn drying kiln in use on hilltop

c. 400 CE: Creation of an enclosure on the southern side; infant burial

c. 500 CE: Site of Tlachtga constructed (probably in a single phase)

c. 950 CE: Significant industrial activity to the east of the site and within the Tlachtga ditches

c. 1200 CE: Massive burning event at Tlachtga.[59]

In medieval Irish lore, the four sites of Tara (*Temair*), Telltown (*Tailtiu*), *Uisneach* and *Tlachtga* were said to have been the location of fortresses constructed by high king *Tuathal Techmar* at the time of the foundation of Meath (*Mide*) in the early decades of the first millennium CE. In the Fragmentary Annals [116] he is described as "Tuathal of Tlachtga." In the tale known as "The Three Finds of Emain," Bres, Nár and Lothár, sons of king Eochaid Feidlech (and triplets born to Queen Medb of Connacht) were said to have dwelt at Tlachtga in the first century CE.[60] The site seems to have been an important location for gatherings, including a national assembly of kings and religious leaders in 1167 organized by the last High King of Ireland, *Ruaidri Ua Conchobair*. Eamon Kelly, former Keeper of Antiquities at the National Museum of Ireland notes that even with Samhain traditions dying out, "Tlachtga must still have had a strong hold on the imagination of the people, with leaders possibly choosing it as a meeting site to symbolically demonstrate power and stability."[61]

Tlachtga in Literary Sources

One of the earliest references to Tlachtga may come from the Metrical Dindshenchas. The literary corpus known as the *Dindshenchas* ("Lore of Places") is comprised of about 176 poems (the "Metrical Dindshenchas"), plus a number of prose commentaries and independent prose tales (the "Prose Dindshenchas"). As a compilation, the Dindshenchas survived in two different recensions. The first comes from The Book of Leinster, with partial survivals in a number of other manuscripts. The text shows signs of having been compiled from a number of sources from the various provinces of Ireland, and the earliest poems date to at least the 11th century. Although known to us from written sources, some of the poems may have been a product of the pre-literary tradition; quite a number of the place names seem to have fallen out of use in the early medieval period. Edward Gwynn compiled and translated Dindshenchas-related poems from *Lebor na hUidre* ("The Book of Dun Cow," dated prior to 1106 CE), The Book of Leinster (dated to the second half of 12th century), the Book of Ballymote (completed in 1390 or 1391), the Yellow Book of Lecan (written down between 1391 and 1401), the Great Book of Lecan (between 1397 and 1418), and the Rennes Manuscript (which dates to the 15th century).

The poem begins by referring to the site as a "noble and distinguished" hill, which had seen the passing of many kings "since Tlachtga possessed it long ago." It then enumerates her father's lineage and family. In the fifth quatrain it refers to a series of very strange events, and says that Tlachtga went with her "great, beloved father" to Simon Magus (no reason is stated). Simon had three sons, who together "gave their love secretly" to Tlachtga and left her pregnant. The next stanza refers to her strength, saying that she was "not weak," and claims that she was one of three people (along with her father and Simon) who created something referred to as "the red well-finished wheel" (more on that anon). It also says that Tlachtga carried with her a fragment of the wheel, along with the Stone of Forcarthain and the Pillar of Cnam-chaill. As regards the wheel, it was said that anyone who saw it would go blind, anyone who heard it would go deaf, and anyone who touched "the rough-bristled pointed wheel" would die.[62] The poem then continues with the story of Tlachtga. It says that when she came westward to Ireland, she bore three sons but died at their birth (a theme seen in connection with other supernatural women, such as Macha and Clothru, and their related sacred sites). A grave was built for her at the hill, and "above every title given to it by a sage" it is called Tlachtga. At the end, the poem says that as long as the names of her sons—Muach (*muich?* "gloom, sadness, grief, affliction, dark-ness, smoke, heaviness"), Cumma (*cummae* "cutting, destroying" or "shaping, fashioning, composing") and Doirb ("hard, difficult, trying, adverse") – were held in honor throughout Ireland, there would come no ruin to her people (*ní tic díbad dia dáinib*).[63]

At the end of a passage concerning Mug Roith in Rawlinson B 502 [157 Z.36], between a story of a journey to visit Simon and a genealogy of Mug Roith (*Genelach Síl Moga Ruith*, 158a 38), we find a reference to lineages and population groups associated with Tlachtga, including *Clann Fir Tlachtga*, "the descen-dants of the men of Tlachtga" (perhaps the same as "her people" noted above):

> The descendants of *Celtchar*, moreover [are] Eogan and Ailill, Sem and the Men of Tlachtga, Cathnia and Uathnia and Druithnia, from which is Muindruine according to [the people of] Connacht. The descendants of Uathne of the Territory and Uaithni Cliach. The descendants of Cathnia Coenruige…. The offspring of the Men of Tlachtga from whom are [descended the] Dál Umain and the two over-tribes of Arad…[64]

In the Book of Ballymote is a poem almost identical to that in the Met-rical Dindshenchas [BB 406], except that it begins with a prose passage per-taining to Tlachtga:

> *Tlachtga canas roainmniged? Ni ansa. Tlachtga ingen Moga Ruith meic Fergusa. For-daroebleingatar tri meic Simoin druad. Doluid lie athair do foglaim druideachta in betha. Ar bith is i do righni do Thriun in Roth Ramach ocus in lia i Forcarthu ocus in Coirthi hi Cnamchaill. Tarlai iarum anair ocus in déde sin lei co toracht Tulach Tlachtgai. Conid and roslamnad ocus ruc tri maca .i. Doirb a quo Mag nDoirb, ocus Cumma a quo Mag Cuma, ocus Muacha a quo Mag Muaich, ocus co ndechsat na tri hanmann sin indermat a hEre nistoraig digal echtrann.*
>
> Tlachtga—from what was it named? Not difficult. [From] Tlachtga daughter of Mog Ruith, son of Fergus. For the purpose of overcoming [her], in violation of her beauty, she was overpowered [by the] three sons of Simon the druid. She went with her father to learn the magic [literally, "druidism"] of the world. For it is she that

made the Three: the *Roth Ramach* and the Stone of Forcarthu and the Pillar Stone in Cnamchaill. She then came west and after that she arrived at the Hill of Tlachtga. So that it was there she gave birth and bore three sons, that is, Doirb from who is [named] Mag Doirb, and Cumma from who is [named] Mag Cuma, and Muacha from whom is [named] Mag Muaich, and until these three names vanish in forgetting, no foreign vengeance will reach Ireland.[65]

The Rowing Wheel

The Dindshenchas poem refers to the site of Tlachtga as a place that had seen the passing of many a king since Tlachtga possessed it, and describes her as "daughter of the famous slave of kingly Roth." Gwynn's translation of *mug/mog* as "slave" refers to the common usage of the word to denote a male slave or servant (in earlier texts generally a serf or bondman). The word was also used of monks or hermits (i.e. "servant of God"). It was frequently used in combination with the genitive form of a word to form masculine proper names or titles, and might denote a person's devotion towards something or someone (hence, a "devotee"). The word could also be used in kennings, like *mug in ena* ("servant/devotee of the water"), a kenning for the salmon. A pun on Mug Roith's name appears in the final stanza of the ninth century poem above, where it states that "he used to be served, he did not serve anyone" … that Mug Roith was "no slave."[66]

Several texts give the meaning of Mug Roith's name as "devotee of the wheel," such as this passage from the Book of Ballymote:{.}

Mug Ruith .i. Roth mac Riguill rodnalt. Is de ba Mogh Ruith … i. Magus Rotarum .i. is a rothaib do-nidh a taiscélad.[67]

Mug Ruith, that is, Roth mac Riguill fostered him. It is from that he was [called] Mogh Ruith, that is, Magician of the Wheel, that is, it is from wheels that he ascertained his divination.

A similar attribution is given in *Silva Gadelica*:

Mogh roth = "magus rotarum," because it was by wheel-incantation that he used to make his observations.[68]

Here we see a wheel associated with divination, rather than the name of his foster-father, as the impetus behind Mug Roith's name. The *Roth Rámach* or "Rowing Wheel" was one of three objects associated with Tlachtga as well. The word *roth* denotes "something circular or wheel-shaped; the wheel of a vehicle; a disc or sphere (such as those of the sun and moon, or of the circular universe?); a circular brooch or neck ornament," while *rámach* means "rowing or oars, plied with oars, boat-frequented, or marine." Mug Roith was even called "Mog Ruith ramhaig."[69]

An excerpt from Cormac's Glossary also refers to the wheel as *Roth Fáil*.

While it is tempting to see *roth fail* as denoting "Wheel of Ireland," in this context it seems more appropriate to interpret it as "Wheel of Learning" (< 4 *fál* "science, learning"). In the Dindshenchas poem on *Tailtiu,* it mentions a number of stones associated with the assembly. These included *Roth Fáil Flaind,* possibly a reference to the *Roth Rámach* (which is referred to as *Roth Fáil*), and to king *Flann Cinach* (whose significance is noted below).[70] The glossary mentions another object, the Pillar of *Cnámchaill* (< *cnám* "act of gnawing, wasting; ravaging, laying waste" + 2 *coll* destruction, injury; violation of a law or taboo").[71] Here the object known as *Cnámchaill* is referred to by the name *Foí,* a word generally denoting "under/beneath it," and reflected in the phrase *fái na gréine* ("sunset").[72] Also of interest are meanings of *fo* pertaining to the taking of oaths: "by (it)/in respect of (it)/in accordance with (it)." Or, if it is a form of *foaid,* it could denote "it stays/abides," "it watches through the night/besieges," or some meaning pertaining to a feast or festival (such as would have taken place at *Cnoc Tlachtga*). Here is the reference:

> *Föi .i. Cnámchaill. Inde dixit Grúibne fili fri Corc mac Luigdech: 'In a fess (a) fo Fói' .i. ba fesach Cnámchaille. Item Mug Roith per[h]ibet quod Roth Fáil perueniet, dicens 'co rí Durlas finn íar Fói' .i. íar Cnamchaill.*[73]
>
> Foí, that is, Cnamcháill, thus said Grúibne the poet to Corc son of Lugaid: "Is the knowledge (that is) about/in respect of] Foi?" i.e., he was [was he?] acquainted with Cnamchoill. Also Mogh Ruith testifies that Roth Fail [will] arrive, saying: "to the king of fair Thurles after Foi," i.e., after Cnamchoill.[74]

In Rawlinson B 502, Mug Roith's lineage and offspring are outlined, along with a mention of the wheel and an altercation between Simon Magus and the apostle Peter.[75] The passage begins with the following statement:

> Mug Roith, son of Fergus, from whom are the Fir Maigi Féine. It is he who went to learn druidic wisdom with Simon the druid and together they made the *roth ramach.*

This is followed by a reference to a fight between Simon and the apostles Paul and Peter, and the suggestion that Mug Roith was blamed for urging Simon in that conflict. The entry then outlines Mug Roith's lineage and family connections, including a passage concerning Tlachtga:

> Cacht daughter of Cathmind, king of Britain, was the mother of Mug Roith. Roth mac Riguill fostered him. It is from him [he] was called Mug Roith. Two sons of Mug Roith: Buan and Fercorb. Derdraigen was the mother of the two sons of Mug Roith and mother of Cairpre Lifechair, who is a kinswoman of the Chorco Barddeine from the Fortress of Chermna. Dron, moreover, daughter of Lairine, was the primary wife of Mug Roith.
>   And the daughter of Mug Roith was Tlachtga (of?) the aforementioned strong hill, who was overpowered/violated (by) three sons of Simon before going west and giving birth to three sons. It is she [who] brought with her the Pillar Stone of Cnam-

chaille, that is, a remnant of the wheel, and it is she who broke it. Blind is everyone who looks at it, deaf everyone who hears it, dead everyone who touches it…[76]

Let us pause to re-examine these intriguing but somewhat confusing references. In the Metrical Dindshenchas it states that Tlachtga went with her father to Simon Magus, with no reason stated for the visit. His three sons "gave their love secretly" to her, resulting in the birth of three sons. Their birth resulted in her death and burial at the Hill of Tlachtga. The memory of their names is said to provide protection for Ireland. In the poem, Tlachtga is described as having strength and being one of three creators of the three magical objects. In addition, she carries with her a fragment of the wheel, as well as the Stone of Forcharthain and the Pillar of Cnamchaill. In this poem, her actions do not seem to carry with them any negative connotation.

In the *Rennes Dindshenchas* and the *Edinburgh Dindshenchas* it says that Tlachtga went on a journey with her father to "learn the world's magic."[77] The Edinburgh Dindshenchas states that she was ravished by the three sons of Simon because she had created the *Roth Ramach*.[78] In the Rennes Dindshenchas it states was ravished by Simon's sons because she had created not one but three objects: the Rowing Wheel, the Stone in Focarthu and the Pillar-Stone in Cnámchoill.[79] In these passages, her creation of the objects carries a connotation sufficiently negative to cause or justify her violation by the sons of Simon Magus.

How did Simon become attached to these Irish figures? Simon was a contemporary of the apostles and was said to have offered money to Peter to purchase for himself spiritual grace, as well as the ability to perform miracles. A heretical cult of "Simonians" ensued, its chief tenet being that Simon himself was the supreme deity.[80] As Chadbourne notes, "his scuffle for precedence over Peter and Paul was energized by the attraction he held for crowds of the uncertain and the curious."[81] This was the result of magical acts he was said to have performed, making images of stone and brass move around (including that of a serpent) and assuming the appearance of flying through the air.[82] At first glance, this seems like a straight-forward way for the medieval Irish to account for the prodigious amount of magical knowledge and power Mug Roith was said to possess, attributing it to mysterious lands to the east rather than to the beliefs or practices of their own ancestors. One could therefore denounce Mug Roith and his magic, as Biblical tradition denounced the magic of Simon. But perhaps there is more to it than that.

Birds, Druids and Ancestors

Marina Smyth notes that the notion of flying druids may have been of special significance to the Irish Augustine, who was almost certainly a monk in one of the foundations of Saint Carthach, probably at Lismore. She writes: "It is perhaps no mere coincidence that the fifteenth-century manuscript now known as the Book of Lismore contains the account of *The Siege of Druim Damgaire,* in which the blind druid Mug Roith assisted Munster with his magical powers against the army of Ulster's king Cormac and his druids." According to the genealogies, Mug Roith was the ancestor of the tribe of the *Fir Maige Féne,* who were based in the area of Fermoy near Lismore.[83] Smyth notes that at a critical stage in the saga:

> …Mug Roith covered himself with the pelt of a brown hornless bull, put on his var-iegated bird's headdress and rose up into the air, chanting as he went, in order to better control the druidic fire he had set against the invaders. We are reminded of the cloak of bird feathers which Irish poets are reported to have worn, as well as of the Siberian shamans who donned a special feather costume for their ritual "flight" to the Otherworld. There is more at work here than simply the association of druids with the magic of Simon Magus; it is far more likely that a local tradition of "flying" druids evoked the parallel of the apocryphal story. Shape-changing was nothing unusual in early Irish vernacular literature, and it frequently involved transforma-tion into a bird.[84]

These are all points well taken, for there is another important aspect to consider pertaining to druids or magicians being credited with the ability to fly through the air. As we saw in *Forbhais Dromma Damhgháire,* after Mug Roith dons his brown bull-hide, his speckled bird-mask with billowing wings, and the rest of his "druidic gear," he proceeded to "fly up into the air." An intriguing and potentially relevant passage comes from a treatise entitled *On the Miracles of Holy Scripture,* attributed to Saint Augustine of Hippo (but in actuality the work of an Irishman writing in the year 655). The treatise is concerned with providing "natural" explanations for all of the miracles in the Bible, postulating that all of God's acts after the creation must have been in accordance with nature and not in violation of its laws. John Carey writes:

> Particularly impressive, and so far as I know unparalleled in the early Christian West, is his vision of nature as a harmonious whole whose integrity even God will not violate: I do not think that it is farfetched to see here the early foreshadowing, tentative and isolated, of an ecological sensibility.[85]

In Chapter 17 of the treatise, the writer discusses miracles attributed to Moses, including being able to change his staff into a snake. Simon was cred-ited with creating a magical snake, and Mug Roith changed a stone into an eel. Chapter 18 discusses Moses changing water into blood. In the saga, Mug Roith created a cloud that could shower blood. A passage from Chapter 17 is of particular interest as the writer considers Moses and his staff (the italics are mine):

The staff [that] changed into a serpent, and the serpent [that] changed back again to wood, constitute a problem for those who inquire into nature—unless it be that each, the staff and the serpent, appears to be made from earth; for being made from the same material, they would by the power of God the Governor be changed into each other by turns. But if it be conceded that all things made from earth can be changed into one another by turns—as for instance animal to tree, bread to wine, man to bird—then none of these could remain firmly bound of its own nature.

We would seem, indeed, to give our assent to the laughable *tales told by the druids, who say that their forebears flew through the ages in the form of birds;* and in such cases we would speak of God not as the Governor but as the Changer of natures. Far be it from us to do so, lest we believe that after the first establishment of the natures of all things he made anything new, or not contained by its own nature.[86]

Marina Smyth has written about the importance of birds in native Irish cosmology, as well as a variety of episodes in which saints and druids engage in contests of power (which may involve staffs, as well as flight or levitation).[87] She writes:

Must we conclude that all Irish associations of druids with flight originate in the Simon Magus story? It would seem not, because the Irish Augustine is not talking about *magi* merely flying about, but actually transforming into the substance of birds. Moreover, the reference to the "ancestors of druids" gives the claim a definite aura of immediate relevance.[88]

In addition, Carey notes that this remarkable statement seems to indicate that:

…in the middle of the seventh century, there were still in Ireland Druids (in Irish the word *magus* regularly corresponds to Old Irish *druí*) preaching some form of the doctrine of transmigration attributed to their continental counterparts by Greek and Roman authors. The implications of this for our understanding of the pace and character of the conversion in Ireland has yet to be explored; the passages seems however to lend support to the suggestions regarding this period in the general introduction.[89]

The suggestions he is referring to are as follows:

If the process of conversion began well before Patrick, it continued for at least two centuries after him; it could scarcely have happened otherwise, in a country with no centralized political authority, dozens of petty kingdoms, and a well-entrenched pagan priestly hierarchy. There is considerable disagreement regarding the stages by which the native druid priesthood gave way to the Christian church, but it is at any rate reasonably clear that druids were still active in certain capacities down into the seventh and eighth centuries, a period in which they are mentioned in legal and penitential treatises.[90]

Carey goes on to note that it is apparent "that the Irish druids had not yet dwindled to being mere local conjurors or 'fairy doctors,' for they are described as 'teaching what sounds like a doctrine of metempsychosis or reincarnation." This is a fascinating thing to contemplate, for Classical authors also mentioned this theme in relation to the Continental Celts. Strabo, writing in the 1st century BCE–1st century CE, states that the druids (and others) said that the soul, like the universe, was immortal, though at some time or another both fire and water will overwhelm them.[91] Pomponius Mela, also writing in the first century CE, says that one of the things the druids taught ("which has become common knowledge among the masses") is that the soul was eternal and that there was an afterlife among the shades. Lucan, in his *Pharsalia* (1st century CE), wrote that the Celts taught that the soul goes on after death to inhabit another body in another world, and "if what they sing of is true," death is but a midpoint of a long existence.[92] Valerius Maximus (early 1st century CE) states that the people in Gaul were in the habit of lending money to be repaid in the next world. He says the reason for this is that they are convinced that the souls of men are immortal. He adds, "I should call them stupid were it not for the fact that these trouser-wearing folk have exactly the same belief as that held by Pythagoras."[93] Diodorus Siculus, writing in the late 1st century CE, said that the Pythagorean doctrine prevailed among the Celts in Gaul, namely "that the souls of men are immortal and that after a period of time they live again, since the soul enters another body."[94] As we saw in an earlier chapter, the stories of Fintan and Tuan, and the conversation between Saint Columba and the mysterious youth "provide tantalizing hints regarding beliefs and practices which may have been associated with a pre–Christian doctrine of rebirth."[95]

Druids, Women and Poets

Returning to the theme of druids in early medieval Ireland and the dates associated with their continuing presence, in a collection of canons (of uncertain date), Christian and pagan communities in Ireland are portrayed as existing side by side. The canons also mention the custom of taking "soothsayers" as witnesses to confirm legal agreements.[96] Carey writes that although it is impossible to state with certainty when paganism became extinct in Ireland, written sources suggest that conversion had largely been completed by the early years of the eighth century. Nonetheless, ecclesiastics continued to allude to the old religion, "sometimes in ways which suggest a continuing loyalty to some of its elements." And, while the old religion lingered on in some parts of Ireland, "the very sources which bear witness to this residual paganism testify also to the rapid expansion and precocious intellectual fecundity of the church in Ireland."[97] Carey also notes that down to modern times, "as is well known, it has still been possible for many Irish people to believe both in the One God and in a host of supernatural beings, and to attribute daunting powers to the latter."[98]

Regarding the role of druids in early Irish law, Fergus Kelly writes as follows:

> Traditions preserved in the sagas and saints' lives indicate that the druids of pre–Christian Ireland had a similarly high status to their British and Continental counterparts, the *druides* of Latin sources. The druid (Old Irish *druí*) was priest, prophet, astrologer and teacher…. According to the sixth century *First Synod of Saint Patrick,* oaths were sworn in his [the druid's] presence. By the time of the law-texts (seventh and eighth centuries) it is clear that the advance of Christianity had reduced his position to that of sorcerer or witchdoctor. He is discriminated against in law…. However, he retains enough influence to secure inclusion among the *dóernemeds* of *Uraicecht Becc*…[99]

The term *doérnemed* refers to a lower class of free persons in early Irish society (contrasted with *sóernemed*). In some texts, physicians, judges, harpists, blacksmiths, coppersmiths, carpenters and other craftsmen were included in this category. Although possessing some prestige, they do not have full *nemed* status, something that was afforded to kings, poets, clerics and nobles. Written sources indicate that the magic spells of druids were feared. An eighth century hymn asks God for protection from the spells of women, blacksmiths and druids. There are also references to a type of magic or sorcery known as *corrguinecht,* "heron (or crane) killing," in which the druid or poet recited a satire while standing on one leg, with one arm raised and one eye shut (possibly in imitation of a heron's stance). However, the druids' power could be useful in war. The *Annals of Ulster* (s.a. 560/561) record the use of a druidic fence (*erbe ndruad*) in the battle of *Cúil Dremne.* Any warrior who leaped over the fence was killed. And according to *Bretha Nemed Toísech,* a druid could ensure victory for the weaker side in battle.[100] In *Forbhais Dromma Damhgáire,* Mug Roith's magic was utilized in battle and he did in fact ensure victory for the weaker side.

In terms of the old religion, there are numerous references to practices associated with oath taking which are particularly interesting. The Old Irish sagas make numerous references to the practice of swearing by the elements, as we saw in Chapter 1. Anyone who broke such an oath could be punished by the elements themselves. There are also references to swearing by a local deity. Fergus Kelly feels that although no direct (historical) evidence has survived of this practice, it is likely that such forms of oath-taking were used in early Irish law. He notes that in the sixth century *First Synod of Saint Patrick,* a Christian who swore an oath before a druid in the pagan manner had to do a year's penance.[101] A discussion of evidence for druids and druidic belief in seventh and eight century Ireland (with some evidence possibly dating to the early ninth century) is found in an excellent article by Bridgette Slavin and an essay by John Carey.[102]

In the seventh century, druids were apparently still active as transmitters of tradition; in the eighth, their place within the framework of society was still being negotiated by legal writers; and ninth-century manuscripts contain incantations which are in effect supplications to pagan deities.[103]

If Mug Roith served as a symbol of the knowledge, beliefs and practices associated with the druidic class, in the eyes of some clerics he may have been maligned for this perceived power. Like Simon, he asked for payment before assisting the people of Munster. Like Simon, he used magic to fly through the air (something the druids attributed to their ancestors). With all this in mind, his strange association with Simon Magus becomes more understandable. As for Tlachtga, she was the daughter of an arch-druid and associated with a site at which the pagan Irish were believed to hold rituals associated with Samhain. In addition, she was a woman who sought forbidden or arcane knowledge (as did Boand and Sinann). All three women perished as a result. The influence of the story of Eve undoubtedly played a role in these contexts. While both the druid and filid classes consisted almost exclusively of men, there are instances in which women hold those roles in both historical and legendary contexts. There was no law prohibiting women from doing so, but most women would have been occupied with the responsibilities of house-holding and child-rearing (especially if they were not wealthy and/or did not have the means to pay for training). It may be that if a woman showed exceptional skill or promise in relation to these vocations, she may have had the option to choose a career over marriage (if she had the status or wealth to do so or if an exception was granted due to her abilities).

Some women who composed verse (at least according to the law texts) were not legally recognized poets but satirists who used verse for malicious purposes. Although usually feared and condemned, female satirists were legally recognized to have the right to satirize the head of kin of a person for whom she had given a pledge, if that pledge became forfeit. There are also historical records of female poets. Around 934 CE the Irish annals record the death of a woman named *Uallach,* who was described as a "woman poet of Ireland" (*banfili Érenn*). A woman, therefore, could be recognized as a full-fledged poet-seer. A woman's role as a poet would have afforded her more legal rights than other women, as was the case with female rulers, physicians, wrights, judges, military rulers and hostage negotiators.[104] And with those rights came more power and independence.

Wheels, Stones and Judgment

As we have seen, the association of Mug Roith with magic and aerial feats, and the connection of Tlachtga with Samhain and the pursuit of occult knowledge, may have made these two figures targets in the eyes of the church.[105] This helps explain their artificial connection with Simon Magus. But what about the objects they created? The Metrical Dindshenchas states that Tlachtga was one of three (along with Simon and her father) who made the *roth rámach*. In the Edinburgh Dindshenchas, she was said to have been ravished by the sons of Simon because she alone had created the *Roth Ramach* ("Rowing Wheel").[106] In the Rennes Dindshenchas she was ravished because she had created not one, but all three of the objects: the Rowing Wheel, the Stone in Focarthu, and the Pillar-Stone in Cnámchoill.[107] The blame directed at Tlachtga becomes even more intense, for in the *Bansenchus* (c. 1147) it states that she was the wife of Simon, and from her, because of the martyr she slew, is named the hill of the flocks.[108] The martyr in question is John the Baptist, whose feast day was the Summer Solstice.

The blame for John's death takes on a different form in two poems from the 14th century *Book of Uí Maine*. These poems relate the tale of how Salome demanded the head of John the Baptist as a reward for her dancing, and adds that the only person who would agree to execute the saint was Mug Roith (not Tlachtga). In addition, it states that he demanded a fee for his services (something which Simon did, and which Mug Roith does in the saga).[109] Perhaps the episode about Mug Roith's student cutting off the head of an enemy with a flaming axe provided some context for this connection with the beheading of John the Baptist. Mug Roith's association with Simon is mentioned only briefly in the ninth century poem, in two stanzas inserted in an otherwise non–Simonian narrative. These say that Mug Roith waged war with Simon against Peter to obtain a blessing on his wisdom and weapons. As a result of that conflict ("from which no brightness was born"), it states that the Irish made him (Mug Roith) a god of druidry.[110] In *Forbhais Dromma Damhgháire* there is just a brief mention of Simon, which is quite different from the references above. As Mug Roith prepares to create magical dogs to counteract the supernatural sheep, he uses the tinder box of Simon, the flint of Daniel, and the kindling wood of *Eitheoir Ilchruthaigh* ("The Many-Shaped").[111]

Do the sources provide any additional information about the magical objects that Tlachtga and/or Mug Roith were said to have created? As regards the *roth rámach* ("rowing wheel"), Gwynn translates the phrase *in roth rúad rogrinn* as "the red well-finished wheel." There are other shades of meaning for *rúad* ("red, of a brownish or dark red, as opposed to *derg*, "bright red"; often of blood-stains, as opposed to *fland,* the color of freshly shed blood; red-haired; in poetry and rhetorical style, "strong, mighty, formidable; adventurous, or difficult, dangerous, journey). *Grind* can be translated as "accurate, exact; intent, diligent; pleasant, lovely; swift, quick; strong, vigorous." The wheel could be "red and well-finished," or it could be "strong/mighty/formidable" and "very accurate, swift or fierce." Later in the poem, Gwynn translates the phrase *roth garb-grennach gráinne* as "rough-jagged dreadful wheel," which seems to be at odds with the description of it as being "red and well-finished." I suggested above that a translation for the latter phrase as "rough-bristled pointed wheel" may work better, with the "bristles" potentially signifying the spokes of a wheel (although this is just a suggestion).

A prophecy attributed to Saint Columba stated that the Rowing Wheel and the other two objects would come to Ireland prior to the Day of Judgment, during the reign of *Flann Ciothach,* the last king. On Saint John's Day—the Summer Solstice—adherents of Simon's cult would be crushed by the Rowing Wheel and other instruments of divine vengeance. O' Curry wrote that the rowing wheel was a ship containing a thousand beds, with a thousand men in each bed, a ship that could sail on both sea and land. It would not furl its sails until it was destroyed by the Pillar-Stone of Cnámchoill. They (Simon's believers) would be met by the brave chief of Cnámchoill who would cut them all off, so that not one of them should ever cross the sea again.[112]

Carey has edited a poem called "Colum Cille's Warning to Baíthín," which also refers to this scenario. It says that in Flann Cithach's time, the Judgement and the *Roth Rámach* will come. Due to the thousand beds on the ship, it will be very difficult and unsupportable. However, "the outlandish ungentle vessel" sails equally well on sea and land. The poem says that the Pillar-Stone of Cnámchaill will break it, and Congalach of Cnámchaill will overtake and kill the men at Mag nElta. Two and a half years after the Roth Rámach comes, the fleet of Inber Domnann arrives, with thousands of vessels that circle Ireland twice. The ensuing events are a bit unclear: a shipping settlement will be in the west of Inber Domnann, gathering the cattle and daughters of the Gaels. At Tara, Flann Cithach will wage combat beside the stronghold of Cormac.[113] Such are the vagaries of medieval prophecy.

The three objects also play a role in a prophetic poem attributed to Colum Cille known as "The Fleet of Inber Domnann," where the events alluded to at the end of the above poem are spelled out in more detail. *Inber Domnann* (Malahide Bay in north County Dublin) seems to have had a reputation in the tales as a traditional gateway for invaders or incomers to Ireland. In *Lebor Gabála,* the *Fomoire* (Fomorians), the *Fir Bolg* and *Tuathal Techtmar* were all said to have landed at this site. In addition to events associated with the victory of Flann Cinach/Cithach over an invading fleet, the poem mentions the three magical objects. In the second stanza it refers to "*Roth Rámach with smoothness,*" perhaps supporting the reference to the "red well-finished wheel." It is clear that a great battle is in process; in stanza five it says that "until they reach the pillar-stone of Mug Roith, a truly mighty utterance [there], the *Roth Rámach* will break, the idol will perish." Stanza six says that Mug Roith smashes the *Roth Rámach,* which was made by

Simon.[114] It seems we can get no relief to this tangle of stories! This statement clearly contradicts other accounts in which it is Tlachtga who broke the wheel, bringing a piece of it back to Ireland with her and setting it up as the pillar of Cnámchaill. It was prophesied that when the wheel itself came westward in the final days, it would be broken against the pillar. In the original text of *Immacallam in Dá Thuarad,* a calamity at Cnámchail is foretold; a gloss describes the event as the wheel's collision with the stone.[115] There is much action afoot, but little clarity.

The Thunder of the Wheel

A less apocalyptic tale is contained in "The Lore of the Fiery Arrow." This prose account states that in the time of Flan Cinach three objects will come: the Rowing Wheel, the Broom from Fanat, and the Fiery Arrow. It proceeds to give a detailed account of the lore concerning the Fiery Arrow. As the story goes, Cliach was a musician of Smirdub mac Smáil, king of the Three Rosses from *Síd Báine.* He went to woo the daughter of *Bodb* [possibly *Bodb Derg,* a son of the Dagda] in *Síd ar Femen.* After that he was playing his stringed instrument outside the *síd* for a full year. However, he came no closer to *Bodb* on account of the greatness of his power, and was able to gain nothing from the company of girls. But Cliach continued playing, until the earth burst beneath him. This is the origin of the lake on top of the mountain known as *Loch Bél Sét.*

The account then provides a second tale associated with the site, which tells of *Caer Abarbaeth,* daughter of *Etal Anbuail* of the *Side* in Connacht, who was "a powerful girl of many shapes." She had three times fifty girls around her, and every other year the company of girls would be in the shape of birds, and the next year in the shape of humans. In this supernatural bird-flock there was a chain of silver between each pair of birds. One bird among them was the fairest of all the birds of the world, with a collar of red gold around its throat from which came three times fifty chains, and an apple [apple-shaped metal object] of red gold at the end of each chain. While in bird form, the supernatural bird-flock would be on *Loch Crotta Cliach,* and they would say, "There are many remarkable treasures (*sét*) in front of (*ar bélaib*) *Loch Crotta,* so that is why it was called *Loch Bél Sét.*[116]

What do all of these unusual and disparate sources tell us about the objects that Tlachtga and her father are said to have created? The Roth Rámach and the Pillar-Stone of Cnámchaill became connected with apocalyptic events. The ongoing development of this theme has been explored by a number of scholars, but is beyond the further scope of this chapter.[117] The Stone of Forcarthain is referred to in the version of the story summarized by

O' Curry.[118] In his notes on the Metrical Dindshenchas poem, Gwynn states that the account of the *Roth Rámach* in O'Curry makes it clear that it was connected in Irish legend with the early Christian story of Simon's attempt to fly. Simon falls from the air and his body is broken into four pieces, which are turned into four blocks of stone.[119] This may be the origin of the two stones, as well as the statement that Tlachtga broke the wheel (against the stone?) and carried a fragment of it with her.

In his notes to the Dindshenchas, Gwynn mentions that the Pillar Stone of Forcarthain is said to be near Rathcoole on the road from Dublin to Naas.[120] I have not yet been able to find any local traditions connected with the stone. However, in the glossary passage on *Foí*, Stokes notes that the place name of Cnámchaill is now Cleghile (or Cleghill), two miles east of the town of Tipperary, and that its exact situation is laid down in the Book of Lismore.[121] A strangely shaped stone pillar does exist in the townland of Dromline, County Tipperary, a neighboring townland to Clegeile. It is about one meter in height, carved so as to taper slightly near the top, with one side rounded and the other side square. The owners of the land on which the stone is located note that it was originally located in an adjacent field close to the field boundary, but in 1973, during land reclamation, it was moved to its present location. Local tradition records that nothing ever grew on the stone, even though the ditch was very overgrown with ivy. In addition, when the stone was moved, it was left lying on the ground for several years, reputedly causing the withering and death of the grass in the immediate area.[122]

But what of the Rowing Wheel? One suggestion, originally made by Macalister, was that the "wheel" was perhaps reflective of some object associated with druidic craft; specifically an object similar to the "bull-roarer" used in various indigenous cultures. The bull-roarer is a flat lath of wood attached to a string that is whirled about in a wheel or circle. The whirling produces a remarkable sound which was considered to be the voice of a god (and in some cases, likened to the sound of thunder). One of its most common uses was in initiation rituals. Initiates would have never before heard the remarkable sound it emits, and due to its relatively small size it could be easily concealed by the initiators. The bull-roarer was used for other ritual and practical purposes as well.[123] The bull-roarer was often regarded with fear and awe, and at least in an Australian Aboriginal context, women were prohibited from touching it, being present for its use, or even looking at it. These prohibitions existed alongside myths in both Australian and southern New Guinea cultural contexts in which the bull-roarer was said to have been first discovered or used by a woman, but later stolen by a man for his exclusive ownership and use. This may reflect Tlachtga's "breaking" of the wheel, as well as the passage that said that those who saw the wheel would go blind, those who heard it would go deaf, and those who touched it would die. Most

interesting of all for our exploration is the fact that the bull-roarer was sometimes called "the oar," on account of its shape.[124]

Now, Macalister's suggestion could be easily swept under the rug of
"well-intentioned but misinformed perceptions concerning traditional cultures," especially during the early 1900s (and earlier periods as well). However,
there does happen to be solid physical evidence for the use of the bull-roarer
in Ireland during the Iron Age. This first came to my attention during a grant-
funded research trip to Ireland and Scotland, in which I was researching very
early aspects of instrumental and vocal music in Celtic cultures. In the Ulster
Museum in Belfast, while examining objects pertaining to Iron Age Irish culture, I was stunned to see several bull-roarers in a display case. They were
very similar in design to bull-roarers from other cultural contexts, and were
in fact labeled as "bull-roarers" by the museum. This is quite an important
realization to consider, in relation to these Irish accounts of "the rowing
wheel."

Haddon described specimens from Counties Antrim and Cork (prob-
ably those that ended up in the museums in Belfast and Dublin). E. Estyn
Evans also noted the existence of these type of objects in early 20th century
Ireland, where they were primarily (but not exclusively) considered to be
children's toys. These objects consisted of a thin lath of wood with serrated
edges that was swung around on a string so as to produce a buzzing noise.
It was known as a "boomer" in County Down and a "whee-doodle" in County
Carlow. In County Down, a boy playing with one was reproved by an old
woman who told him that he was "meddling with a sacred thing." In County
Carlow, it seems to have also been regarded formerly as a "sacred thing."
Raftery noted that in 1921 a young boy was whirling it around and an old
man who saw him became very angry. He told the child to take the thing
home and burn it, as otherwise he would bring bad luck on the country-side.
Its Modern Irish name was the *Clairín Búirthe* (< *cláirín* "a little board, short
stave; flat part, palm (of the hand)" + *búirthe* "bellowing, roaring," used of
the sound of the lion and the bull) giving "Board/Stave of Bellowing/Roar-
ing").[125]

Wheel, Broom and Arrow

If we revisit the prose account of the Fiery Arrow, it states that in the
time of Flan Cinach the Rowing Wheel (*Roth Rámach*), the Broom from Fanat
(*Scuap a Fanait*) and the Fiery Arrow (*Saignen Tenntige*) will come. Here the
Rowing Wheel is connected with two other objects, but they are not stones.
The Fiery Arrow is connected with two native origin stories that have no
connection at all with Simon Magus or the apocalypse, but instead have to

do with the origin of a lake which erupted due to the playing of a musician from the *Síd* (and whose name was connected with magical birds from the Otherworld). Perhaps there is some connection between the Fiery Arrow and the eruption of a lake, with the spear thrown by Mug Roith from which a water source ensues. Here we should pause to note that the word *saignén* means "lightning, a flash of light, a sudden blast," and the phrase *saighnéan teintighe* denotes "a flash of lightning." The word *scúap* often denotes "a brush or broom," as well as a "flax sheaf or bundle," or in reference to human or animal hair. Interestingly (I believe due to the association with a broom or besom), it can also denote "a gust of wind." If the *scúap* is associated with gusts of wind, and the fiery arrow is associated with lightning, it may be that the rowing wheel was associated with thunder, due to the noise it made.

Perhaps these three objects played a role in native traditions pertaining to the end of the world (or the end of ages or cycles of time). In Tírechán's seventh century account of a discussion between Saint Patrick and King Loegaire about baptism, the king refers to "the day of *erdathe* according to the druids, that is, the day of … judgement…."[126] We have abundant evidence concerning Norse ideas about the end of times, and it is reasonable to assume that people in Celtic-speaking cultures also had their own traditional concepts regarding the end of the world (whether that was a final event, or a series of ages or cycles). Carey suggests that "ancient pagan beliefs about world destruction may have reinforced Christian expectations of Doomsday."[127] The passage is cryptic, and the word *erdathe* is rare and difficult to parse. It is not even clear where to separate the word into syllables.

The prefix *er-* could reflect either 1 *ér* ("noble, great"), 2 *ér/áer-* (an intensifying prefix), or *air-* ("before," or an intensifying prefix). Not entirely impossible in a purely symbolic fashion would be a connection with the word *úr* "fresh, new; a beginning." *Dath* denotes "colour, hue; brightness; outward appearance; degree, rank, order." Or we might consider a derivation from *daithe* "nimbleness, swiftness, deftness" or some form related to *dathad* "a bestowing, giving." This might suggest a meaning along the lines of "Great Swiftness" or "Guarding Order," both allusive but fairly non-specific terms.

However, if we separate the word in a different way, perhaps the first syllable is reflective of *ard*, "high, elevated, lofty; noble, distinguished; great, extensive." The second syllable might reflect *áth* "ford, open space or hollow between two objects," or *athaig/athad* "interval, space, usually of time." This could give a meaning of "Great/Extensive + Space between two intervals of Time." However, variant spellings of *erdath* (*airdach, airddach*) point to Old Irish *airtach*, "act of refreshing, restoring; act of celebrating; festival, ceremony," which would be most fitting in terms of pagan beliefs about the cycles of time.

As we saw above (and in Chapter 1) there are a number of early references pertaining to the beliefs of the Continental Celts in relation to the possible conditions associated with the end of the world (or of cycles of time). The earliest is Strabo's first century BCE *Geographia* [IV.iv.4], where he states that the druids of Gaul said that "souls and the cosmos are indestructible, but that sometime(s) fire and water will overpower them." Perhaps the Rowing Wheel, whose sound was often likened to that of thunder, represented thunder in this type of cosmogonic context. There is ample evidence in early Celtic artwork for deities associated with wheels, which are believed to be celestial or solar symbols.[128] As we saw above, the phrase *saighnéan teintighe* denotes "a flash of lightning," and *scúap* could refer to a gust of wind. Perhaps this three-fold combination of thunder, lightning and wind had something to do with early Irish perceptions about cosmogonic events.

Clerics and scribes who did not know precisely what the Rowing Wheel was, ascribed to it the shape of a ship with many oars, due to the inclusion of the word *rámach.* It is reasonable to suggest that these three objects were not originally associated with Simon, Flan Cinach or the Apocalypse, but had to do with native beliefs or tales, such as those connected with the Fiery Arrow. The association of "the Rowing Wheel" and other such objects with pagan rituals or beliefs may have led to their inclusion in medieval Irish concerns regarding the Day of Judgment. Some of the details of those pagan tales also led to a connection with Simon Magus. Simon actually has only a very small role in the ninth century poem and the saga. Perhaps earlier versions of Mug Roith's story—in prose or poetic form—were similar to the attested versions, but without the diversion of Simon or Salome. In addition, if we consider the evidence of Iron Age Irish bull-roarers, it may be that the etymological note suggesting that Mug Roith was a *magus rotarum* who made his prognostications by way of wheels was not entirely a linguistic speculation.

The Continental Celts believed that the world could possibly be overwhelmed by water and fire; these two elements play a very large role in the saga of Mug Roith. He also uses his breath to achieve his magical ends, and is cited as fashioning "druid's arrows." There are also several references to his chariot (and its fittings), a vehicle which could go as fast as the March wind. If we look back at the three objects related to the Lore of the Fiery Arrow, we have the following trio: the Rowing Wheel, the Broom from Fanat, and the Fiery Arrow:

The Rowing Wheel—sound of thunder/bull-roarer/Mug Roith's chariot wheels

The Broom of Fanat—"gust of wind"/Mug Roith's use of the druidic breath

The Fiery Arrow—"flash of lightning/Mug Roith's fashioning of druid's arrows

As for Tlachtga, her association with a site connected with Samhain was of course highly problematic for the incoming religion. Archaeological evidence from the period between 400 BCE (the earliest date from that site to which we could comfortably assign Gaelic language and culture) and 500 CE (when paganism would still have been current in Ireland), shows changes in the use of the site, including the creation of the southern enclosure (and the infant burial), and the construction of the site as we now have it. Very little about Tlachtga's role regarding Samain or its rituals has survived, other than Keating's passage (which, if true, is quite informative). He states that the fire of Tlachtga was ordained to be kindled at the site, and the purpose of the sacred fire was to summon the priests, seers and druids of Ireland come to *Cnoc Tlachtga,* to assemble on the eve of Samhain in order to consume (and presumably preside over or assist with) the sacrifices that were offered to the pagan gods.

The passage seems to be reasonably accurate, based on what we know about Samain and other Irish Feast days from various written sources. Notably, we have a text from the 11th century that refers to throngs of people (especially women) offering prayers (*itched,* a native rather than Christian term) on the eve of Samain, which were addressed to a woman of the *Síd* known as *Mongfind* ("Bright Mane"). In the tale *Aided Chrimthainn* ("The Death of Crimthann"), Mongfind was a woman of the *Síd* who died at Samhain. It states that: "Samhain is called the feast of Mongfhinn by the rabble, for she was powerful, and was a witch, for as long as she was in a body; and that is why women, and the rabble, utter prayers to her on the night of Samain."[129] Around the same time period the Irish were said to still seek oracles from the god Oengus mac Óg at Newgrange.[130] The details in these accounts are too specific to be summarily dismissed.

It is lamentable that no other Dindshenchas poem about Tlachtga's pre–Simon adventures has survived. It seems as though her traditional lore—her *senchas*—has been rent into pieces, presumably because of her association with Samain, and her identity as a woman associated with occult knowledge. And while her lore may have been broken into fragments (like the fragment of the Rowing Wheel she was said to carry with her), perhaps her story may be recovered if we sift carefully through the remnants. If Tlachtga was in fact a supernatural or divine female figure associated with the site where the early Irish held their Samain assemblies, she would have been considered very powerful. She may have had her own association with learning and hidden knowledge, separate from any association with Simon. We know that one form of the *ogam* alphabet was named after her: *Taebogam Tlachtga .i. d' aentaeb uile na fega-sa sis,* the "Side Ogham of Tlachtga," that is, on one side all these letters below.[131] Undoubtedly there were more tales and traditions associated with Tlachtga, to which we do not currently have access.

Perhaps it was she who created the *Roth Rámach;* it might have even been used during the Samain ritual at her assembly site. Tlachtga may have learned some of her wisdom from her father, who received training from the Otherworldly druidess Banbhuana ("Everlasting Woman") in the realms of the *Áes Síde.* The Rowing Wheel, the Fiery Arrow, and the Broom of Fanat may have symbolized the powers of thunder, lightning and wind—perhaps associated with cosmic events in Irish tradition—as well as the power of the druid—the Devotee of the Wheel—and his daughter at whose site the Samhain fires were kindled.

9

Cauldron of Awen, Stream of Imbas

The Symbolism of Water and Divine Inspiration

In Irish and Welsh literary sources, bodies of water are credited with a variety of practical and esoteric qualities, including healing, purification, wisdom and transformation. In this final chapter, we will explore several streams of thought pertaining to this phenomenon. These will include the connection between rivers and poetic or divinely-inspired wisdom, wells or springs associated with sacred knowledge, imagery in descriptions of whirlpools and sacred vessels, and prophetic or other divine qualities associated with sites located near waterfalls.[1]

Rivers of Sacred Knowledge

A number of early Irish texts describe rivers that were held in great esteem and were associated with sacred or poetic wisdom and inspiration. Two of the most well-known accounts come from the *Dindshenchas* poems pertaining to the goddesses *Boand* (an origin legend of the River Boyne) and *Sinann* (an origin legend of the River Shannon). In the story of Sinann, she is described as a woman of the Túatha Dé Dannan who approaches a particular well. In her pursuit of knowledge she follows a stream that issues from the well and is drowned, thereby becoming the eponymous spirit of the river.[2] A somewhat similar story is told about Boand, who is also a member of the Túatha Dé Danann. She approaches a sacred well and unadvisedly walks around it three times in a counter-sunwise direction. As a result, the waters rise up and she is disfigured, drowned, and transformed into the spirit of the river.[3]

These wells possessed a dualistic attribute of being able to provide wisdom or cause harm. In the story of Boand, the well was guarded by her husband *Nechtan* (whose name is cognate with *Neptune*) and his three cupbearers *Flesc* ("rod, wand"), *Luam* ("pilot, steersman"), and *Lam* ("hand, arm," or "prowess, valour, accomplishment").[4] The well's powers were so potent that the eyes of anyone who looked into the well would burst (other than Nechtan and the cupbearers). Even by moving to the left or the right, a person would not be able to come away from the well without blemish. In addition, the poem states that "every secret or mysterious evil" would "burst forth" from the well (*maided cech mí-rún*).[5]

A lesser-known reference to a well of power occurs in the *Dindshenchas* poem of *Cend Febrat*. In this poem, the poet relates how during his sleep he was shown every fairy-mound in Cend Febrat. He was also shown a variety of gravesites, and a well or spring famous for its beauty and its never-failing properties. Whoever had the well on their right would remain free from spells or disease, while those who had it on their left hand side would experience quick decay or a shortening of their days. The well was said to have special virtues or properties, as well as specific prohibitions or spells (*búada is búangesse*).[6]

Regardless of the potentially dangerous attributes of these wells and rivers, they were considered extremely venerable. The perceived power of the Boyne is reflected in the fact that in the first *Dindshenchas* poem pertaining to Boand, the river was said to have no fewer than fifteen names (according to medieval Irish conceptions). At the site of the spring from which it issued, the river had the same name as the well: *Segais* (perhaps < *sed/seg* "strength, vigour" + *fis* "knowledge"). After this it was referred to as the *Arm of Nuadu's Wife* and then the *Leg of Nuadu's Wife*. Further along it was called the *Great Silver Yoke*, the *White Marrow of Fedlimid*, *Stormy Wave*, *River of the White Hazel* and *Banna* (as far as Lough Neagh). At this point in the story, the estuary appears to expand beyond its purely physical bounds, and its symbolic power grows to include waterways from other regions. These regions include Scotland (where the river was known as *Roof of the Ocean* and *Lunnand*) and Britain (where it included *Sabrann*, the River Severn). The account then proceeds to include rivers known to medieval scribes from Biblical or Classical sources, such as the Tiber, the Jordan, the Euphrates and the Tigris.[7]

In the *Dindshenchas,* the well associated with Sinann is presented in a somewhat less sinister light than the well approached by Boand. In the poem, Sinann is said to possess every sort of fame or reknown except for *imbas/immus* ("great knowledge," presumably referring to the specialized power known as *imbas forosnai*).[8] In one version of the tale, the power she seeks is called "great wisdom by means of streams" (*imma sóis co srethaib*). This was apparently an important or eminent activity (*gním nóis*) that was needed for her "new life" (*núa-bethaid*).[9] Perhaps the attainment of this power would enable her to transform herself through specialized knowledge or ability.

The phrase *imma sóis co srethaib* may also refer to knowledge associated with an ordering or arrangement (*sreth*) of poetic words or of divinely inspired words, such as may have been used in spells or incantations. The word *sreth* occurs in a number of contexts associated with the craft of the poet: *sreth rann* ("a series of parts [of speech]"), *sreth senchais* ("a series of stories"), and *sreathaibh roscaigh ocus fasaigh ocus airchetail* ("a series of proverbs, commentaries and poetic compositions"). It also occurs in the phrase *iar sreth na súad*, "according to the threads of poetic arts/compositions," which means "handed down by tradition." The words *sreth* and *imbas* occur together in sources other than the story of Sinann. The metrical term *sreth immais* referred to the alliteration of all of the words in a particular line, and the phrase *sreth immais* could refer to a general "spreading of knowledge."[10]

In these place-name stories, the wells were perceived of as sources of wisdom, and the flowing rivers were the method of conveying that wisdom. The concept of the "flowing of wisdom" is referred to in other sources as well. In a group of early Irish poems referred to as *The Cauldron of Poesy*, a specialized vessel was reputed to be the source of "courses of excellent knowledge" (*rethaib sofis*) as well as " a river or current of great knowledge."[11] It was said to sing or chant (*ar-cain*) by way of "a stream of honour or pre-eminence" (*sruaim n-ordan*). The word *srúaim* ("stream") appears in other sources in relation to these concepts, as in the phrases *srúaim sois* ("a stream of great knowledge"), *srúaim ecna úaigh* ("stream of pure wisdom") and *srúaim mór ind forcitil spirdáldi* ("a mighty stream of spiritual doctrine"). In The Book of Leinster, a short entry refers to the "fourteen streams" of poetic ability.[12]

The idea that wisdom should "flow" from the enlightened or inspired person is visible in the phrase *sruth sulbaire ind labartha*, "a stream of eloquence of speaking" (< *sruth* "stream, river, current, torrent"). One of the higher poetic grades, a subdivision of *sóerbard* (as well as a poetic meter) were both referred to as *sruth di aill*.[13] In *Immacallam in Dá Thuarad*, the poet *Néde* states that one of the arts he practices is *sruth fail* ("a stream of science"), a term which is glossed as "many metres, or the abundance of science." Interestingly, one of the activities the poet says he hopes to undertake is to "go among the streams of knowledge" (*etir sruthu íuil*).[14]

The Well of Wisdom

In the texts, the place of origin of these specialized types of wisdom is described as a well or spring (*topar/tobar*), a word which can also denote a "source." One such well is described in detail in the first *Dindshenchas* account of Sinann. This well was said to be located under the sea and at the edge of a river, and it had seven primary streams flowing from it. In the well could be found *immus na Segsa* (the great knowledge of *Segais*), and over it stood the "melodious hazel of the poets" (*coll n-écsi n-ilcheólach*).[15] The nuts of the trees burst forth all at once, along with leaf, flower and fruit, and the nuts fell from the trees into the "honoured well." From the seven streams came a "whispering" (*cocur*) of musical wisdom or inspiration (*ceól-éicse*).[16] The word *éicse*, used here in connection with a musical aspect, has a number of relevant meanings: "divination; wisdom, the profession of a seer; revelation, lore, learning (especially poetry/poetic composition, the poetic art, skill or calling); the poetic profession, poets, the bardic order."[17]

In the second version of Sinann's tale, the well is referred to as *Tipra Chonnlai*, the "Well of Connla," and is likewise located beneath the ocean. Seven streams rose from the well, "six streams, with the seventh being that of Sinann." In this version there are nine hazel trees around the well, which were associated with *Crimall* the sage (*fir glic*). These trees also manifested nuts, leaves and flowers at the same time. They dropped their nuts into the well under the command of some obscure druidical force or knowledge (*le doilbi smachta fo cheó doirchi dráidechta*). The nuts were scattered on the bottom of the well and eaten by the salmon that lived in the well.[18]

There is an unusual detail in the second account of Sinann. In this poem, the juice of the nuts were said to have formed "bubbles of wisdom" (*bolca immaiss*) which flowed down the streams. Sinann, who lacked only the power of *imbas*, saw the bubbles of wisdom and went after them into the water where she was drowned.[19] These "bubbles" of wisdom or inspiration are mentioned in several other sources, where they are referred to as *bolg fis* ("bubble of wisdom") or *bolg imbais* ("bubble of great knowledge").[20] These terms, "a bubble or ball of wisdom," may be a poetic kenning for the hazelnut. However, as I have argued elsewhere, these kennings could be coded references to a type of entheogenic substance, the *Amanita Muscaria* mushroom, which was utilized in various pan-EurAsian contexts for trance induction and the acquisition of sacred or occult knowledge.[21]

One of the most memorable descriptions of a well of wisdom comes from "Cormac's Adventures in the Land of Promise." Cormac is lured away from the royal fortress at Tara and into a magical mist. He then finds himself inside a royal dwelling made from beams of bronze and wattles of silver, and thatched with the wings of white birds. There he sees a fountain with five streams flowing from it and the inhabitants of the Otherworld drinking its water. Nine purple or crimson (*corcor*) hazel trees grow over the fountain, which are referred to as the "hazels of *Buan*" ("everlasting, enduring"). The trees drop their nuts into the fountain, and the five salmon that live in the streams sever their husks and send them floating down the streams. As in the first *Dindsenchas* account of Sinann, there is a musical component. In *Sinann's* tale, a "whispering" of musical wisdom or inspiration is heard; in Cormac's tale it states that the sound of the falling of the streams was "more melodious than any music that men sing."[22]

At the end of the tale, the meaning of this mythic scenario is explained to Cormac by a supernatural informant, who is a pre–Christian deity:

> I am Mannanán mac Lir, king of the Land of Promise; and to see the Land of Promise was the reason I brought thee hither…. The fountain which you saw, with the five streams out of it, is the Fountain of Knowledge, and the streams are the five senses through which knowledge is obtained. And no one will have knowledge who drinks not a draught out of the fountain itself and out of the streams. The folk of many arts are those who drink of them both.[23]

There is a very interesting correspondence between these early literary depictions and an historical account of a healing well on the Isle of Skye. In 1695, Martin Martin mentioned that there were many springs and fountains on the island, the most celebrated of which was the *Loch Siant* well. It was visited by the inhabitants of the island, as well as by numerous mainlanders, who believed it had the power to cure a variety of ailments. Those who knew the customs of the well walked three times around it in a sun-wise direction and drank its water, leaving a small offering on the stone that covered the well. Nine springs issued from the hill above the well, and the local inhabitants paid a tribute of water from the nine springs to a small stream that issued from the well itself. Near the well was a small lake in which lived a number of trout that were highly esteemed and protected by those who visited and tended the well.[24]

The Vessel of Knowledge

In Irish and Welsh literary sources, there is also ample evidence for the association of wisdom and inspiration with cauldrons, cups or vessels. One of the most famous is the medieval Welsh tale known as the *Story of Gwion Bach*. In the tale, the magician *Cerridwen* brews a magical elixir of prophetic knowledge for her otherwise ungifted son. However, when the brew inside the cauldron is ready, Cerridwen has fallen asleep. The magical drops fall on a young boy who was tending the fire, and he acquires the gifts of poetry, prophecy and shapeshifting.[25] Later, in his new incarnation as the legendary poet-seer *Taliesin* ("Shining Brow"), the young man proclaims his abilities in a number of remarkable medieval poems.[26]

A famous poet by the name of Taliesin appears to have been an historical figure, and some of his praise poetry (which may date to the sixth century) still exists. Over the centuries, Taliesin becomes a mystical, legendary figure, and a number of remarkable poems (including some containing allusions to wisdom and specialized knowledge) are attributed to him. These were created by later medieval Welsh poets writing in the "voice of Taliesin," a fairly common poetic occurrence seen in both Irish and Welsh traditions.[27]

In one of the legendary poems, Taliesin states that he obtained something called *awen* from the cauldron of Cerridwen. This is a Middle Welsh word meaning "poetic inspiration." The word *awen* is cognate with the Old Irish word *aí* (earlier form **auí*), which means "blowing, breath, wind" (or in the words of Patrick Ford, "in-spiration").[28] In the Middle Welsh poem *Angar Kyfundawt*, the poetic voice of Taliesin says that God bestowed *awen*, but the divisions of awen were "ranged" (i.e. arranged, put in order) and created in *Annwfn* (the Welsh or early British pagan Otherworld domain). These statements reflect the Christian milieu of Welsh society at the time the poem was written, as well as aspects of native Welsh tradition. In either case, it is clear that the poet considers *awen* to be something that comes from the realms of the divine.

> *Ef a'e rin rodes,*
> *awen aghymes...*
> *Yn Annwfyn y diwyth,*
> *yn Annwfyn y gorwyth,*
> *yn Annwfyn is eluyd,*
> *yn aer uch eluyd...*

> He with his miracles bestowed
> Immeasurable inspiration...
> In Annwfyn he ranged them
> In Annwfyn he made them
> In Annwfyn below the earth
> In the air above the earth...[29]

The poet also states that he has knowledge of these matters, and refers explicitly to the "flowing" of poetic inspiration:

> *Gogwn dedyf radeu*
> *Awen pan deffreu...*

> I know the set gradations
> Of inspiration when it flows...[30]

Later in the poem, Taliesin says that he "sings" *awen*, and brings it forth from the depths (perhaps referring to an Underworld aspect of Annwfyn, or the poet's inner depths of knowledge and ability). This is followed by lines describing knowledge of the river that was believed to flow around the world in medieval times, as well as other mysteries of the natural world:

Awen a ganaf
O dwfyn ys dygaf
Auon kyt beryt
Gogwn y gwrhyt
Gogwn pan dyueinw
Gogwn pan dyleinw...
Gogwn pet pegor
Yssyd y dan vor...
Pet paladyr yg kat
Pet dos yg kawat...
Pwy enw y deu eir
Ny eing yn vn peir...

I sing inspiration
I bring it forth from the depths
The connected river which flows
I know its might
I know how it ebbs
I know how it flows...
I know how many creatures
are under the sea...
How many shafts in a battle
How many drops in a shower...
(and) what the name of the two words are
that can't be fitted into a single cauldron...[31]

The cognate term *aí/ae* is mentioned in a number of early Irish texts. In *Tecosca Cormaic* ("The Instructions of Cormac") it states that a king should support this skill or power (*bíathad cech n-aí*).[32] There are also several figures who possess this word as a name. In the Battle of Mag Tuired, a member of the *áes dána* from the Túatha Dé Danann was called *Aí mac Olloman* ("Poetic Inspiration, son of *Ollam* [a master poet]").[33] In *Lebor Gabála*, a great grandson of Ogma had almost the identical name: *Aí mac Ollam*.[34] A figure named *Ae Fhind mac Deadad* was also mentioned in *Lebor Gabála*.[35]

The concept of *aí* is referred to in a medieval Irish training manual for the *filid* (the medieval Irish poet-seers) known as *Auraceipt na n-Éces*. For instance, it occurs in the phrase *in cetna ae for seis*, "the first science of learning."[36] Seven "sciences" (*seacht n-ae*) or "prime meters of the poetic art" (*primeillge na filideachta*) are mentioned in the text.[37] In one section, *aí* is said to be a science that should be perceived in the mind. The text also states that there are five separate forms of *aí/ae*:

"*ae* that nourishes, *ae* that sings, *ae* that sues, *ae* that judges and *ae* that sits."[38]

The veneration of poetic inspiration found expression in two early Irish invocations to *aí*. Both poems belong to a "creed of poetry" (*crédha na filid-heachta*), and in both cases *aí* is personified as a woman.[39] In several lines, the poet makes veiled references to specific techniques or terminology associated with poetic art. For example, in the first verse, the word *gnúis* ("face, countenance; aspect, kind, form") can in poetic contexts refer to grammatical forms. In such contexts, the word *brecht* may not always be distinguished from *bricht* ("incantation, charm, magical spell"). The word *nasc* ("fastening, tie, ring; legal bond, obligation") may refer obliquely to a type of alliteration known as "binding alliteration." In this technique, the first letter of the last word in a line would be the same as the first letter of the first word in the next line, thus "linking" or "binding" the lines phonetically and sonically. This type of alliteration occurs in some parts of the poem (as does alliteration between stressed words in subsequent lines). I have altered the arrangement of the lines from a layout suggested by Breatnach, in order to highlight the alliteration, which would have been very important in the oral performance of the poem.[40]

Subsequent stanzas also contain references to poetic concepts. In the third verse, *fíad* ("honour, respect, reverence") can refer specifically to the honor bestowed upon a guest according to their rank. This word occurs in a stanza that alludes to the poet's recitation at a noble or royal court, where each person is seated according to their rank. In the fourth verse, the word *míad* ("honour, dignity, elevation, rank, status of an individual") also refers to this scenario. However, the word can also refer to an "elevation of mind," possibly referring to the poet's training and ability (or the effect of the poetic recitation upon the audience). In the same line, the word *rún* ("something hidden or occult, a mystery") may also denote "a mystic or hidden meaning," something the poets were very fond of including in their poems (and which occurs in this poem as well). To my knowledge, this is the first complete translation of this poem:

> *Fo-chen aí*
> *ilchruthach*
> *ilġnúisech*
> *ilḃrechtach*
> *Bé ṡaer*
> *ṡonaisc.*
> *Ar dligid*
> *túarastal*
> *Ar ni tualaing*
> *as-rinde*
> *cen túarastal*
> *Ar dligid*
> *cach aisnéis*
> *a túarastal.*
>
> *For-reith, for-reither*
> *(fo) fiadibh*
> *saímne suidigther*

Ar as fuirired ann sin
subae i clúasib caich.

Rofítir cach
ránnaide recht
cach miad
cach máisrechtach
rán-rúnach
Ro saithe
subaigther

Fo-gleinn, fo-glenar
Do-eim, do-emar
For-reith, for-reiter
Fo chúartaib cloth

Fo-suidethar
be dúisech
duthrachtach
Ar dligid
a h-étsecht
a h-attlugud
i túaith
a túarastal
toraib[41]

Welcome, poetic inspiration!
Of many shapes
Many forms
Many variations;
A female artificer
of excellent binding.

With regard to the right
of remuneration
(For she is not able
to declare [poetry]
without compensation)
By virtue of prerogative,
every narration
has its reward.

It proceeds, it is proceeded
In accordance with honours
Peace is established,
for that is brought about;
A pleasure in the ear of each.

She is aware of every
lawful apportioning,
Every elevation,
Every finely-formed
Splendid, mysterious (one);

A great multitude
is made to rejoice.

It gathers, it is gathered
It protects, it is protected
It supports, it is supported
On circuits of reknown.

A generous woman
Abounding in treasures
Provides sustenance;
By virtue of tradition,
Listening to her
A rejoicing
among the túath:
The renumeration of hosts.[42]

A second poem, which is also an invocation to *aí*, contains a fragment of a symbolic "poetic lineage" (my translation):

Fo chen aí
Ingen sois
Siur chéile
Ingen menman
Míadach, mórdae...[43]

Welcome, Poetic Inspiration!
Daughter of Great Knowledge,
Sister of Wisdom,
Daughter of Mind,
Honourable, exalted...

The motif of a "lineage of wisdom" also occurs in *Immacallam in Dá Thuarad*. In this tale, the poet Néde boasts that he is the son of Poetry, son of Scrutiny, son of Meditation, son of Lore, son of Enquiry, son of Investigation, son of Great-Knowledge, son of Great Sense, son of Understanding, son of Wisdom, son of the three gods of Poetry.[44] Arranged in vertical form, the lineage reads:

Three Gods of Poetry
Wisdom
Understanding
Great Sense
Great Knowledge
Investigation
Enquiry
Lore
Meditation
Scrutiny
Poetry
Poet

The concept of *aí* is mentioned elsewhere in the *Immacallam*. Here it appears as a gloss on a poetic name for the poet Néde—*Tene feth* ("Fire of Speech")—which is glossed *loscud inna ai* ("burning of *aí*").[45] The concept of poetic heat, breath and inspiration also occurs in relation to an Otherworldly cauldron in the medieval Welsh poem *Preiddau Annwn* ("The Spoils of Annwn"), as we discussed previously. King Arthur and his retinue travel to the Otherworld to obtain a magical cauldron from the Chief of Annwn. The cauldron, which would not boil food for a coward, was said to be kindled by the breath of nine maidens. It appears to have had a possible connection with the ocean, for it was said to be "dark about its edge with pearl."[46]

In the "The Caldron of Poesy," the voice of the legendary Irish poet *Amairgen Glungél* ("Song-Born, White-Knee") mentions a cauldron which pours forth "the oral language (*aí*) of poetry."[47] In the text, three special cauldrons are mentioned: *Coire Goriath* ("The Cauldron of Warming"), *Coire Érmae* ("The Cauldron of Motion") and *Coire Sois* ("The Cauldron of Excellent Knowledge"). These cauldrons were said to be the source of poetic art and every other type of knowledge, and were believed to exist within the body of a person.[48]

In one of the poems, *Coire Goriath* was said to have been given to Amairgen directly from the divine (from "the mysteries of the elements"), and could be used to compose poetry "with many great chantings."[49] From *Coire Érmae* issued "accumulations of knowledge" (*rethaib sofis*), "strewings of wisdom" (*srethaib imbais*), "an estuary of knowledge" (*indber n-ecnai*), a "river of splendour" (*srúaim n-ordan*) and "streams of scholarship" (*srúamannaib suíthi*). It was also connected with the mastery of language, the "darkening" or obscurity of poetic speech, and the propagation of knowledge. It was referred to as a "noble brew in which is brewed the basis of all knowledge."[50] *Coire Sois* was associated with the laws of the arts, an increase in prosperity due to the rewards that come from practicing as a fully-trained poet, and the exaltation of people of artistic knowledge or skill.[51]

One passage states that *Coire Érmae* turns or changes position according to the amount of knowledge a person possesses, and that this change could take place as the result of an experience of extreme joy or sorrow. When this occurs, the Cauldron of Motion is converted into the Cauldron of Knowledge. The four types of sorrow that can turn the vessel are longing, grief, jealousy and "exile for the sake of God" (i.e. separation from the Divine).[52] The four types of joy are listed as: the force of sexual longing; safety and freedom from care, and ample food and clothing (until one begins the pursuit of *bairdne*, bardic composition or craft); joy at the prerogatives of poetry after a good study of it; and the arrival of *imbas*. It was said to accumulate in the nine hazels of Segais in the realms of the *síd*, and then sent upstream along the surface of the Boyne. A gloss on the fourth type of joy mentions a "bubble" on the herbs or plants caused by the sun, as well as the fact that "whoever consumes them will have an art or skill (*dán*)," a statement that may support the theory previously mentioned pertaining to entheogens.[53] These very early Irish poems are extremely detailed and cryptic, and a new translation and detailed exploration of "The Cauldron of Poesy" is being prepared for publication in an upcoming work.[54]

In addition to these connections with wisdom and poetry, the word *coire* ("cauldron") has a secondary meaning of "whirlpool." One of the most well-known instances of its use as a place-name is in the *Dindshenchas* account of *Coire Breccáin* (Corryvreckan). In this poem the whirlpool is referred to as the "cauldron of a hundred measures," a place the poet says he does not wish to go until he dies. It was believed that four seas gathered together at the site of the whirlpool, and that no one could cover the space between the edges of the cauldron within the span of a month. No "generous chieftain" who reached it ever returned, and even if the "hosts of the three parts of the world" were set side by side with all those who had yet to be born, this would still not fill the cauldron.[55]

In Scottish folk tradition, Coire Breccáin was associated with the legendary figure of the *Cailleach Bhéara*. She was said to wash her blankets in the whirlpool, perhaps accounting for the inclusion of the Scottish Gaelic word *breacan* ("tartan") in the place-name. Before her washing began, the roar of a coming tempest was heard by people on the shore for a distance of twenty miles for three days before the cauldron "boiled."[56] One legend stated that Breccán, a son of Partholón, drank a draught from the whirlpool and was drowned. In one stanza, he is referred to as *Breccán of Bérre*.[57]

Interestingly, glosses associated with the poems relating to "The Caldron of Poesy" mention that *Coire Goriath* ("The Cauldron of Warming") had the potential quality of being "variegated" (*brecc*). This refers to the three "colours" or varieties of poetry which could praise, warn or satirize the subject of the poem. White referred to praise poetry, variegated was a mixed assessment or a warning, and black referred to satire. As we saw above, Coire Goriath was associated with "many chantings of poetry," and these were described as "numerous displays out of the great seas of poetry."[58]

Cascades of Creation

Another body of water with legendary properties in Celtic literary and folklore contexts is the waterfall. The word *es(s)* denotes a cataract or rapid, as well as a rapidly flowing stream.[59] Waterfalls are mentioned in a poem in *Lebor Gabála Érenn*, as Amairgen magically invokes the features of the land in preparation for its inhabitation by the Gaels:

I invoke the land of Ireland;
Surging is the mighty sea,
Mighty is the upland full of meadows,
Full of meadows is the rainy wood,
Rainy is the river full of waterfalls,
Full of waterfalls is the spreading lake,
Spreading is the spring of multitudes,
The assembly of the king of Tara...[60]

The *Dindshenchas* contains several versions of a place-name story associated with a waterfall known as *Ess Ruaid* (< *ruad* "red" or "strong/mighty,"
modern Assaroe). In the first version, the waterfall was said to be located
near a *síd*-mound associated with a figure by the name of *Aed Ruad* ("Red/
Strong Fire"). The son of *Badurn*, he is a handsome, wealthy and generous
figure, and was described as being "honorable among the men of *Emain*
[Macha]" (*fíal na fír-Emna*).[61] *Aed Ruad* also features in a *Dindsenchas* poem
pertaining to *Emain Macha*, where he is said to be the father of *Macha Mongruad* (Macha "Red-Mane") The account tells how Macha overcame the five
sons of *Dithorba* and forced them to build her a fortress. It then gives a brief
version of the famous story of Macha's race against the king's horses.[62]

The tradition that Aed Ruad was Macha's father is also mentioned in
the Prose *Dindshenchas* account of Emain Macha. Here, three kings were ruling in joint-sovereignty over Ireland: *Dithorba mac Dímmán* (of Uisneach in
Meath), *Cimbaeth mac Fintan*, son of Argatmar (of Finnabair of Mag Inis),
and *Aed Ruad mac Bádurn*, son of Argatmar (of Tír Aeda). Aed Ruad was
said to have been the first of the three kings to die. He drowned in Ess Rúaid,
and from there his body was borne into the adjacent *síd*-mound (*Síd-Aeda*).
He had no children except a single daughter, Macha Mongruad, who
demanded her father's turn at the kingship.[63]

In the *Dindsenchas* poem on *Ard Macha,* Macha gives birth to twins
after winning a race against the king's horses. The twins are called *Fir* and
Fial,[64] perhaps reflecting concepts associated with truth and honor (< 1 *fír*
"true" and 1 *fíal* "noble, honourable"). However, it is possible that the names
reflect some connection or confusion with Macha's father, who was described
as *fíal na fír-Emna*. Another strong possibility is that the names reflect a form
of the word *fer* ("man, person") and 3 *fíal* "kin, related." This would be particularly appropriate in light of the widespread Indo-European myth of the
divine twins, whose names usually reflect the words for "man" and "twin."[65]
(The word "twin" occurs in the place name *Emain Macha,* "The Twins of
Macha"). Interestingly, in a number of Indo-European contexts, the divine
twins are often associated with horses and with a female figure.[66]

The significance of the divine twins in Indo-European mythology is
underscored by their association with foundation or creation myths. In many

cases they were believed to be the progenitors of the human race.[67] Aed Ruad may therefore be the grandfather of the divine twins. Interestingly, in the *Dindchenchas* poem on Emain Macha, Macha states that she is the daughter of someone called *Sainrith mac Inboith* ("Pre-Eminence, Son of Existence"? < *sainred* "special, pre-eminent," *in-* "worthy of/capable of/fit or proper for" + 1 *buith* "being, existing"), a figure potentially associated with creation or existence.[68]

Aed Ruad is described as the son of *Badurn* (perhaps a form of *báidid*, "drowns, submerges" "extinguishes, quenches" "destroys, overwhelms."). This association with water is also seen in connection with Macha. In the *Dindshenchas* of Emain Macha she was said to have been summoned to the king's horse race from "beneath the ocean waves," and that her domain was a "roofless dwelling in the west."[69] As Patrick Ford points out, there is another Celtic goddess associated with horses and sovereignty who may also have had a connection with the ocean. The widely venerated goddess Epona was associated with horses, sovereignty, and journeys to the Otherworld (possibly those that took place after death). She was so popular with Roman cavalry stationed in Britain and other Roman occupied regions that she was actually given a feast day in the Roman calendar. That feast day was December 18, situated between the Consualia (December 15) and the Opalia (December 19). As Consus was identified with Poseidon Hippios, the placement of Epona's feast day near that of a deity associated with water and horses was probably no coincidence.[70]

In addition to the symbolism of water and wisdom, in these sources we have also encountered themes pertaining to fire, heat, boiling and inspiration. Georges Dumézil and Patrick Ford have written about various Indo-European manifestations of the esoteric concept of "fire in water." This was a potent essence that was believed to be maintained in certain bodies of water. It was accessible only to a select few, and had the power to endow them with extraordinary powers. This "fire in water" possessed characteristics associated with potential danger and destruction, as well as heat, burning, illumination, and other concepts pertaining to the attainment of wisdom and the manifestation of poetic or prophetic skill.[71]

Literary references to Boand, Sinann, Taliesin and Amairgen, and other Celtic sources support a connection between fire, water and divine wisdom. As we saw above, the Well of Wisdom was often associated with salmon who cracked open the hazelnuts of wisdom. In early Irish tradition we encounter the *eó fis,* or "salmon of wisdom," which inhabited certain wells, springs or rivers. One of its traditional habitations was at the waterfall of *Ess Ruaid.*[72] In addition to being the abode of *Aed Ruad,* this waterfall was associated with a mythical figure known as *Aed Álaind* ("Lovely/Splendid Fire"). This name refers to a figure who is a well-known member of the Túatha Dé Danann.

The Dagda was known by many titles, including *In Ruad Rofhessa* ("The Red/Noble One of Great Knowledge"), *Echu Ollathair* (perhaps "Great Father of Many Horses"), as well as the epithet *Aed Álaind* of Ess Ruaid.[73] A few sources state that *Aed Álaind* was a son of the Dagda,[74] or one of his grandsons (the offspring of the Dagda's son *Bodb Derg*, "Red Raven").[75] However, the correlation between the Dagda himself and the name *Aed Álaind* is supported by another traditional habitation of the *eó fis*, which was the pool of *Linn Féic*. In one account, the Dagda was referred to as "the king of Linn Féic" (*rig Féic-Linne*).[76] In other sources, the Dagda is clearly associated with wisdom. In the Second Battle of Mag Tuired he described as a "god of druidry."[77] In Cormac's Glossary he is said to be the father of Brigit, a "female sage," "woman of wisdom" and "the goddess whom poets adored"[78]; in the *Immacallam,* Brigit was said to be a *ban-fili*.[79]

A connection between waterfalls and wisdom is also evident in a number of interesting accounts describing divination rites from early modern Scotland. In Pennant's journey through Scotland in 1769, he describes a divinatory practice he witnessed on the Isle of Skye (although he is dismissive of what he sees):

> A wild species of magic was practiced in the district of Trotternish that was attended with horrible solemnity: a family who pretended to oracular knowledge practiced these ceremonies. In this country is a vast cataract whose waters falling from a high rock, jet so far as to form a dry hollow beneath, between them and the precipice. One of these imposters was sewed up in the hide of an ox, and, to add terror to the ceremony, was placed in this concavity; the trembling enquirer was brought to the place, where the shade, and the roaring of the waters, increased the dread of the occasion. The question is put, and the person in the hide delivers his answer. And so ends this species of divination styled *Taghairm*.[80]

A similar practice, common to the western islands of Scotland, was described almost a century earlier by Martin Martin in 1695 (although his account does not mention the waterfall):

> The second way of consulting the oracle was by a party of men who first retired to solitary places, remote from any house, and there they singled out one of their number, and wrapped him in a big cow's hide, which they folded about him; his whole body was covered with it except his head, and so left in this posture all night until his invisible friends relieved him by giving a proper answer to the question in hand, which he received, as he fancied, from several persons that he found about him all that time. His consorts returned to him at break of day, and then he communicated his news to them, which often proved fatal to those concerned in such unwarrantable inquiries.[81]

Another version of the *taighairm* reflects the importance of the waterfall in the rite:

The divination by the *taghairm* was once a noted superstition among the Gael, and in the northern parts of the Lowlands of Scotland. When any important question concerning futurity arose, and of which a solution was, by all means, desirable, some shrewder person than his neighbors was pitched upon, to perform the part of a prophet. This person was wrapped in the warm smoking hide of a newly-slain ox, and laid at full length in the wildest recess of some lonely waterfall. The question was then put to him, and the oracle was left in solitude to consider it. Here he lay for some hours with his cloak of knowledge around him, and over his head, no doubt, to see the better into futurity; deafened by the incessant roaring of the torrent; every sense assailed; his body steaming; his fancy in a ferment; and whatever notion had found its way into his mind from so many sources of prophesy, it was firmly believed to have been communicated by invisible beings who were supposed to haunt such solitudes.[82]

The Scottish Gaelic term *taghairm* comes from Old Irish *togairm,* which refers to an act of calling, invoking, petitioning, inviting or summoning. These folklore accounts display similarities with descriptions of the *tarb-feis* ("bull-sleep"), an early Irish rite in which a bull was sacrificed and a priest (or druid?), after eating of its flesh, dreamt of the identity of the future king.[83] Divinatory sleep was also involved in the rites associated with *imbas forosnai,* in which the *fili* chewed upon a piece of raw flesh, chanted an incantation and went into a prophetic sleep or trance state.[84] There may also be some connection with the divinatory sleep or incubation in a darkened place practiced by poetic candidates in accounts pertaining to poetic schools which existed up to the early 17th century in Ireland and the mid–18th century in Scotland.[85]

As we can see, evidence from a variety of literary and ethnographic sources suggests that bodies of water were physically and metaphorically associated with creation and destruction, healing and transformation, and the acquisition and manifestation of divine wisdom and poetic skill. The archetypal scenario suggested by these sources is an Underworld well of wisdom which was believed to be the source of these powers. Sites where the water bubbled up to the surface of the earth (wells, springs and river sources) were considered potent and sanctified locations where the inhabitants of this world might gain access to the powers of the Otherworld. The attributes and powers of the water flowed through the realms of humankind by way of the streams and rivers of the inner and outer landscape. These powers seem to have intensified where they congregated in whirlpools or rushed over the edge of the earth in waterfalls or cascades. The symbol of the vessel or cauldron played an important role in many of these scenarios, as did the hazel of knowledge and the salmon of wisdom. The gift of poetic inspiration known as *awen* in Wales and *aí* in Ireland, and the illuminating power of knowledge called *imbas* (*forosnai*), seem to have played an important part in these scenarios, suggesting that these powers, like so many others, traced their origin to the domain of the *Áes Síde,* the realms of the Celtic Otherworld.

Chapter Notes

Chapter 1

1. Lucien Lévy-Bruhl, *L'Experience Mystique et Les Symboles chez les Primitifs* (Paris: Librairie Felix Alcan, 1938), 183, cited in Conor Newman, "The Sacral Landscape of Tara: A Preliminary Exploration," in *Landscapes of Cult and Kingship*, ed. Roseanne Schot, et al. (Dublin: Four Courts Press, 2011), 23. A note in regards to the title of this chapter: the word "dreamtime" is of course an English term used to refer to Australian aboriginal concepts pertaining to the "understanding of the world ... the beginning of knowledge from which came the laws of existence ... the old time of the Ancestor beings" (http://www.aboriginalart.com.au). The term was utilized by archaeologist J.P. Mallory in the title of his book, *In Search of the Irish Dreamtime: Archaeology and Early Irish Literature* (London: Thames & Hudson, 2016). No disrespect or cultural appropriation is intended towards Aboriginal cultures or tradition bearers; an analogous term in relation to Celtic cultures is not currently known, and the term is used here with full knowledge of its origins.

2. Tomás Ó Cathasaigh, "Pagan survivals: The Evidence of Early Irish Narrative," in *Coire Sois: The Cauldron of Knowledge: A Companion to Early Irish Saga*, ed. Mattheiu Boyd (Notre Dame: University of Notre Dame Press, 2014), 36; originally published in *Ireland and Europe: The Early Church*, ed. P. Ní Catháin, et al. (Stuttgart: Klett-Cotta, 1984), 291–307.

3. See Mark Williams, *Ireland's Immortals: A History of the Gods of Irish Myth* (Princeton/Oxford: Princeton University Press, 2016), 45–49 for an excellent discussion of vernacular writing and the role of the *filid* in bridging the secular and ecclesiastical worlds.

4. Elva Johnston, *Literacy and Identity in Early Medieval Ireland* (Woodbridge, 2013), 20.

5. Williams, *Ireland's Immortals*, 49, 192.

6. Marina Smyth, "The Earliest Written Evidence for an Irish View of the World," in *Medieval Studies—Cultural Identity and Cultural Integration: Ireland and Europe in the Middle Ages,* ed. Doris Edel (Dublin: Four Courts Press, 1995), 30.

7. A discussion of Indo-European religious belief may be found in James Mallory, *In Search of the Indo-Europeans* (New York/London: Thames & Hudson, 1991), particularly Chapter Five (Indo-European Religion), 128–142. A detailed and thoughtful exploration of naming as a part of creation is found in Proinsias Mac Cana, "Placenames and Mythology in Irish Tradition: Places, Pilgrimages and Things," *Proceedings of the First North American Congress of Celtic Studies*, ed. Gordon MacLennan (Ottawa: 1986): 319–341.

8. For an excellent discussion of native belief within the pseudohistorical traditions of *Lebor Gabála Érenn*, see John Carey, "Native Elements in Irish Pseudohistory," in *Medieval Studies—Cultural Identity and Cultural Integration: Ireland and Europe in the Middle Ages* (Dublin: Four Courts Press, 1995), ed. Doris Edel, 45–60. For myths pertaining to the origins of poetry and culture, see John Carey, "Donn, Amairgen, Íth and the Prehistory of Irish Pseudohistory," *Journal of Indo-European Studies* 38 (2010): 319–341.

9. Roseanne Schot, "From Cult Centre to Royal Centre: Monuments, Myths and Other Revelations at Uisneach," in *Landscapes of Cult and Kingship*, ed. Roseanne Schot, et al. (Dublin: Four Courts Press, 2011), 91.

10. Mac Mathúna, Liam, "The Christianization of the Early Irish Cosmos? *muir mas, nem nglas, talam cé*," *Zeitschrift für celtische Philologie* 45–50 (1997): 532–547; Liam Mac Mathúna, "The Irish Perception of the Cosmos," *Celtica* 32 (1999): 174–187; R. Mark Scowcroft, "Leabhar Gabhála—Part II: The Growth of the Tra-

dition," *Ériu* 39 (1988): 1–64; Alwyn and Brinley Rees, *Celtic Heritage* (New York: Thames & Hudson, 1995), 112–115.

11. Scowcroft, "Leabhar Gabhála—Part II," 40, *n*11.

12. John Carey, "The Location of the Otherworld in Irish Tradition," *Éigse* 19 (1982): 36–43.

13. Williams, *Ireland's Immortals*, 30–34, 40–43, 89–92 regarding *síd* mounds and Otherworld beings.

14. J.J. Tierney, "The Celtic Ethnography of Posidonius," *Proceedings of the Royal Irish Academy*, Vol. 60 (1960), Section C: 196.

15. Tierney, "The Celtic Ethnography of Posidonius," 194–195.

16. R. Atkinson, ed., *The Passions and the Homilies from Leabhar Breac: Text, Translations and Glossary* (Dublin: Royal Irish Academy, 1887), 269–273.

17. Mac Mathúna, "The Christianization of the Early Irish Cosmos?" 532–547; Mac Mathúna, "The Irish Perception of the Cosmos," 174–187; Liam Mac Mathúna, "The Irish Cosmos Revisited: Further Lexical Perspectives," in *Celtic Cosmology: Perspectives from Ireland and Scotland*, ed. Jacqueline Borsje, et al. (Toronto: Pontifical Institute of Medieval Studies, 2014), 10–33.

18. Mac Mathúna, "The Christianization of the Early Irish Cosmos?," 532.

19. Mac Mathúna, "Irish Perceptions of the Cosmos," *Celtica* 23, 1999, 174–187.

20. Cecile O'Rahilly, ed. *Táin Bó Cúailgne: Recension 1* (Dublin: Dublin Institute for Advanced Studies, 1976), 103.

21. O'Rahilly, *Táin Bó Cúailgne: Recension* 1, 216.

22. O'Rahilly, *Táin Bó Cúailgne: Recension* 1, 104.

23. O'Rahilly, *Táin Bó Cúailgne: Recension* 1, 217.

24. See Cecile O'Rahilly, ed. *Táin Bó Cúailgne from the Book of Leinster* (Dublin: Dublin Institute for Advanced Studies, 1967), ll. 4041–4047.

25. O'Rahilly, *Táin Bó Cúailgne: Recension* 1, 36.

26. O'Rahilly, *Táin Bó Cúailgne: Recension* 1, 157.

27. William Sayers, "Netherworld and Otherworld in early Irish literature," *Zeitschrift für celtische Philologie* 59 (2012): 203, referring to William Sayers, "Tripartition in early Ireland: cosmic or social structure," in *Indo-European Religion after Dumézil*, Edgar C. Polomé, ed. (Washington, D.C.: Institute for the Study of Man, 1996), 156–183.

28. Mac Mathúna "The Christianization of the Early Irish Cosmos?" 539.

29. Atkinson, *The Passions and the Homilies from Leabhar Breac*, 989.

30. Scowcroft "Leabhar Gabhála—Part II," 39–45. Scowcroft notes that the world of the *síd* was represented as drawing together "the celestial and infernal elements of the supernatural into an Otherworld the opposite and counterpart of this, and thus converts a triune moral and theological system into a binary cosmology." This process of converting a triune system into a binary one plays out in the invasion saga of the *Túatha Dé Danann*, which he describes as involving "far more complex literary processes than the mere euhemerization of pagan mythology: a complete merger between the natural and the supernatural, which creates a new synthesis and a new mythology. This comprises a system of implicit analogy based on the correlation of aetiological conflicts in (and between) this world and the Other, which is further complicated by the movement of the Túatha Dé into the *síd*, and the resulting ambiguity of both in Irish tradition."

31. Scowcroft "Leabhar Gabhála—Part II," 44–45. This complicates efforts to interpret any evidence which may reflect the nature and function of the gods, or to reconstruct a pantheon from the information we have (which is, in part, divorced from its narrative context). Scowcroft points out that in these types of endeavors it is important to perform a synchronic analysis of text and tradition, and in the service of such, to look at original native concepts of deity and Otherworld (as much as is possible) when analyzing divine figures, attributes, roles and relationships.

32. Victor Kalygin, "Some archaic elements of Celtic cosmology," *Zeitschrift für celtische Philologie* 53 (2003): 70.

33. Kalygin "Some archaic elements of Celtic cosmology," 71.

34. Eric P. Hamp, "Welsh *elfydd, elfydden,* Scottish Gaelic *Alba,*" *Bulletin of the Board of Celtic Studies* 36 (1989): 109–110; Eric P. Hamp, "Welsh *elfydd* and *albio-*," *Zeitschrift für celtische Philologie* 45 (1992): 87–89.

35. Marged Haycock, ed. and trans., *Legendary Poems from the Book of Taliesin* (Aberystwyth: CMCS, 2007), 114.

36. Kalygin, "Some archaic elements of Celtic cosmology," 73–74.

37. Kalygin, "Some archaic elements of Celtic cosmology," 74–75.

38. John T. Koch, "New Thoughts on *Albion, Ierne,* and the Pretanic Isles—Part 1 (The Pre-La Tène Period)," *Proceedings of the Harvard Celtic Colloquium*, Vol. VI (1986): 3–4.

39. Koch, "New Thoughts on *Albion, Ierne,* and the Pretanic Isles," 4.

40. Some observations pertaining to early Irish perceptions of the heavens may be found in Fergus Kelly, "The beliefs and mythology of

the early Irish with special reference to the cosmos," *Astronomy, cosmology and landscape: Proceedings of the SEAC 98 Meeting* (Dublin: European Society for Astronomy in Culture, 1998): 167–172.

41. John Waddell, "The Cave of Crúachan and the Otherworld" in *Celtic Cosmology: Perspectives from Ireland and Scotland*, ed. Jacqueline Borsje, et al. (Toronto: Pontifical Institute of Medieval Studies, 2014), 84–88. See Timothy Darvill, *Prehistoric Britain* (London: Routledge, 1996) regarding changes in religious practice starting in the late Bronze Age and into the Iron Age.

42. Koch, "New Thoughts on *Albion, Ierne, and the Pretanic Isles*," 12–15; See also Darvill, *Prehistoric Britain* on related topics.

43. For an interesting discussion of concepts associated with Lower World locations, see John Waddell, *Archaeology and Celtic Myth* (Dublin: Four Courts Press, 2014), 56–73.

44. For comparison of Classical, Christian and Irish perceptions related to this theme see John Carey, "Ireland and the Antipodes: The Heterodoxy of Virgil of Salzburg," in *The Otherworld Voyage in Early Irish Literature*, ed. Jonathan Wooding (Dublin: Four Courts Press, 2014), 133.

45. See Edel Bhreathnach, *Ireland in the Medieval World AD 400–1000: Landscape, Kingship and Religion* (Dublin: Four Courts Press, 2014) for a discussion of the social use of boundaries associated with north and south and how kingship was associated with the four/five provinces.

46. Muireann Ní Bhrolcháin, "Death-tales of the early kings of Tara," in *Landscapes of Cult and Kingship*, ed. Roseanne Schot, et al. (Dublin: Four Courts Press, 2011), 45.

47. Reverence for the sacred center is attested by the existence of central offering pits and centrally located wooden pillars in ritual sites or assembly grounds. The "fifth" province (Meath < OIr *Mide* "middle") was associated with kingship and sacred sites.

48. Rees, *Celtic Heritage*, 118–139.

49. Grigory Bondarenko, *Studies in Irish Mythology* (Berlin: Currach Bhán, 2014), 43–56.

50. Proinsias Mac Cana, *The Cult of the Sacred Centre: Essays on Celtic Ideology* (Dublin: Dublin Institute for Advanced Studies, 2011), 91–2, 98, 109–112, 124–134, 138–141.

51. R. I. Best, "The Settling of the Manor of Tara," *Ériu* 4 (1910): 121–172.

52. Best, "The Settling of the Manor of Tara," 146–147.

53. Best, "The Settling of the Manor of Tara," 146–151.

54. Kuno Meyer, ed, *Hibernica Minora, Being a Fragment of an Old-Irish Treatise on the Psalter with Translation, Notes and an Appendix Containing Extracts Hitherto Unpublished from MS. Rawlinson, B. 512 in the Bodleian Library* (Oxford: Clarendon Press, 1894), 39–41.

55. Mary M. Delaney, *Of Irish Ways* (New York: Dillon Press/Barnes & Noble, 1973), 333.

56. John Carey, "A Tract on the Creation," *Éigse* 11 (1986): 1–9; John Carey, "Cosmology in *Saltair na Rann*," *Celtica* 17 (1985): 33–52.

57. Carey, "A Tract on the Creation," 3.

58. Mallory, *In Search of the Indo-Europeans*, 140.

59. Carey, "A Tract on the Creation," 3, 7.

60. The specific section in *De natura rerum* is 31.2 [*PL* 83. 1004A]

61. Carey, "Cosmology in *Saltair na Rann*," 38.

62. John Carey, "The Three Sails, The Twelve Winds, and the Question of Early Irish Colour Theory," *Journal of the Warburg and Courtauld Institutes,* Vol. 72 (2009): 229–231.

63. Carey "Cosmology in *Saltair na Rann*," 37.

64. I would like to thank Dr. Benjamin Bruch for providing me with a copy of his paper, "An Analysis of Color Terms in the Vankh Dialect of Eastern Armenia," *Annal of Armenian Linguistics*, Vol. 22/23 (2003): 17–28, in which the work of Brent Berlin and Paul Kay, *Basic Color Terms: Their Universality and Evolution* (Berkeley: University of California Press, 1969), is concisely set out.

65. See also Heidi Ann Lazar-Meyn, "Colour Terms in Táin Bó Cúailgne," *Ulidia* (1994): 201–205; and Heidi Ann Lazar-Meyn, "The Colour Systems of the Modern Celtic Languages—Effects of Language Contact," in *Language Contact in the British Isles: Proceedings of the Eighth International Symposium on Language Contact in Europe*, ed. P.S. Ureland, et al. (Tübingen, Germany: Max Niemeyer Verlag, 1988), 227–241.

66. Mallory, *In Search of the Indo-Europeans*, 133; Jaan Puhvel, *Comparative Mythology* (Baltimore: Johns Hopkins University Press, 1987), 159–160; Emily Lyle, *Archaic Cosmos: Polarity, Space and Time* (Edinburgh: Polygon, 1990), 8–11.

67. I have written about this topic elsewhere: "*Éisce, Gáeth ocus Muir*: Three Notes on Archaic Celtic Cosmology," *Cosmos* 18 (2002): 103–119.

68. Elizabeth Gray, ed. and trans., *Cath Maige Tuired: The Second Battle of Mag Tuired* (Naas: Irish Texts Society, 1982), 24–25.

69. For concepts associated with "northern islands," see F.M. Le Roux, "Les Îles au Nord du Monde," in *Hommages à Albert Grenier*, ed. Marcel Renard (Brussels: Latomus, 1962), 1051–1062.

70. Gray, *Cath Maige Tuired*, 74; Vernum, Hull, "The Four Jewels of the *Túatha Dé Danann*," *Zeitschrift für celtische Philologie* 18 (1929): 73–89.

71. See Williams, *Ireland's Immortals*, 148–152 for additional discussion of these texts.

72. E.G. Quinn, et al., *Contributions to a Dictionary of the Irish Language, derived mainly from Old and Middle Irish materials* (Dublin: Royal Irish Academy), hereinafter referred to as DIL. DIL 4 *gor*: this meaning may derive from 2 *gor* "pious, dutiful," but is used in the sense of "fire" in the *Dindshenchas* and O'Davoren's Glossary. Unless otherwise noted, all translations of Old and Middle Irish words will be assumed to derive from DIL.

73. Gray, *Cath Maige Tuired*, 24–25, 74–75.

74. Gray, *Cath Maige Tuired*, 38–43.

75. William W. Goodwin, ed., *Plutarch: De defectu oraculorum* (Cambridge: Little, Brown and Co., 1874), Section 23 (accessed via http://www.Perseus.tufts.edu).

76. Another text which may have influenced (or been influenced by) native associations with the four cardinal directions is discussed in: J.G. O'Keefe, "The Four Custodians of Knowledge in the Four Quarters of the World," *Irische Texte* 4 (1934): 33–35.

77. For a discussion of Irish cosmology, see my article, "*Éisce, Gáeth ocus Muir*," 103–119. Additional information is included in Chapter Eleven of my book, *Celtic Myth and Religion: A Study of Traditional Belief* (Jefferson, NC: McFarland, 2012).

78. Grigory Bondarenko, "Roads and Knowledge in *Togail Bruidne Da Derga*," in *Celtic Cosmology: Perspectives from Ireland and Scotland*, ed. Jacqueline Borsje, et al. (Toronto: Pontifical Institute of Medieval Studies, 2014), 193–194. See also Rees, *Celtic Heritage*, 149–153.

79. Mac Cana, *The Cult of the Sacred Centre*, 76–79.

80. Best, "The Settling of the Manor of Tara," 128–155.

81. See *Landscapes of Cult and Kingship*, ed. Roseanne Schot, et al. (Dublin: Four Courts Press, 2011), 93–94, regarding the role of Uisneach as the comogonic center of Ireland.

82. DIL *trefhuilngid*.

83. R. Thurneysen, *Mittelirische Verslehern*, Irische Texte III, 45.4.

84. Kuno Meyer, *The Triads of Ireland* (Dublin: *Todd Lecture Series* 13, 1906), 26–27.

85. Whitley Stokes, "Adomnán's Second Vision," *Revue Celtique* 12 (1891): 440, n.12.

86. Kevin Murray, ed. *Baile in Scáil: The Phantom's Frenzy* (London: Irish Texts Society, 2004), 33.

87. Edward Gwynn, *Metrical Dindshenchas*, Part III (Dublin: Dublin Institute of Advanced Studies, 1991), 146–149; Bondarenko, "Roads and Knowledge in *Togail Bruidne Da Derga*," 69–76.

88. Gwynn, *Metrical Dindshenchas*, Part IV, 240–247.

89. Damian McManus, *A Guide to Ogam* (Maynooth: An Sagart, 1997), 1–2, 19–35, 42–44, 51, 129, 132, 138–139, 154–159, 162.

90. George Calder, *Auraicept na n-Éces* (Dublin: Four Courts Press, 1995), 289–313.

91. Calder, *Auraicept na n-Éces*, 88–93. While there are a few inconsistencies in the listings and descriptions of the trees and plants, in general they align with the categories given here.

92. Anne Ross, *Pagan Celtic Britain* (Chicago: Academy, 1996), 59–65; A.T. Lucas, "The Sacred Trees of Ireland," *Journal of the Cork Historical and Archaeological Society* LXVIII (1963); Mac Cana, *The Cult of the Sacred Centre*, 76–80; Michael Newton, *Handbook of the Scottish Gaelic World* (Dublin: Four Courts Press, 2000), 191–193, 211–212; Michael Newton, *Warriors of the Word: The World of the Scottish Highlanders* (Edinburgh: Birlinn, 2009), 237–242.

93. Rees, *Celtic Heritage*, 146–172; Bhreathnach, *Ireland in the Medieval World*, 72.

94. Stuart Piggott, *The Druids* (New York: Thames & Hudson, 1993), 63–64, 105.

95. Piggott, *The Druids*, 63–64, 105.

96. See Mac Cana, *The Cult of the Sacred Centre*.

97. H.E. Davidson, *God and Myths of Northern Europe* (New York: Penguin, 1965), 26–29.

98. Davidson, *Gods and Myths of Northern Europe*, 26–29.

99. Kuno Meyer, ed., "Finn and the Man in the Tree," *Revue Celtique* 25 (1904): 344–349.

100. Patrick Logan, *The Holy Wells of Ireland* (Gerrards Cross: Colin Smythe, 1980), 121–126.

101. F. Marian McNeill, *The Silver Bough: A Four Volume Study of the National and Local Festivals of Scotland*, Vol. One (William MacLellan, Glasgow, 1977), 76–77. This substitution is primarily seen in the folk tradition, rather than in earlier literary sources, where the symbolism of the serpent may be influenced by Biblical or Medieval sources. A fine example of the appearance of the serpent in a Scottish context (where the salmon would be in Irish sources) see *Scottish Traditional Tales*, ed. A.J. Bruford and D.A. McDonald (1994, Polygon, Edinburgh), 288–291.

102. Sharon Paice MacLeod, "The Descent of the Gods: Creation, Cosmogony and Divine Order," *Proceedings of the Harvard Celtic Colloquium*, Vol. 21 (2001): 354–359.

103. MacLeod, "The Descent of the Gods," 354–359.

104. Kathryn Chadbourne, "The Celtic Otherworld," *Cosmos: Journal of the Traditional Cosmology Society*, Vol. 14, No. 2 (1998): 157–177.

105. Chadbourne, "The Celtic Otherworld," 163; John Carey, "The Irish 'Otherworld': Hiberno-Latin Perspectives," *Éigse* 25 (1991): 154–159.

106. John Carey, "Time, Space and the Otherworld," *Proceedings of the Harvard Celtic Colloquium*, Vol. 7 (1987): 2; John Carey, "The Otherworld in Irish Tradition," *Éigse* 19 (1982): 39–42; Séamus Mac Mathúna, "The Relationship of the Chthonic World in Early Ireland to Chaos and Cosmos," in *Celtic Cosmology: Perspectives from Ireland and Scotland*, ed. Jacqueline Borsje, et al. (Toronto: Pontifical Institute of Medieval Studies, 2014), 53–54.

107. Myles Dillon, ed., *Serglige Con Culainn* (Dublin: Dublin Institute for Advanced Studies, 1975), 17–18. For a translation: Tom Pete Cross and Harris Slover, *Ancient Irish Tales* (New York: Barnes & Noble, 1996), 176–198.

108. Séamus Mac Mathúna, ed., *Immram Brain—Bran's Journey to the Land of the Women* (Tubingen: Niemeyer, 1985); Kuno Meyer, *The Voyage of Bran* (London: David Nutt, 1895).

109. Patrick Sims-Williams, "Some Celtic Otherworld Terms," in *Celtic Language, Celtic Culture: A Festschrift for Eric P. Hamp*, ed. Matonis, et al. (Van Nuys, CA: Ford and Bailie, 1990), 62–63.

110. Sims-Williams, "Some Celtic Otherworld Terms," 61–65.

111. Tomás Ó Cathasaigh, "The Semantics of 'Síd,'" *Éigse* 17, Part 2 (1978): 149–150.

112. Ó Cathasaigh, "The Semantics of 'Síd,'" 49.

113. Ó Cathasaigh, "The Semantics of 'Síd,'" 140–144.

114. Ó Cathasaigh, "The Semantics of 'Síd,'" 144–145.

115. Ó Cathasaigh, "The Semantics of 'Síd,'" 144, 146.

116. Ó Cathasaigh, "The Semantics of 'Síd,'" 147–148.

117. Marion Deane, "From sacred marriage to clientship: a mythical account of the establishment of kingship as an institution," in *Landscapes of Cult and Kingship*, ed. Roseanne Schot, et al. (Dublin: Four Courts Press, 2011), 5.

118. Chadbourne, "The Celtic Otherworld," 171; Patrick K. Ford, "Prolegomena to a Reading of the *Mabinogi: Pwyll* and *Manawydan*," *Studia Celtica* 16/17: 117.

119. Chadbourne, "The Celtic Otherworld," 170–171.

120. John Carey, "The Origin and Development of the Cessair Legend," *Éigse* 22 (1987), 37–48.

121. Carey "Native Elements in Irish Pseudo-history," 45–60. Both Carey and Scowcroft make reference to a number of elements present in Lebor Gábala and other sources which, although often analyzed as having a Biblical origin, may in fact be native parallels.

122. Carey, John, "The Origin and Development of the Cessair Legend," 37–48; Gregory Toner, "Landscape and Cosmology in the Dindshenchas," in *Celtic Cosmology: Perspectives from Ireland and Scotland*, ed. Jacqueline Borsje, et al. (Toronto: Pontifical Institute of Medieval Studies, 2014), 276–278, 282.

123. John Koch and John Carey, eds. and trans., *The Celtic Heroic Age* (Oakville, CT/Aberystwyth: Celtic Studies Publications, 2000), 235–237.

124. Carey, "The Origin and Development of the Cessair Legend," 38.

125. Carey, "The Origin and Development of the Cessair Legend," 39.

126. Gwynn, *The Metrical Dindshenchas* Part IV, 58–63.

127. Gwynn, *The Metrical Dindshenchas* Part IV, 62–63.

128. Gwynn, *The Metrical Dindshenchas* Part IV, 62–69.

129. Gwynn, *The Metrical Dindshenchas* Part III, 210–215.

130. Carey, "The Origin and Development of the Cessair Legend," 46.

131. John Carey, "The Names of the Plains Beneath the Lakes of Ireland," in *Cín Chille Cúile: Texts, Saints and Places—Essays in Honour of Pádraig Ó Riain*, ed. Carey, et al. (Aberystwyth: Celtic Studies Publications, 2004), 44–57.

132. John Carey, "The Lough Foyle Colloquoy Texts: *Immacaldam Choluim Chille ocus ind Óclaig oc Carraic Eolairg* and *Immacaldam in druad Brain ocus inna banfatho Febuil ós Loch Febuil*," *Ériu* 52 (2002): 53–87.

133. Carey, "The Lough Foyle Colloquoy Texts," 76–77.

134. Carey, "The Lough Foyle Colloquoy Texts," 76–77.

135. Carey, "The Lough Foyle Colloquoy Texts," 60–61.

136. Carey, "The Lough Foyle Colloquoy Texts," 60–61.

137. Carey, "The Lough Foyle Colloquoy Texts," 60–61.

138. Carey, "The Three Sails, The Twelve Winds," 221.

139. Carey, "The Three Sails, The Twelve Winds," 224.

140. Carey, "The Origin and Development of the Cessair Legend," 46.

141. Carey, "Time, Space and the Otherworld," 47 n47.
142. Koch and Carey, *Celtic Heroic Age,* 235–236.
143. Bondarenko, *Studies in Irish Mythology,* 219–220.
144. Joseph Vendryes, ed., *Airne Fingein: Fingen's Nightwatch* (Dublin: Dublin Institute for Advanced Studies, 1953), 4–7. See Carey, "Time, Space and the Otherworld," 46–47, n45 for other references to Fintan.
145. Best, "The Settling of the Manor of Tara," 126–129.
146. Best, "The Settling of the Manor of Tara," 128–133.
147. Best, "The Settling of the Manor of Tara," 134–135.
148. Best, "The Settling of the Manor of Tara," 134–139.
149. Best, "The Settling of the Manor of Tara," 150–153. I have emended a few words of his translation. *Ess Ruaid* (modern Assaroe) is a waterfall that is mentioned in a number of literary sources, and often associated with the acquisition of divine wisdom or inspiration.
150. Best, "The Settling of the Manor of Tara," 154–155.
151. Best, "The Settling of the Manor of Tara," 158–161.
152. Best, "The Settling of the Manor of Tara," 160–161.
153. Koch and Carey, *Celtic Heroic Age,* 238–241.
154. John, Carey, "*Scél Tuain meic Chairill,*" *Ériu* 35 (1984): 92–111.
155. Kuno Meyer, "Mitteilungen aus irischen Handschriften: Die Verwandlungen des Tuan mac Cairill," *Zeitschrift für celtische Philologie,* Vol. 3 (1901): 31.
156. Carey, "*Scél Tuain meic Chairill,*" 92–111.
157. Eleanor Hull, "The Hawk of Achill, or The Legend of the Oldest Animals," *Folklore* XLIII (1932): 392–395.
158. Hull, "The Hawk of Achill," 395–397.
159. Hull, "The Hawk of Achill," 398.
160. Hull, "The Hawk of Achill," 399–402.
161. Hull, "The Hawk of Achill," 382 [fo. 14s, 7 and H.3.18, fo. 35, T.C.D.]
162. Hull, "The Hawk of Achill," 382 [Egerton 33, Art. 20]
163. Hull, "The Hawk of Achill," 380 [Book of Lismore, fo. 151, b 2]
164. Rachel Bromwich, ed. and trans., *Trioedd Ynys Prydein: The Triads of the Island of Britain* (Cardiff: University of Wales Press, 2014), 235–236.
165. Patrick K. Ford, ed. and transl., *The Mabinogi and other Medieval Welsh Tales* (Berkeley: University of California Press, 1977), 147–148.
166. Hull, "The Hawk of Achill," 381 (citing Douglas Hyde, *Legends of Saints and Sinners* Legends of Saints and Sinners, 56–57).
167. Hull, "The Hawk of Achill," 380 (citing Alexander Nicolson, *Gaelic Proverbs and Familiar Phrases*).
168. John Shaw, "A Gaelic Eschatological Folktale, Celtic Cosmology, and Dumézil's "Three Realms,"" in *Celtic Cosmology: Perspectives from Ireland and Scotland,* 43; Marina Smyth, "The Word of God and Early Medieval Irish Cosmology: Scripture and the Creating World," in *Celtic Cosmology: Perspectives from Ireland and Scotland,* 120.
169. Dáibhí Ó Cróinín, ed., *The Irish Sex Aetates Mundi* (1983, Dublin Institute for Advanced Studies), 4.
170. Rees, *Celtic Heritage,* 83–106; Patrick K. Ford, my notes from his course on Celtic Paganism, Harvard University, Spring Term, 2000.
171. Carey, "Time, Space and the Otherworld," 1–27. See John Carey, *A Single Ray of the Sun: Religious Speculation in Early Ireland* (Aberystwyth: Celtic Studies Publications, 2011), 85–89, regarding Christian speculation on cyclical existence, which may have derived from the symbolism of nature, but also involved perceptions of God as the beginning and the end.
172. Carey, "Time, Space and the Otherworld," 2–3.
173. Carey, "Time, Space and the Otherworld," 8.
174. Carey, "Time, Space and the Otherworld," 6–7.
175. Carey, "Time, Space and the Otherworld," 7.
176. M. Sticker-Jantscheff, "Magdalenenberg: an examination of archaeological and archaeoastronomical interpretations of a Halstatt period burial mound," *Spica: Postgraduate Journal for Cosmology in Culture,* Vol. III, No. 1 (Spring 2015). Additional information is available at http://www.worldarchaeology.com, "Magdalenenberg: Germany's ancient moon calendar," Nov. 2011.
177. A great deal of academically-supported information pertaining to lunar symbolism in Celtic contexts may be found in the following work: S.M. NicMhacha, *Queen of Night* (Boston: Red Wheel/Weiser, 2005).
178. Eóin Mac Neill, "On the Notation and Chronography of the Calendar of Coligny, *Ériu* 10 (1926–8): 1. Other studies include: J. Loth, "L'année celtique d'après les textes irlandais, gallois, Bretons, et le calendrier de Coligny," *Revue Celtique* 25 (1904): 113–162; J. Cuillandre, "Étude de la concordance du calendrier de Coligny," *Revue Celtique* 47 (1930): 10–29; Rudolf

Thurneysen, "Der Kalender von Coligny," *Zeitschrift für celtische Philologie* 2 (1899): 523–544.

179. Mac Neill, "On the Notation and Chronography of the Calendar of Coligny," 2–3.

180. Mac Neill, "On the Notation and Chronography of the Calendar of Coligny," 3.

181. Mac Neill, "On the Notation and Chronography of the Calendar of Coligny," 4, 33–34.

182. Mac Neill, "On the Notation and Chronography of the Calendar of Coligny," 36–37.

183. Mac Neill "On the Notation and Chronography of the Calendar of Coligny," 10.

184. Mac Neill, "On the Notation and Chronography of the Calendar of Coligny," 11–13. Mac Neill's theory that the sixth day of the moon—the day which Pliny reports the Gaulish druids ceremonially harvested mistletoe—coincided with the full moon, has been disputed. For an argument disproving this notion, see my article, "*Éisce, Gáeth ocus Muir:* Three Notes on Archaic Celtic Cosmology," *Cosmos* 18 (2002): 103–106.

185. Stanley, Ireland, *Roman Britain: A Sourcebook* (New York: Routledge, 1996), 184.

186. I.F. Grant, *Highland Folk Ways* (London: Routledge, 1989), 355; Margaret Bennett, *Scottish Customs—From the Cradle to the Grave* (Edinburgh: Polygon, 1992), 123; Tess Darwin, *The Scots Herbal—Plant Lore of Scotland* (Edinburgh: Mercat Press, 1996), 46; F. Marion McNeill, *The Silver Bough* (Glasgow: William MacLellan, 1977), 57–58.

187. I would like to thank Dr. Joseph Eska for clarifying linguistic aspects of the month names *Anagontios, Cutios, Edrini, Elembiv* and *Simivisonna.* I have notated this information in the specific endnotes. I alone am responsible for additional theories and derivations pertaining to the month names, and any shortcomings (or merit) therein.

188. Calvert Watkins, *Dictionary of Indo-European Roots* (Boston: Houghton Mifflin, 2000), 75.

189. Watkins, *Dictionary of Indo-European Roots,* 19.

190. Watkins, *Dictionary of Indo-European Roots,* 18–19.

191. Nerys Patterson, *Cattle Lords and Clansmen: The Social Structure of Early Ireland* (Notre Dame/London: University of Notre Dame Press, 1994), 129–135.

192. Many thanks to Joseph Eska for this clarification.

193. Watkins, *Dictionary of Indo-European Roots,* 41.

194. Watkins, *Dictionary of Indo-European Roots,* 31.

195. Watkins, *Dictionary of Indo-European Roots,* 28.

196. Watkins, *Dictionary of Indo-European Roots,* 38.

197. My thanks to Joseph Eska for this clarification.

198. Watkins, *Dictionary of Indo-European Roots,* 75.

199. Máire MacNeill, *The Festival of Lugnasad* (Dublin: University College, 2008), 6, 143, 243–249, 251–254, 258–259, 262, 305, 319, 326, 328–329, 337–338, 341, 344–345, 426–427, 619, 624, 626.

200. My gratitude to Joseph Eska for this clarification.

201. Watkins, *Dictionary of Indo-European Roots,* 11.

202. Watkins, *Dictionary of Indo-European Roots,* 23.

203. Watkins, *Dictionary of Indo-European Roots,* 1.

204. Watkins, *Dictionary of Indo-European Roots,* 71.

205. Piggott, *The Druids,* 112, 116.

206. Smyth, "The Earliest Written Evidence for an Irish View of the World," 45–60. An excellent discussion of native celestial observations occurs on pp. 30–37. This may be compared with non-native elements that also formed part of early medieval Irish belief in Marina Smyth, *Understanding the Universe in Seventh-Century Ireland* (Woodbridge: Boydell Press, 1996).

207. Rees, *Celtic Heritage,* 105–106.

208. John Carey, *A New Introduction to Lebor Gabála Érenn* (Irish Texts Society, Dublin, 1993), 2; John Carey, "Native Elements in Irish Pseudohistory," 45–60.

209. Vernum Hull, "De Gabáil in t-Sída (Concerning the Seizure of the Fairy Mound)," *Zeitschrift für celtische Philologie,* 19 (1933): 55–57.

210. J.C. Watson, ed., *Mesca Ulad* (Dublin: Dublin Institute for Advanced Studies, 1941), 1.

211. Carey, *A New Introduction to Lebor Gabála Érenn,* 1–21. The nature of such a belief may be reflected in the 1st century BCE statement of the Alexandrian scholar Timagenes, in which he states that the druids of Gaul maintained that part of the population was indigenous while others were said to come from remote islands and the region beyond the Rhine. In addition, there is Caesar's report that the Gauls stated that they were all descended from a common ancestor or divine father figure ("*Dis Pater*"), and that this was the tradition of the druids. See H.J. Edwards, tr., *Caesar—The Gallic War;* Book VI, 342–3.

Chapter 2

1. An earlier version of this research was originally published in *The Proceedings of the Harvard Celtic Colloquium*, Vol. XXI (Cambridge: Department of Celtic Languages and Literatures, Faculty of Arts and Sciences, Harvard University, 2001): 311–365.

2. Roy Willis, ed., *World Mythology* (New York: Henry Holt and Co., 1993), 18–19.

3. A mythical analogy between macrocosmic elements and parts of the body appears in a number of Indo-European settings, including Norse, Greek and Hindu mythology. See Bruce Lincoln, *Myth, Cosmos and Society: Indo-European Themes of Creation and Destruction* (Cambridge: Harvard University Press, 1986), 1–40.

4. H.E. Davidson, *Gods and Myths of Northern Europe* (London: Penguin, 1964), 27–29.

5. H.J. Rose, *Handbook of Greek Mythology* (New York: E.P. Dutton, 1959), 18–23.

6. Calvert Watkins, *Dictionary of Indo-European Roots* (Boston: Houghton Mifflin, 2000), 22. Watkins points out that in many Indo-European cultures, the name of this archetypal deity derives from the Indo-European root *dyeu-* ("to shine") with many derivates pertaining to "sky," "heaven" or "god." These include the names of Zeus, Jupiter and Jove, as well as words like July ("descended from Jupiter"). From the related root **deiwos* ("god") are Tyr (a Norse Sky god), Old English Tiw (a god of war and the sky, from which we get the word Tuesday), Latin Diana (a moon goddess), the Hindu goddess name Devi, and English words such as "deity" and "divine."

7. Willis, *World Mythology*, 70–84. See also Wendy O'Flaherty, *Hindu Myths* (New York: Penguin, 1980), particularly Chapter One and the Appendices.

8. Willis, *World Mythology*, 19.

9. John Koch, and John Carey, eds., *The Celtic Heroic Age: Literary Sources for Ancient Celtic Europe and Early Ireland and Wales* (Oakville, CT and Aberystwyth: Celtic Studies Publications, 2000), 226–271.

10. R. Mark Scowcroft, "Leabhar Gabhála—Part II: The Growth of the Tradition," *Ériu* 9 (1988): 1–64 (see pp. 12–14 and 63–64 in particular); John, Carey, *A New Introduction to Lebor Gabála Érenn* (Dublin: Irish Texts Society, 1993), 1–21 (see pp. 1–3, 7, and 17–19 in particular).

11. Scowcroft, "Leabhar Gabhála—Part II: The Growth of the Tradition," 1.

12. Scowcroft, "Leabhar Gabhála—Part II: The Growth of the Tradition," 13.

13. Dáibhí Ó Cróinín, ed., *The Irish Sex*

Aetates Mundi (Dublin: Dublin Institute for Advanced Studies, 1983), 4.

14. Scowcroft, "Leabhar Gabhála—Part II: The Growth of the Tradition," 1–64.

15. Alwyn Rees and Brinley Rees, *Celtic Heritage* (New York: Thames & Hudson, 1961), 95.

16. Rees, *Celtic Heritage*, 104.

17. These traditions may have been preserved by the *filid* or other formal guardians of native tradition, who steadfastly and conservatively guarded and transmitted a great deal of other lore, including genealogy, social customs, place-name traditions and poetry; as well as by professional, local or family storytellers, or local lay-persons who maintained pride and interest in ancient history and traditions (local or national, as may still be found in certain parts of Ireland).

18. Rees, *Celtic Heritage*, 104.

19. Rees, *Celtic Heritage*, 104.

20. Carey, John, ed. and transl., "The Book of Invasions (First Recension) *Lebor Gabála Érenn*," in *Celtic Heroic Age*, 226–271.

21. Scowcroft, "Leabhar Gabhála—Part II: The Growth of the Tradition," 32.

22. Scowcroft, "Leabhar Gabhála—Part II: The Growth of the Tradition," 104–5.

23. Scowcroft, "Leabhar Gabhála—Part II: The Growth of the Tradition," 2.

24. Scowcroft, "Leabhar Gabhála—Part II: The Growth of the Tradition," 12.

25. Scowcroft, "Leabhar Gabhála—Part II: The Growth of the Tradition," 35.

26. Scowcroft, "Leabhar Gabhála—Part II: The Growth of the Tradition," 29–32. The five ages presented in *Lebor Gabála* may have been influenced by the five ages known to Irish clerics from Classical sources. The invasions of Partholón, Nemed, the Fir Bolg and the Milesians may also have corresponded with the foundation of the great world-kingdoms of the Third Age (Assyrian, Median, Persian and Alexandrian Greek), a tradition which would have been well known to medieval literati. In either case, the "invasion" of the Túatha Dé Danann seems to have been added into the scheme later, making them the last group to join an already established sequence of "invaders."

27. Pamela S. Hopkins and John T. Koch, ed. and trans., "Historia Brittonum" in *Celtic Heroic Age*, 275–290.

28. Hopkins and Koch, "Historia Brittonum," 275–290. See also Carey, *A New Introduction to Lebor Gabála Érenn*, 4–6; and John Carey, "Native Elements in Irish Pseudohistory," in *Medieval Studies—Cultural Identity and Cultural Integration: Ireland and Europe in the Middle Ages* (Dublin: Four Courts Press, 1995), 49.

29. Carey, "Native Elements in Irish Pseudo-history," 47.

30. Carey, "Native Elements in Irish Pseudo-history," 32.

31. Carey, "Native Elements in Irish Pseudo-history," 53–54.

32. Carey, "Native Elements in Irish Pseudo-history," 53–54. The ensuing confusion is evident in the story of Túan where we are told that "the men of learning do not know their origin, but think it is likely they are exiles from heaven." This same speculative musing was recorded in connection with the fairies in Irish and Scottish folklore. It may also have been influenced by accounts in which the Túatha Dé Danann are said to have arrived "in dark clouds."

33. Carey, "Native Elements in Irish Pseudo-history," 54.

34. Carey, "Native Elements in Irish Pseudo-history," 54. See also Koch and Carey, *Celtic Heroic Age,* 252.

35. See Rees, *Celtic Heritage,* 107, where an alternate interpretation of the tradition of "five invasions" is provided. Here the authors compare the five pre-Gaelic peoples with the tradition of the "Five Kindreds" known in India. In the *Rig Veda* they are spoken of as immigrants who come from another location "across the waters" and who settle and till the lands on the other shore. It is understood that this does not represent an historical invasion but a crossing over from one form of being to another. In voyages to the sacred realms, a crossing of water often implies a change of state or status. The Five Kindreds travel by way of ship ("across the water," "from distant lands") or in a heavenly chariot. This is similar to descriptions of the invasions in LG, including that of the Túatha Dé Danann who are said to have come from a distant location ("the northern islands of the world," which implies travel across water), either arriving in ships, or "in dark clouds" (the latter possibly interpreted as indicating "from the sky").

36. It is interesting to note that in LG tradition, the Gaels and the non-Gaels are descended from two different grandsons of Noah, Gomer and Magog. Gomer's son *Ibath* ("yew") has two sons *Bodb* (a native word meaning "raven") and *Baath* (a native word meaning "death" or perhaps more appropriately, "sea"). *Bodb* has a son *Dói* ("unskilled, inartistic'?) who has no descendants. *Baath,* on the other hand, has an extremely skilled son, Fénius Farsaid, a sage associated with poetry and languages. It is through this more reputable line that the Gaels claimed their descent. The non-Gaels are descended from Magog, a name which appears in the Old Testament as a place-name, denoting a northern kingdom ruled by a figure known as Gog (*Ezekiel* 38:2 and 3, and *Ezekiel* 39:1). In *Revelations* 20, Gog and Magog are mentioned as destructive figures whose names symbolize the gentile nations leagued against the church at the end of time. Thus the non-Gaels (including the Túatha Dé Danann, the pagan gods of the Irish) descend from a shadowy figure who is, in one Biblical context, associated with paganism. I am grateful to former Br. Bartholomew Mallio for information and references pertaining to Gog and Magog.

37. Henry Wansbrough, ed., *The New Jerusalem Bible* (New York: Darton, Longman and Todd, 1985), 28–9. We cannot be sure exactly which books of the Bible (or other associated works) early Irish scribes had in front of them, that may have been influential in the formation or interpretation of whatever sources or pseudo-historical texts they may have been referencing or drawing from. Other learned influences may well have come into play. In this chapter, I have referred to the *New Jerusalem Bible,* performing a careful reading of Genesis and other pertinent sections, including the index of persons. A computer search and close reading of pertinent sections of the Vulgate also formed part of this research. Clearly some of these medieval adaptations resulted from the challenges facing the newly-converted Irish of finding a place for themselves among the descendants of Noah, as well as coordinating their traditions with the new system which was based on Biblical authority, Greco-Roman historiography and other medieval sources.

38. Hopkins and Koch, *Historia Brittonum,* 275–290; M.A. O'Brien, ed., *Corpus Genealogiarum Hiberniae,* Vol. 1 (Dublin: Dublin Institute for Advanced Studies, 1976), 1–7; P.C. Bartrum, *Early Welsh Genealogical Tracts* (Cardiff: University of Wales Press, 1966). Names which appear in *Historia Brittonum,* as well as in Irish and/or Welsh genealogies, may have their origin in earlier sources or traditions, which may reflect Biblical, medieval and/or native elements. The Welsh were also known for their predilection for genealogies (including models along similar pseudo-historical lines), and would certainly have been familiar with early histories (such as Isidore of Seville) which circulated in learned circles on the continent and elsewhere. The Welsh also traced themselves back to Adam through the offspring of Noah (although sometimes through different sons of Japheth than those who figure in Irish tradition). However, other than the sole mention of a figure called Seru in the Welsh Life of Saint Cadog, and a figure by the

name of Enos, a grandson of Adam (as well as the name Enoc) in the Genealogies from *Hanes Gruffudd ap Cynan* (both of whom are also mentioned in the pedigrees from Mostyn MS. 117), the names from LG do not seem to figure in the Welsh genealogical tracts. I am indebted to Dr. Charlene Eska for references pertaining to medieval Irish Biblical sources and traditions, including *Historia Brittonum* and information contained in the Genealogies in Rawlinson B. 502. I would also like to thank Dr. Katherine Olsen and Dr. Benjamin Bruch for their help with sources pertaining to the Welsh genealogies.

39. Koch and Carey, *Celtic Heroic Age*, 252–263.

40. In comparing information from different sections of the text, the data was more than 90% accurate in terms of reliability and uniformity. There is some overlap in the information provided in these passages, as well as complementary data which fills in gaps in other sections. Cross-checking all the data presented in the First Recension of LG pertaining to the Túatha Dé Danann, the material was found to be remarkably consistent. The few instances of confusion or omission were easily rectified by referring to other texts such as *Cath Maige Tuired* and *Accalam na Senórach*. This high level of accuracy is quite remarkable in light of the processes of accretion, amalgamation and modification which took place over time.

41. Hopkins and Koch, *Historia Brittonum*, 279.

42. If the alternate spellings reflect the original more closely than the form that appears in LG, perhaps there is some connection with the word *aitecht* "tutorage, instruction" or *aittecht* "act of returning; act of expounding, lesson, instruction." *Aithech*, most commonly known as a word signifying "vassal, peasant," may also mean "giant or monster" (bringing to mind early races of gods who, in some traditions, were a race of giants). In certain usages *aithech* may refer to a husband or master of the house, or a warrior or fighting man. See also *airthechta* "privilege, perogative, due, right" and *airthach* "oath of confirmation or denial; guarantee." These variants open up a number of possible interpretations.

43. John Carey, "The Ancestry of Fénius Farsaid," *Celtica* 22 (1990), 106. In his examination of genealogical traditions pertaining to Fénius Farsaid, Carey discusses the pedigree of the Sons of Mil, variants of which are found in a number of sources (including the first recension of *Lebor Gabála*, *Historia Brittonum*, *Auraicept na nEces*, *Scéla Mosauluim*, and the dynastic poems edited by Kuno Meyer in the

first part of his *Uber die alteste irische Dichtung*). In the lineage of the Sons of Mil, a pair of similar (or potentially related) names appear: those of a father and son duo. The father's name is variously spelled Aurthecht, Aurtacht, Athiecht, Aurtecht, Arthecht, Aurthach, while the son's name appears as Ethecht, Ethiecht, Athecht, or Ethach. The relationship of these names to that of *Faithecht* is unclear. Here I would like to state that these pedigrees, and their sources, dating and interrelationships (as well as the origins of various borrowings or variations) constitute a vast and complex topic which I am not attempting to unravel in totality in this chapter.

44. Elizabeth Gray, *Cath Maige Tuired* (Naas: Irish Texts Society, 1982), 24–5.

45. *Ess Ruad* was one of the places where *Finn mac Cumaill* was said to have caught the salmon of knowledge. Words denoting "red" may be used figuratively to mean "great," "mighty" or "noble."

46. Koch and Carey, *Celtic Heroic Age*, 223–225.

47. My thanks to Dr. Dorothy Africa for this intriguing suggestion.

48. Scowcroft, "Leabhar Gabhála—Part II: The Growth of the Tradition," 59.

49. See Robin Chapman Stacey, *Dark Speech: The Performance of Law in Early Ireland* (Philadelphia: University of Pennsylvania Press, 2007).

50. A.L.F. Rivet, and Colin Smith, *The Place-Names of Roman Britain* (Princeton NJ: Princeton University Press, 1979), 329. For an in-depth discussion of *danu-* river names found throughout the Celtic region, and a possible association with the Irish figure Danu, see my article "*Mater Deorum Hibernensium:* Identity and Cross-Correlation in Early Irish Mythology " in *The Proceedings of the Harvard Celtic Colloquium*, Vol. 19 (1999), 340–384.

51. Rees, *Celtic Heritage*, 107.

52. Lincoln, *Myth, Cosmos and Society*, 1–40.

53. Grigory Bondarenko, *Studies in Irish Mythology* (Berlin: Currach Bhán, 2014), 1–14.

54. George Calder, ed. and trans., *Auraicept na n-Éces: The Scholar's Primer* (Dublin: Four Courts Press, 1995), 7–9, 17, 101–3.

55. Calder, *Auraicept na n-Éces*, 17.

56. Koch and Carey, *Celtic Heroic Age,* Sections 49, 53, 54.

57. Carey, "The Ancestry of Fénius Farsaid," 108–110. Carey examines discrepancies and variants found in the pedigree of the Sons of Mil, whose genealogy shares a few figures in common with that of the Túatha Dé Danann: Baath, Esru, Sru, and Tait. In particular, Carey discusses the *Liber Antiquitatum Biblicarum*, a work written in Hebrew around the time of

Jesus which was translated into Latin probably around the third or fourth century and which circulated as one of the writings of Philo of Alexandria. It is an account of sacred history from the creation to the time of David, with much apocryphal detail. In one version of the text (where the names of Japeth's sons and grandsons are frequently garbled), three grandsons of Japheth's son Javan are listed as *Itheb* (or perhaps *Iabat*), *Beath* and *Fenech*. Carey sees a resemblance between these names and those of the figures *Ibath, Baath* and *Fénius* (*Farsaid*). Both trios of names are unique in their respective literatures, and Carey feels that earlier versions of the *Liber* may have contained readings even closer to the Irish version. However, he also points out that he is unaware of any other convincing indication of knowledge of the text by the early Irish, and it is possible that only a fragment reached them. I would add that it is possible that passing similarities existed between the names of Biblical characters and those of native origin, resulting in subsequent confusion, substitution and alternate spellings (a phenomenon which undoubtedly took place, and for which Carey gives at least one example in this setting).

58. *Genesis* 5:18.

59. Anne Ross, *Pagan Celtic Britain* (Chicago: Academy, 1996), 54–5, 59–66; Fergus Kelly, "The Old Irish Tree-List," *Celtica* 11 (1976): 107–124; Calder, *Auraicept na n-Éces*, 89–93; Michael Newton, *A Handbook of the Scottish Gaelic World* (Dublin: Four Courts Press, 2000), 92–6, 191–2.

60. A.T. Lucas, "The Sacred Trees of Ireland," *Journal of the Cork Historical and Archaeological Society*, LXVIII (1963): 16–54.

61. Ross, *Pagan Celtic Britain*, 60.

62. Davidson, *Gods and Myths of Northern Europe*, 162, 165, 168, 170, 179, 215, 224.

63. Davidson, *Gods and Myths of Northern Europe*. 25.

64. Damian MacManus, "Irish Letter-Names and their Kennings," *Ériu* 39 (1988): 127–145.

65. MacManus, "Irish Letter-Names and their Kennings," 163.

66. MacManus, "Irish Letter-Names and their Kennings," 147.

67. MacManus, "Irish Letter-Names and their Kennings," 147.

68. MacManus, "Irish Letter-Names and their Kennings," 164.

69. Kelly, "The Old Irish Tree-List," 110.

70. MacManus, "Irish Letter-Names and their Kennings," 164.

71. MacManus, "Irish Letter-Names and their Kennings," 164.

72. The yew (*éo*) is connected with a number of kennings that refer to the salmon, a creature associated with divine knowledge, poetry and prophecy. The salmon often appears in connection with rivers or bodies of water associated with wisdom or prophecy. A number of salmon are described as living in an Otherworld well of wisdom (which was often located near sacred trees).

73. Lucas, "The Sacred Trees of Ireland," 18. In a similar vein, the yew is mentioned in an early riddle: "Which are the two trees whose green tops do not fade until they become withered?" "Éo-Rossa and Fidh-Sidheang: Yew and Holly."

74. MacManus, "Irish Letter-Names and their Kennings," 136–7, 147. The yew is renowned for the great age it may attain, and accordingly was placed last in the "Alphabet of the World."

75. John White, *Forest and Woodland Trees in Britain* (Oxford: Oxford University Press, 1995), 207.

76. Newton, *A Handbook of the Scottish Gaelic World*, 191, 211, 214. Dr. Newton was kind enough to point out to me that in addition to the association of a yew tree with the central point of Scotland, a number of place-names containing the element *nem-* ("sacred," as in *nemed* and *nemeton*) are also found near Fortingall.

77. Lucas, "The Sacred Trees of Ireland," 17.

78. White, *Forest and Woodland Trees in Britain*, 207.

79. Carey, "Native Elements in Irish Pseudo-history," 47–8.

80. R A Stewart MacAlister, *Lebor Gabála Érenn*, Part IV (Naas: Irish Texts Society, 1997), 165.

Chapter 3

1. An earlier version of this research was originally published in *Proceedings of the Harvard Celtic Colloquium*, Vol. 23 (Cambridge: Harvard University Press, 2003): 257–283.

2. Nerys Patterson, *Cattle Lords and Clansmen: The Social Structure of Early Ireland* (Notre Dame: University of Notre Dame Press, 1994), 118.

3. References from later accounts of Irish and Scottish Highland folk practices (which reflect, to some degree, the conservative nature of the traditional way of life), agricultural histories from other parts of Europe, and information from medieval Irish historical sources help fill in our understanding of early Irish life.

4. Patterson, *Cattle Lords and Clansmen*, 119.

5. Patterson, *Cattle Lords and Clansmen*, 119.

6. Patterson, *Cattle Lords and Clansmen*, 135–6.

7. This is a very old European practice which may have originated in communities that emphasized the raising of sheep, as sheep naturally move uphill in early spring. In fact, they are so difficult to restrain, that farmers who wanted their milk and wool had to follow them and remain with them in the higher elevations.

8. Patterson, *Cattle Lords and Clansmen*, 136.

9. Patterson, *Cattle Lords and Clansmen*, 136–7.

10. Patterson, *Cattle Lords and Clansmen*, 138. Temporary marriages could end on this date as well.

11. Patterson, *Cattle Lords and Clansmen*, 141–2.

12. Some sources refer to the festival taking place for two weeks on either side of that date, or a week on either side of the date, with Lugnasad at the center.

13. Patterson, *Cattle Lords and Clansmen*, 136–145. Flax was a valuable crop and an object of women's work. It was reaped in mid–August at which time some women could return from the summer pastures to assist with harvesting flax as well as wheat (due to the decline in the production of sheep and cow's milk).

14. Patterson, *Cattle Lords and Clansmen*, 145–6.

15. Patterson, *Cattle Lords and Clansmen*, 141–145.

16. Patterson, *Cattle Lords and Clansmen*, 145. Temporary marriages were often entered into at this time. These could be dissolved at Beltaine by the payment of wages to the woman, without loss of honour-price or reason for the divorce.

17. Edward Gwynn, *The Metrical Dindshenchas*, Part III (Dublin: Dublin Institute for Advanced Studies, 1991), 1–2, 8–9, 24–25; Trefor M. Owen, *Welsh Folk Customs* (Llandysul Dyfed: Gomer Press, 1987), 123.

18. Patterson, *Cattle Lords and Clansmen*, 143.

19. The fresh supply of milk at this time of year would coincide well with the human mother's need for nutrition for the nursing of her young.

20. There were also sex and fertility overtones at Lugnasad due to marriages and subsequent sexual unions between humans (and animals) at this time of year.

21. Patterson, *Cattle Lords and Clansmen*, 119.

22. Patterson, *Cattle Lords and Clansmen*, 121–122.

23. Only the occasional cow was allowed to stay in milk over winter with its winter calf, thus prolonging lactation beyond October.

24. Patterson, *Cattle Lords and Clansmen*, 122, 136.

25. Deer were protected from hunting to some degree during snow falls, when they came down from the mountains in search of food. This encouraged hunting during the summer when animals were in peak condition, but they were left alone to breed.

26. Patterson, *Cattle Lords and Clansmen*, 124–5.

27. Patterson, *Cattle Lords and Clansmen*, 122.

28. Patterson, *Cattle Lords and Clansmen*, 123–5.

29. Patterson, *Cattle Lords and Clansmen*, 128.

30. Although Samain was the official end of the raiding and warring season, and few large battles are recorded as taking place during this time, some plotting and violence no doubt occurred.

31. Patterson, *Cattle Lords and Clansmen*, 123–5.

32. Patterson, *Cattle Lords and Clansmen*, 120, 126–7.

33. Patterson, *Cattle Lords and Clansmen*, 123–6.

34. Patterson, *Cattle Lords and Clansmen*, 131. Guesting and feasting largely ended between Imbolc and Beltaine.

35. Patterson, *Cattle Lords and Clansmen*, 130. Early calving (before the first week in March) could be dangerous, due to low vegetation levels, as it may be four to six weeks before the cows have sufficient milk to feed their young.

36. Patterson, *Cattle Lords and Clansmen*, 131.

37. Patterson, *Cattle Lords and Clansmen*, 131–2.

38. Patterson, *Cattle Lords and Clansmen*, 130; Eric P. Hamp, "imbolc, óimelc," *Studia Celtica*, Vol. 14/15 (1979/1980): 106–113.

39. Patterson, *Cattle Lords and Clansmen*, 129–30.

40. Patterson, *Cattle Lords and Clansmen*, 129

41. It was best to settle disputes and rivalry before engaging in the larger campaigns of summer and fall, when the raiding of well-fed cattle was worth the effort of driving them over great distances.

42. Patterson, *Cattle Lords and Clansmen*, 133–4.

43. Patterson, *Cattle Lords and Clansmen*, 132–3.

44. I am indebted to Nerys Patterson for her excellent research on the seasonal cycles of

work. It was here that I first encountered the idea that there may have been male and female halves or cycles in the yearly work pattern (Patterson, *Cattle Lords and Clansmen*, 19).

45. Patterson, *Cattle Lords and Clansmen*, 135.

46. Patterson, *Cattle Lords and Clansmen*, 139.

47. Kevin Danaher, *The Year in Ireland* (Dublin/Cork: Mercier Press, 1972), 88–9. Certain Beltaine customs were observed in which the whole community could participate, such as the gathering of May flowers or boughs, or the setting up of a May bush to ensure an abundance of milk throughout the summer.

48. Patterson, *Cattle Lords and Clansmen*, 139–140; Danaher, *The Year in Ireland*, 95–6; Alexander Carmichael, ed. and trans., *Carmina Gadelica* (Edinburgh: Lindisfarne Press, 1992), 586–7; F. Marian McNeill, *The Silver Bough, Vol.* Two (Glasgow: William MacLellan, 1959), 55–58, 61; Owen, *Welsh Folk Customs*, 97.

49. Patterson, *Cattle Lords and Clansmen*, 139; McNeill, *The Silver Bough*, 58–9.

50. Danaher, *The Year in Ireland*, 116–117.

51. Danaher, *The Year in Ireland*, 116–117; Carmichael, *Carmina Gadelica*, 83–4.

52. McNeill, *The Silver Bough*, 60.

53. Donald Monro, ed., *Martin Martin—A Description of the Western Islands of Scotland circa 1695* (Edinburgh: Birlinn, 1999), 73.

54. Patterson, *Cattle Lords and Clansmen*, 137–40. Beltaine traditions often focused on a fear of theft of milk by witches or fairies, and therefore included propitiatory rites and the recitation of prayers to protect dairy products. Various agreements were re-negotiated on May 1, such as those between tenants and lords. Many lords received part of their tribute at this time, in the form of milk, butter, curds and cheese. A number of Beltaine traditions included the offering of "first fruits" to the head of the household to ensure luck and abundance in the coming year (first water from the well, first milk from the dairy, etc.). This was considered highly preferable to having these go "out of the house" or farmstead (to "others"), and may reflect anxieties associated with the payment of tributes at this time.

55. Monro, *Martin Martin*, 16.

56. McNeill, *The Silver Bough*, 61.

57. Patterson, *Cattle Lords and Clansmen*, 139–40; Danaher, *The Year in Ireland*, 99–103.

58. Patterson, *Cattle Lords and Clansmen*, 139–40; Danaher, *The Year in Ireland*, 99–103.

59. There are a number of folk traditions that take place at Samain pertaining to horses or mares (one of the symbols of the Goddess of Sovereignty). There are also some Beltaine rites associated with horses, such as the "'Obby 'Oss" festival of Cornwall. These are often associated with fertility, perhaps symbolizing the union or linking of the energies of the sexes before the women leave the community (and before the yearly cycle moves fully into the male half of the year).

60. Danaher, *The Year in Ireland*, 175–6. For a thorough examination of Lugnasad, see Máire MacNeill, *The Festival of Lughnasa* (Dublin: University College Dublin, 2008).

61. McNeill, *The Silver Bough*, 97–8.

62. McNeill, *The Silver Bough*, 98–9. The embers of this fire were put into an old pot along with bits of old iron and carried sunwise around the fields and flocks by the man of the house.

63. Danaher, *The Year in Ireland*, 167; Patterson, *Cattle Lords and Clansmen*, 142.

64. Patterson, *Cattle Lords and Clansmen*, 136.

65. Patterson, *Cattle Lords and Clansmen*, 138; Danaher, *The Year in Ireland*, 169.

66. McNeill, *The Silver Bough*, 120–128.

67. Danaher, *The Year in Ireland*, 200, 205.

68. Danaher, *The Year in Ireland*, 202, 218–227; McNeill, *The Silver Bough* (Vol. Three), 31–39.

69. Danaher, *The Year in Ireland*, 210–212; McNeill, *The Silver Bough* (Vol. Three), 24–5.

70. McNeill, *The Silver Bough*, 56–62.

71. McNeill, *The Silver Bough*, 17–20; Danaher, *The Year in Ireland*, 206.

72. McNeill, *The Silver Bough*, 20.

73. Danaher, *The Year in Ireland*, 204–6.

74. McNeill, *The Silver Bough*, 21–2.

75. Danaher, *The Year in Ireland*, 213; Owen, *Welsh Folk Customs*, 49–56. The procession associated with the *Láir Bhán* in Ireland has a number of similarities with the procession of the *Mair Lwyd* (perhaps "Grey Mare") in Wales. In early Irish legends, light colors (such as white or grey) often denoted the sacredness or significance of an animal or thing. In addition, many Christmas or New Year's customs were likely originally associated with Samain (the old Celtic New Year).

76. Owen, *Welsh Folk Customs*, 49–56.

77. Danaher, *The Year in Ireland*, 15.

78. Danaher, *The Year in Ireland*, 31–3.

79. Danaher, *The Year in Ireland*, 15–23.

80. Danaher, *The Year in Ireland*, 24–31. In parts of southern and western Ireland, young men went about in the procession; in earlier times they dressed in women's clothing. Some carried the Bridget figure with them, but their procession involved music and laughter, and was quite different from the solemn women's ceremony.

81. Monro, *Martin Martin*, 81.

82. McNeill, *The Silver Bough*, 130–131: In

some cases, the last sheaf of the harvest was the one used to create the Bridget doll. In other cases, the last sheaf was finally disposed of at Imbolc.

83. Carmichael, *Carmina Gadelica*, 580–583. At dawn a hymn is sung, and the remnants of the feast were distributed to poor women.

84. Danaher, *The Year in Ireland*, 13–14. This custom is the foundation of Groundhog Day in the United States.

85. Carmichael, *Carmina Gadelica*, 583–5.

86. Patterson, *Cattle Lords and Clansmen*, 139–40.

87. Whitley Stokes, ed. and trans., *Sanas Chormaic* (Calcutta: Irish Archaeological and Celtic Society, 1868), 29.

88. Jeffrey Gantz, trans., *Early Irish Myths and Sagas* (London: Penguin, 1981), 39; Elizabeth Gray, ed. and trans., *Cath Maige Tuired* (Naas: Irish Texts Society, 1982), 44–45. In *Cath Maige Tuired*, the Dagda's epithet is explained as referring to his many powers and abilities ("good" meaning "good at many things.")

89. Gantz, *Early Irish Myths and Sagas*, 40: Uisnech Mide "with Ériu extending equally far in every direction, north and south, east and west."

90. Gray, *Cath Maige Tuired*, 24–5, 47.

91. Anne Ross, *Pagan Celtic Britain* (Chicago: Academy, 1996), 78, 83, 203, 213, 224, 235–6, 257–8, 463, 466–7, 470–2; Calvert Watkins, *Dictionary of Indo-European Roots* (Boston: Houghton Mifflin, 2000), 9. Here we might note the figure of Belenus, a widely-worshipped Celtic deity who was venerated in Gaul, Italy and Britain. There are 31 dedications to him throughout Europe, an unusually high number in terms of survivals. The root of his name (and presumably also of the word *Beltene*) means "to shine or burn; shining white." Here we might recall the association of the direction of south with the color white, and the possible association with Beltaine in yearly symbolic associations (as discussed in Chapter One). It is possible that the word *bel* (as utilized in the name of the holiday) was originally a descriptive term, which in later times suggested the existence of a divine figure associated with these qualities. The root also occurs in the name of another divine figure, *Belatucadros* ("Bright Beautiful One"?), a deity associated with war and protection. Dedications to this god are found in many areas where images of the horned god (in his warrior aspect) also occur. These images also suggest an association with protection and fertility.

92. Gwynn, *The Metrical Dindsenchas*, Vol. IV, 146–161.

93. Gwynn, *The Metrical Dindsenchas*, Vol. III, 40–54.

94. Elizabeth Gray, "Cath Maige Tuired: Myth and Structure," *Eigse* 18–19 (Vol. XVIII, Pt 1, 1980): 201–208. Bres is the son of a Fomorian king named Elatha (a word meaning "art, science, acquired craft or skill") and a Túatha Dé Danann woman (Ériu). Bres turns out to be an unfit ruler (possibly due to his father's ancestry, although later in the tale his father rebukes him for his actions). Lug is also of mixed ancestry, but his father is a member of the Túatha Dé Danann, which is what appears to matter most. In addition, Bres is the offspring of a union that took place without the consent of either family. In both divine and mortal marriage, a couple's union had consequences for both families.

95. Gray, *Cath Maige Tuired*, 66–69.

96. Danaher, *The Year in Ireland*, 169–171. Many of the Lugnasad assemblies were held on hills, heights or mountains.

97. Gwynn, *The Metrical Dindshenchas* (Vol IV): 147–163, 415.

98. The mixed imagery of the harvest sheaf (maiden/hag) may symbolize an ambivalent attitude towards the presence of women during this season, perhaps due to the impending arrival/encroachment of energies associated with the female half of the year. In addition, the Goddess of Sovereignty has a dual aspect associated with life and death, beneficence and fierceness, and so forth. Regarding the possible association of Lug's wife Bui with the Cailleach and/or the Goddess of Sovereignty, see Tomás O'Cathasaigh, "The Eponym of Cnogba," *Éigse* (Vol. 23, 1989): 27–38.

99. Gwynn, *The Metrical Dindshenchas* (Vol. III), 48–53. Bui's name is spelled "*bua*" and "*búa*" in the Dindshenchas of Cnogba (40–47). *Nas* is a poetical term for death. *Bu* may also signify "death" (or be related to *bó* "cow"). See O'Cathasaigh's article cited in the previous footnote for a discussion of this term.

100. Gwynn, *The Metrical Dindshenchas* (Vol III), 2–9.

101. Gwynn, *The Metrical Dindshenchas* (Vol III), 11–17. The women's fair was followed by the fair of the Leinstermen, the fair of princes, the fair of various companies of Ireland, and the fair of Clann Condla.

102. Gwynn, *The Metrical Dindshenchas* (Vol. IV), 3–7, 125–131. Macha's father's name, in various accounts, is given as Midir or Aed Ruad. Thomas Kinsella, trans., *The Táin* (Oxford: Oxford University Press, 1977), 7: In a pre-tale to the *Táin*, Macha describes herself as the daughter of *Sainrith mac Imbaith*. The word *imbaith* may signify "ocean" (relating to *imbádud* "wallowing, drowning" or *bádud* "act of submerging, drowning"). Interestingly, the

swimming of horses took place at many Lugnasad gatherings. In the Dindsenchas of Ard Macha (Gwynn, *The Metrical Dindshenchas,* Vol. IV, 124–131), Macha is said to have been summoned from "the waters" or "the ocean waves." The sale of foals took place at numerous Lugnasad fairs, and the racing or swimming of mares or stallions may have taken place to help establish the value of their offspring (Patterson, *Cattle Lords and Clansmen,* 144). The clearing of plains is mentioned in the tale of Macha (as the wife of Nemed) and in accounts pertaining to Tailtiu.

103. Gray, *Cath Maige Tuired,* 44–47; Alwyn and Brinley Rees, *Celtic Heritage* (New York: Thames & Hudson, 1989), 32.

104. Gray, *Cath Maige Tuired,* 44–47. While the timing of some of these events is not certain, the union of the Dagda and the Mórrigan is clearly stated to have taken place just before the Eve of Samain. The summoning of the gods of power by the Mórrigan is said to have taken place a week before Samain.

105. Gray, *Cath Maige Tuired,* 65–71.

106. Cecile O'Rahilly, transl., *Táin Bó Cúailgne* (Dublin: Dublin Institute for Advanced Studies, 1976), 62, 181.

107. For more information on the Mórrígan and the war goddesses, see my article, "Mater Deorum Hibernensium: Identity and Cross-Correlation in Early Irish Myths," *Proceedings of the Harvard Celtic Colloquium,* Vol. 19 (1999) and its accompanying bibliography. An excellent chapter on the topic was written by Proinsias MacCana, "Celtic Goddesses of Sovereignty," in *Goddesses Who Rule,* ed. Elisabeth Bernard, et al. (Oxford: Oxford University Press, 2000).

108. Gwynn, *The Metrical Dindshenchas* (Vol. I), 187–191; Kathryn Chadbourne, "Giant Women and Flying Machines," *Proceedings of the Harvard Celtic Colloquium,* Vol. XIV (1994): 106–114.

109. Silva Gadelica, quoted in Rees 1989: 165.

110. Maire Herbert, "Transmutations of an Irish Goddess," in *The Concept of the Goddess,* ed. Sandra Billington, et al. (London: Routledge, 1996), 141–151.

111. Early references to Imbolc are scarce, and do not seem to suggest the existence of large tribal assemblies. It is interesting to note that as the seasons progress, Bridget's quarter of the year gives way to that of her father, The Dagda. It may be that his staff or club, which wielded the power of life and death, was transferred to his daughter in the form of a staff that was placed beside her, the tracks of which were sought in the ashes of the hearth on Imbolc morning.

Chapter 4

1. A version of this research was originally published in *Proceedings of the Harvard Celtic Colloquium,* Vol. 19 (1999), 340–384.

2. DIL, *Danann II: is ón Danann fá máthair don triar so.* The Irish themselves saw in Danann a feminine personal name: *Danann inghean Dealbhaoith.*

3. Elizabeth Gray, ed. and trans., *Cath Maige Tuired* (London: Irish Texts Society, 1982), 122.

4. John Carey, "Lebor Gabála Érenn (First Recension): The Book of Invasions," in *The Celtic Heroic Age,* ed. John T. Koch and John Carey (Malden, Massachusetts: Celtic Studies Publications, 2001), 258: "Donann, daughter of that same Delbáeth…"

5. Edward Gwynn, ed. and trans., *The Metrical Dindshenchas* (Dublin: Dublin Institute for Advanced Studies, 1991), 268–271; Gray, *Cath Maige Tuired,* 122; Carey, "Lebor Gabála Érenn," 258.

6. Gray, *Cath Maige Tuired,* 122; Carey, "Lebor Gabála Érenn," 248. In *Lebor Gabála,* the three are associated with a place-name: "Donann … was the mother of the last three of them, i.e., of Brian and Iuchar and Iucharba. They were the three gods of skill (*trí dee dána*) after whom Sliab na Trí nDé is named." An interesting description of the three (referred to as *Trí Dee Donand*) is found in R.I. Best, Osborn Bergin, and M.A. O'Brien, eds. and transl., *The Book of Leinster, formerly Lebar na Núachongbála* (Dublin: Dublin Institute for Advanced Studies, 2007), 124. In *Immacallam in dá Thuarad* ("The Colloquoy of the Two Sages"), they are said to be three sons of Bres and Bríg; in LG they are said to be the offspring of Bres. While initially this seems to be another inexplicable element of early Irish literature, there may be something to it. The kingship of Bres was not distinguished by those things which made a good king: generosity, entertainment, and contests of arts and martial feats. As a result he was satirized, and from that point on there was no prosperity in his reign. Bres was not a suitable leader or a fit king, and despite his attempts to remain installed in office, he is removed from the kingship. Nuadu reigns after him. At this point, Lug comes to Tara and is honored for his many skills by Nuadu. Lug becomes a primary character in the proceedings, and is instrumental in assisting the Túatha Dé in the Battle of Mag Tuired. Lug plots the murder of Bres, but spares him in return for valuable information pertaining to agriculture (the time when plowing, sowing and reaping should take place). It is not inconceivable that Bres was angry at Lug. If Brian, Iuchar and Iucharba are indeed Bres' sons, they

may well have killed Lug's father in retaliation. Certainly this makes more sense than the sons of Danu performing such a deed for no apparent reason. It is also interesting to think about these characters in terms of the seasonal celebrations of Irish tradition. Lugnasad was said to have been instituted by Lug to honour his foster-mother Tailtiu, who died from the exertion of clearing many plains (possibly symbolizing the preparation of the land for agriculture). The Feast Day of Lugnasad (associated with Lug) and the Feast Day of Imbolc (associated with Brigid) are located at opposite points of the yearly cycle. Bríg's husband Bres is threatened by and almost killed by Lug, whose abilities and reputation outshine his own. We might envision Bres as possibly having once been in the position opposite to that of his wife Bríg in the seasonal cycles, only to be supplanted by the young, brilliant god Lug. Perhaps the story of the encounter between Bres and Lug formed part of some early traditional tales pertaining to the seasonal holidays. There is a Dindshenchas poem that provides a different tale in which Bres is bested by Lug through trickery and magic: Gwynn, *The Metrical Dindshenchas*, Vol. III, 216–223.

7. Gray, *Cath Maige Tuired*, 44–45, 50–53.

8. DIL *ecna(e)* I: wisdom, knowledge, enlightenment, frequently Divine wisdom or of spiritual knowledge, but also applied to human learning in its widest sense; rarely intelligence, skill. Personified: Ecna mac na tri nDea nDana; Ergna mac Ecnai. Of persons, wise, enlightened. As a substantive, a wise man, philosopher, sage. DIL *érgna* (cf. ecnae, egne): "understanding, discrimination, discernment. Personified: Ergna mac Ecnai .i. is tuisechu do neoch in t-ecna do bith i n-anmain quam a thasselbad* ("wisdom must be in a man's soul before he can display it"). *Érgna* is the exhibition of wisdom, ecna is the gift itself.

9. Wendy O'Flaherty, *Hindu Myths* (New York: Penguin, 1980), 25: "The Father Commits Incest with his Daughter: One concept of creation which begins in the Rg Veda and persists through later Hindu mythology is the idea of primeval incest.... Heaven and earth, once so carefully and safely propped apart, meet here in an act which is creative but dangerous..."

10. Other than parallels suggested by other Indo-European mythological contexts, to my knowledge there is no evidence connecting Delbaeth with the sky or celestial realms.

11. DIL *Danann* III: Danann bandrúi (Keating), Danand bantúathach (LL); Gray, *Cath Maige Tuired*, 122.

12. DIL *dess*: (a) right (as opposed to left) (b) south (the south being on the right to a person facing east), and by derivation (c) in a

figurative sense "right, just, meet." Hence, a sunwise (or clockwise) circle or circuit was said to be performed *dessel*, "the direction of the sun, right-hand course" (towards the south or right, in relation to a person facing the east). From the idea that sun-wise was a lucky or auspicious direction comes the extended or more generalized meaning "what is lucky, favourable, propitious." Conversely, 2 *túath* "northern, left, on the left; perverse, wicked, evil" finds expression in the term *túaithbel* (*túath* + *sel)* "a turning, lefthand-wise, against the sun, withershins," found in phrases implying wrongness, awkwardness, even chaos or confusion. In early tales, turning the left side of one's chariot towards another (i.e. making a circle left-hand wise) indicates a possible insult or affront, and may show malicious intent. It is this form of *túath* (2) from which comes the words *túaithe* "witchcraft, sorcery" and *túathaid* "magician, witch" (used to describe Danu, the witch or sorceress). The fairies are also described as "the folks that turn withershins" (*arna gentib impadhas tuaithbil, na sidhaighi*). Druidical knowledge or craft is also described in similar terms: *tuathcheird .i. ceird thúathamhail, no dráoidheachta*, "left-hand craft, or druidic magic" (from *druídecht* "secret lore and arts of the druids; in wider sense, occult science, wizardry.") The *Túatha Dé* are said to have come from the "northern islands of the world" (*i n-indsib túaschertachaibi an domuin*), where they studied magic, sorcery, witchcraft and the like. In this case, "northern" may simply mean "far away, from an obscure or mysterious location," but the connection with magic is notable.

13. Gray, *Cath Maige Tuired*, 52–3: In *Cath Maige Tuired*, Lug inquires of "his two witches" (*bantúathaid*), Bé Chuille and Díanann, what power they will provide in the battle.

14. DIL *Danann* III: Donand Mathair na ndea; Carey, "Lebor Gabála Érenn," 255: "Donann mother of the gods."

15. Anne Ross, *Pagan Celtic Britain* (Chicago: Academy, 1996), 290, 293: "Anu and Danu, the divine mother of early Irish mythology find their parallel in Dôn, mother of certain of the Welsh divinities." Patrick K. Ford, *The Mabinogi and other Medieval Welsh Tales* (Berkeley: University of California Press, 1977), 89: "In this branch we are concerned with the family of Dôn, a goddess whose name is equivalent to the Irish Danu, mother of the gods known as the Túatha Dé Danann." Also 189–194, where Dôn is the mother of several important figures: Gwydion, a powerful magician, Gofannon (the smith god, equivalent of the Irish Goibhniu), Ar(i)anrhod ("Silver Wheel," mother of Dylan Eil Ton and Lleu Llaw Gyffes), Gilfaethwy, and Amaethon (the Divine Ploughman); and 172,

where Dôn is referenced in a poem uttered by the inspired poet Taliesin, referring to his past history or incarnations: "I know the stars' names from the North to the South ... I was in the court of Dôn before the birth of Gwydion...." See also Proinsias MacCana, *The Mabinogi* (Cardiff: University of Wales Press, 1992), 51: "...most of the main incidents in the Four Branches belong to the mythological layer of British tradition. The family of Dôn evidently corresponds to the divine people of the Irish known as Túatha Dé Danann, Man-awydan is the British equivalent of the Irish god of the sea Manannán mac Lir, Rhiannon (from *Rigantona "Divine Queen")* and *Teyrnon* (from *Tigernonos* "Divine Lord") with their son Mabon (from *Maponos* "Divine Son") are central to the whole concept of deity among the Celts."

16. John Carey, "The Name "Túatha Dé Danann," *Éigse* 18:2 (1981): 291–294. Carey refers to a number of interesting points made by Stern (c. 1900) regarding the name *Danu*. He mentions that Stern considered Sir John Rhys's suggestion (also c. 1900) that the Welsh Dôn is a cognate of Danann "possible, but unproven." In 1933, W.J. Gruffydd derived Dôn from *Dánuvia via Donwy, and cited *Dánu as a cognate. He was followed by Rachel Bromwich (*Studies in Early British History*, 1954) and Alwyn and Brinley Rees (*Celtic Heritage,* 1961). In more recent times, few seem to have commented further on whether the names are definitively linked, but they are often mentioned as cognate, and arguments could certainly be made for such a case (see endnote 43 below). The fact that *Donann* appears to be an earlier form than *Danann* may help support a linguistic connection (although this may also be due to confusion with tribal names such as *Túath Domnann,* discussed below). Also in support of their association is the fact that *Dôn* is the mother of the Divine Smith *Gofannon,* and *Danu* is said to be the mother of *na trí dée dána,* which presumably included the figure Goibniu, the Irish Smith god.

17. DIL *Danann* III: Danann, gen. Danainne, in the place-name Dá Chích Danainne in Co. Kerry. DIL *Danann* II: Dá Chích Danann, two mountains in County Kerry.

18. Carey, "Lebor Gabála Érenn," 259: "...fair, generous Donann..."; R.A.S. Macalister, transl., *Lebor Gabála Érenn,* Part IV (London: Irish Texts Society, 1941), 226–7: *Donand chomlán cáin,* "perfect, fair Donand. DIL *cáin:* "fine, good, fair, beautiful; *comlán:* "complete, perfect"; *lán* I: full (of), filled (with), ample, enough; II (a) the full, complement, whole (b) In general sense of "abundance, plenty." The descriptive term *comlán* could also

mean "Very Full, Ample" or "Great Abundance or Plenty."

19. Lecture notes from Patrick K. Ford's *Celtic Paganism* class, Harvard University, Spring, 2000: "Túatha Dé Danann, Tribe(s) of the Goddess Danu—explicitly a race of gods. As in Welsh literature—the Children of Dôn."

20. DIL *dán;* Fergus Kelly, *A Guide to Early Irish Law* (Dublin: Dublin Institute for Advanced Studies, 1995), 43–48, 51–56, 57–63.

21. DIL *dán: Ro hordaigheadh cach dib for a dhan dileas, ib. ferr dán orbba,* "A trade or profession is better than farming." Several sources also record the distinction between *dée* (gods, those of skill) and *andée* (non-gods, or husbandmen).

22. Mary E. Byrne, "*Airec menman Uraird maic* Coisse" in *Anecdota from Irish Manuscripts*, Vol. 2, ed. Osborn Bergin, et al. (Halle and Dublin, 1908), 50.

23. A.L.F. Rivet and Colin Smith, *The Place-Names of Roman Britain* (Princeton, New Jersey: Princeton University Press, 1979), 329. A root *dánu-* meaning "bold" (perhaps giving "rapidly flowing") was postulated by Jackson. Rivet and Smith felt that due to its extremely widespread occurrence, repetition and connection with rivers, the meaning "river" may be a safer assumption (rather than an adjective which is not necessarily related to water, and which may not accurately describe all the waters in question). They find Elkwall's linking of Celtic *dánu-* with Sanskrit *danu* "rain, moisture" unwarranted.

24. Rivet and Smith, *The Place-Names of Roman Britain,* 329.

25. Rivet and Smith, *The Place-Names of Roman Britain,* 336–7.

26. Rivet and Smith, *The Place-Names of Roman Britain,* 338.

27. Rivet and Smith, *The Place-Names of Roman Britain,* 338.

28. W.F.H. Nicolaisen, *The Picts and Their Place-Names* (Groam House Museum Trust, Scotland, 1966), 18, 21–22.

29. Christina Hole, *Encyclopedia of Superstitions* (New York: Barnes & Noble, 1961), 141–2 (quoting G.F. Black, *Orkney and Shetland Folk-Lore,* 1901), and 218–19 (quoting *Folk-Lore* Volume 15, 1904). Sheila Livingstone, *Scottish Customs* (New York: Birlinn/Barnes & Noble, 1996), 124: Similar traditions were associated with other Scottish rivers. The Spey and the Tweed were said to demand one human life annually, while the Till demanded two: *Tweed says to Till,* "What gars ye rin sae still?" Says Till to Tweed, "Though ye run wi' speed, and I run slaw, Whaur ye droon ae man, I droon twa."

30. R. Mark Scowcroft, "Leabhar Gabhála—

250 Chapter Notes—4

The Growth of the Tradition," *Ériu* 34 (1988): 2, 8, 14.

31. Scowcroft, "Leabhar Gabhála—The Growth of the Tradition," 17–18. In regards to information about Scythia, the *literati* relied on Orosius and Isidore of Seville, whose works inspired the itineraries in tract I of *Lebor Gabála*. Orosius locates the Scythians east of the Caspian Sea. It was believed that the northern ocean (to which the Caspian Sea was thought to be connected) was part of the great ocean which encircled the known world. Orosius' descriptions must have inspired the strange voyage of the Gaedil from Scythia to Spain by way of the northern ocean, Sliab Riphi (the Montes Riphaei at the source of the *Tanais* or Don, in LG located right on the ocean shore), and the Black and Mediterranean Seas.

32. As the tale continues, sacred rivers are again a focus. Íth, son of Bregon, sails with his chieftains and retinue, and invade Ireland. They land at Inber Scéne, the mouth of the Shannon. Éremon mac Miled sails to the northeast and lands at Inber Colptha, the mouth of the Boyne.

33. J.P. Mallory, *In Search of the Indo-Europeans* (New York: Thames & Hudson, 1991), 195, 239, 262–264.

34. Dáibhí Ó Cróinín, ed., *The Irish Sex Aetates Mundi* (Dublin: Dublin Institute for Advanced Studies, 1983), 1–7, 116, 133. The Danube is also mentioned in the Irish *Sex Aetates Mundi* ("Six Ages of the World"), as one of the borders of the peoples of Europe in medieval pseudo-historical tradition. Of the family of Japheth it was said: "They occupied many lands in Asia, from Mount Imai and from Mount Tur to the river Danube and as far as Scythia," as well as the whole of Europe including Spain and Britain. The Danube serves as a border or line of demarcation of an important early territory.

35. Mallory, *In Search of the Indo-Europeans*, 95–6, 106–7 (regarding languages); and Barry Cunliffe, *The Ancient Celts* (New York: Oxford University Press, 1997), 43–51 (regarding material culture).

36. Cunliffe, *The Ancient Celts,* 42–48, 51, 53–57, 64, 73–5, 78–80, 294.

37. I would like to express my thanks to Professor Tomás Ó'Cathasaigh for pointing out this fact. See Carey, "Lebor Gabála Érenn," for an example of this attestation.

38. Alwyn Rees and Brinley Rees, *Celtic Heritage* (New York: Thames & Hudson, 1989), 52–3.

39. Gwynn, *Metrical Dindshenchas*, 286–9, 292–5.

40. John Carey, "The Location of the Oth-erworld in Irish Tradition," *Éigse* XIX (1982): 36–43.

41. Eric P. Hamp, "The Dag(h)d(h)ae and his relatives," in *Donum grammaticum: Studies in Latin and Celtic Linguistics in Honor of Hannah Rosen,* ed. L. Sawick, L., et al. (Peters, 2002), 163–169.

42. My thanks to Professor Joseph Eska for clarifying this information. See also Calvert Watkins, *Dictionary of Indo-European Roots* (Boston: Houghton Mifflin, 2000), 20.

43. Carey, "Lebor Gabála Érenn"; Gray, *Cath Maige Tuired*, 117; Gerard Murphy, ed., *Duanaire Finn* (Dublin: Irish Texts Society, 1953), 208–210; T.F. O'Rahilly, *Early Irish History and Mythology* (Dublin: Dublin Institute for Advanced Studies, 1984), 308–317.

44. Later versions contain various forms of the name *Túatha Dé Danann.*

45. Carey, "Lebor Gabála Érenn," 292. These earlier forms (*aes síde, Túath(a)/Fer Dé(a)* occur in 9th c., or possibly even 8th c. sources, with the exception of two references in *Tochmarc Étaine* assigned by Thurneysen to the 9th century (but which seem like interpolations and may therefore stem from the 11th century revision of the text). Interestingly, in *Cath Maige Tuired,* Lug, Dagda, Ogma, Goibniu and Dian Cécht are referred to as *Fer nDéa,* "The Men of the Goddess" (Gray, *Cath Maige Tuired*, 42–3).

46. Carey, "Lebor Gabála Érenn," 294 n. 36. Carey suggests that perhaps the poet Eochaid ua Flainn introduced the figure of Donann. A prose description of the Dagda's reign in LG enumerates the various members of the Túatha Dé Danann. Immediately following this is Eochaid's poem, which also lists the members of the Túatha Dé. The two lists correspond, with the exception of Donann, who is absent from the earlier prose version, possibly suggesting that Eochaid added her to his later listing. However as we shall see, Donann/Danu goes by other names, one of which is listed in the prose description.

47. Murphy, *Duanaire Finn,* 210.

48. Whitley Stokes, transl., *Sanas Chormaic* (Calcutta: Irish Archaeological and Celtic Society, 1868), 4.

49. I am grateful to Dr. Mark Williams for pointing out this information, which will appear in his book, *Ireland's Immortals: A History of the Gods of Irish Myth* (Princeton: Princeton University Press, 2016).

50. Marie-Louise Sjoestedt, *Gods and Heroes of the Celts* (Berkeley: Turtle Island Foundation, 1982), 38.

51. DIL *sonus*; DIL *Ana: is innti* (i.e. in Munster) *nó adhradh bandía in tsónusa .i. Ana a hainm-sein agus is uaithi sidhe isberar Da Chigh Anann ós Luchair Degad,* Cóir Anm. 1.

52. DIL *Ana*: name of a goddess; *íath Anann*, name for Ireland: *Anann .i. Ereann* (O'Cl.). 1 *íath*: land, country; territory; in many poetical names of Ireland: *Iath nAnann .i. Eiriu* (O'C. 1409). John Carey, "Notes on the Irish War-Goddess," *Éigse* 19:2 (1983), feels that the phrase *brúctaidh fri híath nAnann*, "bursts against the land of Anu" from the Old Irish poem "Ail tighe tres filidhecht" may have inspired later glossators to explain the term *íath nAnann* as "Ireland."

53. DIL, *dag/deg*.

54. Gwynn, *Metrical Dindshenchas*, Vol. IV, 274–275, 448; Stokes, *Sanas Chormaic*, 17.

55. Gray, *Cath Maige Tuired*, 55.

56. See Carey, "Lebor Gabála Érenn."

57. MacAlister, *Lebor Gabála Érenn*, 155.

58. Hole, *Encyclopedia of Superstitions*, 301–2.

59. Ann Dooley and Harry Roe, eds. and trans., *Tales of the Elders of Ireland: A New Translation of Accalam na Senórach* (Oxford: Oxford University Press, 1999), 24–6.

60. An oblique reference to Anu occurs in *Tochmarc Emire*. In a series of riddles between Emer and Cú Chulainn, he claims to have journeyed *eter ríg nAnann ocus a gníed* ("between the king of Anu and his servant") perhaps referring to a location ruled by this figure. See: Best, Bergin and O'Brien, *Lebor na hUidre: Book of the Dun Cow*, 310; and Tom Cross and Clark Slover, trans., *Ancient Irish Tales* (New York: Barnes & Noble, 1996), 157.

61. Dooley and Roe, *Tales of the Elders of Ireland*, 25–26.

62. Dooley and Roe, *Tales of the Elders of Ireland*, 27.

63. Proinsias MacCana, *Celtic Mythology* (London: Hamlyn, 1973), 131.

64. A longer example of this, in relation to *aí*, is discussed in Chapter Nine of this book.

65. Calvert Watkins, *How to Kill a Dragon* (Oxford: Oxford University Press, 1995), 262.

66. Whitley Stokes, *"Immacalam in Dá Thuarad:* Colloquoy of the Two Sages," *Revue Celtique* 26 (1905): 28.

67. William Gillies, "The Classical Irish Poetic Tradition," *Proceedings of the Seventh International Congress of Celtic Studies* (Oxford, 1983): 114.

68. J.E. Caerwyn Williams, "The Court Poet in Medieval Ireland," *Sir John Rhys Memorial Lecture* (London: Oxford University Press, 1972), 23. See also M.L. West, *Indo-European Poetry and Myth* (Oxford: Oxford University Press, 2007), 35–36.

69. Stokes, *Immacalam in Dá Thuarad*, 31.

70. As an example, neither Danu nor Anu appear in any poems in the Metrical Dindshenchas, while The Mórrígan appears in a number of them.

71. DIL, *Morrígan*: In the Middle Irish Period the first syllable seems to have been commonly equated with *mór* "great," and the vowel is often accented. Frequently used with the article (*in Morrígan*).

72. Macalister, *Lebor Gabála Erenn*, 122–123, 182: "Badb and Macha and Morrigu and Ana, the three [*sic*] daughters of Ernmas the witch." Carey, "Lebor Gabála Érenn," 255: "Nemain of the...; Donann mother of the gods. Badb and Macha, great wealth; the Morrígan, foundation of sorcery; the guides of savage battle, the splendid daughters of Ernmas."

73. DIL *Morrígan*: np. Morrignae, morrigna. *hi Ross Bodbo .i. na Morrighno*. In Táin Bó Regamna, she is called *"in Morrígan"* in Eg., *"in badb"* in YBL. DIL, badb: *Machae .i. badb nó asi an tres morrigan*; *ind Neamain (.i. in Badb)*. This helps show that Nemain is the proper name of the third sister who is referred to as such throughout Lebor Gabála (Nemain wife of Néit).

74. MacCana, *The Mabinogi*, 86.

75. Macalister, *Lebor Gabála Érenn*, 154–155: *Trí hingena aile hic Ernmaiss, .i. Badb ocus Macha ocus Mórrígú*. Carey, "Lebor Gabála Érenn," 255: "Badb and Macha, great wealth; the Morrígan ... the guides of savage battle, the splendid daughters of Ernmas."

76. Macalister, *Lebor Gabála Érenn*, 182–3: *Badbh ocus Macha ocus Morrighan ... tri hingeana Earnmhais na ban-thuathaighe*. Carey, "Lebor Gabála Érenn," 254: "the three daughters of Ernmas the witch," and 255: "the Mórrigan, foundation of sorcery." DIL, *badb: Nemain Danand Badb is Macha, Morrígu ... bantuathecha Túathe De Danand*, LL.

77. Máire Herbert, "Transmutations of an Irish Goddess," 143, and Patricia Lysaght, "Aspects of the earth-goddess in the traditions of the banshee in Ireland," 161–2, in *The Concept of the Goddess*, ed. Sandra Billington, et al. (London: Routledge, 1996).

78. Gray, *Cath Maige Tuired*, 129.

79. Thomas Kinsella, trans., *The Tain* (Dublin: Oxford University Press/Dolmen Press, 1969), 132–3.

80. The young woman in this episode identifies herself as the daughter of King Buan, a name reminiscent of Anu's epithet *Buanan*. Ross, *Pagan Celtic Britain*, 291, identifies Buanan along with Scáthach as the two powerful women who train Cú Chulainn in the arts of war. The connection may be strengthened in remembering Buanan's description as the "nurse of heroes" (*mumu na fian*).

81. MacAlister, *Lebor Gabála Érenn*, 130–131, 160–161; Carey, "Lebor Gabála Érenn," 259, "Ernmas had three more daughters; Badb and Macha and Morrígu (whose name was Anann)"

and 254, "Badb and Macha and Anann (from whom are the Cíche Anann in Luchair), the three daughters of Ernmas the witch."
82. Macalister, *Lebor Gabála Érenn*, 188–189; Gray, *Cath Maige Tuired*, 122.
83. Rees, *Celtic Heritage*, 83–89.
84. Here we might recall the alleged union of Danu and Delbaeth, perhaps symbolic of a goddess of the land (the daughter) and a god of the sky realm (the father) uniting in an act of creation.
85. Gray, *Cath Maige Tuired*, 44–5.
86. Gwynn, *The Metrical Dindshenchas*, Part 3, 148: *unnius Uisnig.*

Chapter 5

1. A version of this paper was originally published in *Proceedings of the Harvard Celtic Colloquium*, Vol. 28 (2008): 185–199.
2. Wolfgang Meid, *The Romance of Froech and Findabair, or The Driving of Froech's Cattle: Táin Bó Froích* (Innsbruck: Institut für Sprachen und Literaturen der Universität Innsbruck, 2015); Jeffrey Gantz, *Early Irish Myths and Sagas* (Middlesex: Dorset Press, 1985), 114–126.
3. Nancy Power, "Classes of Women described in the *Senchas Már*," in *Studies in Early Irish Law*, ed. Thurneysen, et al. (Dublin: Royal Irish Academy, 1936), 88.
4. Fergus Kelly, *A Guide to Early Irish Law* (Dublin: Dublin Institute for Advanced Studies, 1995), 70.
5. Fergus Kelly, *A Guide to Early Irish Law*, 71.
6. Nancy Power, "Classes of Women described in the *Senchas Már*," 88.
7. Nancy Power, "Classes of Women described in the *Senchas Már*," 88–90.
8. Kelly, *A Guide to Early Irish Law*, 70–72.
9. Angela Bourke, et al., eds., *The Field Day Anthology of Irish Writing*, Vol. IV (New York: New York University Press, 2002), 26.
10. DIL, *finn, síabair.*
11. Rachel Bromwich, *Trioedd Ynys Prydein* (Cardiff: University of Wales Press, 1978), 380–381.
12. Patrick K. Ford, *The Mabinogi and other Medieval Welsh Tales* (Berkeley: University of California Press, 1977), 2, 125–126, 131; Richard M. Loomis, "Culwch and Olwen," in *The Romance of Arthur: An Anthology of Texts in Translation*, James J. Wilhelm, ed. (New York: Garland, 1994), 25; Brynley F. Roberts, "*Culhwch ac' Olwen*, The Triads, Saints' Lives," in *The Arthur of the Welsh*, Bromwich, et al., eds. (Cardiff: University of Wales Press, 2008), 73–95.

13. Rachel Bromwich, "The Welsh Triads," in *Arthurian Literature in the Middle Ages*, Roger S. Loomis, ed. (Oxford: Oxford University Press, 2001), 46.
14. Bromwich, *Trioedd Ynys Prydein*, 144.
15. Ford, *The Mabinogi and other Medieval Welsh Tales*, 131.
16. Bromwich, *Trioedd Ynys Prydein*, 145.
17. Bromwich, *Trioedd Ynys Prydein*, 206.
18. Bromwich, *Trioedd Ynys Prydein*, 147.
19. Bromwich, *Trioedd Ynys Prydein*, 154.
20. Whitley Stokes, ed. and trans., *Sanas Chormaic* (Calcutta: Irish Archaeological and Celtic Society, 1868), 23.
21. Bromwich, *Trioedd Ynys Prydein*, 196–206.
22. Bromwich, *Trioedd Ynys Prydein*, lxix, lxxxi–lxxxii.
23. Bromwich, *Trioedd Ynys Prydein*, 154–155.
24. Bromwich, "The Welsh Triads," 46 n5.
25. Bromwich, *Trioedd Ynys Prydein*, 154–155.
26. Richard J. Loomis, "Arthur in Geoffrey of Monmouth," in *The Romance of Arthur*, 71–72, 80, 92.
27. Bromwich, *Trioedd Ynys Prydein*, 385, 455. The name Medrawd or Modred also occurred as a personal name (as well as in place-names), possibly supporting earlier positive characterizations.
28. Bromwich, *Trioedd Ynys Prydein*, 154, 380.
29. Bromwich, *Trioedd Ynys Prydein*, 154, 382; Bromwich, "The Welsh Triads," 46. For a discussion of the *Gogynfeirdd* see Ceri W. Lewis, "The Court Poets: Their Function, Status and Craft," in *A Guide to Welsh Literature*, Vol. 1, Jarman, et al., eds. (Cardiff: University of Wales Press, 1992), 123–156.
30. Bromwich, *Trioedd Ynys Prydein*, xxviii, 382.
31. Bromwich, *Trioedd Ynys Prydein*, 381–382; Brynley F. Roberts, "Geoffrey of Monmouth, *Historia Regum Britanniae* and *Brut y Brenhinedd*," in *The Arthur of the Welsh*, 97–116 (p. 110 in particular).
32. Bromwich, *Trioedd Ynys Prydein*, 382–384.
33. Bromwich, *Trioedd Ynys Prydein*, 384–5.
34. Tom P. Cross and Clark H. Slover, trans., *Ancient Irish Tales* (New Jersey: Barnes & Noble, 1996), 382–383.
35. Bromwich, *Trioedd Ynys Prydein*, 455. For an excellent discussion of early references to Arthurian materials in poetic form, see Patrick Sims-Williams, "The Early Welsh Arthurian Poems," in *The Arthur of the Welsh*, Bromwich, et al., eds. (Cardiff: University of Wales Press, 2008), 33–71.

36. Lewis Thorpe, trans. *Geoffrey of Monmouth—The History of the Kings of Britain* (Hammondsworth: Penguin, 1982), 221.

37. Tomás Ó Cathasaigh, "The Sister's Son in Early Irish Literature," in *Coire Sois,* Matthieu Boyd, ed. (Notre Dame: University of Notre Dame Press, 2014), 65–94.

38. Bromwich, *Trioedd Ynys Prydein,* 132–133.

39. Ford, *The Mabinogi and other Medieval Welsh Tales,* 151.

40. John Carey, "Nodons in Britain and Ireland," *Zeitschrift fur Celtische Philologie* 40 (1984): 1–22.

41. Ford, *The Mabinogi,* 45; Sioned Davies, ed. and trans., *The Mabinogion* (Oxford: Oxford University Press, 2007), 11.

42. Bromwich, *Trioedd Ynys Prydein,* 154; Davies, *The Mabinogion,* 230; DIL, *rígan.* See also: Glyn E. Jones, "Early Prose: The Mabinogi," in *A Guide to Welsh Literature,* Vol. 1, Jarman, et al, eds. (Cardiff: University of Wales Press, 1992), 189–202.

43. Anne Ross, *Pagan Celtic Britain* (Chicago: Academy, 1996), 281–285; MacLeod, Sharon Paice, "*Mater Deorum Hibernensium*: Identity and Cross-Correlation in Early Irish Mythology," *Proceedings of the Harvard Celtic Colloquium* 19 (1999): 377–381.

44. Patrick K. Ford, "Celtic Women: The Opposing Sex," *Viator: Medieval and Renaissance Studies* 19 (1988): 425–427.

45. Máire Herbert, "Goddess and King: The Sacred Marriage in Early Ireland," *Cosmos* 7 (1992): 266; Edel Bhreathnach, *Ireland in the Medieval World AD 400–1000: Landscape, Kingship and Religion* (Dublin: Four Courts Press, 2014), 55.

46. Gantz, *Early Irish Myths and Sagas,* 119.

47. Ford, *The Mabinogi and other Medieval Welsh Tales,* 45; Davies, *The Mabinogion,* 11.

48. Ford, "Celtic Women: The Opposing Sex," 425; Ross, *Pagan Celtic Britain,* 387; DIL, *feis.*

49. Ford, *The Mabinogi and other Medieval Welsh Tales,* 126; Roberts, "*Culhwch ac'Olwen,* The Triads, Saints' Lives," 106, 110. See also James J. Wilhelm, "Wace: *Roman de Brut,*" in *The Romance of Arthur,* 106; Valerie Krishna, "The Alliterative *Morte Arthure,*" in *The Romance of Arthur,* 503.

50. Timothy Darvill, *Prehistoric Britain* (London: Routledge, 1996), 122, 132.

51. James J. Wilhelm, "Sir Thomas Malory: *Le Morte D'Arthur,*" in *The Romance of Arthur,* 567–568.

52. Gantz, *Early Irish Myths and Sagas,* 121.

53. John O'Meara, ed. and trans., *Gerald of Wales: The History and Topography of Ireland* (London: Penguin, 1982), 110.

54. J.P. Mallory, *In Search of the Indo-Europeans* (London: Thames & Hudson, 1989), 132.

55. Proinsias Mac Cana, *The Mabinogi* (Cardiff: University of Wales Press, 1992), 55–57, 121.

Chapter 6

1. Primary sources include: Johan Corthals, ed. and trans., "*Táin bó Regamna und Táin bó Flidais: zwei altirische Erzählungen,*" diss. (unpublished): Hamburg University (1979); Ernst Windisch, ed. and trans., "Táin Bó Flidais," in *Irische Text mit Worterbuch,* vol. 2:2, Ernst Windisch, et al., eds. (Leipzig, 1887), 206–223 (based on LL, Egerton 1782 and LU, with extracts in TCD 1337); Richard I. Best and Osborn Bergin, eds. and trans., *Lebor na hUidre: Book of the Dun Cow* (Dublin: Hodges, Figgis, 1929); Rudolf Thurneysen, Rudolf, ed., *Zu irischen Handschriften und Litteraturdenkmälern* [1] (Berlin: Abhandlungen der königlichen Gesellschaft der Wissenschaften zu Göttingen, Philologisch-Historische Klasse 14.2, 1912), 95–96 [RIA 23 O 48 text]; A.H. Leahy, trans., *Heroic Romances of Ireland,* 2 vols. (London: Irish Saga Library 2, 1905–1906).

2. Secondary sources: Ernst Windisch, "Nachträge," in *Irische Text mit Worterbuch,* vol. 2:2, Windisch, et al., eds. (Leipzig: 1887), 225–226; Rudolf Thurneysen, *Die Irische Helden- und Königsage bis zum siebzehnten Jahrhundert* (Halle: Niemeyer, 1921); Noémie Beck, *Goddesses in Celtic Religion—Cult and Mythology: A Comparative Study of Ancient Ireland, Britain and Gaul* (PhD Thesis, Université Lumière Lyon 2 and University College Dublin, 2009); Maire Ní Bhain, *Táin Bó Flidais,* unpublished M.A. Thesis (University College Galway, 1976), Closed Access Theses Collection, TH 670.

3. *Lebor na hUuidre* (The Book of the Dun Cow), Dublin, Royal Irish Academy, MS 23 E 25 (1229), [s. xi/xii], ff. 21a-22a (interpolated version of TBF, which lacks the beginning). Irish vellum manuscript dating to before 1106, written at Clonmacnoise; the earliest surviving manuscript containing literature written in Irish, contains the oldest version of TBC, the Voyage of Bran, the Feast of Bricriu, and other religious, mythological and historical material. *Lebor Laignech* (The Book of Leinster), properly *Leabhar na Nuachongbhála*; Dublin, Trinity College MS 1339 (H 2.18), [s. xiii²], ff. 247a-248a. The earliest manuscript written entirely in Irish, dated to the latter half of 12th c. (c. 1160?). MS Egerton 1782, London, British Library, ff. 82r-82v. A miscellany containing

more than 60 tales, hymns, poems and other literature, by the scribes of the Ó Maoil Chonaire (O'Mulconry) family, c. 1516–1518. In spite of its relatively late date (as compared to LL, LU and YBL) it is one of the most important documents for the study of early Irish literature. Yellow Book of Lecan, Dublin, Trinity College, MS 1318 [H 2.16], a composite miscellany dating to the 14th and 15th centuries.

4. A discussion of Fergus mac Róich, and the formation and evolution of TBF, may be found in Ruairí Ó hUiginn, "Growth and Development in the Late Ulster Cycle: The Case of *Táin Bó Flidais*," CSANA Yearbook 5 (Dublin: Four Courts Press, 2006): 143–161.

5. Margaret Dobbs, "On Táin Bó Flidais," *Ériu* 8 (1915), 133. See also: Dublin, Royal Irish Academy, MS 23 O 48, part 1, ff. 26ra–26rb (pp. 21–22 in facsimile), c. 1435–1440; Dublin, Trinity College, MS 1337 (19), pp. 565–628 (H 3.18) [s. svi (?)] pp. 603–604 (glossed extracts), 15th and 16th centuries; and Dublin, Trinity College, MS 1287 (H 1.13) [1746] p. 347, copy from the former, c. 1746, transcribed by Aodh Ó Dálaigh (Hugh O'Daly). Contents include Egerton 1782. For comparative textual relationships: *Cf.* the early Modern Irish recension *Táin bó Flidaise*, which tells quite a different version of the story, and its sequel, *Tóraigheacht tána bó Flidaise*.

6. Some useful sources concerning Fergus include: Whitley Stokes, ed. and trans., "The Tidings of Conchobar son of Ness," *Ériu* 2 (1908); Kuno Meyer, ed., "Mitteilungan aus irischen Handschriften: Fergus macc Róig," *Zeitschrift fur Celtische Philologie* 12 (1918): 375; Cecile O' Rahilly, trans., *Táin Bó Cuailgne:* Recension 1 (Dublin: Dublin Institute for Advanced Studies, 1976); Ruairí Ó hUiginn, "Fergus, Russ and Rudraige: A Brief Biography of Fergus Mac Róich," *Emania* (1993): 31–40; Patricia Ní Mhaoileaoin, "Patterns and Problems in the Heroic Biography of Fergus mac Róich," *Proceedings of the Harvard Celtic Colloquium*, Vol. 32 (2012): 214–228; Patricia Ní Mhaoileaoin, "The heroic biography of Fergus mac Róich: A case study of the heroic-biographical pattern in Old and Middle Irish literature" (NUI Galway, 2015).

7. Windisch, "Táin Bó Flidais," 206–223.

8. Leahy, *Heroic Romances of Ireland,* 103–124.

9. Additional materials may be found in Ní Bhain, Maire, *Táin Bó Flidais*.

10. Fergus Kelly, *A Guide to Early Irish Law* (Dublin: Dublin Institute for Advanced Studies, 1998), 139.

11. Kelly, *A Guide to Early Irish Law*, 139.

12. Kelly, *A Guide to Early Irish Law*, 70.

13. Kelly, *A Guide to Early Irish Law*, 74.

14. Kelly, *A Guide to Early Irish Law*, 76, 104, 186–187.

15. Kelly, *A Guide to Early Irish Law*, 75–77.

16. Kelly, *A Guide to Early Irish Law*, 75–77.

17. Dobbs, "On Táin Bó Flidais," 142; Anne Ross, *Pagan Celtic Britain* (Chicago: Academy, 1996), 286, 410. His attributes are evident in his name (<*virogustus* "choicest of men").

18. Dobbs, "On Táin Bó Flidais," 141–143; Ross, *Pagan Celtic Britain,* 277, 286. Fergus' virility is described in the following manner: "Seven women were his desire in wedlock, until he came to Cruacha and sojourned with Medb, accommodation for that seven was assigned to him." His size and appetite were evidently prodigious as well, as it took seven bushels to bathe his head, the food of seven ordinary persons to fill him, and the drink of nine ordinary persons as well. Fergus' strength and deeds are praised and enumerated, and he is said to be the equal of seven hundred soldiers in battle.

19. John Carey, "A Túath Dé Miscellany," *Bulletin of the Board of Celtic Studies* 39 (1992): 24, 28. The *Miscellany* is probably the work of a single compiler working with learned lore from the glossaries, grammars and other arcane bodies of linguistic speculation like *Auraceipt na nÉces* and the expanded *Sanas Cormaic*. The text is an enumeration of individuals associated with the Túatha Dé Dannan, along with other miscellaneous material. Despite its brevity, Carey believes that it "repays careful scrutiny: it sheds considerable light not only on the mythical background of Irish legend, but on the attitudes brought to this problematical material by its heirs and transmitters."

20. Carey, "A Túath Dé Miscellany," 28.

21. Carey, "A Túath Dé Miscellany," 35

22. Carey, "A Túath Dé Miscellany," 27.

23. Carey, "A Túath Dé Miscellany," 35.

24. Carey, "A Túath Dé Miscellany," 26–27.

25. Carey, "A Túath Dé Miscellany," 35.

26. Edward Gwynn, *The Metrical Dindshenchas*, Vol. IV (1991, Dublin Institute for Advanced Studies), 70–71. DIL: *garb*, "rough, rugged, harsh" or 2 *garb* "a torrent'; *grésach* "lasting, perpetual, constant, habitual."

27. Katherine Briggs, *An Encyclopedia of Fairies* (New York: Pantheon, 1976), 134–135. Briggs notes that there appear to be two classes of Otherworld or "fairy" animals: domesticated animals bred and used by the fairies, and wild supernatural creatures, which exist for their own purposes and in their own right. It is sometimes difficult to distinguish between them, as the fairies are said to let their creatures roam freely. Fairy cattle were, in general, less threatening than fairy horses, and were sometimes considered lucky or beneficial. At

other times, though, they could be quite dangerous.

28. R.A. S. Macalister, ed. and trans., *Lebor Gabála Érenn*, Part IV (Dublin: Irish Texts Society, 1997), 133, 151, 159, 183, 197, 231. The information occurs in Paragraph 62, between references to the two wives of Nét and a reference to two supernatural oxen.

29. Johm Carey, "Myth and mythography in *Cath Maige Tuired*," *Studia Celtica*, Vol. 24/25 (1989/90): 58, *n*54. Carey refers to this as an example of the development of a personal name from a common noun or phrase. He suggests that the king (whose name is spelled *Amadair Flidais)* comes into existence due to a reinterpretation of the phrase *a máthair Flidais*. See also: Eoin Mac Néill, "Reconstruction and date of the Laud synchronisms," *Zeitschrift für Celtische Philologie* 10 (1914).

30. Whitley Stokes, ed. and trans., "*Cóir Anman*: The Fitness of Names," in *Irische Text mit Übersetzungen und Wörterbuch,* Stokes, et al., eds. (Leipzig, 1897), 295.

31. Carey, "A *Túath Dé* Miscellany," 7.

32. Stokes, "*Cóir Anman*: The Fitness of Names," 294–295.

33. Stokes, "*Cóir Anman*: The Fitness of Names," 295.

34. DIL, "*os*": A somewhat obsolete term, used primarily in poetry. It is also attested in the name of Finn Mac Cumhall's son Oisín "Little Deer."

35. Briggs, *An Encyclopedia of Fairies,* 143; Tess Darwin, *The Scots Herbal: The Plant Lore of Scotland* (Edinburgh: Mercat Press, 1996), 105–109, 151–2. The other ingredients of the "fairy banquet" included Silverweed (*potentilla anserina*) a common herb with a nutritious root, known in Scottish Gaelic as *an seachdamh aran*, "the seventh bread," considered one of the "seven breads of the Gael," referring to its importance in the diet of the Highlands and Islands of Scotland (before potatoes became common). Heather was prized for its many uses, including tea, ale, medicine, animal fodder and bedding, and in many folklore accounts, barley is said to be the preferred grain of the fairies.

36. Thurneysen, *Die irische Helden und konigsage,* 318–321.

37. Beck, "Goddesses in Celtic Religion," 185.

38. Daithi Ó hÓgain, *The Lore of Ireland: An Encyclopedia of Myth, Legend and Romance* (Suffolk UK: Boydell Press, 2006), 162.

39. Beck, "Goddesses in Celtic Religion," 185.

40. Macalister, *Lebor Gabála Érenn,* 197.

41. Donald MacKinnon, "The Glenmasan

Manuscript," *The Celtic Review,* Vol. Four (1907–1908): 109–111.

42. Dobbs, "On Táin Bó Flidais," 148.

43. MacKinnon, "The Glenmasan Manuscript," Vol. Three: 125.

44. Beck, "Goddesses in Celtic Religion," 186; Edel Bhreathnach, *Ireland in the Medieval World AD 400–1000: Landscape, Kingship and Religion* (Dublin: Four Courts Press, 2014), 43–44.

45. DIL, *séd/ség*.

46. Ó hOgain, *The Lore of Ireland,* 231.

47. Carey, "A *Túath Dé* Miscellany," 35.

48. It might also refer to the spilling of Oilill's blood, which resulted from drink ingested at a feast in the later versions of TBF.

49. Margaret Dobbs, ed. and trans., "The Ban-Senchus," *Revue Celtique* (1930): 322.

50. Flidais' son Nia Segamuin is mortal, or at least half-mortal (his father is human, rather than divine).

51. Carey, "A *Túath Dé* Miscellany," 35; Alfred Holder, *Alt-celtischer Sprachschatz* (Leipzig: 1896–1907), 188.

52. Carey "A *Túath Dé* Miscellany," 35. He points out that while *Arduinna* should give OIr *ardan(n)*, *Airden* could be based on an archaic spelling *Arden*.

53. Miranda Green, *Celtic Goddesses* (New York: George Braziller, 1995), 165–7.

54. Carey, "A *Túath Dé* Miscellany," 35.

55. Elizabeth Gray, ed. and trans., *Cath Maige Tuired* (Naas: Irish Texts Society, 1982), 52–55; Macalister, *Lebor Gabála Érenn,* 133, 151, 159, 183, 197, 231.

56. DIL, 1 *coll*, m-o, gs. *cuill.* Examples are found in the place names *Ath Cuille* and the intriguing phrase *Coll na nIngen*, "The Hazel of the Daughter."

57. Gwynn, *The Metrical Dindshenchas,* Vol. IV, 329.

58. In previously quoted sources, Flidais' father is either *Oilill Dubh*, son of Find, or *Garb*, son of Gréssach. Fainche, also the mother of *Currech mac Cathair* and *Fothad Cananne*, is said to be the daughter of *Airmora* of *Arada Cliach*.

59. Gwynn, *The Metrical Dindshenchas,* Vol. IV, 328–333.

60. Ann Dooley, Ann and Harry Roe, eds. and trans., *Tales of the Elders of Ireland: A New Translation of Accalam na Senórach* (Oxford: Oxford University Press, 1999), 115–116.

61. Perhaps this alludes to the references to blood which exist in connection with her mother. An example referring to the meaning of *fuil* "blood" gives: *a fuluo .i. flann derg* (O'Mulc. 591)

62. Dooley and Roe, *Acallam na Senórach,* 201.

63. Green, *Celtic Goddesses*, 103–4, 134–6, 170, 182.

64. Kuno Meyer, "*Ein altirischer Heilsegen*," Sitzb. 17 (1916): 420–422.

65. Ross, *Pagan Celtic Britain*, 57, 52, 62, 207, 228–229, 246, 271, 280. British and Continental goddesses associated with healing and curing were often connected with healing waters (and in some cases, sacred groves). One goddess of this type was associated with a horned deity. *Nemetona* ("Goddess of the Grove/Sacred Place") was a goddess of the *Nemetes* and the *Treveri*, worshipped in Britain and Gaul. In Germany she was venerated along with Mars (who appears in his role as healer, rather than warrior). At the British healing sanctuary of *Aquae Sulis* at Bath, Nemetona and *Mars Leucetius* were invoked as a divine couple. An unidentified relief at Aquae Sulis of a seated goddess and a horned god may represent Leucetius and Nemetona. The British Goddess *Arnemetia* ("She who dwells near/against the sacred grove") was also venerated at the site of healing waters (*Aquae Arenemetiae*, Buxton, Derbyshire). This water source was dedicated to the goddess, who presided over the curative waters (comprised of two springs with different kinds of water). While these deities may not appear to be specifically associated with animals, their names suggest a possible connection with forested areas. Iconography uncovered at these places of worship suggest attributes of fertility as well as healing. Here we might recall the healing power attributed to Flidais' daughter Flann, who heals Cailte by washing his head. In the folklore associated with Irish healing wells, there are sometimes accounts of heads once having been present in the wells.

66. Calvert Watkins, *How to Kill a Dragon* (Oxford: Oxford University Press, 1995), 519–539. See also M.L. West, *Indo-European Poetry and Myth* (Oxford: Oxford University Press, 2007), 334–339.

67. Watkins, *How to Kill a Dragon, passim.*

68. Watkins, *How to Kill a Dragon*, 537–544.

69. Watkins, *How to Kill a Dragon*, 543–545.

70. Watkins, *How to Kill a Dragon*, 542.

71. Meyer, "*Ein altirischer Heilsegen*," 420–422; Carey, "A *Túath Dé* Miscellany," 35; Jacqueline Borsje, "A Spell called Éle," in *Ulidia 3: Proceedings of the Third International Conference on the Ulster Cycle of Tales*, Toner, et al., eds. (Coleraine: University of Ulster, 2009), 193–212.

72. Gwynn, *The Metrical Dindshenchas*, Vol. Three, 260–265.

73. Myles, Dillon, ed., *Serglige Con Culainn* (Dublin: Dublin Institute for Advanced Studies, 1975); Tom P. Cross and Clark H. Slover,

Ancient Irish Tales (New York: Barnes & Noble, 1996), 176–198. Fand is the daughter of *Aed Abrat*, a figure who must be one of Flidais's sexual partners. It is unclear if Fand's brother Oengus and sister Lí Ban are also the children of Flidais, or whether they are the offspring of Aed with another female partner.

74. Cross and Slover, *Ancient Irish Tales*, 179–181.

75. Cross and Slover, *Ancient Irish Tales*, 182–183.

76. Cross and Slover, *Ancient Irish Tales*, 190

77. Cross and Slover, *Ancient Irish Tales*, 194–195.

78. Cross and Slover, *Ancient Irish Tales*, 195.

79. Cross and Slover, *Ancient Irish Tales*, 196–197.

80. Cross and Slover, *Ancient Irish Tales*, 197–198.

81. An excellent and concise overview of deer imagery may be found in Miranda Green, *Dictionary of Celtic Myth and Legend* (London: Thames & Hudson, 1992), 198–199.

82. J.G. McKay, "The Deer Cult and the Deer-Goddess of the Ancient Caledonians," *Folklore* XLIII (1932): 144–174. McKay points out that throughout the Scottish Highlands, supernatural beings associated with deer are almost always female, whether they appear as giants, hags or small green-clad fairy women.

83. James MacKillop, *Dictionary of Celtic Mythology* (Oxford: Oxford University Press, 1998), 313–314.

84. Gwynn, *The Metrical Dindshenchas*, Vol IV, 136–143.

85. Ross, *Pagan Celtic Britain*, 190, 276. A connection has been postulated between Cernunnos (who may play a role as "lord of animals") and a figure from the Welsh tale "The Lady of the Fountain." The Welsh figure is described as a large man who sits on a mound in a great clearing. He demonstrates his power over the animals by striking a great stag, whose cry summons a multitude of animals that then pay homage to the man on the mound.

86. Miranda Green, *Animals in Celtic Life and Myth* (New York: Routledge, 1992), 47–50, 62–5, 166–168. The stag is virile and aggressive during mating season, and in some contexts is considered the king of the forest. His spreading antlers may have been perceived as symbolizing the branches of trees, and the growth and shedding of antlers may have suggested imagery associated with regeneration or seasonal cycles. Stags also seem to have been associated with fertility, prestige, speed, and the abundance of the forest.

87. Ross, *Pagan Celtic Britain*, 190 295; Green, *Celtic Goddesses*, 132.

88. Ross, *Pagan Celtic Britain*, 295. A horned male head was found at the same site.

89. Ross, *Pagan Celtic Britain*, 190, 295; Beck, *Goddesses in Celtic Religion*, 191–192.

90. Beck, *Goddesses in Celtic Religion*, 191–192.

91. Ross, *Pagan Celtic Britain*, 190. Horned gods are generally depicted alone. In one representation of Cernunnos from Saintes, he is accompanied by a female consort. The antlered goddesses are also frequently depicted alone, although some are accompanied by a male deity (whose identity varies).

92. Green, *Celtic Goddesses*, 170.

93. Ross, *Pagan Celtic Britain*, 179, 216 n23.

94. Green, *Dictionary of Celtic Myth and Legend*, 170.

95. Ross, *Pagan Celtic Britain*, 295.

96. Calvert Watkins, *Dictionary of Indo-European Roots* (Boston: Houghton Mifflin, 2000), 40.

97. Beck, *Goddesses in Celtic Religion*, 193.

98. Ross, *Pagan Celtic Britain,* 295.

99. John Carey, "Horned Fairy Women," *Ériu* 34 (1988): 203–4.

100. Carey, "Horned Fairy Women," 278–9.

101. For an excellent, detailed discussion of horned or antlered deities and their attributes see Ross, *Pagan Celtic Britain*, 172–220.

102. Carey, "A *Túath Dé* Miscellany," 35; Thurneysen, *Die Irische Helden- und Königsage,* 318; Ross, *Pagan Celtic Britain*, 277.

103. Ross, *Pagan Celtic Britain,* 277 n 39, 295; Green, *Celtic Goddesses*, 165–167.

104. Thurneysen, *Die Irische Helden- und Königsage*, 318.

105. Marie-Louise Sjoestedt, *Celtic Gods and Heroes* (Mineola NY: Dover, 2000), 36.

106. Ross, *Pagan Celtic Britain*, 66, 420.

107. Ross, *Pagan Celtic Britain*, 277.

108. Mark Morford and Robert Lenardon, *Classical Mythology* (New York: Longman, 1991), 173–184.

109. Ross, *Pagan Celtic Britain*, 277.

110. Ross, *Pagan Celtic Britain*, 69, 277–279, 295; Green, *Celtic Goddesses*, 110, 165–167. In one instance Diana is accompanied by the hunter god Apollo Cunomaglus. Diana's image was also found with a statuette of a triple-horned bull. As we have seen, Flidais was the owner of a supernatural bull.

111. Ross, *Pagan Celtic Britain*, 303. Aquatic birds often appear in connection with the wagons, as well as composite animals of birds and horned beasts.

112. Green, *Celtic Goddesses*, 161. Behind the deer held by the two women is the figure of another woman wearing large earrings, as well as a man with an erect phallus who holds an axe. They are surrounded by pairs of mounted warriors with spears, shields and conical helmets.

113. Green, *Celtic Goddesses*, 351–2, 355–6, 363–4.

114. The reference to a chariot may have defined or suggested Flidais' range of attributes, rather than constituting a specific element of her representation.

115. Ross, *Pagan Celtic Britain*, 303.

116. Ross, *Pagan Celtic Britain*, 303–304.

117. Hilda Ellis Davidson, *Gods and Myths of Northern Europe* (New York: Penguin, 1964), 202.

118. Wikipedia, "Vahana."

119. Davidson, *Gods and Myths of Northern Europe*, 30, 39–40.

120. Davidson, *Gods and Myths of Northern Europe*, 106–7.

121. Davidson, *Gods and Myths of Northern Europe*, 94–6.

122. Davidson, *Gods and Myths of Northern Europe*, 95–6. A similar wagon dating to the ninth century was buried inside a ship, along with other wooden objects of ceremonial intent. These accompanied the burial of a woman of high rank. With the burial were tapestries depicting a man and woman standing beside the wagon, perhaps representing a ceremonial procession or religious activity.

123. Gearóid Ó Crualaoich, "Non-Sovereignty Queen Aspects of the Otherworld Female in Irish Hag Legends: The Case of the Cailleach Bhéarra," *Béaloideas* Vol. 62–3 (1994–5): 151–158.

124. Tomás Ó Cathasaigh, "The Eponym of Cnogba," *Éigse* 23 (1989): 34–35. The Cailleach's association with supernatural cattle is suggested by a variety of associated place names, including *An Tarbh* (previously *Tech nDuinn*) and *Inis Buí* (perhaps associated with the cow known as *Bó Buí*). The *Cailleach Bhéarach's* chthonic nature is expressed through her association with funerary buildings and cairns in various parts of Ireland.

125. Ó Crualoich "Non-Sovereignty Queen Aspects of the Otherworld Female in Irish Hag Legends," 151. This occurs in the tale "The Chase of Ben Gulbin."

126. Ross, *Pagan Celtic Britain*, 296.

127. Ross, *Pagan Celtic Britain*, 293; McKay, "The Deer Cult and the Deer-Goddess of the Ancient Caledonians," 166. In 1917 a gamekeeper in Invernesshire reported that the Cailleach of Ben Breck had cleaned out one of her wells that year and afterwards washed herself in it. The Cailleach of Lochaber was still well known in her district as late as 1927.

128. McKay, "The Deer Cult and the Deer-Goddess of the Ancient Caledonians," 152. For an in-depth study of the Cailleach, see Gearóid

Ó Crualaoich, *The Book of the Cailleach* (Cork: Cork University Press, 2007), including many useful articles in his bibliography.

129. McKay, "The Deer Cult and the Deer-Goddess of the Ancient Caledonians," 149. One tale describes a *cailleach* singing about her deer; another refers to the animals as "my darling deer" or "the beast of my love."

130. McKay, "The Deer Cult and the Deer-Goddess of the Ancient Caledonians," 168. While most cailleachs primarily have dealings with men (hunters), the Cailleach of Ben Breck was also seen by women, who complained that when in deer form she stole their dulse and kail. While the appearance of this *Cailleach* was considered inauspicious for hunters, she was said to protect outlaws (which may suggest her connection with that which is outside of society).

131. McKay "The Deer Cult and the Deer-Goddess of the Ancient Caledonians," 153–154.

132. McKay "The Deer Cult and the Deer-Goddess of the Ancient Caledonians," 153–154.

133. McKay "The Deer Cult and the Deer-Goddess of the Ancient Caledonians," 153–154. The hunters would share their catch with other women, as it was considered incorrect or mean to refuse to share with a woman who had asked for a portion (especially a married woman). Perhaps the hunters feared they might be a Cailleach in disguise. In some cases, the witch is too greedy and a conflict ensues, during which she may be driven off by the hunter and his hounds.

134. McKay "The Deer Cult and the Deer-Goddess of the Ancient Caledonians," 170. Prior to providing responses to her petitioners, the *Iorosglach-Urlair* would strike the ground three times, perhaps summoning assistance from underworld powers from whom she may have received her inspiration.

135. Ó Crualoich, "Non-Sovereignty Queen Aspects of the Otherworld Female in Irish Hag Legends," 157.

136. McKay "The Deer Cult and the Deer-Goddess of the Ancient Caledonians," 173.

137. Jean Louise Brunaux, *The Celtic Gauls: Gods, Rites and Sanctuaries* (London: Seaby, 1987), 96–7; Green, *Celtic Goddesses,* 163.

138. W. Dansey, *Arrian on Coursing. The Cynegeticus of the Younger Xenophon* (London: Bohn, 1831), http://www.archive.org.

139. Ross, *Pagan Celtic Britain,* 293, 420. On p. 140, Ross remarks that certain tales seem to contain "genuine memories of the powerful female deities who when they ceased to be actively propitiated, became embedded in the folk memory and perpetuated in the tales and especially in the topographical legends of the country. Such early divinities as Áine, Grian and Macha found a permanent place in the names for the natural features with which they were associated, and in the stories accounting for the origins of these names. The same principle operated in the case of numerous local goddesses who became transformed into *cailleachs*, who might be encountered at the wells of which they were considered to be the guardians or driving their herds of deer over the hills where they were once propitiated."

Chapter 7

1. Marged Haycock, ed. and trans., *Legendary Poems from the Book of Taliesin* (Aberystwyth: CMCS, 2007), 21, 36, 40, 433–451.

2. A.O.H. Jarman and Gwilym Rees Hughes, *A Guide to Welsh Literature,* Vol. 1 (Cardiff: University of Wales Press, 1992), 18–19, 32, 34–35, 52–66; Patrick K. Ford, *The Mabinogi and other Medieval Welsh Tales* (Berkeley: University of California Press, 1977), 1–2, 17, 19–21, 159–187.

3. Patrick Sims-Williams, "Some Celtic Otherworld Terms," in *Celtic Language, Celtic Culture: A Festschrift for Eric P. Hamp,* ed. Matonis, et al. (Van Nuys: Ford and Bailie, 1990), 57–81.

4. Haycock, *Legendary Poems from the Book of Taliesin,* 435; Oliver J. Padel, *Arthur in Medieval Welsh Literature* (Cardiff: University of Wales Press, 2000), 34–35.

5. Haycock, *Legendary Poems from the Book of Taliesin,* 434–437.

6. Haycock, *Legendary Poems from the Book of Taliesin,* 434–435; John K. Bollard, "Arthur in the Early Welsh Tradition," in *The Romance of Arthur: An Anthology of Medieval Texts in Translation,* ed. Wilhelm (New York/London: Garland, 1994), 19–20.

7. Haycock, *Legendary Poems from the Book of Taliesin,* 434–437.

8. Haycock, *Legendary Poems from the Book of Taliesin,* 434- 436.

9. Bollard, "Arthur in the Early Welsh Tradition," 20.

10. Haycock, *Legendary Poems from the Book of Taliesin,* 435–436.

11. Barry Raftery, *Pagan Celtic Ireland* (London: Thames & Hudson, 1994), 10, 22, 25–27, 31–32, 37, 114–115, 149, 153, 184; Timothy Darvill, *Prehistoric Britain* (London: Thames & Hudson, 1987), 123, 157; Ruth and Vincent Megaw, *Celtic Art* (London: Thames & Hudson, 1996), 74–177, 185–186; Michael Ryan, ed., *The Illustrated Archaeology of Ireland* (Dublin: Country House, 199), 93–125.

12. Elizabeth Gray, *Cath Maige Tuired* (Naas: Irish Texts Society, 1982), 24–25.

13. Ford, *The Mabinogi and other Medieval Welsh Tales*, 63, 69.

14. Ford, *The Mabinogi and other Medieval Welsh Tales*, 162–164.

15. John T. Koch and John Carey, eds. and trans., *The Celtic Heroic Age: Literary Sources for Ancient Celtic Europe and Early Ireland and Wales* (Oakville, CT/Aberystwyth: Celtic Studies Publications, 2000), 7.

16. Koch and Carey, *The Celtic Heroic Age*, 12.

17. Alwyn and Brinley Rees, *Celtic Heritage* (London: Thames & Hudson, 1989), 194.

18. Rees, *Celtic Heritage*, 192–194.

19. Sioned Davies, ed. and trans., *The Mabinogion* (Oxford: Oxford University Press, 2007), 65–102; and see Jonathan Wooding, ed., *The Otherworld Voyage* (Dublin: Four Courts, 2000), 87, regarding a seeress associated with the eruption of a lake (Lough Neagh).

20. Edward Gwynn, *The Metrical Dindsenchas*, Vol. II (Dublin: Dublin Institute for Advanced Studies, 1991), 26–29.

21. Gwynn, *The Metrical Dindsenchas* (Vol. II), 28–33.

22. Richard M. Loomis, "Arthur in Geoffrey of Monmouth," in *The Romance of Arthur: An Anthology of Medieval Texts in Translation*, ed. Wilhelm (New York/London: Garland Publishing, 1994), 93.

23. James J. Wilhelm, "Arthur in the Latin Chronicles," in *The Romance of Arthur: An Anthology of Medieval Texts in Translation*, ed. Wilhelm (New York/London: Garland Publishing, 1994), 7–8.

24. Basil Clarke, ed., *Vita Merlini* (Cardiff: University of Wales Press, 1975).

25. A.L.F. Rivet and Colin Smith, *The Place-Names of Roman Britain* (London: Batsford, 1979), 42, 81.

26. http://brittanica.com, *Cronus.* Cronus became king of the Titans and took his sister Rhea as his consort. He swallowed his children because his parents warned him that he would be overthrown by his own child. When Zeus was born, Rhea hid the child and tricked Cronus into swallowing a stone instead. When Zeus grew up, he forced Cronus to disgorge his siblings and successfully waged war against him. There are several versions of the story of Briareus, the name by which the gods referred to him (mortals calling him Aegaeon). He was also a son of Uranus and Gaea, and one of the three hundred-armed fifty-headed Hecatoncheires. In Homer and Hesiod, Briareus and his brothers help Zeus against an attack by the Titans. Callimachus makes him an opponent of Zeus, and one of the assailants of Olympus. Another tradition makes him a giant of the sea, an enemy of Poseidon and the inventor of warships.

27. In this account, Cronus is bound in sleep on the island by Briareus, who may have represented the powerful forces of nature that manifested in earthquakes or the motion of sea-waves.

28. Horace L. Jones, ed., *The Geography of Strabo* (Cambridge MA: Harvard University Press, 1960), 250–251 [4.4.6].

29. Mark Morford and Robert J. Lenardon, *Classical Mythology* (White Plains NY: Longman, 1991), 288–295.

30. Morford and Lenardon, *Classical Mythology*, 288–295.

31. Morford and Lenardon, *Classical Mythology*, 343. The next oldest of the Greek mysteries after those at Eleusis, were those associated with the *Cabiri,* whose cult center was on the island of Samothrace (associated with the area around the city of Pergamum). Little is known about any specifics of belief or practice. The Cabiri were frequently referred to as *theoi megaloi* ("the great gods"), and sometimes identified with the *Dioscuri* (Castor and Pollux). They were especially associated with the protection of seafarers during ocean voyages, as well as the earth and the hope of a new life.

32. Benjamin Fortson, trans., "*Strabo-Geography*," in Koch and Carey, *The Celtic Heroic Age*, 15.

33. Barry Cunliffe, *The Ancient Celts* (Oxford: Oxford University Press, 1997), 202–208; Peter Harbison, *Pre-Christian Ireland* (London: Thames & Hudson, 1988), 154–158; Barry Cunliffe, *The Celtic World* (New York: Greenwich House, 1986), 94–5; Raftery, *Pagan Celtic Ireland*, 180.

34. F.E. Romer, ed., *Pomponius Mela's Description of the World* (Ann Arbor: University of Michigan Press, 1998), 115.

35. Rivet and Smith, *The Place-names of Roman Britain*, 455.

36. Cunliffe, *The Ancient Celts*, 72, 77, 243.

37. Cunliffe, *The Ancient Celts*, 243, 245.

38. Christina H. Roseman, ed. and trans., *Pytheas of Massilia* (Chicago: Ares, 1994), 67–68.

39. Barry Cunliffe, *The Extraordinary Voyage of Pytheas* (New York: Walker and Co., 2002), 59; Cunliffe, Barry, "The First Eight Thousand Years, 7000 BC–AD 1000," in *A People of the Sea—The Maritime History of the Channel Islands*, ed. Jamieson (London: Methuen, 1986), 8. Pytheas mentions one of the promontories of Armorica, Kabaion, which may be the port at *Corbilo,* at the mouth of the Loire. This may tie in with Strabo's report of an island near mouth of Loire.

40. Cunliffe, *The Extraordinary Voyage of Pytheas*, 59.

41. Rivet and Smith, *The Place-names of Roman Britain*, 90.

42. Rivet and Smith, *The Place-names of Roman Britain*, 80.

43. Rivet and Smith, *The Place-names of Roman Britain*, 90.

44. Rivet and Smith, *The Place-names of Roman Britain*, 455.

45. Cunliffe, "The First Eight Thousand Years," 3–7.

46. Barry Cunliffe, "Guernsey and the Channel Islands in the First Millenium BC," in *Guernsey: An Island Community of the Atlantic Iron Age*, ed. Burns, et al. (Oxford: Oxford University Committee for Archaeology, Monograph No. 43/Guernsey Museum, Monograph No. 6, 1996), 125–126. Excavations on Alderney suggest the presence of a community living near the harbor on the south side of the island, an excellent haven for those sailing north from Guernsey towards the northern coast of Lower Normandy, but not useful for those traveling from Guernsey to the Solent. The available evidence suggests that there may have been somewhat less contact and trade with the Continent and Britain during the middle of the Iron Age (c. 400–120 BCE). As a result, Channel Islands culture may have become somewhat more "insular" during this period. In the Later Iron Age, however, trade and outside contact were reinvigorated, possibly due to contact with the Romans and the Mediterranean world.

47. Cunliffe, "Guernsey and the Channel Islands in the First Millenium BC," 120.

48. Cunliffe, "Guernsey and the Channel Islands in the First Millenium BC," 11, 16.

49. Cunliffe, "Guernsey and the Channel Islands in the First Millenium BC," 81–82.

50. Burns, Cunliffe, de Jersey, and Hill, "Gazetteer of Iron Age Sites and Finds on Guernsey, Herm and Sark," in *Guernsey: An Island Community of the Atlantic Iron Age*, ed. Burns, et al., 117–119.

51. R.B. Burns, "The Excavation," in *Excavations at Jerbourg, Guernsey*, ed. Burns (Cardie Gardens, Guernsey: Guernsey Museum Monograph No. 1, 1988), 1–2, 46.

52. Burns, "The Excavation," 119.

53. Burns, "The Excavation," 126–127.

54. Burns, "The Excavation," 92–99, 104–108.

55. Barry Cunliffe, "The Iron Age Burials of Guernsey," in *Guernsey: An Island Community of the Atlantic Iron Age*, 83–88.

56. Cunliffe, "The Iron Age Burials of Guernsey," 114.

57. Cunliffe, "The Iron Age Burials of Guernsey," 116.

58. Edgar MacCulloch, *Guernsey Folklore* (London: Elliot Stock, 1903), 129–133; John Utt-

ley, *The Story of the Channel Islands* (New York: Frederick Praeger, 1967), 16, 18.

59. MacCulloch, *Guernsey Folklore*, 129–133; Uttley, *The Story of the Channel Islands*, 16, 18.

60. Steven J. Cox, *Guernsey Folklore* (St. Peter Port, Guernsey: Guernsey Historical Monograph No. 12, 1882), 11.

61. Uttley, *The Story of the Channel Islands*, 18.

62. Stephen Dewar, *Witchcraft and the Evil Eye in Guernsey* (St. Peter Port: Guernsey Historical Monograph No. 3, 1968), 4.

63. MacCulloch, *Guernsey Folklore*, 296–304; Dewar, *Witchcraft and the Evil Eye in Guernsey*, 5–10.

64. There are currently 267 permanently inhabited islands off the coasts of Britain and Ireland (including the Channel Islands), as well as hundreds of smaller islands. Numerous islands also exist off the coasts of France, several dozen of which are inhabited (some only seasonally).

65. Averie Cameron, *Procopius* (Berkeley: University of California Press, 1985), 214–215.

66. Cameron, *Procopius*, 214–215.

67. Cameron, *Procopius*, 214–215.

68. Cunliffe, *The Extraordinary Voyage of Pytheas*, 145–149.

69. Cunliffe, *The Extraordinary Voyage of Pytheas*, 145–149

70. Haycock, *Legendary Poems from the Book of Taliesin*, 435.

71. Stanley Ireland, *Roman Britain* (London: Routledge, 1992), 23 (re: Tacitus, *Agricola*, 10–12).

72. Rees, *Celtic Heritage*, 194. Here we might bring to mind the Scottish folk tradition of kindling the *teine eigin* or "need fire" at Beltaine from nine types of sacred wood, an act that was ritually performed by nine (or nine times nine) men.

73. Patrick K. Ford, *The Celtic Poets* (Belmont, MA: Ford and Bailie, 1999), xxvii

74. Ford, *The Celtic Poets*, xxvii.

75. John T. Koch, trans., "The Tablet of Larzac," in Koch and Carey, *The Celtic Heroic Age*, 3–4; Bernard Mees, "The Women of Larzac," *Keltische Forshungen* 3 (2008): 169–188; LeJeune, Fleuriot, Lambert, Marichal and Vernhet, *Le plomb magique du Larzac et les sorcières gauloises* (Paris: C.N.R.S., 1985), reprint in *Études Celtiques* XXII: 88–177.

76. Many of these Classical accounts would benefit from a more in-depth exploration of their contents, as well as the intentions, biases and worldview of their authors, than is possible in this setting. Additional comparisons with Classical, Celtic and other Indo-European evidence would undoubtedly also prove fruitful.

77. Patrick Sims-Williams, *The Celtic Inscriptions of Britain* (Oxford: The Philological Society, 2003), 205 *n*1264.

78. For a more detailed exploration, see D. Ellis Evans, *Gaulish Personal Names* (Oxford: Oxford University Press, 1967). Online information may be obtained from the article "Name Constructions in Gaulish" by Tangwystyl verch Morgant Glasvryn (Heather Rose Jones), 2001 at http://www.s-gabriel.org>tangwystyl.

79. It is unclear whether the beginning of the inscription refers specifically to "underworld magic" or simply using a word denoting "below," to refer to the list of female names which follow. One reference that supports the first interpretation comes from the Annals of Ulster" for the year 737: *Cernach filius Foghartaigh a suis scleratis sociis dolose iugulatur, qm uaccarum uituli ocus infimi orbis mulieres tediose fleuerunt.* In his article, "The Irish Otherworld: Hiberno-Latin Perspectives" (*Éigse* 25, 1991, p. 154–156), John Carey translates this as follows: "Cernach son of Fogartach is treacherously slain by his wicked companions; the calves of cows and the women of the lowest world wearisomely lamented him." He takes this as a reference to the *mná side,* or "banshees" who were traditionally believed to keen the members of certain noble Irish families, and sees the term *infimus orbis* as the Hiberno-Latin equivalent of *síd(e),* "Otherworld mounds," which "appears to be evidence for an idea that *come* single realm, here visualized as lying beneath the surface of the earth, was the home of the immortals."

80. Haycock, *Legendary Poems from the Book of Taliesin*, 110–123.

Chapter 8

1. I am indebted to an excellent article about Tlachtga published by Dr. Kathryn Chadbourne in *Proceedings of the Harvard Celtic Colloquium*, Vol. XIV (1994), which has stayed with me and served as the impetus for this research. In addition, the work of John Carey and Marina Smythe proved invaluable for the completion of this work.

2. Chatsworth, Derbyshire; Book of Lismore [s.xv] f. 168 (126).

3. Proinsias Mac Cana, *The Learned Tales of Medieval Ireland* (Dublin: Dublin Institute for Advanced Studies, 1980), 45, 94.

4. Marie-Louise Sjoestedt, ed. and trans., "Le siege de Druim Damhghaire: Forbuis Droma Damhghaire [part I]," *Revue Celtique*, Vol. 43 (1926), 1–123; and [part II], *Revue Celtique,* Vol. 44 (1927), 157–186.

5. Séan Ó Duinn, ed. and trans., *Forbhais*

Droma Dámhgáire: The Siege of Knocklong (Cork: Mercier Press, 1992).

6. Kate Müller-Lisowski, ed., "Texte zur Mog Ruith Sage 3: Verse über Mog Ruith," *Zeitschrift für celtische Philologie* 14 (1923), 145–163.

7. Kathryn Chadbourne, "Giant Women and Flying Machines," *Proceedings of the Harvard Celtic Colloquium,* Vol. XIV (1994), 106–114.

8. See: Ó Corráin, Donnchadh, "Creating the Past: The Early Irish Genealogical Tradition," *Peritia* 12 (1998), 194–196.

9. John Carey, "An Old Irish Poem about Mug Ruith," *Journal of the Cork Historical and Archaeological Society,* Vol. 110 (2005), 113–134. Carey notes that the poem in the Book of Lecan (Dublin, RIA MS 23.P.2; cat. 535), is found on the *verso* of folio 124.

10. Carey, "An Old Irish Poem about Mug Ruith," 113. He notes that in addition to the version found in the Book of Lecan (Dublin, RIA MS 23.p.2 (fos 123vb-124rb), Mug Roith's genealogy is found in other manuscripts, including: Dublin, Trinity College MS 1298 (H.2.7), 142–143, and The Book of Uí Maine (Dublin, RIA MS D.ii.1; cat. 1225), fo. 19v. Müller-Lisowski, "Texte zur Mog Ruith Sage," 163, notes a reference from Rawlinson B 502 [157 Z. 36] dating to around 1100, that provides information about Mug Roith's genealogy, and which reflects several different strands of tradition: 1) Cú Allaid son of Laisre son of Finain Bec son of Laithre son of Dathuil Suire son of Saiglenn son of Dee son of Dere son of Labrada son of Caiss son of Buen son of *Mug Ruith* son of Fergusa; 2) *Mug Roith* son of Cuinisc Firthechet son of Firglainn son of Loga son of Mathlam son of Mathrai Magdoin son of Matheirm son of Alloit son of Noende [or else] *Mug Roith* mac Ceithirn son of Fintan son of Aillil Nertlaim son of Trichim. For links to more genealogical passages concerning Mug Roith: www.ucc.ie/celt/texts.

11. Carey "An Old Irish Poem about Mug Ruith," 113–114. TCD MS 1298 also includes a copy of *De fabulis Moga Ruith,* which Carey notes is clearer in some places than that in the Book of Lecan. Neither manuscript, however, includes the poem (two sections of which were inserted in *Forbais Dromma Damgaire* in a simplified and modified form).

12. Carey, "An Old Irish Poem about Mug Ruith," 114.

13. Carey, "An Old Irish Poem about Mug Ruith," 113–116.

14. Carey, "An Old Irish Poem about Mug Ruith," 123–124. In some sources Mug Roith is said to be the son or descendant of Fergus Mac Roich. In Bodleian MS Laud 610, Cacht (whose name means "captive") is daughter of Cath-

mann, king of the Britons. In *Imthechta Moga Ruith*, she was said to have been seized during a raid on the Britons of the Isle of Man, and that she was a slave in the house of *Roth*.

15. Carey, "An Old Irish Poem about Mug Ruith," 117.

16. Carey, "An Old Irish Poem about Mug Ruith," 118–122. For varying accounts of Mug Roith's wives and sons: 127–130.

17. Whitley Stokes, ed. and trans., "Accalamh na Senórach," *Irische Texte mit Wörterbuch*, Vol. 4 (Leipzig, 1900), 72 [ll. 2544, 2552].

18. Ann Dooley and Harry Roe, ed. and trans., *Tales of the Elders of Ireland: A New Translation of "Accalam na Senórach,"* (Oxford: Oxford University Press, 1999), 78.

19. Ó Duinn, *Forbhais Droma Dámhgáire*, 12–13.

20. Ó Duinn, *Forbhais Droma Dámhgáire*, 12–13.

21. Ó Duinn, *Forbhais Droma Dámhgáire*, 14–15.

22. Ó Duinn, *Forbhais Droma Dámhgáire*, 14–15.

23. Ó Duinn, *Forbhais Droma Dámhgáire*, 16–17.

24. Ó Duinn, *Forbhais Droma Dámhgáire*, 16–21.

25. Ó Duinn, *Forbhais Droma Dámhgáire*, 20–25.

26. Ó Duinn, *Forbhais Droma Dámhgáire*, 24–27.

27. Ó Duinn, *Forbhais Droma Dámhgáire*, 26–31.

28. Ó Duinn, *Forbhais Droma Dámhgáire*, 32–37.

29. Ó Duinn, *Forbhais Droma Dámhgáire*, 38–43.

30. Ó Duinn, *Forbhais Droma Dámhgáire*, 44–51.

31. Ó Duinn, *Forbhais Droma Dámhgáire*, 52–53.

32. Ó Duinn, *Forbhais Droma Dámhgáire*, 53–59.

33. O Duinn, *Forbhais Droma Dámhgáire*, 59–67.

34. Ó Duinn, *Forbhais Droma Dámhgáire*, 68–71.

35. Ó Duinn, *Forbhais Droma Dámhgáire*, 72–75.

36. Ó Duinn, *Forbhais Droma Dámhgáire*, 75–79.

37. Ó Duinn, *Forbhais Droma Dámhgáire*, 79–85.

38. Ó Duinn, *Forbhais Droma Dámhgáire*, 86–91.

39. Ó Duinn, *Forbhais Droma Dámhgáire*, 92–95.

40. Ó Duinn, *Forbhais Droma Dámhgáire*, 95–99.

41. Ó Duinn, *Forbhais Droma Dámhgáire*, 98–99.

42. Ó Duinn, *Forbhais Droma Dámhgáire*, 100–103.

43. Ó Duinn, *Forbhais Droma Dámhgáire*, 104–105.

44. Ó Duinn, *Forbhais Droma Dámhgáire*, 106–107.

45. Ó Duinn, *Forbhais Droma Dámhgáire*, 108–109.

46. Ó Duinn, *Forbhais Droma Dámhgáire*, 110–111.

47. Müller-Lisowski, "Texte zur Mog Ruith Sage," 157.

48. Müller-Lisowski, "Texte zur Mog Ruith Sage," 157. "The reign of nineteen kings concluded thereafter, the lifetime of Mug Roith he fought(?) from Ruth mac Rigo, great the fame, to strong Coirpre Lifechair. A wand of wood, estates in Sliab Alpa, to/for Simon's cows is snow, his one capable eye is broken, ten years to him with Simon."

49. Patrick S. Dinneen, ed., *Forus Feasa ar Éirinn: The History of Ireland by Geoffrey Keating* ii (London: Irish Texts Society VIII, 1908), 318–321.

50. RIA MS 23 H 18, "An Leabhar Muimhneach," 101–102 (Scribe: Uilliam mic Cairteáin)

51. National Library of Ireland MS G 22, "Leabhar Ghearr na Pailíse," 100–101 (Scribe: Tomás Ó Súilleamháin, 1773)

52. Chadbourne, "Giant Women and Flying Machines," 106.

53. Dinneen, *Forus Feasa ar Éirinn*, 325.

54. Erin Mullally, "Samhain Revival: Looking for the roots of Halloween in Ireland's Boyne Valley," *Archaeology.org*, October 17, 2016; http://www.excavations.ie, "Tlachtga, The Hill of Ward, Meath'" (2014:026).

55. Mullally, "Samhain Revival"; "Tlachtga, The Hill of Ward, Meath (2014:026)"

56. http://www.excavations.ie, "Tlachtga, The Hill of Ward, Meath (2014:026)."

57. http://www.excavations.ie, "Tlachtga, The Hill of Ward, Meath (2015:171)."

58. http://www.sketchfab.com, "Tlachtga (Hill of Ward), Excavations 2016."

59. "Excavations at Tlachtga," postings at "Excavations at Tlachtga Facebook site, The official page of the UCD School of Archaeology excavations at Tlachtga, the Hill of Ward, Co. Meath; 10/17/16 and 11/16/16.

60. http://www.ucd.ie; UCD School of Archaeology, "The Hill of Ward Project," Principal Investigator: Dr. Steve Davis.

61. Mullaly, "Samhain Revival."

62. Edward Gwynn, Edward, *The Metrical Dindshenchas*, Vol. IV (Dublin: Dublin Institute for Advanced Studies, 1991), 186–189. Gwynn translates *roth garb-grennach gráinne*

as "rough-jagged dreadful wheel." However, a previous passage says it is "well-finished," not rough. The word *grendach* "bristled" seems preferable to *grennach* "bearded," and may refer to the spokes of the wheel. In addition, the word *gráinne* "repulsiveness, ugliness" could apply, but perhaps *grinne* "pointed" is a better choice.

63. Gwynn, *The Metrical Dindshenchas*, Vol. IV, 188–191.

64. My translation from the Old Irish.

65. My translation from the Old Irish.

66. Carey, "An Old Irish Poem about Mug Ruith," 123

67. The Book of Ballymote, Dublin, RIA, 23 P 12, 253a 17.

68. Standish O'Grady, ed., *Silva Gadelica— A Collection of Tales in Irish with extracts illustrating persons and places* (London: Williams and Norgate, 1892), 511.

69. Edward Gwynn, "The Dindshenchas in the Book of Uí Maine," *Ériu* Vol. 10 (1926–1928), 77, par 11.

70. Gwynn, *The Metrical Dindshenchas*, Vol. IV, 154–155.

71. It may be useful to consider 1 *caill* "wood, forest," used of weapons or a group of people, as well as the phrase *fo chaill,* "in outlawry, in hiding, at large."

72. The preposition *fo* is most often translated as "under, beneath," but has a wide range of meanings in varying circumstances: "into, through/out; about, around; subject to/under a name; less than; according to/in accordance with; like, corresponding to; at, by; in respect of/as regards; along with/including." It was used in the declaration of oaths ("by it/in respect of"). Another possibility is that the word is a form of *foaid*, "spends the night; entertainment; feast/festival; stays, abides, sojourns; watches through the night/besieges" (during the Middle Irish period the stem is variously written *foí, faí, foé,* etc.).

73. Osborn J. Bergin, R.I. Best, Kuno Meyer, and J.G. O'Keefe, eds., *Anecdota from Irish Manuscripts*, Vol. 4 (Halle/Dublin: Max Niemeyer/Hodges Figgis, 1912), 49, Item 598.

74. Whitley Stokes, ed. and trans., *Sanas Chormaic: Cormac's Glossary* (Calcutta: Irish Archaeological and Celtic Society, 1868), 74. Thurles is the modern name for *Durlas,* a town in Munster built on a crossing of the River Suir. Located in mid-county Tipperary, it is surrounded by the Silvermine Mountains to the northwest and the Slieveardagh Hills to the southeast. It was the territory of Éile in early times, which at its greatest extent stretched from Croghan Hill in Offaly to just south of Cashel. By the eight century, the territory had broken up into a number of petty kingdoms occupied by the O'Carrolls, the O'Spillanes, the O'Fogarties and the *Eóganacht.* Towards the end of the 12th century and start of the 13th, the Norman Butler dynasty came to be the most powerful in the region. The Annals of the Four Masters mentions a battle that was "gained in Magh-Uatha" by Fearghal, son of Domhnall, and Sichfraidh, son of Uathmharan (i.e. the son of the daughter of Domhnall) over Muirchertach, son of Niall, where Maelgarbh, son of Gairbhith, lord of Dearlas, Conmhal, son of Bruadhran; and many others were slain. [M931.9]. Perhaps our reference is to the Battle of Thurles in 1174.

75. Oxford, Bodleian Library, Rawlinson B 502, 157–158.

76. Müller-Lisowski, "Texte zur Mog Ruith Sage," 162–163.

77. Whitley Stokes, Whitley, "The Rennes Dindshenchas," *Revue Celtique* XVI (1895), 61; Whitley Stokes, Whitley, "The Edinburgh Dindshenchas," *Folklore* 4 (1893), 491.

78. Stokes, "The Edinburgh Dindshenchas," 491.

79. Stokes, "The Rennes Dindshenchas," 61.

80. Angelo Di Bernardino, ed., *Encyclopedia of the Early Church*, Vol. II (Oxford: Oxford University Press, 1992), 180.

81. Chadbourne, "Giant Women and Flying Machines," 108.

82. Robert Atkinson, ed., *The Passions and Homilies of the Leabhar Breac* (Dublin: Royal Irish Academy, 1887), 333.

83. Marina Smyth, "The Earliest Written Evidence for an Irish View of the World," in *Cultural Identity and Cultural Integrity,* ed. Doris Edel (Dublin: Four Courts, 1995), 38.

84. Smyth, "The Earliest Written Evidence for an Irish View of the World," 38–39.

85. John Carey, *King of Mysteries: Early Irish Religious Writings* (Dublin: Four Courts Press, 2000), 51.

86. Carey, *King of Mysteries,* 58.

87. Smyth, "The Earliest Written Evidence for an Irish View of the World," 36–40.

88. Smyth, "The Earliest Written Evidence for an Irish View of the World," 38.

89. Carey, *King of Mysteries,* 58 n7.

90. Carey, *King of Mysteries,* 12

91. Stanley Ireland, *Roman Britain: A Sourcebook* (London/New York: Routledge, 1996), 179.

92. Ireland, *Roman Britain,* 181.

93. Ireland, *Roman Britain,* 182. There are some differences between the beliefs described in these accounts and Pythagoras' teachings; nonetheless, the general concept was recognized by Classical authors from both sources.

94. Ireland, *Roman Britain,* 182

95. Carey, John, *A Single Ray of the Sun:*

Religious Speculation in Early Ireland (Aberystwyth: Celtic Studies Publications, 2011), 3–10.

96. Carey, *King of Mysteries*, 12.

97. Carey, *King of Mysteries*, 12–13.

98. John Carey, "From David to Labraid: Sacral Kingship and the Emergence of Monotheism in Israel and Ireland," in *Approaches to Religion and Mythology in Celtic Studies*, ed. Ritari, et al. (Newcastle: Cambridge Scholars, 2008), 2–27.

99. Fergus Kelly, *A Guide to Early Irish Law* (Dublin: Dublin Institute for Advanced Studies, 1995), 59–61.

100. Kelly, *A Guide to Early Irish Law*, 59–61.

101. Kelly, *A Guide to Early Irish Law*, 198.

102. Bridgette Slavin, "Coming to Terms with Druids in Early Christian Ireland," in *Australian Celtic Journal* 9 (2010), 1–27; Carey, *A Single Ray of the Sun*, 1–38.

103. Carey, "From David to Labriad," 11–12. See also: John Carey, "Téacsanna Draíochta in Éirinn sa Mheánois Luath," *Léachtaí Cholm Cille* 30 (2000), 98–117

104. Kelly, *A Guide to Early Irish Law*, 43–49.

105. For a discussion about magical terminology in relation to stories about Mug Roith, see Bridgette Slavin, "Supernatural art, the landscape and kingship in early Irish texts," in *Landscapes of Cult and Kingship*, ed. Schot, et al. (Dublin: Four Courts Press, 2011), 66–86. A few references are noted in T.F. O'Rahilly, *Early Irish History and Mythology* (Dublin: Dublin Institute for Advanced Studies, 1946), 45, 94.

106. Stokes, "The Edinburgh Dindshenchas," 491.

107. Stokes, "The Rennes Dindshenchas," 61.

108. Margaret C. Dobbs, ed. and trans., "The Ban-Senchus," *Revue Celtique* 47:3–4 (1930), 318.

109. R.A.S. Macalister, "Temair Breg: Remains and Traditions of Tara," *Proceedings of the Royal Irish Academy* 34 (1919), 352.

110. Carey, "An Old Irish Poem about Mug Ruith," 118.

111. Ó Duinn, *Forbhais Droma Dámhgáire*, 88–89.

112. Eugene O'Curry, *Lectures on the Manuscript Materials of Ancient Irish History* (Dublin: Hinch/Traynore, 1878), 401–402, 421–428.

113. John Carey, ed., *The End and Beyond: Medieval Irish Eschatology* (Aberystwyth: Celtic Studies Publications, 2014), 701–702.

114. Máire Herbert, ed. and trans., "'The Fleet of Inber Domnann," in *The End and Beyond: Medieval Irish Eschatology* (Aberystwyth: Celtic Studies Publications, 2014), 715–717.

115. Herbert, "The Fleet of Inber Domnann," 716.

116. Carey, *The End and Beyond*, 709.

117. Kate Müller-Liskowski, "La legend de St Jean dans la tradition irlandaise et le druide Mog Ruith," *Études Celtiques* 3 (1938): 46–70; M. McNamara, *The apocrypha in the Irish Church* (Dublin: Dublin Institute for Advanced Studies, 1975), 168–170; A. O'Leary, "Mog Ruith and apocalypticism in eleventh-century Ireland," in *The Individual in Celtic Literatures*, ed. Nagy (Dublin: CSANA Yearbook 1, 2001): 51–60; Carey, "An Old Irish Poem about Mug Ruith," 113–134; and Carey, *The End and Beyond*.

118. O'Curry, *Lectures on the Manuscript Materials of Ancient Irish History*, 403.

119. Gwynn, *The Metrical Dindshenchas*, Vol. IV, 526; Atkinson, *The Passions and Homilies of the Leabhar Breac*, 1840 *seq.*, lines 33–36.

120. Gwynn, *The Metrical Dindshenchas*, Vol. IV, 426 n35.

121. Stokes, *Sanas Chormaic*, 74.

122. John Gilroy, *Tlachtga: Fire Festival* (Pikefield Publications, 2000), 81, 127 (also viewable at http://www.newgrange.com). While not all of the information in this book is academically sound, the information presented in this section derives from Gilroy's exploration of the area and interactions with the owners of the property.

123. See: Mircea Eliade, *Rites and Symbols of Initiation* (Woodstock CT: Spring Publications, 1998).

124. Macalister, "Temair Breg: Remains and Traditions of Tara," 344–349; Alan Dundes, "A Psychoanalytic Study of the Bullroarer," *Interpreting Folklore* (Bloomington: Indiana University Press, 1980), 181–182; Eliade, *Rites and Symbols of Initiation;* Chadbourne, "Giant Women and Flying Machines."

125. E. Estyn Evans, *Irish Heritage: The Landscape, the People and Their Work* (W. Tempest: Dundalgan Press, 1967). A few pieces of information were derived from John W. Hurley, *The Irish Bullroarer: An Clairín Búirthe* (West Long Branch NJ: Caravat Press, 2004), 1–2, 10. While the book contains quite a bit of speculation, one interesting theory is that the "screaming" of the Stone of Fál against a chariot wheel in the presence of the rightful king could be related to the sound of the bullroarer during an ordeal or initiation ritual.

126. Ludwig Bieler, ed. and tr., "Tírechán, *Collectanea* 12 (2)," in *The Patrician Texts in the Book of Armagh* (Dublin, 1979), 132; John Carey, "Saint Patrick, the Druids, and the End of the World," *History of Religions* 36 (1996): 42–53.

127. Carey, *The End and Beyond,* 20; Edel Bhreathnach, *Ireland in the Medieval World* AD *400–1000: Landscape, Kingship and Religion* (Dublin: Four Courts Press, 2014), 151.

128. Anne Ross, *Pagan Celtic Britain* (Chicago: Academy, 1996), 132, 181, 205, 228, 252, 346–347, 418, 421, 475–476.
129. O'Grady, *Silva Gadelica*, Vol. 1, 332.
130. Whitley Stokes, ed. and trans., *The Annals of Tigernach*, Vol. 2 (Felinfach: Llanerch Press, 1971), 308–309.
131. George Calder, ed. and trans., *Auraicept na n-Éces: The Scholar's Primer* (Dublin: Four Courts Press, 1995), 309.

Chapter 9

1. An earlier version of this research was published in *Proceedings of the Harvard Celtic Colloquium,* Vol. XXVII (Cambridge: Harvard University Press, 2010): 337–355.
2. Edward Gwynn, *The Metrical Dindshenchas,* Vol. III (Dublin: Dublin Institute for Advanced Studies, 1991), 286–297.
3. Gwynn, *The Metrical Dindshenchas,* Vol. III, 26–39
4. Georges Dumézil, "Le Puits de Nechtan," *Celtica,* Vol. VI (1963): 59.
5. Gwynn, *The Metrical Dindshenchas,* Vol. III, 28–31.
6. Gwynn, *The Metrical Dindshenchas,* Vol. III, 226–231.
7. Gwynn, *The Metrical Dindshenchas,* Vol. III, 26–29.
8. Gwynn, *The Metrical Dindshenchas,* Vol. III, 294–295.
9. Gwynn, *The Metrical Dindshenchas,* Vol. III, 288–289.
10. DIL, *sreth*; George Calder, ed. and trans., *Auraceipt na n-Éces: The Scholar's Primer* (Dublin: Four Courts Press, 1995), 24–25.
11. Liam Breatnach, "The Caldron of Poesy," *Ériu* 32 (1981): 68–69; P.L. Henry, "The Caldron of Poesy," *Studia Celtica,* Vol. 14–15 (1979–1980): 126.
12. DIL *srúaim;* R.I. Best, Osborn Bergin, M.A. O'Brien, eds., *The Book of Leinster* (Dublin: Dublin Institute for Advanced Studies, 2007), 124.
13. DIL, *sruth.* One type of poetic composition was *sruth déc* ("a stream of ten, tenth stream") and a lower poetic grade known as *sruth-bard* (a division of *dóerbard*).
14. Whitley Stokes, ed., "The Colloquy of the Two Sages," *Revue Celtique,* Vol. 26 (1905): 22–27.
15. Gwynn, *The Metrical Dindshenchas,* Vol. III, 286–289.
16. Gwynn, *The Metrical Dindshenchas,* Vol. III, 288–289.
17. DIL, *éicse.*
18. Gwynn, *The Metrical Dindshenchas,* Vol. III, 292–293.
19. Gwynn, *The Metrical Dindshenchas,* Vol. III, 294–295. The word *bolg* can mean "bag," "bellows," "berry or bud," "blister" or "ball."
20. DIL, *bolg.*
21. Sharon Paice MacLeod, "Gods, Poets and Entheogens: Ingesting Wisdom in Early Irish Literary Sources," forthcoming in *Thinking about Celtic Mythology in the 21st Century,* ed. Emily Lyle (University of Wales Press). An earlier version of the research was presented as an honorarium lecture, "The Hazel of Immortality," Ford Foundation/GSAS Lecture Series, Department of Celtic Languages and Literatures, Harvard University, 2000.
22. Tom P. Cross and Clark H. Slover, trans., *Ancient Irish Tales* (Totowa: Barnes & Noble, 1969), 504–505.
23. Cross and Slover, *Ancient Irish Tales,* 507.
24. Donald Munro, ed., *Martin Martin: A Description of the Western Islands of Scotland* (Edinburgh: Birlinn, 1999), 93.
25. Patrick K. Ford, *The Mabinogi and other Medieval Welsh Tales* (Berkeley: University of California Press, 1977), 162–164.
26. The definitive translations and editions of these poems are in: Marged Haycock, *Legendary Poems from the Book of Taliesin* (Aberystwyth: CMCS, 2007).
27. A.O.H. Jarman and Gwilym Rees Hughes, *A Guide to Welsh Literature,* Vol. 1 (Cardiff: University of Wales Press, 1992), 106–107; Haycock, *Legendary Poems from the Book of Taliesin,* 9–10, 34–36.
28. Patrick K. Ford, *The Celtic Poets* (Belmont MA: Ford and Bailie, 1999), xxvii.
29. Haycock, *Legendary Poems from the Book of Taliesin,* 112–115.
30. Haycock, *Legendary Poems from the Book of Taliesin,* 114.
31. Haycock, *Legendary Poems from the Book of Taliesin,* 119–120.
32. Kuno Meyer, ed., "Tecosca Cormaic," *Royal Irish Academy Todd Lecture Series* (Vol. XVI), 4.
33. T.F. O'Rahilly, *Early Irish History and Mythology* (Dublin: Dublin Institute for Advanced Studies, 1984), 316.
34. John Carey, ed. and trans., "Lebor Gabála Érenn," in *The Celtic Heroic Age,* ed. John T. Koch and John Carey (Oakville/Aberystwyth: Celtic Studies Publications, 2001), 258.
35. R.A.S. Macalister, ed. and trans., *Lebor Gabála Érenn,* Part IV (London: Irish Texts Society, 1997), 188–189.
36. Calder, *Auraceipt na n-Éces,* 6–37.
37. Calder, *Auraceipt na n-Éces,* 56–57.
38. Calder, *Auraceipt na n-Éces,* 30–31.
39. Calvert Watkins, *How to Kill a Dragon: Aspects of Indo-European Poetics* (Oxford: Oxford University Press, 1995), 262. Originally

published in Edward Gwynn, "An Old Irish Tract on the Privileges and Responsibilities of the Poet," *Ériu* 13.38f and 39f, 1–60 and 220–236 (CIH 1128.20ff and 1129.11ff.); printed and discussed in Breatnach, "The Caldron of Poesy," 58–59 and Calvert Watkins, "Indo-European Metrics and Archaic Irish Verse," *Celtica* VI (1963): 239–240.

40. Breatnach, "The Caldron of Poesy," 58.

41. Breatnach, "The Caldron of Poesy," 58–59; Watkins, *How to Kill a Dragon*, 262. I have revised a number of words to reflect standard Old Irish spelling.

42. Breatnach, "The Caldron of Poesy," 59, suggests the last verse be translated: "The generous lady, abounding in treasures—for it is her right that she be listened to, that thanks be given to her—is maintained in the *túath* by masses of rewards." The concept of the audience/patron giving thanks (and rewards) is attractive.

43. Watkins, *How to Kill a Dragon*, 262; Watkins, "Indo-European Metrics and Archaic Irish Verse," 239–240.

44. Stokes, "The Colloquy of the Two Sages," 30–31.

45. Stokes, "The Colloquy of the Two Sages," 20–21.

46. John K. Bollard, "Arthur in the Early Welsh Tradition," in *The Romance of Arthur*, ed. James J. Wilhelm (New York/London, Garland, 1994), 20.

47. Ford, *The Celtic Poets*, xxvii.

48. Breatnach, "The Caldron of Poesy," 48–49, 65.

49. Breatnach, "The Caldron of Poesy," 62–63.

50. Breatnach, "The Caldron of Poesy," 68–71.

51. Breatnach, "The Caldron of Poesy," 62–63.

52. Breatnach, "The Caldron of Poesy," 66–67.

53. Breatnach, "The Caldron of Poesy," 66–67.

54. Sharon Paice MacLeod, *Early Celtic Poetry and Wisdom Texts: The Three Cauldrons, The Song of Amairgen, and Other Literary Creations* (McFarland, forthcoming).

55. Edward Gwynn, *The Metrical Dindshenchas*, Part IV (Dublin: Dublin Institute for Advanced Studies, 1991), 80–87.

56. K.W. Grant, "The Myth of Cailleach Bheur," in *Myth, Tradition and Story from Western Argyll* (Oban: Oban Times Press, 1925), 8.

57. Gwynn, *The Metrical Dindshenchas*, Vol. IV, 80–87.

58. Breatnach, "The Caldron of Poesy," 62–63.

59. DIL, *es(s)*.

60. Carey, "Lebor Gabála Érenn," 267.

61. Gwynn, *The Metrical Dindshenchas*, Vol. IV, 2–6.

62. Gwynn, *The Metrical Dindshenchas*, Vol. IV, 308–311.

63. Whitley Stokes, "The Rennes Dindshenchas," *Revue Celtique*, Vol. 16 (1895), 281–282.

64. Gwynn, *The Metrical Dindshenchas*, Vol. IV, 126–129.

65. Mallory, J.P., *In Search of the Indo-Europeans* (London: Thames & Hudson, 1989), 132, 135, 140.

66. Mallory, J.P., *In Search of the Indo-Europeans*, 132, 135, 140.

67. Mallory, J.P., *In Search of the Indo-Europeans*, 132, 135, 140.

68. Gwynn, *The Metrical Dindshenchas*, Vol. IV, 126–129.

69. Gwynn, *The Metrical Dindshenchas*, Vol. IV, 126–129.

70. Ford, *The Celtic Poets*, 5.

71. Patrick K. Ford, "The Well of Nechtan and *La Gloire Lumineuse*," in *Myth in Indo-European Antiquity*, ed. Gerald J. Larson (Los Angeles: University of California Press, 1974), 67–74; Dumézil "Le Puits de Nechtan."

72. O'Rahilly, *Early Irish History and Mythology*, 319; DIL, *eicne, bratán*.

73. Elizabeth Gray, ed. and trans., *Cath Maige Tuired* (Naas: Irish Texts Society, 1982), 121; O'Rahilly, *Early Irish History and Mythology*, 320.

74. Gwynn, *The Metrical Dindshenchas*, Vol. IV, 92–95; Macalister, *Lebor Gabála Érenn*, 150–151.

75. O'Rahilly, *Early Irish History and Mythology*, 320, n2.

76. O'Rahilly, *Early Irish History and Mythology*, 320, n5.

77. Gray, *Cath Maige Tuired*, 121.

78. Whitley Stokes, ed. and trans., *Sanas Chormaic* (Calcutta: Irish Archaeological and Celtic Society, 1868), 23.

79. Stokes, "The Colloquy of the Two Sages," 30–31.

80. Anne Ross, *The Folklore of the Scottish Highlands* (New York: Barnes & Noble/Batsford, 1976), 58.

81. Munro, *Martin Martin*, 77.

82. O'Rahilly, *Early Irish History and Mythology*, 324; Edward Dwelly, ed. *Faclair Gaidhlig gu Bearla le Dealbhan* (Glasgow: Gairm Publications, 1994), 920.

83. Cross and Slover, *Ancient Irish Tales*, 97; J.E. Caerwyn Williams and Patrick K. Ford, *The Irish Literary Tradition* (Cardiff: University of Wales Press/Belmont MA: Ford and Bailie, 1992), 30.

84. Stokes, *Sanas Chormaic*, 94.

85. Munro, *Martin Martin*, 79–80; Ford, *The Celtic Poets*, xxvi.

Bibliography

Atkinson, R., ed. *The Passions and the Homilies from Leabhar Breac: Text, Translations and Glossary* (Dublin: Royal Irish Academy, 1887).

Bartrum, P.C. *Early Welsh Genealogical Tracts* (Cardiff: University of Wales Press, 1966).

Beck, Noémie. *Goddesses in Celtic Religion—Cult and Mythology: A Comparative Study of Ancient Ireland, Britain and Gaul* (PhD Thesis, Université Lumière Lyon 2 and University College Dublin, 2009).

Bennett, Margaret. *Scottish Customs: From the Cradle to the Grave* (Edinburgh: Polygon, 1992).

Bergin, Osborn J., Best, R.I., Meyer, Kuno, and O'Keefe, J.G., eds. *Anecdota from Irish Manuscripts*. Vol. 4 (Halle and Dublin: Max Niemeyer/Hodges Figgis, 1912).

Berlin, Brent, and Kay, Paul. *Basic Color Terms: Their Universality and Evolution* (Berkeley: University of California Press, 1969).

Best, R.I. "The Settling of the Manor of Tara," *Ériu* 4 (1910): 121–172.

Best, R.I., and Bergin, Osborn. *Lebor na hUidre: Book of the Dun Cow* (Dublin: Dublin Institute of Advanced Studies, 1992).

Best, R.I., Bergin, Osborn, O'Brien, M.A., eds. *The Book of Leinster: Lebar na Núachongbála* (Dublin: Dublin Institute for Advanced Studies, 2007).

Bhreathnach, Edel. *Ireland in the Medieval World AD 400–1000: Landscape, Kingship and Religion* (Dublin: Four Courts Press, 2014).

Bieler, Ludwig. "Tírechán. *Collectanea* 12 (2)," in *The Patrician Texts in the Book of Armagh* (Scriptores Latini Hiberniae, 10). Ed. and trans., Ludwig Bieler (Dublin: Dublin Institute for Advanced Studies, 1979).

Bollard, John K. "Arthur in the Early Welsh Tradition," in *The Romance of Arthur: An Anthology of Medieval Texts in Translation*. Ed. James J. Wilhelm (New York: Garland, 1994), 11–24.

Bondarenko, Grigory. "Roads and Knowledge in Togail Bruidne Da Derga," in Borsje, Jacqueline, Dooley, Ann, Mac Mathúna, Séamus, and Toner, Gregory, eds. *Celtic Cosmology: Perspectives from Ireland and Scotland* (Toronto: Pontifical Institute of Medieval Studies, 2014), 186–206.

Bondarenko, Grigory. *Studies in Irish Mythology* (Berlin: Currach Bhán, 2014).

Borsje, Jacqueline. "A Spell Called Éle," in *Ulidia 3: Proceedings of the Third International Conference on the Ulster Cycle of Tales*. ed. G. Toner and S. Mac Mathúna (Coleraine: University of Ulster, 2009), 193–212.

Borsje, Jacqueline, Dooley, Ann, Mac Mathúna, Séamus, and Toner, Gregory, eds. *Celtic Cosmology: Perspectives from Ireland and Scotland* (Toronto: Pontifical Institute of Medieval Studies, 2014).

Bourke, Angela, Kilfeather, Siobhan, Luddy, Maria, Mac Curtain, Margaret, Meaney, Geraldine, Ní Dhonnchadha, Máirin, O'Dowd, Mary, and Wills, Claire, eds. *The Field Day Anthology of Irish Writing*. Vol. IV (New York: New York University Press, 2002).

Breatnach, Liam, ed. and trans. "The Caldron of Poesy," *Ériu* 32 (1981): 45–93.

Briggs, Katherine. *An Encyclopedia of Fairies* (New York: Pantheon, 1976).

Bromwich, Rachel. "The Welsh Triads," in *Arthurian Literature in the Middle Ages*. Ed. Roger S. Loomis (Oxford: Oxford University Press, 2001), 44–51.

Bromwich, Rachel, ed. and trans. *Trioedd Ynys Prydein* (Cardiff: University of Wales Press, 1978).

Bruch, Benjamin. "An Analysis of Color Terms in the Vankh Dialect of Eastern Armenia," *Annal of Armenian Linguistics*. Vol. 22/23 (2003): 17–28.

Bruford, A.J., and McDonald, D.A., eds. *Scottish Traditional Tales* (Edinburgh: Polygon, 1994).

Brunaux, Jean Louis. *The Celtic Gauls: Gods, Rites and Sanctuaries* (London: Seaby, 1987).

Burns, Bob, Cunliffe, Barry, and Sebire, Heather, eds. *Guernsey: An Island Community of the Atlantic Iron Age* (Oxford: Oxford University Committee for Archaeology, Monograph No. 43/Guernsey Museum, Monograph No. 6, 1996).

Burns, R.B. "The Excavation" in *Excavations at Jerbourg, Guernsey*. Ed. Bob Burns (Cardie Gardens, Guernsey: Guernsey Museum Monograph No. 1, 1988).

Burns, R.B., Cunliffe, Barry, de Jersey, Philip, and Hill, Mike G. "Gazetteer of Iron Age Sites and Finds on Guernsey, Herm and Sark," in *Guernsey: An Island Community of the Atlantic Iron Age*. Eds. Bob Burns, Barry Cunliffe, and Heather Sebire (Oxford: Oxford University Committee for Archaeology, Monograph No. 43/Guernsey Museum, Monograph No. 6, 1996b).

Byrne, Mary E., "*Airec Menman Uraird maic Coisse*," in *Anecdota from Irish Manuscripts*. Vol. 2. Eds. Osborn Bergin. R.I. Best, Kuno Meyer and J.G. O'Keeffe (Halle and Dublin, 1908).

Caerwyn Williams, J.E. "The Court Poet in Medieval Ireland," *Sir John Rhys Memorial Lecture* (London: Oxford University Press, 1972).

Calder, George, ed. and trans. *Auraicept na n-Éces: The Scholar's Primer* (Dublin: Four Courts Press, 1995).

Cameron, Averie. *Procopius* (Berkeley: University of California Press, 1985).

Carey, John. "The Ancestry of Fénius Farsaid." *Celtica* 21 (1990): 104–112.

Carey, John. "Cosmology in *Saltair na Rann*." *Celtica* 17 (1985): 33–52.

Carey, John. "Donn, Amairgen, Íth and the Prehistory of Irish Pseudohistory." *Journal of Indo-European Studies* 38 (2010): 319–341.

Carey, John. "From David to Labraid: Sacral Kingship and the Emergence of Monotheism in Israel and Ireland," in *Approaches to Religion and Mythology in Celtic Studies*. Katja Ritari, and Alexandra Bergholm, eds. (Newcastle: Cambridge Scholars, 2008): 2–27.

Carey, John. "Horned Fairy Women," *Ériu* 34 (1988): 203–4.

Carey, John. "Ireland and the Antipodes: The Heterodoxy of Virgil of Salzburg," in *The Otherworld Voyage in Early Irish Literature*. Jonathon Wooding, ed. (Dublin: Four Courts Press, 2014).

Carey, John. "The Irish Otherworld: Hiberno-Latin Perspectives," *Éigse* 25 (1991): 154–159.

Carey, John. *King of Mysteries: Early Irish Religious Writings* (Dublin: Four Courts Press, 2000).

Carey, John. "The Location of the Otherworld in Irish Tradition." *Éigse* XIX (1982): 36–43.

Carey, John. "The Lough Foyle Colloquoy Texts: Immacaldam Choluim Chille ocus ind Óclaig oc Carraic Eolairg." *Ériu* 52 (2002): 53–87.

Carey, John. "Myth and Mythography in *Cath Maige Tuired*," *Studia Celtica*. Vol. 24/25 (1989/90): 53–69.

Carey, John. "The Name 'Túatha Dé Danann.'" *Éigse* 18:2 (1981): 291–294.

Carey, John. "The Names of the Plains Beneath the Lakes of Ireland," in *Cín Chille Cúile: Texts, Saints and Places—Essays in Honour of Pádraig Ó Riain*. John Carey, Máire Herbert, and Kevin Murray, eds. (Aberystwyth: Celtic Studies Publications, 2004), 44–57.

Carey, John. "Native Elements in Irish Pseudohistory," in *Cultural Identity and Cultural Integration: Ireland and Europe in the Middle Ages*. Doris Edel, ed. (Dublin: Four Courts Press, 1995), 45–60.

Carey, John. *A New Introduction to Lebor Gabála Érenn* (Dublin: Irish Texts Society, 1993).

Carey, John. "Nodons in Britain and Ireland." *Zeitschrift für Celtische Philologie* 40 (1984): 1–22.

Carey, John. "Notes on the Irish War-Goddess." *Éigse* 19:2 (1983): 263–275.

Carey, John. "The Origin and Development of the Cessair Legend." *Éigse* 22 (1987): 37–48.

Carey, John. "Saint Patrick, the Druids, and the End of the World." *History of Religions* 36 (1996): 42–53.

Carey, John. "*Scél Tuain meic Chairill*," *Ériu* 35 (1984): 92–111.

Carey, John. *A Single Ray of the Sun: Religious Speculation in Early Ireland* (Aberystwyth: Celtic Studies Publications, 2011).

Carey, John. "Téacsanna Draíochta in Éirinn sa Mheánois Luath." *Léachtaí Cholm Cille* 30 (2000): 98–117.

Carey, John. "The Three Sails, The Twelve Winds, and the Question of Early Irish Colour Theory." *Journal of the Warburg and Courtauld Institutes.* Vol. 72 (2009): 221–232.

Carey, John. "Time, Space and the Otherworld," *Proceedings of the Harvard Celtic Colloquium.* Vol. 7 (1986): 1–27.

Carey, John. "A Tract on the Creation," *Éigse* 11 (1986): 1–9.

Carey, John. "A *Túath Dé* Miscellany." *Bulletin of the Board of Celtic Studies* 39 (1992): 24–45.

Carey, John, ed. *The End and Beyond: Medieval Irish Eschatology* (Aberystwyth: Celtic Studies Publications, 2014).

Carey, John, ed. "An Old Irish Poem about Mug Ruith." *Journal of the Cork Historical and Archaeological Society.* Vol. 110 (2005): 113–134.

Carey, John, trans. "The Book of Invasions (First Recension). *Lebor Gabála Érenn*," in *The Celtic Heroic Age: Literary Sources for Ancient Celtic Europe and Early Ireland and Wales.* John T. Koch, and John Carey, eds. (Oakville, CT, and Aberystwyth: Celtic Studies Publications, 2000), 226–271.

Carmichael, Alexander, ed. and trans. *Carmina Gadelica* (Edinburgh: Lindisfarne Press, 1992).

Chadbourne, Kathryn. "The Celtic Otherworld," *Cosmos: Journal of the Traditional Cosmology Society.* Vol. 14, No. 2 (1998): 157–177.

Chadbourne, Kathryn. "Giant Women and Vol Flying Machines," Proceedings of the Harvard Celtic Colloquium. XIV (1994): 106–114.

Clarke, Basil, ed. *Vita Merlini* (Cardiff: University of Wales Press, 1975).

Corthals, Johan (ed. and trans). "*Táin bó Regamna und Táin bó Flidais: zwei altirische Erzählungen*," diss. (unpublished), Hamburg University (1979).

Cox, J. Stevens. *Guernsey Folklore* (St. Peter Port: Guernsey Historical Monograph No. 12, 1882).

Cronus. http://www.brittanica.com.

Cross, Tom P., and Slover, Clark H. *Ancient Irish Tales* (New York: Barnes & Noble, 1996).

Cuillandre, J. "Étude de la concordance du calendrier de Coligny," *Revue Celtique* 47 (1930): 10–29.

Cunliffe, Barry. *The Ancient Celts* (Oxford: Oxford University Press, 1997).

Cunliffe, Barry. *The Celtic World* (New York: Greenwich House, 1986).

Cunliffe, Barry. *The Extraordinary Voyage of Pytheas* (New York: Walker and Company, 2002).

Cunliffe, Barry. "The First Eight Thousand Years, 7000 BC–AD 1000," in *A People of the Sea— The Maritime History of the Channel Islands.* Ed. A.G. Jamieson (London: Methuen, 1986b).

Cunliffe, Barry. "Guernsey and the Channel Islands in the First Millenium BC," in *Guernsey: An Island Community of the Atlantic Iron Age.* Eds. Bob Burns, Barry Cunliffe and Heather Sebire (Oxford: Oxford University Committee for Archaeology, Monograph No. 43/Guernsey Museum, Monograph No. 6, 1996).

Cunliffe, Barry. "The Iron Age Burials of Guernsey," in *Guernsey: An Island Community of the Atlantic Iron Age. Eds.* Bob Burns, Barry Cunliffe and Heather Sebire (Oxford: Oxford

University Committee for Archaeology, Monograph No. 43/Guernsey Museum, Monograph No. 6, 1996b).

Danaher, Kevin. *The Year in Ireland* (Dublin/Cork: Mercier Press, 1972).

Dansey, William. *Arrian on Coursing. The Cynegeticus of the Younger Xenophon* (London: Bohn, 1831), http://www.archive.org.

Darvill, Timothy. *Prehistoric Britain* (London: Routledge, 1996).

Darwin, Tess. *The Scots Herbal: The Plant Lore of Scotland* (Edinburgh: Mercat Press, 1996).

Davidson, Hilda Ellis. *God and Myths of Northern Europe* (New York: Penguin, 1965).

Davies, Sioned, ed. and trans. *The Mabinogion* (Oxford: Oxford University Press, 2007).

Davis, Steve, Principal Investigator. "The Hill of Ward Project," UCD School of Archaeology, http://www.ucd.ie.

Deane, Marion. "From Sacred Marriage to Clientship: A Mythical Account of the Establishment of Kingship as an Institution," in *Landscapes of Cult and Kingship.* Ed. Roseanne Schot, Conor Newman, and Edel Bhreathnach (Dublin: Four Courts Press, 2011), 1–21.

Delaney, Mary M. *Of Irish Ways* (New York: Dillon Press/Barnes & Noble, 1973).

Dewar, Stephen. *Witchcraft and the Evil Eye in Guernsey* (St. Peter Port: Guernsey Historical Monograph No. 3, 1968).

Di Bernardino, Angelo, ed. *Encyclopedia of the Early Church.* Vol. II (Oxford: Oxford University Press, 1992).

Dillon, Myles, ed. *Serglige Con Culainn* (Dublin: Dublin Institute for Advanced Studies, 1975).

Dinneen, Patrick S., ed. *Forus Feasa ar Éirinn: The History of Ireland by Geoffrey Keating* ii (London: Irish Texts Society VIII, 1908).

Dobbs, Margaret. "On Táin Bó Flidais," *Ériu* 8 (1915): 133–149.

Dobbs, Margaret C., ed. and trans. "The Ban-Senchus," *Revue Celtique* 47 (1930), 282–339; 48 (1931), 163–234; 49 (1932), 437–489.

Dooley, Ann, and Roe, Harry. *Tales of the Elders of Ireland: A New Translation of Accalam na Senórach* (Oxford: Oxford University Press, 1999).

Dumézil, Georges. "Le Puits de Nechtan," *Celtica.* Vol. 6 (1963): 50–61.

Dundes, Alan. "A Psychoanalytic Study of the Bullroarer," *Interpreting Folklore* (Bloomington: Indiana University Press, 1980): 177–198.

Dwelly, Edward, ed. *Faclair Gaidhlig gu Bearla le Dealbhan* (Glasgow: Gairm Publications, 1994).

Edwards, H.J., trans. *Caesar: The Gallic War* (Cambridge: Harvard University Press/Loeb Classical Library, 1917).

Eliade, Mircea. *Rites and Symbols of Initiation* (Woodstock CT: Spring Publications, 1998).

Evans, D. Ellis. *Gaulish Personal Names* (Oxford: Oxford University Press, 1967).

Evans, E. Estyn. *Irish Heritage—The Landscape, the People and Their Work* (West Tempest: Dundalgan Press, 1967).

Falileyev, Alexander (in collaboration with Gohil, Ashwin E., and Ward, Naomi). *Dictionary of Continental Celtic Place-Names: A Celtic Companion to the Barrington Atlas of the Greek and Roman World* (Aberystwyth: CMCS, 2010).

Ford, Patrick K. *The Celtic Poets* (Belmont, MA: Ford & Bailie, 1999).

Ford, Patrick K. "Celtic Women: The Opposing Sex," *Viator: Medieval and Renaissance Studies* 19 (1988): 417–438.

Ford, Patrick K. *The Mabinogi and Other Medieval Welsh Tales* (Berkeley: University of California Press, 1977).

Ford, Patrick K. "Prolegomena to a Reading of the *Mabinogi: Pwyll* and *Manawydan*," *Studia Celtica* 16/17 (1981–1982), 110–125.

Ford, Patrick K. "The Well of Nechtan and *La Gloire Lumineuse*," in *Myth in Indo-European Antiquity.* ed. Gerald J. Larson, C. Scott Littleton and Jaan Puhvel (Los Angeles: University of California Press, 1974), 64–74.

Fortson, Benjamin, trans., "Strabo—Geography" in *The Celtic Heroic Age: Literary Sources for Ancient Celtic Europe and Early Ireland and Wales.* Eds. John T. Koch, and John Carey (Oakville, CT and Aberystwyth: Celtic Studies Publications, 2000), 15–19.

Gantz, Jeffrey. *Early Irish Myths and Sagas* (London: Penguin, 1981).

Gillies, William. "The Classical Irish Poetic Tradition," *Proceedings of the Seventh International Congress of Celtic Studies* (1986), 108–120.

Gilroy, John. *Tlachtga: Fire Festival* (Pikefield Publications, 2000).

Goodwin, William W., ed. *Plutarch—De defectu oraculorum* (http://www.perseus.tufts.edu).

Grant, I.F. *Highland Folk Ways* (London: Routledge, 1989).

Grant, K.W. "The Myth of Cailleach Bheur," in *Myth, Tradition and Story from Western Argyll* (Oban: Oban Times Press, 1925).

Gray, Elizabeth. "Cath Maige Tuired: Myth and Structure," Eigse 18–19 (Vol. 18, Pt. 1, 1980): 201–208.

Gray, Elizabeth, ed. and trans. *Cath Maige Tuired* (Naas: Irish Texts Society, 1982).

Green, Miranda. *Animals in Celtic Life and Myth* (New York: Routledge, 1992).

Green, Miranda. *Celtic Goddesses* (New York: George Braziller, 1995).

Green, Miranda. *Dictionary of Celtic Myth and Legend* (London: Thames & Hudson, 1992).

Gwynn, Edward. "The Dindshenchas in the Book of Uí Maine," *Ériu* 10 (1926–1928): 68–91.

Gwynn, Edward. *The Metrical Dindshenchas*. 4 Volumes (Dublin: Dublin Institute for Advanced Studies, 1991).

Gwynn, Edward. "An Old Irish Tract on the Privileges and Responsibilities of the Poet," *Ériu* 13 (1942): 1–60, 220–236.

Hamp, Eric P. "The Dag(h)d(h)ae and His Relatives," in *Donum grammaticum: Studies in Latin and Celtic Linguistics in Honor of Hannah Rosen.* Eds. L. Sawick, and D. Shalev (Peters, 2002), 162–169.

Hamp, Eric P. "imbolc, óimelc," *Studia Celtica.* Vol. 14/15 (1979/1980), 106–113.

Hamp, Eric P. "Welsh *elfydd, elfydden.* Scottish Gaelic *Alba,*" *Bulletin of the Board of Celtic Studies* 36 (1989), 109–110.

Hamp, Eric P. "Welsh *elfydd* and *albio-,*" *Zeitschrift für celtische Philologie* 45 (1992): 87–89.

Harbison, Peter. *Pre-Christian Ireland* (London: Thames & Hudson, 1988).

Haycock, Marged, ed. and trans. *Legendary Poems from the Book of Taliesin* (Aberystwyth: CMCS, 2007).

Henry, P.L. "The Caldron of Poesy," *Studia Celtica.* Vol. 15 (1981): 114–128.

Herbert, Máire. "Goddess and King: The Sacred Marriage in Early Ireland," *Cosmos* 7 (1992), 264–275.

Herbert, Máire. "Transmutations of an Irish Goddess," in *The Concept of the Goddess.* Eds. Sandra Billington and Miranda Green (London: Routledge, 1996), 141–151.

Herbert, Máire. "The Fleet of Inber Domnann," in *The End and Beyond: Medieval Irish Eschatology.* Ed. Carey (Aberystwyth: Celtic Studies Publications, 2014), 715–720.

Holder, Alfred. *Alt-celtischer Sprachschatz* (Leipzig, 1896–1907).

Hole, Christina. *Encyclopedia of Superstitions* (New York: Barnes & Noble, 1961).

Hopkins, Pamela S., and Koch, John T. "*Historia Brittonum*" in *The Celtic Heroic Age: Literary Sources for Ancient Celtic Europe and Early Ireland and Wales.* Eds. John T. Koch, and John Carey (Oakville, CT and Aberystwyth: Celtic Studies Publications, 2000), 275–290.

Hull, Eleanor, ed. and trans. "The Hawk of Achill, or the Legend of the Oldest Animals," *Folklore* 43:4 (1932): 376–409.

Hull, Vernum. "De Gabáil in t-Sída—Concerning the Seizure of the Fairy Mound," *Zeitschrift für celtische Philologie* 19 (1933): 53–58.

Hull, Vernum. "The Four Jewels of the *Túatha Dé Danann,*" *Zeitschrift für celtische Philologie* 18 (1929): 73–89.

Hurley, John W. *The Irish Bullroarer: An Clairín Búirthe* (West Long Branch, NJ: Caravat Press, 2004).

Hyde, Douglas, ed. and trans. *Legends of Saints and Sinners* (New York: Frederick Stokes, 1915).

Ireland, Stanley. *Roman Britain: A Sourcebook* (London: Routledge, 1992).

Jarman, A.O.H., and Hughes, Gwilym Rees. *A Guide to Welsh Literature.* Vol. 1 (Cardiff: University of Wales Press, 1992).

Johnston, Elva. *Literacy and Identity in Early Medieval Ireland* (Woodbridge, 2013), 20.
Jones, Glyn E. "Early Prose: The Mabinogi," in *A Guide to Welsh Literature*. Vol. 1, eds. A.O.H.
    Jarman and Gwilym Rees Hughes (Cardiff: University of Wales Press, 1992), 189–202.
Jones, Heather. "Name Constructions in Gaulish" (2001), http://www.s-gabriel.org.tangwystyl.
Jones, Horace L., ed. *The Geography of Strabo* (Cambridge MA: Harvard University Press, 1960).
Kalygin, Victor. "Some Archaic Elements of Celtic Cosmology," *Zeitschrift für celtische Philolo-
    gie* 53 (2003): 70–76.
Kelly, Fergus. "The Beliefs and Mythology of the Early Irish with Special Reference to the
    Cosmos," *Astronomy, Cosmology and Landscape: Proceedings of the SEAC 98 Meeting*
    (Dublin: European Society for Astronomy in Culture, 1998): 167–172.
Kelly, Fergus. *A Guide to Early Irish Law* (Dublin: Dublin Institute for Advanced Studies, 1995).
Kelly, Fergus. "The Old Irish Tree-List," *Celtica* 11 (1976): 107–124.
Kinsella, Thomas, trans. *The Tain* (Oxford: Oxford University Press, 1977).
Koch, John, and Carey, John, eds. *The Celtic Heroic Age: Literary Sources for Ancient Celtic
    Europe and Early Ireland and Wales* (Oakville, CT and Aberystwyth: Celtic Studies Pub-
    lications, 2000).
Koch, John T. "New Thoughts on *Albion, Ierne*. and the Pretanic Isles—Part 1 (The Pre-La
    Tène Period)," *Proceedings of the Harvard Celtic Colloquium*. Vol. 6–7 (1986): 1–28.
Koch, John T. "The Tablet of Larzac," in *The Celtic Heroic Age: Literary Sources for Ancient
    Celtic Europe and Early Ireland and Wales*. Eds. John T. Koch, and John Carey (Oakville,
    CT and Aberystwyth: Celtic Studies Publications, 2000), 3–4.
Krishna, Valerie. "The Alliterative *Morte Arthure*," in *The Romance of Arthur*. Ed. James J.
    Wilhelm (New York: Garland, 1994), 489–528.
Lazar-Meyn, Heidi Ann. "The Colour Systems of the Modern Celtic Languages—Effects of
    Language Contact," in *Language Contact in the British Isles: Proceedings of the Eighth
    International Symposium on Language Contact in Europe*. Eds. P.S. Ureland and G. Brod-
    erick (Tübingen, Germany: Max Niemeyer Verlag, 1988): 227–241.
Lazar-Meyn, Heidi Ann. "Colour Terms in Táin Bó Cúailgne," *Ulidia* (1994): 201–205.
Le Jeune, Michel, Fleuriot, Léon, Lambert, Pierre-Yves, Marichal, Robert, and Vernhet, Alain.
    Le plomb magique du Larzac et les sorcières gauloises (Paris: C.N.R.S., 1985), reprinted
    in *Études Celtiques* 22 (1985): 88–177.
Le Roux, F.M. "*Les Îles au Nord du Monde*," in *Hommages à Albert Grenier*. Ed. Marcel Renard
    (Brussels: Latomus, 1962), 1051–1062.
Leahy, A.H., ed. and trans. *Heroic Romances of Ireland*. 2 vols. (London, Irish Saga Library
    2: 1905–1906).
Lecture notes from Patrick K. Ford's *Celtic Paganism* class, Harvard University, Spring Term,
    2000.
Lévy-Bruhl, Lucien. *L'Experience Mystique et Les Symboles chez les Primitifs* (Librairie Felix
    Alcan, 1938).
Lewis, Ceri W. "The Court Poets: Their Function, Status and Craft," in *A Guide to Welsh Lit-
    erature*, Vol. 1. Eds. A.O.H. Jarman, and Gwilym Rees Hughes (Cardiff: University of
    Wales Press, 1992), 123–156.
Lincoln, Bruce. *Myth, Cosmos and Society: Indo-European Themes of Creation and Destruction*
    (Cambridge: Harvard University Press, 1986).
Livingstone, Sheila. *Scottish Customs* (New York: Birlinn/Barnes & Noble, 1996).
Logan, Patrick. *The Holy Wells of Ireland* (Gerrards Cross: Colin Smythe, 1980).
Loomis, Richard J. "Arthur in Geoffrey of Monmouth," in *The Romance of Arthur: An Anthol-
    ogy of Texts in Translation* ed. James J. Wilhelm (New York: Garland, 1994).
Loomis, Richard M. "Culwch and Olwen," in *The Romance of Arthur: An Anthology of Texts
    in Translation*. Ed. James J. Wilhelm (New York: Garland, 1994).
Loth, J. "L'année celtique d'après les textes irlandais, gallois, Bretons, et le calendrier de Col-
    igny," *Revue Celtique* 25 (1904): 113–162.
Lucas, A.T. "The Sacred Trees of Ireland," *Journal of the Cork Historical and Archaeological
    Society*. LXVIII (1963): 16–54.

Lyle, Emily. *Archaic Cosmos: Polarity, Space and Time* (Edinburgh: Polygon, 1990).

Lysaght, Patricia. "Aspects of the Earth-Goddess in the Traditions of the Banshee in Ireland," in *The Concept of the Goddess.* Eds. Sandra Billington, and Miranda Green (London: Routledge, 1996), 152–165.

MacAlister, R.A.S. "Temair Breg: Remains and Traditions of Tara," Proceedings of the Royal Irish Academy 34 (1919): 231–399.

MacAlister, R.A. Stewart, ed. and trans. *Lebor Gabála Érenn: The Book of the Taking of Ireland* (Naas: Irish Texts Society, 1997).

Mac Cana, Proinsias. "Celtic Goddesses of Sovereignty," in *Goddesses Who Rule.* Eds. Elisabeth Bernard, and Beverly Moon (Oxford: Oxford University Press, 2000).

Mac Cana, Proinsias. *The Cult of the Sacred Centre: Essays on Celtic Ideology* (Dublin: Dublin Institute for Advanced Studies, 2011).

Mac Cana, Proinsias. *The Learned Tales of Medieval Ireland* (Dublin: Dublin Institute for Advanced Studies, 1980).

Mac Cana, Proinsias. *The Mabinogi* (Cardiff: University of Wales Press, 1992).

Mac Cana, Proinsias. "Placenames and Mythology in Irish Tradition: Places, Pilgrimages and Things," in *Proceedings of the First North American Congress of Celtic Studies.* ed. Gordon MacLennan (Ottawa: 1986): 319–341.

MacCulloch, Edgar. *Guernsey Folklore* (London: Elliot Stock, 1903).

MacKillop, James. *Dictionary of Celtic Mythology* (Oxford: Oxford University Press, 1998).

MacKinnon, Donald. "The Glenmasan Manuscript," *The Celtic Review.* 1904–1908. 1: 12–17, 102–131, 208–29, 296–315; 2: 20–33, 100–121, 202–223, 300–313; 3: 10–25, 114–137, 198–215, 294–317; 4: 10–27, 104–121, 202–219.

MacLeod, Sharon Paice. "Abduction, Swordplay, Monsters and Mistrust," *Proceedings of the Harvard Celtic Colloquium.* Volume 28 (2008): 185–199.

MacLeod, Sharon Paice. *Celtic Myth and Religion: A Study of Traditional Belief* (Jefferson, NC: McFarland, 2012).

MacLeod, Sharon Paice. "A Confluence of Wisdom: The Symbolism of Wells, Whirlpools, Waterfalls and Rivers in Early Celtic Sources," *Proceedings of the Harvard Celtic Colloquium,* Vol. 27 (Cambridge. Harvard University Press, 2010): 337–355.

MacLeod, Sharon Paice. "The Descent of the Gods: Creation, Cosmogony, and Divine Order in *Lebor Gabála,*" *Proceedings of the Harvard Celtic Colloquium.* Volume 21 (2001). 311 – 365.

MacLeod, Sharon Paice. *The Divine Feminine in Ancient Europe: Goddesses, Sacred Women and the Origins of Western Culture* (Jefferson, NC: McFarland, 2014).

MacLeod, Sharon Paice. *Early Celtic Poetry and Wisdom Texts: The Three Cauldrons, The Song of Amairgen, and Other Literary Creations* (Jefferson, NC: McFarland, forthcoming).

MacLeod, Sharon Paice. "*Éisce, Gáeth ocus Muir*: Three Notes on Archaic Celtic Cosmology," *Cosmos* 18 (2002): 103–119.

MacLeod, Sharon Paice. "Gods, Poets and Entheogens: Ingesting Wisdom in Early Irish Literary Sources," in *Thinking About Celtic Mythology in the 21st Century.* Ed. Emily Lyle (University of Wales Press, 2018).

MacLeod, Sharon Paice. "*Mater Deorum Hibernensium:* Identity and Cross-Correlation in Early Irish Mythology," *Proceedings of the Harvard Celtic Colloquium.* Volume 19 (1999): 340–384.

MacLeod, Sharon Paice. "*Óenach Aimsire na mBan:* Early Irish Seasonal Celebrations, Gender Roles and Mythological Cycles," *Proceedings of the Harvard Celtic Colloquium.* Volume 23 (2003): 257–283.

Mac Mathúna, Liam, "The Christianization of the Early Irish Cosmos? *muir mas, nem nglas, talam cé,*" *Zeitschrift für celtische Philologie* 45–50 (1997): 532–547.

Mac Mathúna, Liam. "The Irish Cosmos Revisited: Further Lexical Perspectives," in *Celtic Cosmology: Perspectives from Ireland and Scotland.* Eds. Jacqueline Borsje, Ann Dooley, Séamus Mac Mathúna, and Gregory Toner (Toronto: Pontifical Institute of Medieval Studies, 2014): 10–33.

Mac Mathúna, Liam. "The Irish Perception of the Cosmos," *Celtica* 32 (1999): 174–187.

Mac Mathúna, Séamus. "The Relationship of the Chthonic World in Early Ireland to Chaos and Cosmos," in *Celtic Cosmology: Perspectives from Ireland and Scotland.* Eds. Jacqueline Borsje, Ann Dooley, Séamus Mac Mathúna, and Gregory Toner (Toronto: Pontifical Institute of Medieval Studies, 2014): 53–76.

Mac Mathúna, Séamus, ed. and trans. *Immram Brain—Bran's Journey to the Land of the Women* (Tubingen: Niemeyer, 1985).

Mac Neill, Eóin. "On the Notation and Chronography of the Calendar of Coligny. *Ériu* 10 (1926–8): 1–67.

Mac Néill, Eoin, "On the Reconstruction and Date of the Laud Synchronisms," *Zeitschrift fur Celtische Philologie* 10 (1915): 81–96.

Macneill, Máire. *The Festival of Lughnasa* (Dublin: University College Dublin, 2008).

"Magdalenenberg: Germany's Ancient Moon Calendar," Nov. 2011, http://www.worldarchaeology.com.

Mallory, J.P. *In Search of the Indo-Europeans* (New York: Thames & Hudson, 1991).

McKay, J.G. "The Deer Cult, and the Deer-Goddess of the Ancient Caledonians." Folklore 43 (1932): 144–174.

McManus, Damian. *A Guide to Ogam* (Maynooth: An Sagart, 1997).

McManus, Damian. "Irish Letter-Names and Their Kennings," *Ériu* 39 (1988): 127–145.

McNamara, M. *The Apocrypha in the Irish Church* (Dublin: Dublin Institute for Advanced Studies, 1975).

McNeill, F. Marian. *The Silver Bough: A Four Volume Study of the National and Local Festivals of Scotland* (Glasgow: William MacLellan, 1977).

Mees, Bernard. *The Women of Larzac.* Keltische Forshungen 3 (2008): 169–188.

Megaw, Ruth, and Vincent Megaw. *Celtic Art* (London: Thames & Hudson, 1996).

Meid, Wolfgang. *The Romance of Froech and Findabair or The Driving of Froech's Cattle: Táin Bó Froích* (Innsbruck: Institut für Sprachen und Literaturen der Universität Innsbruck, 2015).

Meyer, Kuno. "*Ein altirischer Heilsegen,*" Sitzb. 17 (1916): 420–422.

Meyer, Kuno. "Mitteilungen aus irischen Handschriften: Die Verwandlungen des Tuan mac Cairill," *Zeitschrift für celtische Philologie.* Vol. 3 (1901).

Meyer, Kuno. *The Triads of Ireland* (Dublin: *Todd Lecture Series* 13, 1906).

Meyer, Kuno. *The Voyage of Bran* (London: David Nutt, 1895).

Meyer, Kuno, ed. "Finn and the Man in the Tree," *Revue Celtique* 25 (1904): 344–349.

Meyer, Kuno, ed. *Hibernica Minora, Being a Fragment of an Old-Irish Treatise on the Psalter with Translation, Notes and an Appendix Containing Extracts Hitherto Unpublished from MS. Rawlinson, B. 512 in the Bodleian Library* (Oxford: Clarendon Press, 1894).

Meyer, Kuno, ed. "Mitteilungan aus irischen Handschriften: Fergus macc Róig." *Zeitschrift fur Celtische Philologie* 12 (1918): 375.

Meyer, Kuno, ed. and trans. "The Instructions of King Cormac Mac Airt : Tecosca Cormaic," *Royal Irish Academy Todd Lecture Series* 15 (Dublin, 1909).

Morford, Mark, and Lenardon, Robert. *Classical Mythology* (White Plains NY: Longman, 1991).

Mullally, Erin. "Samhain Revival: Looking for the Roots of Halloween in Ireland's Boyne Valley." *Archaeology.org.* October 17, 2016.

Müller-Liskowski, K. "La legend de St Jean dans la tradition irlandaise et le druide Mog Ruith." *Études Celtiques* 3 (1938): 46–70.

Müller-Lisowski, Käte, ed. 'Texte zur Mog Ruith Sage 3. Verse über Mog Ruith." *Zeitschrift für celtische Philologie* 14 (1923): 145–163.

Munro, Donald, ed. *Martin Martin—A Description of the Western Islands of Scotland circa 1695* (Edinburgh: Birlinn, 1999).

Murphy, Gerard, ed. and trans. *Duanaire Finn* (Dublin: Irish Texts Society, 1953).

Murray, Kevin, ed. and trans. *Baile in Scáil: The Phantom's Frenzy* (London: Irish Texts Society, 2004).

Newman, Conor. "The Sacral Landscape of Tara: A Preliminary Exploration," in *Landscapes of Cult and Kingship*. Eds. Roseanne Schot, Conor Newman, and Edel Bhreathnach (Dublin: Four Courts Press, 2011), 22–43.

Newton, Michael. *A Handbook of the Scottish Gaelic World* (Dublin: Four Courts Press, 2000).

Newton, Michael. *Warriors of the Word: The World of the Scottish Highlanders* (Edinburgh: Birlinn, 2009).

Ní Bhain, Maire. *Táin Bó Flidais*. Unpublished M.A. Thesis, University College Galway (1976).

Ní Bhrolcháin, Muireann. "Death-tales of the Early Kings of Tara," in *Landscapes of Cult and Kingship*. Eds. Roseanne Schot, Conor Newman, and Edel Bhreathnach (Dublin: Four Courts Press, 2011), 44–65.

Ní Mhaoileaoin, Patricia. "Patterns and Problems in the Heroic Biography of Fergus mac Róich," *Proceedings of the Harvard Celtic Colloquium*. Vol. 32 (2012): 214–228.

NicMhacha, S.M. *Queen of Night* (Boston: Red Wheel/Weiser Press, 2005).

Nicolaisen, W.F.H. *The Picts and Their Place-Names* (Groam House Museum Trust, Scotland, 1966).

Nicolson, Alexander. *Gaelic Proverbs and Familiar Phrases* (Edinburgh, 1881).

O'Brien, M.A., ed. *Corpus Genealogiarum Hiberniae*. Vol. 1 (Dublin: Dublin Institute for Advanced Studies, 1976).

Ó Cathasaigh, Tomás. "Pagan Survivals: The Evidence of Early Irish Narrative," in *Coire Sois—The Cauldron of Knowledge: A Companion to Early Irish Saga*. ed. Matthieu Boyd (Notre Dame: University of Notre Dame Press, 2014), 35–50.

O'Cathasaigh, Tomás. "The Eponym of Cnogba," *Éigse* Vol. 23 (1989): 27–38.

Ó Cathasaigh, Tomás. "The Semantics of 'Síd,'" *Éigse* 17, Part 2 (1978): 137–155.

Ó Cathasaigh, Tomás. "The Sister's Son in Early Irish Literature," in *Coire Sois—The Cauldron of Knowledge: A Companion to Early Irish Saga*. ed. Matthieu Boyd (Notre Dame: University of Notre Dame Press, 2014), 65–94.

Ó Corráin, Donnchadh. "Creating the Past: The Early Irish Genealogical Tradition," *Peritia* 12 (1998): 177–208.

Ó Cróinín, Dáibhi. *The Irish Sex Aetates Mundi* (Dublin: Dublin Institute for Advanced Studies, 1983).

Ó Crualaoich, Gearóid. *The Book of the Cailleach* (Cork: Cork University Press, 2007).

Ó Crualaoich, Gearóid. "Non-Sovereignty Queen Aspects of the Otherworld Female in Irish Hag Legends: The Case of the Cailleach Bhéarra." *Béaloideas Vol.* 62–3 (1994–5): 151–158.

O'Curry, Eugene. *Lectures on the Manuscript Materials of Ancient Irish History* (Dublin: Hinch/Traynore, 1878).

Ó Duinn, Séan, ed. and tr. *Forbhais Droma Dámhgáire: The Siege of Knocklong* (Cork: Mercier Press. 1992).

O'Flaherty, Wendy Doniger. *Hindu Myths* (New York: Penguin, 1980).

O'Grady, Standish, ed. *Silva Gadelica—A Collection of Tales in Irish with Extracts Illustrating Persons and Places* (London: Williams & Norgate, 1892).

Ó hÓgain, Daithi. *The Lore of Ireland: An Encyclopedia of Myth, Legend and Romance* (Suffolk UK: Boydell Press, 2006).

Ó hUiginn, Ruairí. "Growth and Development in the Late Ulster Cycle: The Case of *Táin Bó Flidais*," *Memory and the Modern in Celtic Literatures*. CSANA Yearbook 5, ed. Joseph Falaky Nagy (Dublin: Four Courts Press, 2006): 143–161.

Ó hUiginn, Ruari. "Fergus, Russ and Rudraige: A Brief Biography of Fergus Mac Róich," *Emania* (1993): 31–40.

O'Keefe, J.G. "The Four Custodians of Knowledge in the Four Quarters of the World," *Irische Texte* 4 (1934): 33–35.

O'Leary, A. "Mog Ruith and apocalypticism in eleventh-century Ireland," in *The Individual in Celtic Literatures*. ed. Joseph Falaky Nagy (Dublin: CSANA Yearbook 1, 2001): 51–60.

O'Meara, John, ed. and trans. *Gerald of Wales: The History and Topography of Ireland* (London: Penguin, 1982).

O' Rahilly, Cecile. *"Táin Bó Cúailgne from the Book of Leinster,"* (Dublin: Dublin Institute for Advanced Studies, 1967).

O' Rahilly, Cecile. *Táin Bó Cuailgne:* Recension 1 (Dublin: Dublin Institute for Advanced Studies, 1976).

O'Rahilly, T.F. *Early Irish History and Mythology* (Dublin: Dublin Institute for Advanced Studies, 1984).

Owen, Trefor M. *Welsh Folk Customs* (Llandysul Dyfed: Gomer Press, 1987).

Padel, Oliver J. *Arthur in Medieval Welsh Literature* (Cardiff: University of Wales Press, 2000).

Patterson, Nerys. *Cattle Lords and Clansmen: The Social Structure of Early Ireland* (Notre Dame: University of Notre Dame Press, 1994).

Piggott, Stuart. *The Druids* (New York: Thames & Hudson, 1993).

Power, Nancy. "Classes of Women Described in the *Senchas Már,"* in *Studies in Early Irish Law.* Eds. R. Thurneysen, N. Power, M. Dillon, K. Mulchrone, D.A. Binchy, A. Knoch, and S.J. Ryan (Dublin: Royal Irish Academy, 1936).

Puhvel, Jaan. *Comparative Mythology* (Baltimore: Johns Hopkins University Press, 1987).

Quin, et al. (DIL) *Dictionary of the Irish Language, Based Mainly on Old, and Middle Irish Materials* (Dublin: Royal Irish Academy, 1913-1976).

Raftery, Barry. *Pagan Celtic Ireland* (London: Thames & Hudson, 1994).

Rees, Alwyn, and Brinley. *Celtic Heritage* (New York: Thames & Hudson, 1995).

Rivet, A.L.F, and Smith, Colin. *The Place-Names of Roman Britain* (Princeton, NJ: Princeton University Press, 1979).

Roberts, Brynley F. "Geoffrey of Monmouth. *Historia Regum Britanniae* and *Brut y Brenhinedd,"* in *The Arthur of the Welsh.* Eds. Rachel Bromwich, A.O.H. Jarman, and Brynley F. Roberts (Cardiff: University of Wales Press, 2008), 97–116.

Roberts, Brynley F. *"Culhwch ac' Olwen.* The Triads and Saints' Lives," in *The Arthur of the Welsh.* Eds. Rachel Bromwich, A.O.H. Jarman, and Brynley F. Roberts (Cardiff: University of Wales Press, 2008), 73–96.

Romer, F.E. *Pomponius Mela's Description of the World* (Ann Arbor: University of Michigan Press, 1998).

Rose, H.J. *Handbook of Greek Mythology* (New York: E.P. Dutton, 1959).

Roseman, Christina H. *Pytheas of Massilia* (Chicago: Ares, 1994).

Ross, Anne. *The Folklore of the Scottish Highlands* (New York: Barnes & Noble/Batsford, 1976).

Ross, Anne. *Pagan Celtic Britain* (Chicago: Academy, 1996).

Ryan, Michael, ed. *The Illustrated Archaeology of Ireland* (Dublin: Country House, 1991).

Sayers, William. "Netherworld and Otherworld in Early Irish Literature," *Zeitschrift für celtische Philologie* 59 (2012): 201–230.

Sayers, William. "Tripartition in early Ireland: cosmic or social structure," in *Indo-European Religion after Dumézil.* Ed. Edgar C. Polomé (Washington, D.C.: Institute for the Study of Man, 1996), 156–183.

Schot, Roseanne. "From Cult Centre to Royal Centre: Monuments, Myths and Other Revelations at Uisneach," in *Landscapes of Cult and Kingship.* Eds. Roseanne Schot, Conor Newman, and Edel Bhreathnach (Dublin: Four Courts Press, 2011), 87–113.

Schot, Roseanne, Newman, Conor, and Bhreathnach, Edel, eds. *Landscapes of Cult and Kingship* (Dublin: Four Courts Press, 2011).

Scowcroft, R. Mark. "Leabhar Gabhála: Part II: The Growth of the Tradition," *Ériu* 39 (1988): 1–66.

Shaw, John. "A Gaelic Eschatological Folktale, Celtic Cosmology, and Dumézil's 'Three Realms,'" in *Celtic Cosmology: Perspectives from Ireland and Scotland.* Eds. Jacqueline Borsje, Ann Dooley, Séamus Mac Mathúna, and Gregory Toner (Toronto: Pontifical Institute of Medieval Studies, 2014), 34–52.

Sims-Williams, Patrick. *The Celtic Inscriptions of Britain* (Oxford: The Philological Society, 2003).

Sims-Williams, Patrick. "The Early Welsh Arthurian Poems," in *The Arthur of the Welsh.*

Eds. Rachel Bromwich, A.O.H. Jarman, and Brynley F. Roberts (Cardiff: University of Wales Press, 2008), 33–71.

Sims-Williams, Patrick. "Some Celtic Otherworld Terms," in *Celtic Language, Celtic Culture: A Festschrift for Eric P. Hamp*. eds. A.T.E. Matonis and Daniel F. Melia (Van Nuys: Ford & Bailie, 1990), 57–84.

Sjoestedt, Marie-Louise. *Gods and Heroes of the Celts* (Berkeley: Turtle Island Foundation, 1982).

Sjoestedt, Marie-Louise, ed. and trans. "Le siege de Druim Damhghaire: Forbuis Droma Damhghaire [part I]," *Revue Celtique*. Vol. 43 (1926): 1–123; *Revue Celtique*. Vol. 44 (1927): 157–186.

Slavin, Bridgette. "Coming to Terms with Druids in Early Christian Ireland," *Australian Celtic Journal* 9 (2010): 1–27.

Slavin, Bridgette. "Supernatural Art, the Landscape and Kingship in Early Irish Texts," in *Landscapes of Cult and Kingship*. Eds. Roseanne Schot, Conor Newman, and Edel Bhreathnach (Dublin: Four Courts Press, 2011), 66–86.

Smyth, Marina. "The Earliest Written Evidence for an Irish View of the World," in *Medieval Studies—Cultural Identity and Cultural Integration: Ireland and Europe in the Middle Ages*. Ed. Doris Edel (Blackrock: Four Courts Press, 1995), 23–44.

Smyth, Marina. *Understanding the Universe in Seventh-Century Ireland* (Woodbridge: Boydell Press, 1996).

Smyth, Marina. "The Word of God and Early Medieval Irish Cosmology: Scripture and the Creating World," in *Celtic Cosmology: Perspectives from Ireland and Scotland*. Eds. Jacqueline Borsje, Ann Dooley, Séamus Mac Mathúna, and Gregory Toner (Toronto: Pontifical Institute of Medieval Studies, 2014), 112–143.

Stacey, Robin Chapman. *Dark Speech: The Performance of Law in Early Ireland* (Philadelphia: University of Pennsylvania Press, 2007).

Sticker-Jantscheff, Melanie. "Magdalenenberg: An Examination of Archaeological and Archaeoastronomical Interpretations of a Halstatt Period Burial Mound." *Spica: Postgraduate Journal for Cosmology in Culture*. Vol. III, No. 1 (Spring 2015).

Stokes, Whitley. "Adomnán's Second Vision," *Revue Celtique* 12 (1891): 420–423.

Stokes, Whitley. "*Immacalam in Dá Thuarad*: The Colloquy of the Two Sages." *Revue Celtique* 26 (1905): 4–64.

Stokes, Whitley, ed. *Cóir Anman*: "Fitness of Names," *Irische Text mit Übersetzungen und Wörterbuch, herausgegeben von Wh. Stokes und E. Windisch, dritte Serie*. 2 Heft (Leipzig, 1897).

Stokes, Whitley, ed. "The Edinburgh Dindshenchas." *Folkore* 4 (1893):471–497.

Stokes, Whitley, ed. *Sanas Chormaic* (Calcutta: Irish Archaeological and Celtic Society, 1868).

Stokes, Whitley, ed. and trans. "Accalamh na Senórach," *Irische Texte mit Wörterbuch*. Vol. 4 (Leipzig, 1900): 1–438.

Stokes, Whitley, ed. and trans. *The Annals of Tigernach*. 2 vols. (Felinfach: Llanerch Press, 1971).

Stokes, Whitley, ed. and trans. "Tidings of Conchobar mac Nessa," *Ériu* 4 (1910): 18–38.

Stokes, Whitley, 'The prose tales in the Rennes Dindsenchas,' *Revue Celtique*. Vol. 15 (1894): 272–336, 418–484; Vol. 16 (1895): 31–83, 135–167, 269–312, 468.

Thorpe, Lewis, trans. *Geoffrey of Monmouth—The History of the Kings of Britain* (Hammondsworth: Penguin, 1982).

Thurneysen, R., ed. *Mittelirische Verslehern*. in *Irische Texte mit Wörterbuch*. Vol. III, ed. Ernst Windische and Whitley Stokes (Leipzig, 1891), 1–182.

Thurneysen, Rudolf. "Der Kalender von Coligny." *Zeitschrift für celtische Philologie* 2 (1899): 523–544.

Thurneysen, Rudolf. *Die Irische Helden- und Königsage bis zum siebzehnten Jahrhundert* (Halle: Niemeyer, 1921), 318–321.

Thurneysen, Rudolf (ed.). *Zu irischen Handschriften und Litteraturdenkmälern* [1], Abhandlungen der Königlichen Gesellschaft der Wissenschaften zu Göttingen, Philologisch-Historische Klasse 14.2, Berlin, 1912.

Tierney, J.J. "The Celtic Ethnography of Posidonius," *Proceedings of the Royal Irish Academy.* Vol. 60 (1960): 189–275.

"Tlachtga, The Hill of Ward, Meath" (2014, 2015, 2016), http://www.excavations.ie.

Toner, Gregory. "Landscape and Cosmology in the Dindshenchas," in *Celtic Cosmology: Perspectives from Ireland and Scotland.* Eds. Jacqueline Borsje, Ann Dooley, Séamus Mac Mathúna, and Gregory Toner (Toronto: Pontifical Institute of Medieval Studies, 2014), 268–284.

University College Dublin, School of Archaeology: "Excavations at Tlachtga" Facebook site, The official page of the UCD School of Archaeology excavations at Tlachtga, the Hill of Ward, Co. Meath; 10/17/16, 11/16/16.

Uttley, John. *The Story of the Channel Islands* (New York: Frederick Praeger, 1967).

Vahana. http://www.Wikipedia.

Vendryes, Joseph, ed. *Airne Fingein: Fingen's Nightwatch* (Dublin: Dublin Institute for Advanced Studies, 1953).

Waddell, John. *Archaeology and Celtic Myth* (Dublin: Four Courts Press, 2014).

Waddell, John. "The Cave of Crúachan and the Otherworld" in *Celtic Cosmology: Perspectives from Ireland and Scotland.* Eds. Jacqueline Borsje, Ann Dooley, Séumas Mac Mathúna, and Gregory Toner (Toronto: Pontifical Institute of Medieval Studies, 2014), 77–92.

Wansbrough, Henry, ed. *The New Jerusalem Bible* (New York: Bantam Doubleday, 1985).

Watkins, Calvert. *Dictionary of Indo-European Roots* (Boston: Houghton Mifflin, 2000).

Watkins, Calvert. *How to Kill a Dragon* (Oxford: Oxford University Press, 1995).

Watkins, Calvert. "Indo-European Metrics and Archaic Irish Verse." *Celtica* VI (1963): 194–249.

Watson, J.C., ed. *Mesca Ulad* (Dublin: Dublin Institute for Advanced Studies, 1941).

West, M.L. *Indo-European Poetry and Myth* (Oxford: Oxford University Press, 2007).

White, John. *Forest and Woodland Trees in Britain* (Oxford: Oxford University Press, 1995).

Wilhelm, James J. "Arthur in the Latin Chronicles," in *The Romance of Arthur: An Anthology of Medieval Texts in Translation.* Ed. James J. Wilhelm (New York: Garland Publishing, 1994), 3–10.

Wilhelm, James J. "Sir Thomas Malory: Le Morte D'Arthur," in *The Romance of Arthur: An Anthology of Medieval Texts in Translation.* Ed. James J. Wilhelm (New York: Garland Publishing, 1994), 567–568.

Wilhelm, James J. "Wace: Roman de Brut," in *The Romance of Arthur: An Anthology of Medieval Texts in Translation.* Ed. James J. Wilhelm (New York: Garland Publishing, 1994), 95–108.

Williams, J.E. Caerwyn, and Ford, Patrick K. *The Irish Literary Tradition* (Cardiff: University of Wales Press/Belmont MA: Ford & Bailie, 1992).

Williams, Mark. *Ireland's Immortals: A History of the Gods of Irish Myth* (Princeton, NJ: Princeton University Press, 2016).

Willis, Roy, ed. *World Mythology* (New York: Henry Holt & Co., 1993).

Windisch, Ernst. "Nachträge," in *Irische Text mit Worterbuch.* Vol 2:2 (1887), ed. Ernst Windisch and Whitley Stokes (Leipzig, 1887), 225–226.

Windisch, Ernst (ed. and trans). "Táin Bó Flidais," in *Irische Text mit Worterbuch.* Vol 2:2 (1887). Eds. Ernst Windisch, and Whitley Stokes (Leipzig, 1887), 206–223.

Wooding, Jonathan, ed. *The Otherworld Voyage in Early Irish Literature* (Dublin: Four Courts Press, 2014).

Index

Index